Praise for

Poland 1939

"Exemplary.... About as good as military history can be. Moorhouse has visited the places he writes about, and understands weaponry, tactics and the structures of the German and Polish armed forces.... Like all good histories, Moorhouse's answers an old question and raises a new one."
—Timothy Snyder, *New York Times*

"As Roger Moorhouse relates in *Poland 1939: The Outbreak of World War II*, the short, savage campaign to crush the Poles, who fought against hopeless odds, proved to be 'a five-week struggle that prefaced nearly 300 weeks of slaughter'...He tells a tale of Polish gallantry, German brutality, and what he sees as Anglo-French perfidy."
—Geoffrey Wheatcroft, *New York Review of Books*

"Moorhouse's book remedies that gap [in the history of The Polish War], weaving together archival material, first-hand accounts, perceptive analysis and heartbreaking descriptions of Poland's betrayal, defeat and dismemberment."
—*Economist*

"Chilling...All Poles know that their September war—and of course the many subsequent years of occupation, resistance and exile—was no side-show. Now Moorhouse has expertly laid bare this simple truth: that when two totalitarian regimes make common cause, everyone in their immediate neighbourhood is likely to be trampled underfoot."
—*Times* (UK)

"Excellent...a harrowing, but very needed, account of the first engagement of the Second World War."
—*Telegraph*

"A fascinating book.... There are moments of heroism and defiance here that will put a catch in your throat and a shiver down your spine."
—*Sunday Telegraph*

POLAND
1939

Also by Roger Moorhouse

*The Devils' Alliance: Hitler's Pact with Stalin,
1939–1941* (2014)

Berlin at War (2010)

POLAND 1939

THE OUTBREAK OF WORLD WAR II

Roger Moorhouse

BASIC BOOKS
NEW YORK

For Norman—who planted the seed

———————————

Basic Books
Hachette Book Group
1290 Avenue of the Americas, New York, NY 10104
www.basicbooks.com

Printed in the United States of America

Originally published in 2019 as *First to Fight: The Polish War 1939* by Bodley Head in the United Kingdom

U.S. hardcover and ebook originally published by Basic Books in 2020
First US trade paperback edition October 2022

Published by Basic Books, an imprint of Perseus Books, LLC, a subsidiary of Hachette Book Group, Inc. The Basic Books name and logo is a trademark of the Hachette Book Group.

The Hachette Speakers Bureau provides a wide range of authors for speaking events. To find out more, go to www.hachettespeakersbureau.com or call (866) 376-6591.

The publisher is not responsible for websites (or their content) that are not owned by the publisher.

Print book interior design by Linda Mark

Library of Congress Cataloging-in-Publication Data
Names: Moorhouse, Roger, author.
Title: Poland 1939 : the outbreak of World War II / Roger Moorhouse.
Other titles: Outbreak of World War II
Description: New York : Basic Books, [2020] | Includes bibliographical references and index. Identifiers: LCCN 2019044646 | ISBN 9780465095384 (hardcover) | ISBN 9780465095414 (ebook)
Subjects: LCSH: World War, 1939–1945—Campaigns—Poland. | World War, 1939–1945—Poland. | Poland—Armed Forces—History—World War, 1939–1945.
Classification: LCC D765 .M63 2020 | DDC 940.54/2138—dc23
LC record available at https://lccn.loc.gov/2019044646

ISBNs: 978-0-465-09538-4 (hardcover); 978-0-465-09541-4 (ebook); 978-1-5416-0261-8 (paperback)

LSC-C

Printing 1, 2022

CONTENTS

POLAND 1939
On the Eve of War

BALTIC SEA

DANZIG
FREE STATE

LITHUANIA

Kaunas

Wilno

Gdynia
Danzig
Tczew
Königsberg

EAST
PRUSSIA
(GERMANY)

N

Grodno

Bydgoszcz
Wizna

Toruń
Mława
R. Narew
Białystok

Poznań
R. Vistula
Modlin

R. Warta
Warsaw
R. Bug
Brest
Pińsk

Kock

Łódź
Lublin

Wieluń
Kielce
Frampol

Breslau
Łuck
Równe

Gleiwitz
Częstochowa
R. San
Tomaszów
Lubelski

GERMANY
Katowice
Tarnów
Lwów

Kraków
Przemyśl
Stanisławów
Tarnopol

SLOVAKIA
U.S.S.R.

HUNGARY

0   100 miles

0   200 km

ROMANIA

POLAND 1939
German and Polish Troop Dispositions
and the German Plan

Polish armies

German armies

German line of attack

Red Army Invasion of Poland
17 September 1939

Soviet armies

Red Army line of attack

Polish KOP
(Border Defence Corps) units

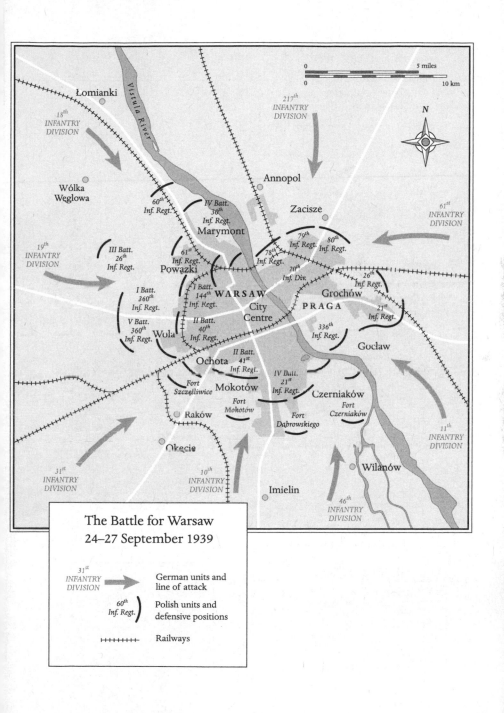

The Battle for Warsaw
24–27 September 1939

Łomianki

18ᵗʰ
INFANTRY
DIVISION

Vistula River

217ᵗʰ
INFANTRY
DIVISION

N

0   5 miles
0   10 km

Wólka
Węglowa

60ᵗʰ
Inf. Regt.

IV Batt.
36ᵗʰ
Inf. Regt.

Marymont

Annopol

Zacisze

61ˢᵗ
INFANTRY
DIVISION

19ᵗʰ
INFANTRY
DIVISION

III Batt.
26ᵗʰ
Inf. Regt.

61ˢᵗ
Inf. Regt.

Powązki

79ᵗʰ
Inf. Regt.

80ᵗʰ

78ᵗʰ
Inf. Regt.

20ᵗʰ
Inf. Div.

26ᵗʰ
Inf. Regt.

I Batt.
360ᵗʰ
Inf. Regt.

I Batt.
144ᵗʰ
Inf. Regt.

WARSAW
City
Centre

Grochów

PRAGA

21ˢᵗ
Inf. Regt.

V Batt.
360ᵗʰ
Inf. Regt.

Wola

II Batt.
40ᵗʰ
Inf. Regt.

336ᵗʰ
Inf. Regt.

Gocław

Ochota

II Batt.
41ˢᵗ
Inf. Regt.

IV Batt.
21ˢᵗ
Inf. Regt.

Czerniaków

Fort
Szczęśliwice

Mokotów

Fort
Mokotów

Fort
Dąbrowskiego

Fort
Czerniaków

11ᵗʰ
INFANTRY
DIVISION

Raków

Okęcie

31ˢᵗ
INFANTRY
DIVISION

10ᵗʰ
INFANTRY
DIVISION

Imielin

Wilanów

46ᵗʰ
INFANTRY
DIVISION

The Battle for Warsaw
24–27 September 1939

31ˢᵗ
INFANTRY
DIVISION

German units and
line of attack

60ᵗʰ
Inf. Regt.

Polish units and
defensive positions

┼┼┼┼┼┼┼┼   Railways

POLAND DIVIDED

Poland under German and
Soviet occupation
September 1939–June 1941

BALTIC SEA

LITHUANIA

R. Neman

Königsberg

Danzig

Wilno

EAST PRUSSIA

Grodno

Białystok

Poznań

R. Vistula

Warsaw

Pińsk

R. Warta

Łódź

N

R. Bug

Łuck

Równe

GERMANY

Kraków

R. San

Przemyśl

Lwów

U.S.S.R.

Tarnopol

SLOVAKIA

0   100 miles

0   200 km

HUNGARY

ROMANIA

Annexed to the Reich

General Government

Occupied by
Nazi Germany

Administered by Lithuania

Annexed by the U.S.S.R.

Poland's pre-war frontier

AUTHOR'S NOTE

WRITING ABOUT A REGION WITH SHIFTING FRONTIERS AND MIXED populations can sometimes be a challenging task. For simplicity, in this book I have employed a policy of using names appropriate to the period under scrutiny. If the modern name differs from that, then it will be given in brackets at first mention.

So, to take the example of what is now the Ukrainian city of L'viv: in September 1939, it was the Polish city of Lwów, so it will be rendered here as Lwów (L'viv) at first mention, and simply as Lwów thereafter. No political statement is thereby intended.

In addition, where there is an accepted Anglicized form—such as Warsaw, Brest, or Moscow—then I have naturally used it throughout.

Polish words look complicated, but their pronunciation is consistent. All vowels are of even length, and their sound is best rendered by the English words "sum" (*a*), "ten" (*e*), "ease" (*i*), "lot" (*o*), "book" (*u*), and "sit" (*y*). Most consonants behave in the same way as in English, except for *c*, which is pronounced "ts"; *j*, which is soft, like the *y* in "yes"; and *w*, which is equivalent to an English *v*. The stress in Polish always falls on the penultimate syllable.

There are also a number of accented letters and combinations peculiar to Polish, such as:

ą = nasal *a*, hence *Piątek* is pronounced "piontek"

ę = nasal *e*, hence *Łęczyca* is pronounced "wenchytsa"

ó = *u*, hence *Kraków* is pronounced "krakoov"

ci = *ch* as in "cheese"

ć = *ch* as in "cheese"

cz = a longer *ch*, as in "catch"

ch = hard *h*, as in "loch"

ł = English *w*, hence *Kałuszyn* is pronounced "kawooshin"

ń = soft *n*, as in Spanish "*mañana*"

rz = soft *j*, as in French "*je*"

si = *sh* as in "ship"

ś = *sh* as in "ship"

sz = a longer *sh*, as in "sheer"

ż = as *rz*, as in French "*je*"

ź = similar to ż, but harder.

PREFACE

THE SECOND WORLD WAR IN EUROPE BEGAN AT DAWN ON SEP-
tember 1, 1939.

It shouldn't need saying, of course, but the date of the start of the
largest war in human history is a subject that is shrouded in confusion across the globe. Every combatant nation has its own narrative
and chronology. In China and Japan, for instance, the war is held to
have begun on July 7, 1937, when Japanese and Chinese forces engaged
following the Marco Polo Bridge Incident. For Americans, the war
started on December 7, 1941, with the Japanese attack on Pearl Harbor; everything before that date is merely a curious, far-off prelude to
the main event. Sometimes, such dissenting views are entirely justifi-
able, dictated by geography and convention; sometimes they are more
mendacious. In the Soviet Union (and in its successor state, Russia), for
example, the fiction has long been maintained that the Second World
War began only with the German attack on June 22, 1941. Stalin's
earlier invasions of Poland, Finland, and the Baltic States have been
skillfully airbrushed from the popular narrative.

Even the British and the French—and their respective former em-
pires—are less than entirely clear on the issue. Though both countries

declared war on Hitler's Germany on September 3, 1939, after the Germans' failure to withdraw from Poland, they did nothing to aid their ally, shamefully leaving Poland to its fate. Thereafter, for the people of Britain and France, nothing much happened until German forces smashed westward across the French border in May 1940. The British called that intervening period the "Phoney War"; the French, the "*Drôle de Guerre*"—the "funny war."

But there was nothing funny—or phony—about the war that Poland fought in the autumn of 1939. As the sun rose on September 1, Hitler's forces crossed the Polish frontier from the north, west, and south, hurtling forward in their tanks and trucks and on foot, while the Luftwaffe scoured the skies, bombing and strafing seemingly with impunity. After little more than two weeks, with Polish armies in disarray and lacking any assistance from their Western allies, the coup de grâce was delivered by Hitler's new confederate, Stalin, and the Red Army invaded from the east on September 17. As German and Soviet forces met on Polish soil and declared their eternal brotherhood—conveniently forgetting the preceding years of rabid antipathy—Poland entered a new totalitarian dark age: a world of persecution, misery, and death. By the end of the Second World War, one in five Poles would be dead.

Poland, then, was—in that neat slogan devised by its wartime propagandists—"First to Fight." Its defensive campaign in September 1939 opened the Second World War in Europe: a five-week struggle that prefaced nearly 300 weeks of slaughter. It cost as many as 200,000 lives on all sides and showcased many of the brutal practices that would feature so strongly in the later conflict: the targeting of civilian populations, indiscriminate aerial bombing, and mass killings.

Invaded and occupied by Europe's two preeminent totalitarian powers, Poland would be exposed to every horror that modern conflict could devise. Just as the Wehrmacht unleashed a race war against the Poles in the west, so the Red Army imported class war in the east. Poland's citizens would be sifted and sorted, with those deemed undesirable subjected to arrest and deportation if they were lucky, state-sanctioned murder if they were not.

The Polish campaign also had a significance well beyond that country's frontiers: it brought Britain and France into the war. The two Western allies had guaranteed Poland's territorial integrity in the spring of 1939 in a vain attempt to halt German expansion. Consequently, it was this defense of Poland—however nominally interpreted—that transformed the war from a Central European squabble into a conflict of worldwide significance.

Bearing all of this in mind, it would be fair to expect that Poland's brave, brief war of 1939 might be well known. But it is not—it has been all but forgotten outside Poland. Despite our collective obsession with all aspects of the Second World War, the "September campaign" always seems somehow to fall through the cracks, ignored or passed over in a few sentences. Consequently, it is barely known or understood in the English-speaking historiography.

A glance at some of the most popular history books of the past few years should serve to illustrate the point. Whereas enthusiastic readers can peruse competing volumes on the Ardennes campaign, Dunkirk, or D-Day, they would search in vain for much modern scholarship on Poland's war of 1939. Aside from a couple of specialist military studies, the last book devoted to the subject, Nicholas Bethell's *The War Hitler Won*, was published in 1972.

General works are little better. An examination of popular histories of the Second World War reveals the scale of the problem. On average, out of some 700 pages of text, they devote just 16 to the defense of Poland in 1939, which often include the wider matter of the entry into the war of Britain and France. Some ignore the subject entirely or are almost comically Anglocentric, describing the outbreak of the war by referring solely to Whitehall politics while making no mention of the very real battles then being fought on Polish soil. Moreover, those that examine the subject in anything more than a cursory manner tend to rely almost entirely on German sources: the usually self-serving memoirs of those who participated in the invasion, and the often turgid regimental histories of the German army that tend to make nonmilitary historians' eyes bleed. The results are predictably myopic: historians repeat Nazi propaganda tropes almost verbatim, ignore the Soviet invasion entirely, and shamefully write the Poles out of their own history. Yet the real problem is more profound. History, as we know, is written primarily by the winners. As Hitler pithily put it on the very eve of the Polish campaign, "The victor will never be asked if he told the truth." And, in the case of Poland, none of the victors had any interest in telling the true story. The Germans spun their narrative of the September campaign as best they could in the early years of the war and produced a host of memoirs, coffee-table books, and pseudo-histories that lauded their victory, extolled the brilliance of the Blitzkrieg, and emphasized the innate inferiority of the enemy. After the war, meanwhile, when the extent of German crimes was known to the world, the invasion of Poland became a quaint overture to the murderous main act. Aside from a few postwar memoirs and the work of a small number of historians, few Germans care to remember the campaign today.

The Soviets, meanwhile, did everything they could to pretend they did not invade Poland in 1939. The postwar narrative, which showed the Soviet Union and its people as the foremost victims of the war, could not permit an acknowledgment that Stalin had facilitated Hitler in starting the conflict, or that he had then assisted his newfound ally in invading, partitioning, and destroying Poland. Consequently, the Red Army's invasion was dressed up as a humanitarian intervention, and any mention of it as anything else was effectively suppressed, both in the Soviet Union and in postwar Communist Poland. That denial continues to our present moment. As recently as 2016, a Russian blogger was prosecuted for sharing a text about German–Soviet collaboration in the invasion of Poland. His alleged crime was the "circulation of false information."

Although not an active suppression of the facts, Britain's own heroic wartime narrative left little popular appetite for, or interest in, its humiliating betrayal of its Polish ally. Even though many Polish veterans of 1939 made their homes in the United Kingdom after their nation's defeat, and after Poland fell to Communist control in 1945, their stories were scarcely heard. The memoirs and histories written by veterans residing in the United Kingdom—such as Władysław Anders, Klemens

Rudnicki, and Józef Garliński—failed to puncture the established Western narrative of the war.

In the end, it was left to the Poles themselves to tell the story of the two invasions of 1939. In the immediate postwar years, Communist Poland was not interested in publicizing those events, except to reflexively damn the "German fascists" and the prewar regime for its supposed foolhardiness. By the 1960s, when a more nationalistic communism prevailed, a new narrative emerged. This narrative, based loosely (and not wholly inaccurately) upon the idea of the ordinary Polish soldier being betrayed by the ineptitude of his superiors and the duplicity of his capitalist allies, vehemently denied any belligerent role for the Red Army. Only after the Communist system collapsed in 1989 were those aspects of Polish history finally open to objective examination, and only then could the story of Poland's war be told in its entirety.

This book, therefore, is an attempt to embrace some of that new Polish historiography, and so to rebalance the wonky Western narrative of the Second World War's opening campaign. It tells a story that is still little known to English-speaking readers—a story of heroism, of suffering, and of a gallant fight against ruthless and superior enemies. And it is an attempt to wrest the story free from the dark shadow of totalitarian propaganda—from the Nazi mythology of an easy Blitzkrieg victory to the Soviet lie that the Red Army never invaded at all. As such, Polish voices—from memoirs, diaries, and archival accounts—are finally brought into the story. One can only hope that future historians will no longer render the Poles as nameless, voiceless victims, bit-part players in their own narrative.

Of course, any work of scale and ambition requires collaborators, and though the words on the page are mine, a huge number of debts were accrued in their preparation that must be acknowledged. Many colleagues and friends were kind enough to share their knowledge, including Grzegorz Bębnik, Sławomir Dębski, Richard Hargreaves,

Tomasz Kuba Kozłowski, Wojciech Łukaszun, Dmitriy Panto, Bill Russ, Ian Sayer, Rob Schäfer, Ben H. Shepherd, Andrzej Suchcitz, Jacek Tebinka, and Anna Zygalska-Cannon.

Others were on hand to give help and advice as I traveled across Poland to visit archives, museums, and the sites where the events I was describing took place, such as Mokra, Wizna, the Bzura battlefields, or Mława. They include Krzysztof Mroczkowski and Jakub Link-Lenczowski at the Muzeum Lotnictwa Polskiego in Kraków, Katarzyna Tomiczek of the Ośrodek Promocji Gminy Węgierska Górka, Emil Makles of the Izba Pamięci Bitwy pod Mokrą, Kazimierz Śwircz at the Muzeum Bitwy nad Bzurą in Kutno, Marcin Sochoń and Dariusz Szymanowski of the Stowarzyszenie "Wizna 1939," Ludwik Zalewski in Nowogród, Wojciech Śleszyński and Łukasz Radulski in Białystok, Katarzyna Myszkowska and Krzysztof Bojarczuk in Sulejów, Andrzej Jarczewski and Mikołaj Ratka at the Radiostacja Gliwice in Gliwice, Tomasz Chinciński at the Muzeum II Wojny Światowej in Gdańsk, Karol Szejko at the Muzeum Westerplatte i Wojny 1939 r. in Gdańsk, Marek Adamkowicz at the Muzeum Poczty Polskiej in Gdańsk, Jan Tymiński and Jacek Waryszak at the Muzeum Marynarki Wojennej in Gdynia, Radosław Wiecki in Tczew, Wojciech Krajewski and Janusz Wesołowski at the Muzeum Wojska Polskiego in Warsaw, Władysław Szarski at the Muzeum Obrony Wybrzeża on Hel, Marcin Owsiński at the Muzeum Stutthof in Sztutowo, and Jacek Wilamowski and Katarzyna Skourpa-Malińska at the Muzeum Ziemi Zawkrzeńskiej in Mława.

In addition, a few people generously gave their linguistic or research help, including Jess Bennett, Will Hobden, Jadwiga Kowalska, Philipp Rauh, Saskia Smellie, Alex Standen, Lyuba Vinogradova, and Axel von Wittenberg at the Polish Institute and Sikorski Museum in London. Thanks, too, to Bill Donohoe for the cartography. My agent, Georgina Capel, was as stoic and supportive as a writer could wish, notwithstanding the myriad crises that I inflicted upon her. My UK editor, Jörg Hensgen, was similarly brilliant, as insightful and deft of editorial touch as ever. Special thanks must also go to my outrageously gifted and indefatigable research assistant Anastazja Pindor, without whom this book would scarcely have been possible. For everything else, I must thank my wife, Melissa, and my children, Oscar and Amelia, and their daily reminders of what really matters.

Lastly, I would like to dedicate this book to someone whose passion for the subject inspired my interest in Polish history nearly three decades ago—my former professor, coauthor, and most esteemed colleague, Norman Davies.

Tring, 2019

AN UNREMARKABLE MAN

T HERE IS ONLY ONE SURVIVING PICTURE OF FRANCISZEK
Honiok. It was taken for a family occasion, or maybe a court visit,
and it shows him in a suit and tie, his dark blond hair beginning to re-
cede at the temples, his pale eyes betraying a determined look. At five
feet two inches, he was a little shorter than average, and he had a slightly
disheveled air, but other than that he was very ordinary. Perhaps that
was what determined his fate.

As the forty-one-year-old bachelor was escorted away that day, it was
said that he looked bewildered. Doubtless he was wondering why he
had been picked up, but he did not say a word.[1] He had most likely been
selected from a file in Gestapo headquarters, far away on Prinz Albrecht
Strasse in Berlin, where an ethnic Pole with a history of anti-German
agitation was urgently required for an undisclosed purpose. If anything,
Honiok was too qualified. Born in the German province of Upper Silesia
in 1898, he had fought on the Polish side during the Silesian Uprisings
that had followed the First World War. After a brief stint in Poland, he
then returned to Germany in 1925, whereupon he was forced to fight
deportation back to Poland, a case he successfully pursued all the way
to the League of Nations in Geneva. Though his firebrand days were

perhaps over by 1939, Honiok was still well known in his home village of Hohenlieben (Łubie) as a staunch advocate of the Polish cause.

As he was taken away on the afternoon of August 30, 1939, Honiok had little idea of what his Gestapo captors had in store for him. He was driven first to the barracks at Beuthen (Bytom), where he was given food and water, and then to the Gestapo headquarters at Oppeln (Opole), where he spent an uncomfortable night locked in a file room. Throughout, his captors noted, he was "apathetic, his head constantly bowed."[2] He never spoke, and no one spoke to him except for curt instructions from his Gestapo escort. Moreover, despite the German obsession with paperwork, he was not registered in any of the locations through which he passed; his guards were under orders that he was to remain anonymous.[3] The following morning, August 31, Honiok was taken to the police station at Gleiwitz (Gliwice), where he was placed in solitary confinement, again with no records taken.[4] It would be the last day of his life.

Later that afternoon, across town in the Haus Oberschlesien Hotel, Schutzstaffel (SS) *Sturmbannführer* (Major) Helmut Naujocks delivered a final briefing to his team of six SS men and policemen. Naujocks—a twenty-seven-year-old from Kiel on Germany's Baltic coast—had been an early convert to Nazism, joining the SS in 1931 after briefly attending university and having his nose flattened by a Communist with an iron bar. Described by one contemporary as "an intellectual gangster," he swiftly fell under the patronage of Reinhard Heydrich, the head of the German police network and one of the darkest figures in the Nazi hierarchy.[5] It was on Heydrich's instruction that Naujocks and his team had arrived in Gleiwitz two days earlier, posing as mining engineers. Their real task, however, was to engineer a "false flag" operation: to make it look as though Polish irregulars had attacked German territory.

Tensions between Germany and Poland—which had been strained at best for some two decades—had spiked over the preceding few months. The ostensible reason for the *froideur* was Germany's territorial losses to Poland from the Versailles Treaty—primarily Upper Silesia, Posen, and the so-called Polish Corridor—all of which had been viewed as a

Helmut Naujocks, the "intellectual gangster" and architect of the Gleiwitz incident.
Library of Congress; public domain

The victim: Franciszek Honiok
private collection

profound humiliation in Germany and had contributed to a gradual poisoning of German–Polish relations. Hitler's ire, however, went deeper, stoked by his racial prejudices and his belief that Germany's national destiny lay in expansion to the east. As he had become more reckless in his saber-rattling, eager to capitalize on what he saw as Western weakness and anxious for the war that he thought would define him and his "Third Reich," Hitler had begun to target Poland more specifically, ramping up the rhetoric and complaining vociferously of Polish barbarism and bad faith.

By the summer of 1939, therefore, territorial concessions by the Poles, had they been offered, would no longer be enough: Hitler wanted his war. He faced two problems, however. For one thing, Poland had allies in Britain and France: both had pledged to defend it in the event of foreign aggression. For another, the vast majority of the German people, though most supported the Nazis wholeheartedly, had no stomach for another world war. Hitler thus had to dress up his belligerent intentions to make them appear defensive: he needed to show Poland as the aggressor and Germany as the innocent victim. In this way, he reasoned, the German people might be persuaded to support the war, and Poland might even be detached from its international alliances. Hitler summed up these ideas in a speech to his senior military commanders at his Alpine residence near Berchtesgaden on August 22. "The destruction of Poland has priority," he said, adding that "the aim is to eliminate active forces, not to reach a definite line. Even if war breaks out in the West, the destruction of Poland remains the primary objective." When it came to public opinion, he assured the commanders, "I shall give a propagandist reason for starting the war, no matter whether it is plausible or not. The victor will not be asked afterwards whether he told the truth."[6]

That summer, the world saw much of Hitler's propaganda offensive. Though the SS took the lead, German military intelligence, the Abwehr, also involved itself in the task of undermining Poland. In the last week of August, it engineered a spate of incidents across the country, which were often intended to look as though they were inspired by anti-German sentiment: a bomb attack was carried out on a war memorial in Cieszyn, another targeted a German book shop in Poznań, yet another damaged a railway bridge in Nowy Sącz.[7]

Its most infamous operation took place on the night of August 28, when one of its agents—an unemployed metalworker of German extraction by the name of Antoni Guzy—left a large bomb, contained in two suitcases, in the left-luggage hall of Tarnów railway station in the south of the country. When the bomb exploded shortly after 11:00 p.m., it destroyed a section of the station building and killed twenty-four people, including a two-year-old girl.[8] Guzy was arrested at the scene, and under interrogation he provided investigators with chapter and verse on the subversive methods of the Abwehr. He explained that he had been recruited via a German trade union organization and had received cursory training in Germany before being assigned to a cell operating out of the town of Skoczów in southern Poland. After receiving his orders in a coded message broadcast by Radio Breslau (Wrocław), he had traveled from Bielsko first to Kraków, where he had collected the cases, and then on to Tarnów, where he had deposited them in the left-luggage hall. Guzy, who claimed not to have known that the cases contained explosives, told his interrogators that he had done what he did because he "felt German."[9]

Guzy was little more than a pawn, but his interrogation would have made it clear to the Poles—if they were not aware already—that the Abwehr was behind the attacks. What was less clear was the precise motivation: the bombing in Tarnów had little discernible military rationale, beyond a wanton destruction of Polish infrastructure—and Guzy gave no hint of a wider goal or plan. It seemed most likely intended to provoke some sort of retaliation by the Poles against the German minority, thereby adding weight to Hitler's propaganda narrative of ethnic persecution and perhaps providing him with grounds for a military intervention.[10]

While the Abwehr recklessly blundered, and Hitler railed about Polish intransigence, the agents of the SS were silently working to drive relations between Berlin and Warsaw to a breaking point. Already that summer, Heydrich had ordered that all "politically unreliable elements" were to be removed from a prohibited area along the German side of the Polish frontier.[11] Within that zone, isolated properties, barns, and farmsteads were identified and earmarked for gasoline-bomb attacks, for which Polish arsonists would then be made responsible.[12] Through the summer of 1939, therefore, German newspapers carried countless lurid reports on what they called "Polish Terror," complaining of "Polish bandits," "growing nervousness," and the "frightful suffering of German refugees." By the end of August, they would claim that some sixty-six Germans had been murdered.[13]

At the same time that the German media was busy slandering the Poles, a training center was established at Bernau, north of Berlin, at which over 300 SS volunteers, mostly from Upper Silesia, were prepared to conduct infiltration operations against Poland. They were trained using Polish weapons and uniforms, and taught the essentials of the Polish language. By late August, they were ready for action. On the night of August 31, the volunteers were deployed in "raids" on the German customs post at Hochlinden (Stodoły), near Rybnik, and the foresters' lodge near Pitschen (Byczyna).[14] By smashing windows, firing into the air, and singing and swearing in broken Polish, they were to simulate border incursions by Polish forces.[15] Were it not for the bodies of six concentration camp inmates, who were dressed in Polish uniforms and then shot and left at Hochlinden to add bloody authenticity to the scene, the playacting would have been almost comical.

Given the orgy of murderous pretense that the Germans engineered on the eve of the war, it is perhaps understandable that generations of historians have persistently gotten the story of the Gleiwitz incident wrong, conflating it with other actions—such as Hochlinden—and speaking erroneously of assailants in Polish uniforms and of multiple Polish victims. Such misconceptions, persistent though they are, are dispelled by referring to the original sources, which clearly show that the assailants there were not in uniform, and that there was only one victim.

Beyond that correction, the action at Gleiwitz held another special significance. By accident or design, it was only there that the attackers—posing, of course, as Polish insurgents—were required to speak, to give voice to their "mission" and broadcast their intentions to the wider world. To this end, Naujocks believed that he had developed the perfect plan. From his earlier reconnaissance, he had identified the Gleiwitz radio transmitting station, with its 111-meter (365-foot) wooden tower, as an ideal target. He and his men could easily take control of the site, lock up the station staff, fire a few shots into the ceiling, and broadcast an incendiary message in Polish over the airwaves before fleeing into the darkness. He had concluded that 8:00 p.m. would be the best time for the assault, reckoning that his men would be aided by the cover of dusk. It would also be a time when most people would be at home listening to their radios.[16]

Initially, Naujocks's plan for Gleiwitz was to go ahead without bloodshed. But his superiors had decided that the attack required the addition of a clinching piece of evidence. Naujocks was informed by the head of the Gestapo himself, Heinrich Müller, that a Pole would be supplied whose bloodied corpse was to be left at the radio station as irrefutable "proof" of Polish responsibility for the attack.[17] For this reason, it was not

"Attention! Here is Gleiwitz!"
akg-images / Interfoto

enough to use one of the concentration camp inmates killed at Hochlinden; it had to be someone with a proven history of anti-German agitation. This, then, was the fate that the SS had in store for Franciszek Honiok.

So, while Honiok spent his final hours in the Gleiwitz police station, Naujocks waited in his hotel room to receive the code words that would launch his mission. At 4:00 p.m., the phone rang, and, on answering, Naujocks heard Heydrich's nasal, high-pitched voice demanding that he call back immediately. On doing so, he heard Heydrich give the code: "Grossmutter gestorben" (Grandmother has died).[18] With that, he called his men together for a final briefing, reiterating their objectives and respective tasks. Later, he and his men changed into their scruffy civilian clothes and climbed into two cars for the short journey northeast to the transmitter station. Arriving precisely at 8:00 p.m., as planned, and with night rapidly falling, they rushed into the building. Pushing past the station manager, who rose to meet them, Naujocks's men overpowered the staff before taking them to the basement, where they were ordered to face the wall as their hands were tied behind their backs. Naujocks and his radio technician, meanwhile, were trying to work out how to make their incendiary broadcast.

One of the problems that Naujocks had needed to solve in his planning was ensuring that the proclamation would be heard. He had considered targeting the main radio station in Gleiwitz—a much larger facility closer to the city center—but had decided against it, not only because of the logistical challenge, but also because of the likelihood that its broadcasts would be cut off by the transmitter station. Consequently, he decided to stage his attack on the transmitter station itself, where there was only a "storm microphone"—used to interrupt local programs to warn of extreme weather—but also a much-reduced possibility that the broadcast would be monitored and interrupted.[19]

Having dealt with the station staff, Naujocks now had to locate the storm microphone and establish how to patch it into the main broadcast. Finding the device in a cupboard, but unable to connect it, he hauled the staff from the basement at gunpoint, one by one, until one of them told him what to do.[20] With that, the group's Polish speaker, Karl Hornack, pulled a crumpled sheet of paper from his pocket and stepped forward. As a pistol was fired into the air to provide an appropriately martial atmosphere, he read:

UWAGA! TU GLIWICE! RADIOSTACJA ZNAJDUJE SIĘ W POLSKICH RĘKACH! [Attention! Here is Gleiwitz! The radio station is in Polish hands!][21]

What followed was supposed to be a call to arms from a fictional "Polish Freedom Committee," demanding that the Polish population in Germany rise up to resist the authorities and conduct sabotage operations, and promising that the Polish army would soon march in as a liberator.[22] However, for reasons that have never been satisfactorily explained, only the first nine words were broadcast, and those were only audible in the district of Gleiwitz itself; the remainder was lost in a cacophony of static. Heydrich, listening in Berlin, heard nothing at all.[23]

While Naujocks had been busying himself with his broadcast, Franciszek Honiok was delivered to the building. Shortly before 8:00 p.m., he had been visited in his cell in the Gleiwitz police station by an SS man in a white coat purporting to be a doctor, who had given him an injection.[24] Unconscious, he was then driven the short distance to the transmitter station, where two of Naujocks's men carried him into the building, laying him down close to the rear entrance. It is not clear who shot Honiok, or precisely when he was killed, but as Naujocks left the radio station, he stopped briefly to examine the dead man, slumped close to the door, his face smeared with his own blood. He would maintain, to his death in 1966, that neither he nor his men had shot Franciszek Honiok. He knew nothing about the man, Naujocks told prosecutors, not even his name: "I was not responsible for him," he said.[25]

So, with barely a thought, Franciszek Honiok was murdered to provide the gloss on Heydrich's nefarious propaganda coup. He was disposable, anonymous, collateral damage in Nazi Germany's headlong drive to war. He would become a footnote to history, his murder demonstrating the sneering, contemptuous brutality of the Nazi regime. It was a grim foretaste of the fate that would befall Poland: a single death that prefaced at least 50 million others.

It didn't matter that the ruse to which Honiok's body had given spurious credence failed: the German media were already primed and ready to run the story regardless. Within hours, the radios were blaring and the newspaper presses were rolling, the latter bearing banner headlines about the Polish "attack" on Gleiwitz and the inevitability of a German response.[26] By the time most Germans had heard or read those words the following morning, Hitler's tanks were already advancing into Poland. The Second World War had begun.

CHAPTER ONE

"WESTERPLATTE FIGHTS ON"

A T 4:43 A.M., SHORTLY AFTER DAWN, ON SEPTEMBER 1, 1939, the German battleship *Schleswig-Holstein* slipped her moorings in the New Port of Danzig (Gdańsk) and moved the short distance to where the Vistula made a southward turn, the Bend of the Five Whistles. There, positioned almost perpendicularly across the channel, she trained her guns on the Polish military transit depot on the Westerplatte some 300 meters (985 feet) away, and—on the command of her captain, Gustav Klcikamp—opened fire.

For those watching events that morning, the *Schleswig-Holstein* must have seemed a strange candidate to fire the opening salvos of the Second World War. She was a survivor of the *Deutschland* class of battleships and had been launched in 1906, before the advent of the HMS *Dreadnought* revolutionized naval warfare. Obsolete even before the start of the First World War, the *Schleswig-Holstein* had participated in the Battle of Jutland in 1916 and had been decommissioned the following year, destined for use as a floating barracks. She had even been earmarked as a "target ship" for the modern vessels of Hitler's navy to practice their gunnery. With her vertical ram bow, the *Schleswig-Holstein* was a naval relic, a throwback to an earlier age, pressed back into service as a training ship for German naval cadets. Moored in Danzig's harbor on a "friendship visit" to the city to commemorate the twenty-fifth anniversary of the Battle of Tannenberg—that salient German victory in the opening months of the First World War—she would scarcely have been seen as a threat.

Yet, though the manner of the attack may have been a surprise, the location certainly was not. Danzig had long been the focus of German–Polish tensions. Though ethnically predominantly German, it had been detached from Germany by the Treaty of Versailles and established as a free state under the League of Nations; at the same time, transport and trade concessions were granted to the newly reconstituted Poland, so that Danzig served, in effect, as Poland's port. This naturally rankled, both in Germany and among the majority German population of Danzig. Strikes among dockworkers in 1920 then led to Poland being granted the peninsula of the Westerplatte—effectively the eastern bank of the Vistula estuary—to serve as a military depot for the secure unloading of munitions and military hardware. As one of the few key Polish sites in and around Danzig, the Westerplatte would inevitably find itself in the firing line in the event of heightened tensions.

And tensions were most certainly heightened in the summer of 1939. After his success in dismantling Czechoslovakia, Hitler had trained his sights on Poland, and Danzig was an obvious target, both for his rhetoric and for the subversive actions of his acolytes. With passions duly inflamed, it was perhaps unsurprising that large numbers of Danzigers turned out to welcome the *Schleswig-Holstein* upon its arrival in the port on the morning of August 25. They would not have suspected that the aged vessel, sailing into dock with her flags flying and her crew immaculately turned out on her upper decks, was concealing a company of 225 marines below her decks.[1] Her "friendship visit" was, in truth, a mission of war.

So it was that the *Schleswig-Holstein*'s main 28 cm guns were brought to bear on the Westerplatte that morning. There was not much for them to aim for. A barracks, mess, and storerooms had been built in the early 1930s along with a ring of five guardhouses to provide a modicum of

4:48 a.m.: the battleship *Schleswig-Holstein* opens fire.
Muzeum Wojska Polskiego, Warsaw

security. In accordance with the original treaty by which it had been established, the Westerplatte depot was permitted a garrison of some eighty-eight officers and men. However, as German–Polish relations had deteriorated from 1938, the site had been surreptitiously reinforced, its garrison raised to 210 through the simple method of smuggling in soldiers, and its defenses augmented by the addition of antitank ramparts, barbed-wire entanglements, an alarm system, and seven reinforced outposts, complete with slit trenches and earthworks. In total, the Polish troops on the Westerplatte possessed 160 rifles, 42 machine guns, 1,000 grenades, 4 mortars, and 2 antitank guns.[2] As one veteran recalled of that summer, every Westerplatte soldier slept with his boots on, "holding his gun, like a lover beneath the blanket, locked and loaded."[3]

At 4:48 a.m., as the Polish garrison slept, the *Schleswig-Holstein*'s guns began their broadside. Over the next seven minutes, they boomed and thundered, raining down over 5 metric tons (5.5 US tons) of shells on the Polish positions, aiming to breach the depot's eastern perimeter wall and soften up the defenders. In addition to the eight salvos from the main guns, 59 shells were fired from the *Schleswig-Holstein*'s medium battery, as well as 600 rounds from its 20 mm flak guns.[4] As one Polish survivor recalled with masterful understatement, "They dropped a lot of iron on Westerplatte."[5] The results were certainly impressive: trees were splintered to matchwood, and many of the barracks and guardhouses were damaged. Despite the point-blank range, however, the initial shelling was not as successful as one might expect. Some of the shells failed to explode, others detonated in the trees, and a few sailed over the peninsula, dropping harmlessly in the Bay of Danzig beyond.[6] Nonetheless, as a veil of smoke and dust enveloped the peninsula, the first military death of the war was registered: a twenty-five-year-old rifleman, Stefan Jezierski, was killed instantly when a 20 mm shell came through the observation window of his position in Guardhouse 3.[7]

Given their dominance in firepower, it is perhaps understandable that the German attackers were confident of taking the depot "in ten minutes."[8] But that optimism was not shared by all of those present. The *Schleswig-Holstein*'s captain, Gustav Kleikamp—a veteran of the Battle of Jutland and a former U-boat officer—had much to say in the ship's log about the lack of adequate preparation and reconnaissance. A few days earlier, he had written that "informants have been given more credibility than the military planners, and no one has been told— even in August 1939—what was intended for the Westerplatte."[9] He was especially concerned about the lack of adequate maps, given that a single example—"old, containing no details of buildings and munition stores"—had been handed to the marine brigade's commanders only the day before the attack.[10] The marines would be advancing blind.

Such concerns would be dramatically realized at 4:55 a.m., when the *Schleswig-Holstein*'s guns fell silent and the first landward assault began. Moving westward along the peninsula, the marines came under fire from all sides as soon as they passed what was left of the 2-meter (6.5-foot) wall that marked the boundary of the Westerplatte depot. If they were expecting a simple mopping-up operation, convinced that no one could have survived the bombardment, they would be sorely disappointed. As they advanced, they soon found themselves under withering fire from the Polish positions, some of which were not visible to them and were not marked on their out-of-date maps.[11] As their commander would later confess, at no time during that first assault did they even see the enemy.[12]

The Poles, however, could see their attackers all too clearly. As one defender, stationed in a forward outpost, recalled, "I saw how the Germans advanced. They had white canvas rucksacks, two long-handle hand grenades each and egg grenades in a bag, also of white canvas. They made very good targets, with their dark uniforms and white canvas bags, very easy to see from a distance. But we didn't have to strain our eyes, because we let them come as close as 30–40 meters [100 to 130 feet] before we opened fire. . . . Few of them came out alive."[13] Moving ahead in plain sight and unaware of their surroundings, the German marines were sitting ducks for the Polish defenders. Watching from the *Schleswig-Holstein,* Captain Kleikamp noted with concern that despite the "continuing heavy fighting . . . the company seems to make only very slow progress."[14]

After an hour of fighting, the advance by the first wave of three marine platoons had ground to a halt just inside the eastern perimeter of the Westerplatte depot. Taking heavy losses, with thirteen dead and fifty-eight wounded, the marines were forced to withdraw; the survivors were convinced that Polish soldiers were even hiding in what remained of the treetops.[15] Kleikamp noted morosely, "The Poles on the Westerplatte will not simply be overrun by a surprise attack."[16]

With that failure, the *Schleswig-Holstein* launched a second, more intensive bombardment of the Polish positions, this time lasting for almost an hour and using some 46 metric tons (50 US tons) of munitions.[17] Again, the effect on the Westerplatte was devastating. As Lieutenant Leon Pająk recalled: "The momentary calm is broken by the roar of cannons and explosions. . . . The soldiers cling to the walls of the trench. A hail of shrapnel, splinters of tree branches and entire treetops rain down from the sky. Fountains of sand, a whirling cloud of smoke, the stench of sulphur and hot iron . . ." Soon after making these observations, Pająk was hit in the stomach and groin and lost consciousness.[18]

When the bombardment was finished shortly before 9:00 a.m., the marine company, now reinforced by sixty men of the SS-Heimwehr

Danzig, a Nazi militia raised from local volunteers, launched another ground assault. Initially the attack fared better than before, with forward units briefly reaching the ring of Polish guardhouses before being repelled. In the chaos that followed, however, the marines' commanding officer, Second Lieutenant Wilhelm Henningsen, was mortally wounded, and the unit was again forced to withdraw.[19] At 1:00 p.m., Henningsen's deputy reported to the *Schleswig-Holstein* that "taking the Westerplatte with the storm company was impossible."[20]

Later that day, the marines' acting commander reported to his superiors that success would only be achieved with the "complete destruction" of the site, and requested that his unit—half of which had been "wiped out"—be removed from the front line.[21] The frustration he showed went all the way to the top. In his diary, the German army's chief of staff, General Franz Halder, recorded the difficulty that the Polish defense of the Westerplatte was causing. "No heavy artillery," he wrote. "*Schleswig* maintains it cannot destroy [the bunkers], *Stuka* liaison maintains that they cannot hit them." With only a little exaggeration, he summed up the problem: "At least 20 modern concrete bunkers, with underground connection. Above ground, wire obstacles within thickly wooded area."[22]

Among the defenders, meanwhile, morale was good and losses comparatively light. Only a few men were wounded and two killed that day: Stefan Jezierski, killed in the opening assault, and Sergeant Wojciech Najsarek, killed during the marines' assault on the perimeter. Two others, Corporal Andrzej Kowalczyk and the rifleman Bronisław Uss, would die of their wounds the following day. "After the baptism of fire," the garrison's commander, Major Henryk Sucharski, recalled, "the crew maintains excellent combat spirit."[23] Clearly, the Westerplatte was not the easy target that the Germans had imagined.

WHILE THE FIGHTING RAGED ON THE WESTERPLATTE THAT morning, another German assault was under way in the city itself, at the so-called Polish Post Office on Heveliusplatz. Poland had been granted an extraterritorial post office in Danzig under the Treaty of Versailles to provide for the secure handling of postal traffic through the city. And as a prominent symbol of the Polish state, the post office inevitably became a target when the crisis peaked in the summer of 1939. In response, a combat engineer, Reserve Lieutenant Konrad Guderski, had been sent to bolster the building's defenses, and army reservists and militiamen had been transferred in to serve as the postal staff. By the morning of September 1, the building contained fifty-eight people—including the manager's wife and adopted daughter, eleven-year-old Erwina—along with rifles, machine guns, and three crates of hand grenades. In the event of an attack, the defenders were ordered to hold out for six hours, by which time they would be relieved by the Polish army.[24]

As at the Westerplatte, the German attackers at the post office— units of the SS-Heimwehr Danzig and the Danzig police—grievously underestimated their opponents. When the muffled boom of the *Schleswig-Holstein*'s guns sounded in the distance at 4:48 a.m., they began their assault, starting with a large-scale raid on the front of the building to serve as a feint for an attempted breach of the rear. Both attacks failed, stymied by the preparedness and fierce resistance of the Polish defenders. Later that morning, two armored cars were brought up along with three artillery pieces, and the Germans attacked again. They achieved little, however. Polish machine-gun positions replied to each German assault with such venom that one attacker described the building as a "fire-spewing mountain."[25] Among the defenders, meanwhile, only Guderski was killed, apparently by the blast of his own grenade while he was halting an attempted German incursion.[26] "Even shelling with the heavy howitzer of the Wehrmacht could not bring the defenders to surrender," one SS veteran of the action recalled, adding that "the Poles defended their Post Office with extraordinary bravery."[27] Surprised by such determined resistance, the German commander, Police General Willi Bethke, ordered the evacuation of the surrounding buildings, fearful of collateral damage and doubtless wary of eyewitnesses to

German troops advance cautiously on the Polish Post Office in Danzig.
Narodowe Archiwum Cyfrowe

his actions. The Poles were then addressed by loudspeaker and informed that they had two hours to surrender. After that, they were told, the building would be destroyed.[28]

In the late afternoon, once it had become clear that the Poles were not going to submit—many of them assumed they would be shot if they did so[29]—the Germans resumed their attacks, with concentrated artillery fire finally forcing the defenders into the cellar. Then Bethke delivered a bestial coup de grâce. Bringing up a tanker, he ordered his men to pump gasoline into the building's basement. A hand grenade would provide the ignition. As one survivor recalled, "Everything went up in flames [and] we in the cellar were suffocating with the gases. We decided, because of the overwhelming German advantage, to give ourselves up. When we cried out that we surrender, the Germans ignored us and continued the attack."[30] In desperation, the post office director, Dr. Jan Michoń, who was already injured, staggered out waving a white cloth. The SS, shouting "Down with the Polish dogs!," gunned him down. Next, the postmaster, Józef Wąsik, attempted to surrender. He, too, was killed, engulfed, according to some accounts, by a blast from a flamethrower.[31]

In the end, five of the defenders were killed outright and a further six would die in the following days of their burns, including eleven-year-old Erwina.[32] A few managed to escape via the rear of the building, but the remainder surrendered, emerging—with singed hair and blackened faces—to be delivered into the hands of the Danzig Gestapo. A month later, these survivors, along with four of those who had attempted to escape and had been recaptured, would be tried before a military court as "irregulars." Thirty-eight of them were subsequently executed by firing squad.[33]

THAT MORNING, AS THE OPENING ATTACKS OF THE WAR RAGED, Hitler took the stage in the Kroll Opera House in Berlin to deliver a speech to the assembled members of the Reichstag. The people of the German capital were in a phlegmatic mood. Many of them would have listened to Hitler's proclamation to his army, broadcast by radio beginning at 5:40 a.m., in which he had raged about the "bloody terror" of the Poles and lauded Germany's fight "for honor."[34] Consequently, when Hitler left the Reich Chancellery for the Kroll, all the usual precautions had been made for the demonstration of popular enthusiasm that was expected to result: barriers had been erected, and Sturmabteilung (SA) and SS men were deployed to hold back the crowds. Except that there were no crowds. As Albert Speer noted, the streets of the capital were "strikingly quiet" that morning, and the few Berliners who were present stared in silence as Hitler passed by. One of the regime's regional party leaders, *Gauleiter* Karl Wahl, went further, claiming that there was "no enthusiasm" for war, and that the entire German people "seemed seized by a paralyzing horror."[35]

If Hitler shared such concerns that morning, he did not readily show them. Though he was outwardly calm and had slept well the night before, the nervous exhaustion of the previous few weeks was manifesting itself in other ways—stomach pains, headaches, and a toothache. As his valet recalled, Hitler's breath at that time was "almost constantly foul." Another member of his entourage remembered that his halitosis was so bad that those around him struggled not to step back in revulsion.[36]

In the Kroll Opera, meanwhile, bedecked with swastika flags, a vast golden eagle spanned the width of the stage, and there was scarcely a seat to be had. Though many deputies were absent—Reichstag president Hermann Göring had only summoned members at 3:00 a.m., and some were serving in the Wehrmacht—the vacancies were taken by eager Nazi bigwigs and ambitious underlings, all keen to witness history. German radio had been alive with accounts of the "Polish attacks" at Gleiwitz and elsewhere the previous night, and it was clear to all that the tensions of the summer were about to boil over. So Hitler, dressed in a smart field-gray tunic and dark trousers, took the podium in an atmosphere of hushed expectation.

He began in rather halting, uncertain tones—as was his style—his rasping staccato delivery contrasting with Göring's mellifluous words of introduction. As his voice rose, he revisited many of the themes that had fed his popularity and driven his rise to power: the iniquity of the Versailles Treaty, the perfidy of the Western Powers, Germany as the eternal victim. He also rounded on Poland: on Warsaw's "unreasonable" refusal to "settle the Corridor question," its "slow strangling" of the Free City of Danzig, and its "oppression of the Germans." "No great power can long stand by passively and watch such events," he warned.[37]

Increasingly interrupted by applause, Hitler grew more impassioned, elaborately rolling his r's as he did so. Arriving at the meat of his speech, he revealed that "Polish atrocities" had once again been committed the previous night: fourteen in total, three of which were "quite serious," referring to Hochlinden, Pitschen, and Gleiwitz. Posing as the innocent party, Hitler stated that his "patience had been mistaken for weakness" and that he was now resolved "to speak to Poland in the same language that Poland for months past has used toward us." After another short digression, he went on:

This night, for the first time, Polish regular soldiers fired on our territory. Since 5:45 a.m. we have been returning fire, and from now on bombs will be repaid with bombs. Whoever fights with poison gas will be fought with poison gas. Whoever departs from the rules of humane warfare can only expect that we shall do the same. I will continue this struggle, no matter against whom, until the safety of the Reich and its rights are secured.[38]

It was a masterpiece of feigned innocence, and it concluded with Hitler piously, and mendaciously, declaring that his air force would "restrict itself to attacks on military targets," as he had no desire to "make war against women and children." The speech was greeted with a chorus of "heils" and applause that, as General Halder noted, was "as ordered, but thin."[39] For all the hyperbole, however, one word that was conspicuously absent from the speech was "war." As a memorandum sent from Berlin to all German embassies and consulates that night made clear, that word was to be scrupulously avoided. "This action is for the present not to be described as war," the instruction read, "but merely as engagements which have been brought about by Polish attacks."[40]

For that reason, perhaps, the speech was met with a degree of indifference on the streets of Berlin. Such had been the tumultuous events of the previous few years that most Germans seemed to overlook its significance; indeed, many of those listening to the radio that morning would not have fully appreciated that the speech heralded war. They would have imagined another bout of saber-rattling, a limited incursion, perhaps, followed by a negotiated victory: that was how Hitler had progressed thus far—in the Rhineland, Austria, and Czechoslovakia—and that was how the broad mass of the population would have wanted him to continue. Consequently, there was little sense of panic, or even any grasp of the momentous nature of the events they were witnessing. The American correspondent William Shirer noted that "the people on the streets . . . were apathetic despite the immensity of the news which had greeted them from their radios." When the newsboys came down the street selling their special editions, he said, "no one laid down their tools to buy one."[41]

If apathy reigned in Germany, the public mood across Poland was a mixture of defiance and optimism. According to one Polish pilot, morale among his comrades that morning was "fantastic"—they did not even mind that they were flying outdated aircraft. "No one cared about that," he said. "We just wanted to fight, we wanted to zoom through the air, to avenge old wrongs and new, to kill for the slander and brazenness."[42] One diarist in Lwów (L'viv), Alma Heczko, summed up the popular spirit, writing, "We are not afraid. We must win and we shall win. We won 20 years ago and we shall win again now. Back then we were weaker and we won Poland back, and now that we are strong we will not give away a single piece of our land." Some were even relieved that the dark, troubled summer had finally come to an end. "One thing is certain," recalled an infantry major: "I felt relaxed, or even happy, that the exhausting wait was over and the game had begun."[43]

That optimism, while not entirely misplaced, was at least partly influenced by the positive spin that the Polish media put on the opening day of the conflict. The morning's newspapers had missed the invasion, of course, and spoke only of Poland's "finger on the trigger" and "Hitler's ludicrous demands." The evening editions carried the news in full banner headlines. "The Whole Nation in Defense of Freedom," proclaimed *Wieczór Warszawski* (Warsaw Evening); "With Faith, Trust and Courage, We Go into Battle," intoned *Echo*. Radio, meanwhile, broadcast patriotic music and accounts of Polish cavalry units advancing into East Prussia, promising that "the hour of victory is at hand."[44]

The morning had begun with the solemn tones of radio announcer Zbigniew Świętochowski proclaiming the outbreak of war: "Hello. Hello. This is Warsaw on all wavelengths. At 5:40 German troops crossed the Polish frontier, breaking the nonaggression pact. A number of cities were bombed. In a moment you will hear a special message." Later, Świętochowski would return to the airwaves to give air-raid warnings. The pianist Władysław Szpilman recalled the first such broadcast he heard on that first morning of war:

The howl of sirens sounded from the loudspeakers installed on lamp-posts, in windows and over shop doorways. Then I heard the radio announcer's voice: "This is an alarm warning for the city of Warsaw. . . . Be on alert! Now on their way are . . ." At this point the announcer read out a list of figures and letters of the alphabet in military cipher that fell on civilian ears like a mysterious cabbalistic threat. Did the figures mean the number of aircraft on their way? Were the letters code for the places where the bombs were about to be dropped? And was the place where we were now standing one of them?[45]

Whether they understood them or not, such coded warnings, with their introduction of "Uwaga! Uwaga!" (Attention! Attention!), would become one of the abiding memories of the war for many Poles.

The proclamations of the commander-in-chief, Marshal Edward Śmigły-Rydz, were another novelty. In his order of the day to Polish troops, he referred to Germany as Poland's "ancient enemy" and insisted that the invader must "pay dearly with his blood for every step he makes on Polish soil." "Our cause is just," he reminded his readers, adding, "Regardless of the length of this war and the sacrifice that must be made, the ultimate victory will fall to us."[46] Posters and billboards reinforced the defiant message. One, showing a portrait of Śmigły-Rydz in full regalia, flanked with images of military hardware and massed ranks of soldiers, declared, "A violent act of force must be resisted with force," along with the mantra, "We shall not relinquish our own. We shall defeat the aggressor."

The confidence was infectious. Warsaw troop trains bore the slogan "Do Berlina!" (On to Berlin!), and one officer recalled that "no-one wanted to hear anything about retreat, let alone think about it."[47] A diarist from Bydgoszcz, in northern Poland, recalling going into his bank on the morning of September 1, wrote, "The branch director and his deputy were in excellent mood. According to their information, the German attack did not surprise our troops on the frontier. The situation in the Corridor was good, and our cavalry had just entered Danzig."[48]

The truth was nowhere near as rosy. The Germans enjoyed an over-whelming numerical superiority in hardware—3:1 in artillery, 3:1 in tanks, 5:1 in aircraft—and, what is more, German equipment was generally more advanced, faster, and more effective than that of their opponent.[49] The disparity was evident in every theater and obliged some Polish forces to avoid battle altogether. The cream of the Polish navy, for example, had already departed Polish waters. "Operation Peking," which had been ordered on August 29, foresaw the transfer of Poland's destroyer fleet to British bases as soon as war appeared imminent. Consequently, three destroyers—ORP *Grom*, the ORP *Błyskawica*, and the ORP *Burza*—departed on the afternoon of the 30th bound for Leith, with orders to engage the Germans in the event of war and to scuttle themselves if they faced capture. After being shadowed by German aircraft through the Baltic, at dawn on September 1 they were already in the North Sea, where they were met by two Royal Navy destroyers, the HMS *Wallace* and the HMS *Wanderer*.[50] Serving under British command thereafter, they would play no part in the defense of Poland. The only significant surface vessels to remain in Polish waters were the destroyer ORP *Wicher* and the minelayer ORP *Gryf*, which remained in the Bay of Danzig to face the invader. Both would be sunk on the afternoon of September 3.

The five-strong submarine flotilla, meanwhile, was not evacuated. Under "Operation Worek," it was ordered that morning to patrol the Bay of Danzig and Poland's Baltic coast to harass German naval operations and prevent any attempted seaborne landings. Unable to be resupplied once war broke out, however, the vessels escaped in the weeks that followed. Three were interned in Sweden, and two, the ORP *Wilk* and the ORP *Orzeł*, made it to Britain—the latter following a daring escape from internment in Tallinn. Despite such heroics, however, the Polish submarines, like their surface fleet, would make only a negligible contribution to Poland's defense in 1939.[51]

The situation was little better in the air. Already that morning, airfields near Warsaw, Kraków, Radom, Łódź, Katowice, and countless other Polish towns and cities had been bombed in an effort by the Luftwaffe to cripple the Polish air force on the ground. Anticipating the attack, the Polish air force had dispersed most of its aircraft, especially the most modern examples, to makeshift airfields, leaving the enemy to bomb largely empty sites. One Polish air force major later noted that it "seem[ed] quite naïve of the Germans to have believed that during the preceding days of high political tension and with their own obviously aggressive intentions, we would leave our units sitting at their peacetime bases."[52] Though the Germans would tell themselves (and the wider world) that they had destroyed the Polish air force on the ground, the truth was rather more complex.

For many Poles, then, the first experience of the war was the sound of bombing. In the capital, Władysław Szpilman woke on September 1 to the distant thud of explosions. Not far away, Alexander Polonius heard the "muffled reports" of what he took to be Polish antiaircraft artillery. Marta Korwin climbed up to the roof of her building to "watch the exciting spectacle," wondering which districts of Warsaw had been hit.[53] To the east, near Lublin, the Olszowski family's first news of the war was seeing aircraft circling above them. "I thought it was manoeuvres," one of them recalled:

> Then I heard some machine guns and everybody came out of the house to see what was happening. Grandpa said, "My God! It's war!" and rushed indoors to switch on the wireless. . . . Everybody was stunned. With ears glued to the loudspeaker we were trying to catch the fading words. The battery or the accumulator, or both, were packing up. When we could no longer hear even a whisper from the wireless set, Grandpa turned the switch off and looked at our anguished faces. He knelt down in front of the picture of Jesus Christ and started to pray aloud. We repeated after Grandpa: "Our Father, Who art in Heaven, hallowed be Thy name . . ."[54]

The first of the German bombing raids, however, was not on Warsaw; it was a strategic attack on the bridges over the Vistula at Tczew, 20 kilometers (12.4 miles) south of Danzig. The bridges—one rail, one road—had been built in the nineteenth century and, side by side,

Unleashing hell: the *Stuka* attack on the Vistula bridge at Tczew.
Narodowe Archiwum Cyfrowe

spanned the 1,000 meters (0.62 miles) of the Vistula. The bridges were crucial crossing points on Poland's largest river, connecting Poland on the west with the Danzig Free State on the east. The Germans considered it essential that the bridges be captured intact, in order to ease the passage of invading troops across the Polish Corridor.[55] The Polish defenders, however, well aware of the site's strategic importance, had the bridges mined with 10 metric tons (11 US tons) of explosives.[56]

So, shortly after 4:30 in the morning of September 1, even before the *Schleswig-Holstein* had opened fire on the Westerplatte, a force of forty-five Junkers Ju-87 *Stukas* assumed their formation in the skies above Tczew. Their primary task was to knock out the power plant and cabling to prevent a detonation of the mines, with diversionary raids to be carried out on signal boxes and the railway station at Tczew itself. At the same time, a goods train, hijacked by German troops, would approach the rail bridge from the eastern side before disgorging its human cargo, men who would attempt to take control of the target.

Despite the boldness of its conception, however, the mission was a failure. Before reaching the bridges, the train was sidelined at Simonsdorf (Szymankowo) by suspicious Polish customs officials, who sent up a flare to alert the nearby garrison at Tczew to the imminent danger. Moreover, as a German pilot, Paul-Werner Hozzel, explained, the blanket of patchy fog over the target meant that the *Stukas* could not hope to be accurate. Though they dropped their bombs as ordered, and watched "the rising mushroom-shaped explosions" on the embankment, they were only able to temporarily disable the charges.[57] An hour later, the Poles blew up the bridges. The opening German operation of the war had been an outright fiasco.

If the raid at Tczew had a limited strategic rationale, the one at Wieluń, a small town some 20 kilometers (12.4 miles) from the German border of Silesia, had a different logic. At 5:40 that morning, as dawn was breaking, a squadron of *Stukas* shattered the silence.[58] According to the account of pilot Oskar Dinort, commanding officer of the dive-bombing squadron Sturzkampfgeschwader 2, the attack followed a well-practiced drill:

Close radiator flap
Turn off supercharger
Tip over to port
Set angle of dive to 70 degrees
Accelerate: 220, . . . 250, . . . 300 mph[59]

Plummeting earthward, their sirens screaming, the *Stukas* released their bombs at around 700 meters (2,300 feet) before pulling out of the dive, climbing into the brightening skies, and repeating the procedure. It was the first of three raids the town would endure that day.

On the ground, the raids caused chaos: one eyewitness said "hell" was unleashed. With no antiaircraft defenses—and no military presence at all—Wieluń, a town of some 16,000, was entirely at the mercy of Hitler's Luftwaffe. Its hospital and church were quickly flattened, and over 300 other buildings (70 percent of the town) were destroyed, including monastery complexes, a synagogue, an Orthodox church, and the old and new market squares.[60] Over 50 metric tons (55 US tons) of bombs were dropped, transforming the heart of Wieluń into a moonscape of smoking rubble. One of those present recalled hurrying to the town center in the aftermath to see what had happened. "It was destroyed," he wrote. "Everywhere there were bodies and body parts: arms, legs, a head."[61] Nobody could be sure how many had been killed, with estimates ranging from a few hundred to 1,600. The *Stuka* crews suffered no losses at all: there was no Polish defensive fire. Indeed, as the Luftwaffe report on the attack would note, there was "no sign of the enemy" whatsoever.[62]

The question of why Wieluń was targeted has long exercised historians. Some have suggested that the raid was a cynical exercise to boost morale in the wake of a dive-bombing demonstration flight by the same *Stuka* squadron two weeks earlier, when thirteen aircraft crashed in a fog with all crews lost.[63] It could also be that the raid was simply made in error. It is clear, for instance, that German military intelligence wrongly believed that Polish army formations and staff headquarters had been stationed in the town over the previous days; one German agent reported the presence of the 8th Uhlan Regiment.[64] Yet such rationalizations ignore the simplest explanation, which is that the Luftwaffe was engaged in an act of psychological warfare: it aimed to break the spirit of the Poles as quickly as possible by sowing panic behind the front lines.[65] Whatever the reason, one conclusion cannot be gainsaid: Hitler's claim that his airmen would restrict themselves to military targets was a barefaced lie.

Wieluń's grim fate could well have been visited upon Warsaw had the weather not intervened. Alongside the strategic targeting of Polish airfields that morning, German plans had foreseen a massive attack on the Polish capital. Codenamed "Operation Waterfront" (*Unternehmen Wasserkante*), it was to utilize both of the Luftwaffe's air fleets to damage the city's industrial capacity and sap civilian morale. In the event, however, low cloud cover and fog over central Poland meant that the operation had to be postponed in favor of more isolated actions by the 1st Air Fleet, some of whose aircraft drew a heavy toll from a spirited defense. The Polish Pursuit Brigade (Brygada Pościgowa) was especially effective, intercepting the formations of Luftwaffe bombers with its own PZL P.11 and P.7 fighters. One of its pilots, Lieutenant Jerzy Palusinski, recalled the scene as his squadron rose to engage the Heinkels and Dorniers of the enemy:

> There was a furious fight in front of us. Something around 200 planes in one place, at the same time. [. . .] On my right, I noticed three fat bombers heading south [. . .] from the distance of 400 feet I fired [at] the target with a long burst of fire. Manoeuvring my machine I aimed at the right engine and once again pulled the trigger. The Heinkel's engine was set [o]n fire and after a while [it] dropped off the formation and crashed to the ground.[66]

In the vicious battle that morning north of Warsaw, the Germans lost fifteen aircraft, and were effectively prevented from dropping their bombs on the capital.[67] The first of those losses, a Heinkel, was shot down by Alexander Gabszewicz and Andrzej Niewiara, both flying P.11s. Gabszewicz excitedly landed his aircraft close to his crashed victim and picked up a souvenir—a piece of the tailplane and a twisted machine gun—before rejoining the fray; he would himself be shot down later that day.[68] In another engagement, the P.11 pilot Stefan Okrzeja engaged a Dornier Do-17 over Radzymin, sending it plunging earthward "like a giant fireball." Such was the excitement of the other members of Okrzeja's squadron that their twelve planes "flew around that . . . pillar of smoke, as if performing a war dance." They estimated that the smoke rose as high as 300 meters (984 feet). It was their first downed enemy: "a beautiful sight."[69] Okrzeja would be shot down and killed four days later over Wyszków, barely 10 kilometers (6 miles) away.

To the south, over Kraków, better weather meant that the German 4th Air Fleet could operate more effectively, but the conditions were just as favorable for the defenders. A heavy German raid on the main airfield at Rakowice early that morning gave rise to the first air victories of the war. Soon after takeoff from Balice airfield, a P.11c fighter, piloted by Captain Mieczysław Medwecki, was shot down by Sergeant Frank Neubert, flying a Ju-87 *Stuka*. Minutes later, Pilot Officer Władysław Gnyś—who had taken off alongside Medwecki—avenged his colleague's death by shooting down two Do-17 bombers.[70]

On that first day of the war, the Luftwaffe launched more than 2,000 sorties, carrying out raids on over 100 Polish towns and cities, including Warsaw, Kraków, Ostrów Mazowiecki, Poznań, Katowice, Grodno, Kielce, and Kutno. At Kutno, their dive-bombers attacked an evacuation train, causing numerous casualties.[71] They also targeted at least 30 Polish airfields, where they destroyed some 180 Polish aircraft. These sites included Małaszewicze, near Terespol, where 9 of the latest PZL.37 Łoś bombers—10 percent of the total available—were destroyed on the ground, and Krosno, where 19 aircraft were lost when a hangar was bombed.[72] At Rakowice airfield in Kraków, meanwhile, two military hangars were destroyed with the loss of some 31 aircraft, with 10 men killed on the ground.[73] The following day, the airfield and air force academy at Dęblin was attacked by around 100 aircraft, causing significant destruction on the ground as well as killing or wounding 30 personnel. No Luftwaffe aircraft were shot down during the attack.[74] With results like that, it is little wonder that German propaganda would proclaim that the air war had already been won.

Yet the Germans did not have everything their own way. Their losses on that first day amounted to some 40 aircraft, compared to 29 combat losses for the Poles. The P.11s and P.7s, though outclassed, had nonetheless proved their worth. Moreover, the dispersal of Polish fighter squadrons had certainly come as a surprise, leaving mainly obsolete models and trainers to be destroyed on the ground. Behind the propaganda, the Luftwaffe knew it had been fooled. As a memorandum of the 1st Air Fleet conceded, "Whereabouts of the enemy air arm largely

"Is that the Polish border, Herr Leutnant?"
Muzeum II Wojny Światowej, Gdańsk

unknown."[75] The Poles were outgunned by the sleek Messerschmitts, Heinkels, and Dorniers of the Luftwaffe, and were outnumbered, but they were still in the fight. And, what was more, they were more than capable of giving their opponents a bloody nose.

WHILE WIELUŃ WAS BEING BOMBED, AND THE WESTERPLATTE and the Polish Post Office were being besieged, German forces also began their land assault of Poland. At dawn, they moved off from their forward positions, many of them sensing the magnitude of the moment. At 4:43 a.m., one officer noted, "I light a cigarette—when it goes out, the war will be on."[76] Crossing the frontier was often momentous. In some instances, German soldiers carried out a ceremonial destruction of the border post—as at Zoppot (Sopot), north of Danzig, where the striped barrier was gleefully ripped from its hinges for the benefit of an accompanying propaganda unit. One Wehrmacht diarist merely recorded his pride at having participated in the invasion: "It is a wonderful feeling, now, to be a German," he wrote.[77]

The morning was particularly memorable for one German officer. Forty-two-year-old Major Ottomar Domizlaff had served in World War I and the postwar German Reichswehr, and was now commander of the 1st Battalion of the 22nd Infantry Regiment, stationed in East Prussia. Overzealous and rather disliked by his men, Domizlaff had already crawled some distance over the Polish frontier north of Mława when the German artillery opened fire to announce the start of the war, and the unfortunate major received a splinter wound in his buttock. "Harmless but painful," wrote a fellow officer, but "the story spread like wildfire throughout the division, which was soon roaring with laughter."[78] Despite being caused by friendly fire, the injury meant that Domizlaff was later awarded a Wound Badge, almost certainly the first of the Second World War.

For others, the war's opening moments might have been wholly uneventful. As their unit moved off, one rifleman asked his officer, "Is that the Polish border, Herr *Leutnant*?" "That *was* the Polish border," came the answer.[79] The experience of Hans von Luck, a company commander in the 2nd Light Division, was perhaps typical. Advancing eastward into the Polish Corridor, he recalled that "the frontier was manned by a single customs official. As one of our soldiers approached him, the terrified man opened the barrier. Without resistance, we marched into Poland. Far and wide, there was not a single Polish soldier in sight."[80]

In some places, German troops advanced virtually unopposed. Elsewhere, they faced stubborn Polish resistance. At Węgierska Górka, for instance, in the Beskid hills of Poland's far south, the advancing forces of the 7th Bavarian Infantry Division, part of the German 14th Army, received a rude awakening. There, among the rolling hills and wooded valleys, a network of defensive bunkers had been belatedly begun by the Poles that summer. Although only four of the planned sixteen had been provisionally completed and manned by the outbreak of war—and they were still lacking power, water, and communications—they nonetheless

German soldiers destroy the border post near Zoppot.
Narodowe Archiwum Cyfrowe

constituted a considerable obstacle to any force seeking to advance north along the valley of the river Soła. Each bunker had a crew of around twenty officers and men and was armed with a 37 mm antitank gun and a selection of light and heavy machine guns.

When German advance forces arrived above the town in the afternoon of September 2, Polish defenders quickly engaged them. "The bullets chirp and whizz close over our heads," one German soldier wrote, "like the cracking of a whip. . . . From minute to minute, we sink deeper into the plowed furrows." After they repelled the initial German assault, the engagement settled into a siege with artillery and tracer fire—"in thick endless streams"—targeting the bunkers, though often with little effect. The official account of the German 7th Army Corps recalled how the artillery fire at Węgierska Górka was accurate, but "the assault troops could see very well how the shells bounced off their targets, like stones against a steel helmet. . . . It was clear that the artillery would not manage it alone."[81]

Meanwhile, the Poles fired back with all they had, fighting off the advancing infantry and pioneers. One by one, however, the bunkers were overpowered and forced to surrender, the survivors staggering out "black as poodles . . . hardly able to see."[82] As a German war correspondent recalled, the engagement amounted to a "baptism of fire" for the Bavarian division: "We battled at Węgierska Górka the entire night. The enemy didn't make things easy for us. The Poles remained in the bunkers. We had to root most of them out. A few survivors left their blown-up concrete castles, smoke blackened, lips pressed together, faces pained."[83]

The last of the bunkers—codenamed *Wędrowiec*, or "Wanderer"— was given up only at 5:00 p.m. on September 3, after its ammunition had been exhausted.[84] It had held out for twenty hours. Across the four manned bunkers at Węgierska Górka, 13 defenders were killed; around 20 more got away under cover of darkness, and the remainder were taken captive, including the commander, Captain Tadeusz Semik. German casualties were estimated at around 300.[85] It was an engagement, the German 7th Army Corps report noted, that "would long be spoken of by German soldiers," but it added, "Brave lads, these Poles."[86] Small wonder, perhaps, that it would become known to its defenders as "the Westerplatte of the South."

Though it ultimately failed to hold up the German advance, the battle at Węgierska Górka nonetheless demonstrated that the Poles could give a good account of themselves, especially if they were defending prepared and fortified positions. It was a lesson that the Germans would learn again, to their cost, at Mława. Located about 100 kilometers (over 65 miles) north of Warsaw and barely 10 kilometers (6 miles) from the southern frontier of East Prussia, Mława stood astride the shortest route from German territory to the Polish capital. For this reason, an extensive system of earthworks and bunkers was planned for the area just north of the town. Although the project was only belatedly begun in July 1939, by September 1 the defenses were already well advanced, with barbed-wire entanglements, antitank trenches, and barriers. In addition, forty-nine concrete bunkers, though rather basic, and armed only with heavy machine guns, were nonetheless completed in their essentials, with interlocking fields of fire and artillery support. A second network of six similar bunkers was established east of Mława, north of the town of Rzęgnowo, with the two defensive systems separated by an impassable area of forests and swamps. In all, the Mława line of defenses—manned by three regiments of infantry, with cavalry brigades protecting the flanks—stretched for over 30 kilometers (18 miles).[87]

Beginning at dawn on September 1, the German invasion near Mława initially proceeded swiftly, with the SS-Deutschland Regiment in the vanguard, sweeping through the villages immediately south of the East Prussian border and skirmishing with those Polish units that were patrolling ahead of the defensive lines. However, when German forces encountered the fortifications—of which they appeared to be largely unaware—their headlong attack foundered. Near Piekiełko, Polish defenders allowed forward units of the German 23rd Infantry Regiment to approach to within approximately 200 meters (650 feet) before opening fire. The result, one Polish sergeant recalled, "was incredible. 8 enemy vehicles were left on the road, 4 of them burnt out, and the rest of the column scattered in panic."[88]

German accounts of Mława were searing. One tank driver recalled the drumming of Polish bullets against his armor, followed by a "powerful explosion" that destroyed the neighboring tank, producing a "thick black cloud of smoke rising from the turret like a fountain." In the heat of the battle, the tank crew had little idea of either their losses or their progress. Suddenly a spark momentarily lit the cabin. When the crew came to their senses, they saw the gunner slumped down with a spreading pool of blood on the floor. Then came another powerful strike: "The transmission grinds. Bloody hell! A shell has bust the track!"[89]

That afternoon, another German assault reached the Mława defenses near the village of Kuklin but found them impenetrable. The tanks of the 7th Panzer Regiment discovered railway tracks embedded vertically in concrete as well as antitank ditches, 6 meters wide and 3 meters deep (about 20 feet by 10 feet), stretching for 500 meters (1,640 feet). In seeking to avoid such obstacles, the 7th Panzer's tanks turned broadside, thereby exposing their lightly armored flanks to the Poles with predictable results. By early evening, the Germans had withdrawn, having lost seven tanks as well as a company commander, and a further thirty-two tanks were damaged.[90] Soon after, the divisional commander, Major-General Werner Kempf, filed his report: "The attack was a disaster," he wrote. "Terrible losses of panzers, numbers unknown. An attack here is hopeless."[91] The Mława line had been held, for now.

To the west of Mława, the German 4th Army was pressing eastward across the Polish Corridor, seeking to cut off the Polish forces in the north and reunite East Prussia with the Reich. Given that they were entering territory that, only a generation before, had been part of the German Empire, for some it was an emotional experience. Approaching the village of Wielka Klonia (Gross Klonia in German), General Heinz Guderian, then commanding the 19th Army Corps, was momentarily lost in reminiscences. As he wrote in his memoir, "Gross Klonia had once belonged to my great-grandfather Freiherr Hiller von Gärtringen. Here, too, was buried my grandfather Guderian. My father had been born in this place. This was the first time I had ever set eyes on the estate, once so beloved by my family."[92]

Once Guderian was finished reminiscing, there was fighting to be done. The German 4th Army, of which his 19th Army Corps was part, had been positioned west of the Tuchola Forest, an area of dense woodland that the Poles had considered largely impassable, and so had defended with only an infantry division and a cavalry brigade.[93] The commander of the Polish "Pomeranian Army" stationed in the Corridor, General Władysław Bortnowski, was well aware that the presence of his forces was intended to act only as a "trip wire": to ensure that any German incursion into the Polish Corridor would not go unnoticed by the outside world.[94] When he had realized that he could be facing a full-scale invasion, however, he had asked that his men be withdrawn southward, to prevent them from being cut off or destroyed. His request was refused. His Pomeranian Army would face the might of Guderian's armored spearhead alone. In the debacle, Bortnowski struggled to evacuate the 9th and 27th Infantry Divisions, then already engaged in the northern half of the Corridor, but the task was beyond him. Such an evacuation, he admitted, was "wishful thinking."[95]

While Guderian's advance through the Tuchola Forest would soon demonstrate the revolutionary potential of the massed armored advance, the morning's first major engagement in the Polish Corridor, at Chojnice, owed a debt to more primitive military methods. The town had been slated to be captured by a surprise attack using an armored train, the *Panzerzug 3*, one of four such trains used by the Germans in the Polish campaign. Though it was a throwback to an earlier age of warfare, the *Panzerzug 3* was a beast: with an armored locomotive at its heart, it was flanked by an artillery car, an antiaircraft car, and assault cars containing men and weaponry.[96] Arriving at Chojnice's railway station shortly after 5:00 a.m., it successfully disgorged its cargo of infantry and a rail-adapted armored car before being engaged by Polish artillery, which destroyed its command turret, killing the train commander. In the pandemonium that followed, the crew members attempted to retreat, but they were soon trapped on a demolished bridge, whereupon Polish guns destroyed the lead wagon and set fire to the remainder. A German surprise attack had failed that morning yet again. The war diary of the 19th Army Corps was quietly damning in its assessment: "The era of deploying rail-bound armored trains against an enemy in a prepared position appears to have passed."[97]

Later that day, near the village of Krojanty northeast of Chojnice, another seemingly anachronistic engagement would provoke enduring controversy. At dusk, two squadrons of the Polish 18th Pomeranian Cavalry Regiment were ordered to engage troops of the German 20th Motorized Division, so as to ease the eastward retreat of a neighboring unit. The skirmish would provide Berlin with a rich seam of propaganda for the entire campaign.

Poland's cavalry regiments—the Uhlans—had a proud military tradition and were still seen in 1939 as the very elite of the Polish army. However, warfare had changed rapidly in the opening decades of the twentieth century, and though all armies still boasted cavalry units in

Showing their mettle: the famed Polish cavalry.
Muzeum Wojska Polskiego, Warsaw

1939—including the Germans—their role had shifted significantly. By 1939, the Polish cavalry was essentially used as mounted infantry. Equipped with field guns, light tanks, and antitank rifles, they fought dismounted, with their horses providing speed and mobility.

Yet, at Krojanty, when the 18th Cavalry faced units of German infantry—apparently at rest—the decision was made to mount a traditional cavalry charge, one of the last of its kind. Though a superior officer attempted in vain to halt the attack, perhaps foreseeing the carnage that was to follow, the order stood, and with the regimental commander, Colonel Kazimierz Masztalerz, leading the way, 200 Polish cavalrymen drew their sabers, spurred their horses, and charged at full gallop.[98] At first, the attack went well. German infantrymen, surprised, if nothing else, by the manner of the assault, fled, desperate to escape the thundering hooves and slashing sabers. Improbably, it seemed that the Poles had won. But then, as a Polish eyewitness recalled, "suddenly enemy tanks came out of hiding, charging our flank with a drumfire barrage. The squadrons instantly scattered toward the nearby wooded height, a good antitank position, but did not escape the effects of the armored attack." When the regimental buglers called a while later, only half the regiment returned.[99]

In the aftermath, twenty-five of the cavalrymen lay dead, including Masztalerz, with a further fifty injured.[100] Major-General Stanisław Grzmot-Skotnicki, whose forces had been relieved by the skirmish at Krojanty, expressed his words of thanks. The 18th Pomeranian Regiment had "etched its name in gold in the pages of history of the Polish cavalry," he said.[101] The Germans, too, were momentarily impressed. Word of the Uhlans' charge spread swiftly that evening. A few kilometers to the south, for instance, near his headquarters at Trzciany, General Guderian discovered his men hurriedly setting up field positions and donning their steel helmets in expectation of an imminent cavalry attack. He did all he could to calm them down.[102] The following day, the German 2nd Division even reported that attacks by Polish cavalry had penetrated their lines as far as the artillery positions.[103]

Such grudging admiration would shift to ridicule in the weeks that followed. Far from being seen—as it might have been—as a fleeting victory for Polish martial élan before the victory of German technological superiority, Krojanty would be portrayed by German propaganda as a symbol of Polish foolishness. This image would be repeated in countless newspaper articles and spurious memoirs. The mythology even infected the official history of the 3rd Panzer Division, which mendaciously spoke of the Polish cavalrymen riding with their sabers drawn, unable to believe that "the German panzers are made of steel."[104]

In truth, the Polish cavalry would show their mettle once again that day far to the south, at the village of Mokra, northwest of Częstochowa. There, the German 4th Panzer Division was advancing northeastward, probing the gap between the Polish Łódź and Kraków Armies, an area held by the Volhynian Cavalry Brigade. Early in the morning, after being held up negotiating antitank ditches dug by Polish scouts close to the border, the 340 or so tanks of the 4th Panzer finally made contact with the enemy west of Mokra.[105] They were mainly Mark I and II Panzers, which—though formidable in their own right—were far removed from the armored behemoths developed later in the war. Neither was particularly generously armed or armored, with less than 15 millimeters (0.6 of an inch) of frontal armor, at best.[106] Moreover, though a handful of their crews may have fought in the Spanish Civil War, for the vast majority Poland would be their baptism of fire.

Facing the tanks of the 4th Panzer that morning was the 8,000-strong Volhynian Cavalry Brigade, which consisted of four cavalry regiments as well as infantry, artillery, and an armored detachment equipped with armored cars and TKS tankettes—small, two-man armored vehicles used for reconnaissance and infantry support.[107] Fighting dismounted, the Polish cavalrymen were armed with the Bofors 37 mm gun and the wz.35 antitank gun, a long-barreled, high-velocity rifle known by its codename, "Uruguay." Both guns were able to penetrate 15 millimeters of armor at 300 meters (985 feet).

First contact was made at 7:30 a.m. when German tanks approaching from the west shelled local villages and machine-gunned fleeing civilians before being halted by the antitank artillery of the 21st Vistula Uhlan Regiment. After a brief withdrawal, the 4th Panzer Regiment was then drawn—by German accident or Polish design—into a large clearing around the three hamlets that made up Mokra, which was surrounded by forest on three sides. More perilously for the Germans, the clearing was bounded to the east by a wooded railway embankment, upon which a Polish armored train—No. 53 *Śmiały* (The Bold)—was positioned.

In the ten-hour engagement that followed, the Germans launched three assaults on the Polish lines, but with only minimal success. As one of the defenders recalled, a stalemate ensued: "A mass of tanks, about forty. . . . Mokra is in flames. Smoke and dust. . . . [T]he tanks, in a frenzy, rake fire from their cannons and machine guns. Our batteries are keeping up, firing head on."[108] For Panzer commander Willi Reibig it was a sobering experience. "The name Mokra had no meaning for us," he wrote. "A village like any other. But if only we had known!"[109] There were two primary reasons for this ruefulness. The first was the effectiveness of the "Uruguay" antitank rifle, which could cut a swath through the German light tanks. It worked not by penetrating the enemy armor directly, but by causing a spall of metal shards to be ejected inside the vehicle, which would kill or injure the occupants and damage the engine and machinery. The results were impressive, as one Polish lancer recalled: "I grabbed the rifle . . . lay down behind a barn and fired at the side of a tank. It burst with a billow of black smoke. While I was still on the ground, the turret hatch opened and one of the crew began to come out. Before he had time to swing his foot out of the tank, a shot was fired and he slumped from the hatch, dead."[110]

The second reason for German soldiers to remember Mokra was the deployment of the armored train, which provided vital supporting fire throughout the battle. Though under constant threat from air attack, the *Śmiały* was able to move into position on the embankment to engage each German advance with a "torrent of cannon and machine-gun fire," shooting until its barrels overheated.[111] Caught in the open space, and threatened on three sides, the tanks of 4th Panzer paid a heavy price. "There's a crashing and smashing like mad," wrote Willi Reibig.[112] In the resulting confusion, "a great number of tanks caught fire, [and] many had snapped tracks and were immobilized. Their crews started jumping out of their turrets, drawing a powerful fire from light and heavy machine guns. In the commotion and smoke, some German tanks lost their sense of direction and ended up ramming into each other and firing at one another."[113]

If the Germans had thought that they would roll over the Polish army with ease, Mokra checked their hubris, a reminder of Helmuth von Moltke's maxim that "no battle plan survives first contact with the enemy." Despite their brave stand, however, by the end of the day the Poles could no longer hold their defensive positions. In danger of being outflanked, with ammunition running low and the *Śmiały* damaged and forced to disengage, the remaining men of the Volhynian Cavalry Brigade executed a surreptitious withdrawal, moving under cover of darkness to new defense lines a few kilometers to the east. Despite being outnumbered and outgunned, they had stopped the German advance at the cost of 190 men killed and a further 300 injured.[114] A cavalry brigade had held off an armored division for ten hours.

German losses at Mokra were estimated at around 500 killed, with some 100 vehicles destroyed. But psychological damage had been inflicted: the confidence of the men of 4th Panzer had been severely dented. That evening, the cry of *"Alarm!"* from a panicked sentry sent the division's support column—including field kitchens and artillery batteries—scurrying westward in fear. As the divisional diary noted, "All too easily, there's a sudden, unexpected, contagious collapse," which was only rectified by the intervention of the commander, General Georg-Hans Reinhardt.[115]

Despite the efforts of senior officers to restore morale, that collapse in confidence could be highly infectious. As a staff officer of the 4th Army noted on the very first night of the war, "Tonight everywhere there are burning villages, houses and barns. Here and there wild shooting, supposedly irregulars. Everywhere there is nervousness."[116] That tension would bring with it baleful consequences, contributing to a trigger-happy climate in which atrocities and executions became grimly commonplace.

The tone was set for the war on its opening days. In the village of Serock, near Bydgoszcz, the Germans executed around thirty-five Poles, mainly soldiers and railwaymen, whom they had captured in a nearby forest, in "retaliation" for a shot fired at them. In Jankowice, near Katowice, twelve Poles were shot in revenge for the killing of a German officer; they included three children, aged ten, twelve, and fourteen.[117] In Wyszanów, near Poznań, seventeen women and children were killed when German soldiers threw hand grenades into a cellar, despite the victims' pleas for mercy.[118]

The slaughter at Wyszanów was triggered, it was thought, by one of the victims trying to run away. But any pretext sufficed. In the village of Torzeniec, near Kępno, men of the Wehrmacht's 41st Infantry Regiment avenged themselves on local inhabitants after a brief nighttime firefight cost three of their men their lives. Believing that the villagers had fired on them, the soldiers responded with "wild shooting" before setting barns and houses alight, and then murdered those who tried to escape the burning buildings. Among the dead were a mother and her two-year-old daughter. The following morning, the Germans arrested all the surviving men from the village, court-martialed them, and sentenced them to death. Then, in a "gesture of mercy," they ordered every other man to step out of line, and those men were executed in front of the rest. Eighteen were killed. One of them, Józef Sadowski, voluntarily gave his life when he realized that his seventy-year-old father, Stanisław, had been selected. In total, 34 villagers in Torzeniec were murdered.[119] A further 13 were murdered in Gostyń, 26 in Łaziska Górne, 38 in Zimnowoda, 75 in Parzymiechy, 159 in Albertów.[120]

Elsewhere, petty scores were settled. At Simonsdorf in the Danzig Free State, German gendarmes executed some 40 Poles. The victims were railway and customs employees, along with their families, who had prevented the hijacked train containing German soldiers from reaching the bridge at Tczew by shunting it into a siding.[121] According to an eyewitness, their bodies were piled up and a sign was erected declaring, "Here lies the Polish minority from Simonsdorf."[122] They paid with their lives for frustrating German ambitions. In all, it is estimated that, in the first three days of the war alone, some 72 mass executions were carried out by German forces, claiming over 800 victims.[123] A brutal benchmark was being set for the remainder of the campaign—and the remainder of the war.

Clearly, beyond the tenuous justification of "retaliation," there was a wider barbarism in evidence. It found its expression not only in the brutal treatment of the Polish population but also in anti-Semitic violence and in the indiscriminate targeting of churches, residential suburbs, hospitals, and civilian trains.[124] As at Wieluń, rural villages and towns with no military significance were flattened as if for sport. Columns of refugees were harried and hounded from the air, with German aircraft strafing them seemingly at will. Germany's new norms of war meant the targeting of entire populations, regardless of the pious words of its leaders about "military targets." The head of the British military mission to Poland, Sir Adrian Carton de Wiart, himself a veteran of the Somme and, as a recipient of the Victoria Cross, no stranger to the horrors of warfare, noted the differences between the war he had known in Flanders and its new form. "I saw the very face of war change," he wrote, "bereft of romance, its glory shorn, no longer the soldier setting forth into battle, but the women and children buried under it."[125]

THE OPENING DAYS OF THE WAR HAD SHOWN THAT GERMAN forces would not be having things all their own way. Their opponents were neither incompetent nor lacking in determination. Though the Wehrmacht's situation reports crowed that advances had been made in every theater, the reality was more complex.[126] Advances had been made, and had been substantial, but they were a far cry from the stereotypical image of an all-conquering German war machine crushing the hapless, inferior Poles. All of the Germans' surprise attacks of that morning—at Chojnice and Tczew and on the Westerplatte—had failed in their objectives, thwarted either by their own complacency and incompetence or by the vigor of the Polish defense. Moreover, though the Poles had suffered considerable reverses, they had nonetheless demonstrated that they were more than capable of fighting back. The image that the world would come to know of the campaign—of an inept, irresolute enemy, unable to resist the German advance and foolhardy enough to charge advancing tanks with cavalry—would be a fiction of Joseph Goebbels's propaganda. The Poles had shown that they were determined to defend themselves. It just remained to be seen how Paris and London would respond to the German attack.

Chapter Two

THE TYRANNY OF GEOGRAPHY

P OLAND WAS WELL ACCUSTOMED TO FIGHTING FOR ITS EXIS-
tence. Though the Polish Republic of 1939 had only been established
after the collapse of the Central Powers and the Russian Empire at the
end of the First World War, it drew upon a political folk memory that
stretched back hundreds of years, much of it involving conflict and the
violent irruptions of its neighbors. For a time in the sixteenth and seventeenth centuries, Poland had been one of Europe's primary military powers—in the Commonwealth with Lithuania from 1569, it stretched from
the Baltic all the way to the Black Sea, and its armies had fought, among
others, against the Teutonic Knights, the Tatars, Muscovy, and the
Kingdom of Sweden. Most famously, perhaps, Poland's iconic "winged
hussars" under King Jan III Sobieski had routed the Turks at the gates of
Vienna in 1683, thereby halting the Ottoman advance into Europe.

While the seventeenth century had been the high-water mark of Polish power in Europe, the century that followed it witnessed a spectacular
ebb tide. As Poland's neighbors, Prussia, the Habsburg Monarchy, and
Russia, consolidated and grew in strength, they increasingly saw Poland
as an arena into which they could project their own influence. Their primary weapon in that process was to exploit the very institutions that had

previously made Poland's "noble democracy" so successful—the elective monarchy and the *liberum veto*, which demanded unanimous assent for all legislation before the Sejm, the Polish parliament. By using bribes and corrupt noblemen, Poland's neighbors could hamstring reform, paralyze the Sejm, and sow chaos, contributing to the Commonwealth's eventual decline. Poland would soon become as familiar with malign foreign interference as it had once been with military success.

From 1772, Poland—whose borders had waxed and waned over the previous seven centuries—began to disappear from the map. In that year, in response to a noble rebellion against Russian influence, a first "partition" of the country was agreed by Prussia, Russia, and Habsburg Austria, which between them annexed 30 percent of Poland's territory and 28 percent—4 million—of its people. The preamble to the Partition Treaty, signed in St. Petersburg that summer, justified the action as a supposed response to the "spirit of faction, the troubles and intestine war which had shaken the Kingdom of Poland for so many years, and the Anarchy which acquires new strength every day."[1] One of the few Polish senators to protest the country's betrayal was Tadeusz Rejtan, who begged his fellow nobles in the Sejm to reject the partition, then tore his clothes open at the chest and threw himself onto the floor of the chamber, imploring the king "on the blood of Christ" not to "play the part of Judas [and] kill the Fatherland."[2] But, the deed was done, and the partition was agreed. The mendacious subtext of the treaty was clear: Poland was collapsing in disarray, and its dutiful neighbors were rightfully stepping in to restore order. It was a narrative that would repeat itself again and again.

In the two decades that followed, that diagnosis of troubles and anarchy would be studiously brought to fruition. Under the client-king Stanisław August Poniatowski—one of the Russian empress Catherine the Great's many lovers—the country was torn between the stranglehold of foreign (predominantly Russian) influence and a reformist urge to survive. The reformers scored some notable successes, not least among them the National Education Commission of 1773 and the constitution of 1791, the first such document in Europe. But the prospect of constitutional reform and the longed-for restoration of national sovereignty so alarmed Poland's autocratic eastern neighbor that, once again, an intervention was engineered; Russian troops invaded in support of a local rebellion and persuaded the pusillanimous king to sue for peace. In the aftermath, the Sejm was forced to revoke the constitution. Poland was partitioned once again—this time between Russia and Prussia, which cost it a further 40 percent of its original territory.

Thus stymied, Polish patriots and reformers were left with little option but to launch a national insurrection—proclaimed in Kraków in 1794—"for gaining national self-rule and for the foundation of general liberty." Soon after, a conscript army under the generalship of Tadeusz Kościuszko—one of the heroes of the American Revolution—defeated the Russian army at Racławice; the revolt then spread to Warsaw and Wilno (Vilnius), where Russian garrisons were violently ejected. Despite such promising successes, however, the insurrection could not be sustained against both Russian and Prussian military intervention. When Kościuszko was taken prisoner at the Battle of Maciejowice, and Warsaw fell to Russian guns, the insurrection collapsed, to be followed by an inevitable third—and final—partition. In 1795, barely a century after Poland's armies had "saved Christendom" at the gates of Vienna, the nation vanished from the map.

Of course, the fact that a Polish state had ceased to exist did not mean that the Polish people disappeared: they continued their lives as peasants and nobles, merchants and intellectuals, either in exile or as subjects of the partitioning powers. In the decades that followed, all of them had to respond to their predicament. Some did so by assimilating to the dominant culture, others by tactically collaborating with the occupier—in the hope that something of "Poland" might thereby be saved—and still others by actively resisting. It would be this spectrum of responses that defined Polish life for the next century.

For those who chose to resist, Poland's military tradition and the more recent insurrections were important inspirations. Yet rarely has martial endeavor met with so little political reward. During the nineteenth century, generation after generation of Poles fought and died for a cause that rarely seemed to materially advance. Under Napoleon, some 25,000 men served in the Polish Legions as France's most loyal lieutenants, taking on—at times—Poland's partitioning powers, but unable to fight directly for a restored, independent Poland. Their sacrifice, though synonymous with the victory at Samosierra in 1808, was perhaps typified by the dark fate of the legionnaires who were sent to quell a rebellion in the distant French colony of Saint-Domingue (Haiti), a mission from which few would return.

Indeed, though the Polish Legions would become an integral part of partitioned Poland's narrative of itself, the legionnaires were mostly fighting far from the country they hoped to resurrect. It was a distance that was symbolized by the song that would later become the reborn Poland's national anthem, "Dąbrowski's Mazurka." Its lyrics open with an iconic line, "Poland is not yet lost, so long as we still live," and in its chorus it contains the demand that the legionnaires' commander—the Dąbrowski of the title—"March! March! . . . from the Italian land to Poland."* For all their efforts in Napoleon's cause, the Legions did little to further the goal of Polish rebirth.

A generation later, Poland took up arms once more. In November 1830, in response to growing Russian repression at home and the rumor that the tsar's Polish soldiers might be used to crush revolutions abroad, a military coup managed to take Warsaw and oust the Russian garrison. In the months that followed, Russia's heavy-handed response succeeded in transforming this local revolt into a national uprising under the inspiring (and inspired) motto "Za naszą i waszą wolność" (For our freedom and yours). When the Russian army returned in February 1831, however, it swiftly regained the initiative, and after Warsaw fell that September, following a bloody siege, the revolt was crushed and the status quo ante restored. Abroad, a wave of liberal sympathy for Poland's plight garnered some high-minded verbiage but little material gain. Meanwhile, the first cohorts of *Sybiracy*—Poles deported to a punitive exile in Siberia—made their way east.[3]

---

* The term *mazurka* refers to a form of music based on a traditional Polish folk dance.

If their fight against Russian occupation was the most pressing and the most vehement, it does not mean that Polish patriots in the other partitions meekly accepted their lot. In 1846, in a prelude to the revolutions that would sweep through Europe two years later—the so-called Springtime of the Nations—Poles rose to demand independence in Kraków, in the Austrian Partition, and in the Wielkopolska region around Poznań, then part of the Prussian Partition. Predictably, the risings were crushed by Prussian and Austrian forces—with extreme brutality in Galicia, where peasants were paid in salt for the heads of Polish nobles.[4] Another rising in Wielkopolska in the spring of 1848, which sought to take advantage of the new revolutionary reality across Europe, was similarly suppressed by Prussian forces.

If those insurrections against foreign rule were perhaps not determined enough, they would pale into insignificance compared to the next Polish uprising. In January 1863, a forced conscription of Polish youth to a twenty-year term of service in the Russian army provoked an angry armed response. This time, however, the insurrection would prove to be more than a purely military adventure. In the intervening years since the last revolts, Polish society had changed; the "national idea" was more widespread and more fervently held than ever, and the insurgents now boasted a full-fledged political program to bolster their cause. Alongside that unifying idea, the revolt had a comprehensive organizational structure that possessed all the attributes of an underground state. The cause of Polish independence, it seemed, had come of age.

That underground state—with its ministries, security cadres, couriers, and tax collectors, often operating under the very noses of the Russian authorities—would set the standard for what would come to be known as *konspiracja*: the clandestine resistance to occupation. It would also prove highly effective at conducting a guerrilla campaign against the Russians, including small-scale engagements and ambushes across the territory of the Russian Partition. It would evoke another wave of international sympathy for Poland's plight, with commentators from the Russian anarchist Mikhail Bakunin to the Italian nationalist Giuseppe Garibaldi cheering the Polish cause from abroad, and favorable opinions also being voiced on the floor of the British House of Commons.[5]

For all the fine words, little in the way of help would be forthcoming, and yet again the weight of Russian force was finally made to tell. The insurrection would have a macabre coda when, on the morning of August 5, 1864, some eighteen months after the revolt had begun, five of its leaders were hanged by the Russians on the ramparts of the Citadel in Warsaw. Ten thousand or so Poles had been killed in fighting the tsar's forces, and a further 35,000 were deported to Siberia. While the members of that new generation of *Sybiracy* struggled to maintain their faith in the cause, their compatriots at home found themselves under suppression, with every expression of Polish patriotic sentiment outlawed. Already removed from the map, Poland was in danger of extinction.

In the aftermath, generations of Poles either emigrated or contented themselves with their lot; at best, they engaged in what became known as "organic work"—advancing the Polish cause through cultural and political collaboration with the partitioning powers. With Germany unifying as an empire in 1871, and Russia growing in strength and significance, it would clearly take a cataclysm to shake their dominance over the Polish lands. Only the Austrian Partition, the most liberal of the three, allowed some leeway to Polish national ambition; only there could Polish patriots breathe more easily.

With the outbreak of the First World War in 1914, the "Polish Question"—as it had now become—came to the fore once again. With large numbers of Polish conscripts serving in the armies of the three partitioning powers, it became politically expedient to all sides to offer some concessions to Polish national sentiment. In the four years that followed, a number of promises were made and a number of Polish soldier-politicians sought to maneuver and scheme as best they could. The most prominent among the latter was Józef Piłsudski, who was at the head of a reformed Polish Legion fighting under German and Austrian auspices. In response, the Western Allies also made promises, notably by agreeing to the principle—enshrined in US president Woodrow Wilson's "Fourteen Points" of January 1918, as one of the conditions for a lasting peace—that Poland should be restored as an independent state. This principle, under Point XIII, specified that the Polish state must have "free and secure access to the sea" and that it must include all those territories "inhabited by indisputably Polish populations." In the event, however, it was the collapse of both the Russian Empire in 1917 and the Central Powers in 1918 that enabled an independent Poland to reemerge after an absence of 123 years. Like V. I. Lenin in Petrograd, Piłsudski found power lying in the street; he merely had to stoop to pick it up.

Nonetheless, Poland's rebirth would be the product of a painful labor. Though the partitioning powers had collapsed, the result on the ground was something of a free-for-all in which competing ambitions had to fight for their realization. As Winston Churchill quaintly put it, "The War of the Giants has ended, the quarrels of the pygmies have begun."[6] Those "quarrels" consisted of rumbling border conflicts with the emergent states of Lithuania and Czechoslovakia; a bloody rising in Wielkopolska against German irregulars and Freikorps; and a short-lived Polish–Ukrainian war, as a result of which Lwów was returned to Polish control. Most quarrelsome of all was the Polish–Soviet War, which ranged across the region for two years before ending in August 1920, thanks to the Polish victory at the gates of Warsaw—the so-called Miracle on the Vistula.

That conflict, a curious, highly mobile mélange of cavalry assaults and armored trains, would witness the emergence of some of the military personalities to achieve prominence in 1939, such as Władysław Langner and Tadeusz Kutrzeba. Foremost among them, however, was Edward Śmigły-Rydz. Born in humble circumstances in Galicia, in the Austrian Partition, in 1886, Edward Rydz (as he was then known) was orphaned in his youth and raised by his grandparents before being informally adopted by the parents of a school friend.

A talented artist, he attended the Academy of Fine Arts in Kraków before his growing interest in politics and philosophy prompted a change to the prestigious Jagiellonian University. By this time already

Poland's peripatetic commander-in-chief,
Edward Śmigły-Rydz.
public domain

an active member of Polish paramilitary organizations, he added the
nom de guerre "Śmigły" (agile) to his surname. Drafted into the Austro-
Hungarian army in 1914, he found his métier: by 1916 he was a colonel
in Piłsudski's Polish 1st Brigade, and he later took charge of the underground Polska Organizacja Wojskowa (Polish Military Organization). By the time of Poland's rebirth in 1918, he had emerged as one
of Piłsudski's most important lieutenants, masterminding the defeat
of the Red Army at Daugavpils and then commanding the Polish 3rd
Army in the summer of 1920, when it captured the Ukrainian capital of
Kiev: the high-water mark of the Polish offensive. Piłsudski would say
of him that "when it comes to strength of character and will, he excels
above all the other generals."[7]

The Polish–Soviet War played a major role in shaping men such as
Śmigły-Rydz who came of age in these years, but its significance went
far beyond the personal. In particular, it dealt a bruising blow to the
Soviet Union's dreams of expanding the communist world. As the Red
Army's order of the day on the eve of the battle for Warsaw made plain,
Soviet ambition did not end with the Polish capital: "Onward to the

west!" it read. "Over the corpse of White Poland lies the road to world-wide conflagration!"[8] Indeed, for the Soviet leadership, the war against the Poles was only the opening phase of a wider offensive that would carry the communist idea westward to Berlin, Paris, and London. The Miracle on the Vistula, therefore, not only saved Central and Western Europe from communism but also dented the Kremlin's ambitions. It was a setback that Stalin, for one, would neither forget nor forgive.[9]

With the victory against the Soviets, and the resulting Treaty of Riga of 1921, Poland was once again secured on the European map. But, to some extent, that rebirth was just the beginning of Poland's difficulties. Though Poland enjoyed the distant support of the Western Allies—its territorial arrangements had been largely rubber-stamped by the Treaty of Versailles in 1920, and Allied military missions had been sent to lend advice in the fight against the Soviets—its more immediate neighbors were much more sinister in their intentions. Neither Germany nor the Soviet Union was reconciled to the territorial losses they had each incurred at the end of the First World War, and the reconstituted Poland represented a large proportion of their irredenta. Little wonder, perhaps, that the Soviet foreign minister, Vyacheslav Molotov, would later describe Poland as "the monstrous bastard of the Peace of Versailles."[10] It was a view that was most certainly shared in Germany even before Hitler came to power. When the Soviets and Germans found common cause and signed the Rapallo Pact in 1922, German general Hans von Seeckt outlined, in a memorandum to German chancellor Joseph Wirth, what he called "one of the firmest guiding principles of German policy," namely, that the existence of Poland was "intolerable and incompatible with Germany's vital interests."[11] The logical basis for German–Russian collaboration, he suggested, was that Poland should be made to disappear.

Perennially threatened from without, the reborn Poland also faced multiple challenges from within, ranging from the difficulty of welding together a single state infrastructure, where previously there had been three, to the problems of industrialization. But perhaps the most pressing problem was how to incorporate the large ethnic minorities. Given the nature of its rebirth and the complex demographic realities in the region, the new Poland was a multiethnic state. Its minorities, constituting nearly 30 percent of the population, included around 4 million Ukrainians, 3 million Jews, 1.5 million Byelorussians, and 800,000 Germans.[12] Yet after the hardships endured in the national cause over more than a century, the ruling ethos of the new state was often instinctively and narrowly "Polish" in nature—and although all essential freedoms and rights were granted to minorities, the tone was often one of tension, with mutual prejudices, recriminations, and even violence commonplace. It was an atmosphere that was typified by the assassination, in 1922, of the first president of the Polish Republic, Gabriel Narutowicz, who was shot by an ultranationalist after it was alleged that he had won the election only thanks to the votes of the country's minorities.[13]

Given such strains, it was unsurprising that the parliamentary democratic system itself only creaked along, with political turmoil and short-lived administrations leading to widespread frustration. The deadlock was broken in 1926, when Józef Piłsudski—the mustached strongman who had led the drive to independence, but had been in brooding retirement since it had been achieved—returned to the political scene at the head of a military coup, dramatically facing down the president in the middle of Warsaw's Poniatowski Bridge. The regime that followed—known as Sanacja, taking its name from a word that means "cleansing"—was a curious hybrid: the constitution, the Sejm, and political parties all remained, albeit under the "guidance" of the clique around Piłsudski, with the latter remaining nominally above politics and taking only the position of minister of defense for himself. But despite its authoritarian trappings—and there was a significant toughening of the regime in later years—Sanacja never became a dictatorship or a one-party state; rather, it might euphemistically be described as a "managed democracy."

Piłsudski generally left domestic policy in the hands of his ministers, to be run in accordance with vague "national principles," and busied himself with the management of foreign policy. In 1921—five years prior to his return—the government in Warsaw had signed an alliance with France that was intended to solidify Poland's international position, deterring both German and Soviet aggression. But Piłsudski went further, formulating the "Doctrine of Two Enemies" to govern Poland's relationship with its revanchist neighbors. According to this doctrine, Poland would maintain correct—even cordial—relations with both Germany and the Soviet Union, but it would ally with neither. Still, Piłsudski signed a nonaggression pact with the USSR in July 1932, and after apparently toying with the idea of conducting a preventive strike against Germany in March 1933, agreed to a similar pact with Hitler in January 1934.[14] By the time Piłsudski died in May 1935, Poland—despite suffering widespread unemployment and ethnic tension—nonetheless appeared to be at least internationally secure.

Aside from foreign policy, Piłsudski liked to devote his attention to the military. The Polish army had emerged in 1920 from the war with the Soviet Union full of confidence and vigor—understandably so, as it had been the army (and armed irregulars) who had realized the dream of independence and drawn the frontiers of the Republic. However, the army spent much of the interwar period essentially preparing for a repeat of the last war—a mobile conflict dominated by cavalry and armored trains. To a large extent, this approach was reinforced by simple economics: with its predominantly agrarian economy, Poland could ill afford the huge costs demanded by mechanization. Polish military spending in the five years before 1939 was less than 3 percent of what Hitler's Germany spent over the same period. More strikingly, perhaps, the amount that Germany would spend to equip a single armored division exceeded the entire annual budget for the Polish army.[15]

There were other factors at play. For one thing, Poland's postwar military leadership had, by and large, not experienced the horrors of trench warfare in the First World War, and so had failed to see that mechanization was the future. For another, the nation that reemerged in 1920—particularly eastern Poland, with its wide-open spaces, extensive marshland, and lack of infrastructure—seemed admirably suited to the continued use of cavalry. In addition, the elevated status of the cavalryman in Polish society, traditionally the *crème de la crème* of military service, ensured that any steps taken toward mechanization tended to be rather halting and tentative.

Despite these difficulties, one should not imagine that the Polish army of 1939 lacked martial spirit. After the long decades of foreign occupation, independence was far too precious to most Poles to be given away without a fight. In any case, the Polish army was not the backward-looking, cavalry-centered anachronism that German propaganda would later have the world believe. With 1 million men under arms, it was the fifth-largest military force on the planet, boasting some thirty divisions of infantry and eleven cavalry brigades.[16] Yes, there were shortages of transport, but the infantry dominated, and the cavalry, of course, fought dismounted, armed with the ferocious 37 mm field gun. Neither was the Polish army shy of innovation. Polish armorers developed the highly effective wz.35 antitank rifle as well as the excellent wz.1928 machine gun. The Vis pistol—a variant of the iconic Browning M1911 Colt—appeared in 1936 and is often described as one of the best handguns of the era.

Where there were more serious shortcomings was in hardware, especially armor. At one time, shortly after the First World War, Poland—thanks largely to French largesse—could boast the fourth-largest tank force in the world. By the late 1930s, however, Poland's tanks, despite totaling nearly 700 in number, would be dwarfed by those available to its totalitarian neighbors. Moreover, most of them would not stand comparison with their rivals. Only the 7TP model—a three-man tank coming in at 10 metric tons (11 US tons), with a 37 mm main gun, of which Polish forces had some 98 examples—might expect to hold its own against the German Panzer IIs. Others, though relatively numerous, were much less formidable, such as the 400 or so TK-3 and TKS tankettes—light reconnaissance tanks weighing under 3 metric tons (3.3 US tons), armed only with a machine gun—or the 45 FT-17 tanks still in service, most of which were remnants of the original French cadre from 1919.[17] The Germans, in contrast, could field over 3,000 tanks in September 1939, and though some 80 percent of them were the relatively primitive Panzer Is and IIs, there were about 300 of the more advanced Panzer III and IV models, which would become the mainstay of German armored forces throughout the war.[18] As if these numerical failings were not enough, Polish tank doctrine—such as it was—followed the French practice of using tanks for infantry support. The emerging German Blitzkrieg doctrine, by contrast, foresaw tanks punching holes in enemy lines, which following infantry could exploit. So while Polish armored crews did not want for bravery, they were wholly unprepared for the coming war of 1939.

The situation in the air was no more comforting. Here, too, Poland's air force had initially been relatively strong, numbering some 700 aircraft in 1919.[19] However, the financial implications of maintaining and updating such a force in the years that followed proved prohibitive. In the 1920s, an ambitious plan to expand the Polish air force to 200 combat squadrons foundered on account of the cost and the dissenting vision of Piłsudski, who was curiously unconvinced of the importance of air power. Later efforts to develop a domestic airline industry bore some fruit, not least the PZL P.7, an all-metal, high-wing, monoplane fighter that was state-of-the-art when it was introduced in 1933, and its more powerful successor, the PZL P.11, which appeared the following year. Another success was the PZL.37 Łoś, or "Moose," an adaptable and capable twin-engine light bomber that entered service in 1938. Nonetheless, given the rapid advances in aeronautical technology in the late 1930s, and the vast amounts of money devoted to rearmament in Hitler's Germany, the Polish air force would go to war in 1939 with obsolete hardware. With 400 or so serviceable Polish combat aircraft facing around 2,500 machines of the Luftwaffe, it was vastly outnumbered and outgunned.[20]

Poland's military and political leaders were well aware of these shortcomings—what one High Command wit called the "doctrine of poverty"[21]—and that awareness influenced their strategic thinking in the late 1930s in two ways. First, Polish defensive planners realized that any coming war most likely had to be a collective effort: Poland could not afford to fight its enemies alone, and urgently needed to secure reliable allies. Second, it became clear that Poland did not have the means to realistically plan for a two-fronted war. Initially, therefore, given that the Soviet Union appeared to be the most pressing threat, an eastern operational plan—named *Wschód*, or "East"—was developed from 1936. This plan foresaw some six army groups concentrated along the eastern frontier to carry out delaying actions and channel any Red Army offensive into more readily defensible and fortified areas, such as that at Sarny, east of Brest.[22]

Following the Austrian *Anschluss* of 1938, when Germany's expansionist tendencies became more obviously manifest, work began on an analogous western operational plan, codenamed *Zachód*, or "West." *Zachód* anticipated German planning for an invasion of Poland, which was in turn predicated on simple geography. Poland was effectively encircled by Germany, with the provinces of Silesia in the southwest and East Prussia in the north forming two jaws of a vast pincer. Hence, it was logical to expect any attack to drive in three general directions: eastward into western Poland, northeastward from Silesia in the direction of Warsaw, and southward from East Prussia, also directed at the capital. Simply flooding those largely indefensible border regions with Polish troops made little strategic sense. Yet the Poles did not want to be accused of a lack of will, which might have compromised any Anglo-French commitment to their defense, so "Plan *Zachód*," completed in the spring of 1939, envisaged a complex balancing act to deal with this strategic predicament.

Polish armies were intended in the first instance to engage any invasion in order to buy time for deeper-lying defense lines to be developed and reserves to be mobilized. They were deployed along Poland's frontiers with the heaviest concentrations in those areas where the German advance was expected. In the north, in the Corridor, the Pomeranian Army was stationed on the lower Vistula, between Bydgoszcz and Tczew. South of East Prussia, the Modlin Army was situated around Mława and Ciechanów, while the Narew Group was strung along the border to the east, from Łomża to Suwałki. To the west, the Poznań Army manned the area of Wielkopolska, protruding like a salient into Germany's eastern flank. To the south of that lay two of the strongest formations: the Łódź Army, to defend the southwestern approaches to Warsaw, the direction from which the main German thrust was expected; and the Kraków Army, tasked with holding the vital industrial area of Upper Silesia as well as the approaches to Poland's second city. Lastly, the Carpathian Army was positioned along the Slovakian frontier to the south, from Nowy Sącz east to Sanok (see Map 2, "Poland 1939: German and Polish Troop Dispositions and the German Plan").

That vigorous defense of the frontiers, though strategically questionable, was deemed politically necessary in order to contradict any suggestion on the part of Poland's would-be allies that the country was unwilling to defend itself. Once those international alliances had been triggered, the logic went, Polish forces were to avoid being encircled and destroyed, and while inflicting maximum losses on the enemy, they would conduct a fighting withdrawal to more defensible lines, such as to the area east of the river Vistula, which bisected the country north to south. In the third phase, there would be a counteroffensive to coincide with the expected entry into the war of Poland's Western allies.[23]

Thus, Poland's strategic planning in 1939 was explicitly predicated upon material military assistance from foreign allies. Boiled down to its essentials, *Zachód* meant holding out until an Allied offensive in the west could relieve the German pressure. Poland, then, was looking for allies in the west just as the British and the French were belatedly looking for active ways to contain Hitler. The two sides found each other in the spring of 1939; the problem was that they were looking for different things.

ANGLO-FRENCH ATTEMPTS TO DEAL PEACEFULLY WITH THE THREAT posed by Hitler's Germany had reached their apogee with the Munich Conference of September 1938, where Czechoslovakia—the then object of Hitler's ire and ambition—was dismembered in the hope of securing a wider peace. For the Poles, Munich provided the opportunity to restore the tiny district of Zaolzie, which had been lost to Czechoslovakia in 1919, to Polish control, but they thereby opened themselves up to damaging accusations, if not of collusion with Hitler, then at least of benefiting from Czechoslovakia's demise. In the process, they squandered a good deal of international sympathy, not least from their eastern neighbor Stalin, who contrived to view Munich as little more than an abject accommodation with fascism.

More importantly, however, the Munich Conference sealed the cession of the Sudetenland to Germany, which Hitler had solemnly declared to be "his last territorial demand in Europe."[24] British prime minister Neville Chamberlain, meanwhile, waved his "piece of paper"— the newly signed Anglo-German Declaration—at Heston Aerodrome and proclaimed "peace for our time." It was a peace that would prove vanishingly short-lived. In March 1939, Hitler's troops marched into Prague and occupied the rump of Czechoslovakia, rendering the Munich Agreement a dead letter. Appeasement had failed, and new ways had to be found to contain Germany.

At the end of March 1939, that new policy became apparent. Addressing the House of Commons, Chamberlain extended a guarantee to Poland, the next likely target of German aggression, that "in the event of any action which clearly threatened Polish independence," the British government would "lend the Polish government all support in [its] power."[25]

Of course, from a British perspective, there was very little that could practically be done to defend Polish independence in the event of conflict: Britain's resources of men and materiel simply did not make an active intervention in Central Europe a realistic prospect. When former prime minister David Lloyd George proclaimed that Chamberlain "could not send a single battalion to Poland" in the event of war, he was right.[26] Neither, one might add, was there much Anglo-French will to launch a vigorous assault on Germany from the west in support of Poland. But for Chamberlain, that was not the point; one might even say that Poland was not the point. For him, the guarantee represented a return to reason and diplomacy, rather than the deployment of brute force. It was an expression of solidarity and support, certainly, not only for Poland but also for France, which had

British prime minister Neville Chamberlain, defending Poland with vowels and consonants alone. *Wellcome Collection Gallery CC-BY-4.0*

long been concerned that Britain's commitment to European affairs was less than solid. But, more than that, it was a signal that further German aggression would not be tolerated. It was a line in the sand, an attempt to contain Hitler through threats—however empty those threats may have been.

Yet, despite this rather hollow guarantee, Poland felt that it had received what it wanted: it had its foreign allies and could now continue its military planning in the firm expectation of their assistance. And, crucially, those expectations were neither dimmed nor contradicted when high-level Franco-Polish discussions began to put flesh on the bones of the promised alliance that spring. On the contrary, they were stoked. In May, the French commander-in-chief, General Maurice Gamelin, and the Polish minister of war, General Tadeusz Kasprzycki, signed the so-called Kasprzycki–Gamelin Convention, which promised an immediate French air attack on Germany in the event of a German invasion, followed by a diversionary land assault on the third day of French mobilization, and then a larger-scale relief offensive, comprising "the bulk" of French forces, to begin after the fifteenth day.[27]

The British, too, made promises, albeit more obliquely. In July 1939, General Edmund Ironside, inspector general of the British army, visited Warsaw for talks. And though he was cautious in private, confessing to his diary that "we can do very little to help the Poles," in public he was perhaps rather too generous in describing his vision of military cooperation.[28] According to the Polish foreign minister, Józef Beck, he undertook to "study the possibility" of transferring Royal Air Force (RAF) formations to Poland, along with a General Staff mission, and promised "to supply . . . 100 bomber aircraft of the newest type," as well as a contingent of Hurricanes. Naturally, his Polish interlocutors considered the talks to be "most satisfactory," and, a month later, inquiries were duly made about an advance RAF bomber force based on Polish soil.[29] None of these aircraft would ever be delivered.

In the summer of 1939, therefore, Poland and Britain were locked in a curious relationship. Poland believed that it had found the ally—along with France—that would assist in its defense; the guarantee had seemed to confirm that assumption, as had all the staff discussions that followed. Yet, for Britain at least, Poland was more of a tool than an ally. Despite all the earnest talk of active support, British politicians and military planners knew full well that there was very little they could or would do to practically help Poland in its hour of need. Instead, they were seeking to use Poland to try to contain Hitler—to conjure up the specter of war to rein in his territorial ambitions, in the hope that that specter alone would prove to be enough of a deterrent.

The problem with this approach was that Hitler was not going to be deterred. Poland, to his mind, did not deserve to exist as a state, let alone to frustrate German ambitions.[30] Consequently, when he received word of Chamberlain's gambit, Hitler wasn't moved to reason; he was infuriated. According to Admiral Wilhelm Canaris, who was present in the Reich Chancellery when news of the British guarantee arrived, Hitler flew into a rage: "With features distorted by fury, he had stormed up and down his room, pounded his fists on the marble table top and spewed forth a series of savage imprecations. Then, with eyes flashing with an uncanny light, he had growled the threat: 'I'll brew them a devil's potion.'"[31]

Backed into a corner, Hitler and his paladins were soon plotting a way out of the impasse, and a rapprochement with Stalin's Soviet Union was emerging as a possible solution. Though first aired as a ruse—what Göring called a *petit jeu*—to intimidate the Poles, the idea soon gained traction, drawing on the traditionally pro-Russian tendencies of many of those in the German Foreign Office. Even the Nazi ideologue and veteran anti-Bolshevik Alfred Rosenberg opined that "when Germany's life is at stake, even a temporary affiliation with Moscow would have to be contemplated."[32] Though initially reluctant to take this path, citing his long years of struggle against communism, Hitler was finally persuaded to allow his new foreign minister, Joachim von Ribbentrop, to have his head and pursue negotiations with Stalin.

When it came, Ribbentrop's approach met Soviet strategic thinking at something of a crossroads. The Munich Conference of the previous year, from whose deliberations the USSR had been omitted, had left a sour taste in Moscow's mouth: it had appeared to provide the final proof that the idea of "collective security" to contain and defeat Hitler was now definitively dead in the water. Increasingly distrustful of the British and the French—as well as the Germans—Stalin was moving toward a policy of simply getting the best deals he could from bilateral negotiations. In essence, this was something of a return to the original ideological principles of the USSR, wherein the outside world was seen as uniformly hostile, with no qualitative differences between Nazism and Western capitalism: according to Marxist-Leninist doctrine, they were two sides of the same malevolent coin, the only difference being that Nazism was further down the road to an inevitable demise. It followed that relations with the outside world—whether democratic or totalitarian—could never be normal; every relationship would be viewed by the Kremlin as a zero-sum game, the only guiding principle being whatever would bring the most benefit and security to the USSR. Now that collective security had failed, *all* options were on the table.

So, as the storm clouds gathered over Europe in the summer of 1939, diplomatic circles would embark upon a rather undignified round of horse-trading, with the British and French on one side and the Germans on the other, seeking to woo Stalin to their camp. The "imperialists" were the first to publicly show their hand, sending a joint delegation, consisting of a British admiral and a French general, to Moscow in early August for negotiations. It was a mission that was almost comically doomed to failure. Not only did the British admiral—Sir Reginald Ranfurly Plunkett-Ernle-Erle-Drax—raise Soviet eyebrows with his quadruple-barreled name, but he and his French counterpart were not granted plenipotentiary powers, and so lacked the authority to conduct serious material negotiations; they had to refer back to London and Paris for any decisions to be made. What was more, the delegation's six-day voyage to the Soviet Union, up the Baltic in an aged British merchantman, did little to convince the Soviets of Western seriousness.

In that assumption, at least, the Soviets were correct. Rarely in history has an international alliance been pursued with less enthusiasm. Given the justified suspicions that many in the British government still harbored toward the USSR, the Anglo-French delegation had been sent with the instruction to "go very slowly."[33] They were going through the motions, holding their noses while talking to the Soviets, in the hope that their mere presence in Moscow might scare Hitler into compliance—or that by talking out the summer, they could rob Hitler of his opportunity for action.

More seriously, however, the Anglo-French delegation could offer very little of substance to Stalin. Hemmed in by their guarantee to Poland, they could offer no territorial inducements, despite Stalin's lengthy list of irredenta; nor could they secure an agreement from the Poles for a suggested passage of the Red Army through the east of the country to meet any German threat. This was not just stubbornness on Warsaw's part; Poland's experience of the previous century and a half suggested that once Russian soldiers arrived, they could be very difficult to dislodge. It was no great surprise, then, that negotiations stalled on this point. Marshal Kliment Voroshilov, the Soviet defense commissar, bemoaned the fact that this "cardinal question" could not be answered satisfactorily.[34]

In truth, what the Anglo-French delegation was offering was a principled preservation of the status quo, and Stalin had very little interest in that. In the circumstances of 1939, with conflict looming once again over the continent of Europe, "business as usual" held little appeal for him. Stalin scented an opportunity. As he laconically explained to the later British ambassador to Moscow, "The USSR wanted to change the equilibrium. . . . England and France wanted to preserve it."[35] As an avid student of the Bolshevik revolution, Stalin knew that war could be a powerful motor in "changing the equilibrium," and he was certainly not averse to encouraging his ideological enemies to fight each other. Later that month, he would outline his reasoning to the Politburo:

> A war is on between two groups of capitalist countries for the redivision of the world, for the domination of the world! We see nothing wrong in their having a good hard fight and weakening each other. It would be fine if, at the hands of Germany, the position of the richest capitalist countries (especially England) were shaken. Hitler, without understanding it or desiring it, is shaking and undermining the capitalist system. . . . We can manoeuvre, pit one side against the other to set them fighting each other as fiercely as possible.[36]

Stalin's foreign minister would be even more explicit. "Lenin was not mistaken when he assured us that the Second World War will help us to gain power throughout all Europe, just as the First World War helped us to gain power in Russia," Molotov explained.[37] As long as the Soviet Union could remain aloof from it, war was something to be welcomed.

While such ideological considerations no doubt provided the background to Stalin's thinking, the immediate material benefits of an arrangement with Hitler would have been extremely persuasive on their own. Already at the beginning of his flirtation with the Soviets, Ribbentrop had flagged up Germany's willingness to make wide-ranging concessions when he told the Soviet attaché in Berlin, Georgy Astakhov, that "there is no question between the Baltic and the Black Sea which cannot be settled to the complete satisfaction of both parties."[38] A few days later, Astakhov spelled out to his superiors in Moscow the opportunity that was opening up, explaining that Germany was willing to pay any price to prevent an alignment between the USSR and the Western Powers, and that Berlin would give up the Baltic states, Bessarabia, and eastern Poland "if we can give them the promise not to interfere in the conflict."[39] Negotiations were evidently much easier if what you were willing to "give up" wasn't yours to begin with.

By the time Ribbentrop arrived in Moscow on the afternoon of August 23, 1939, the German–Soviet relationship was already blossoming. Meetings had been conducted with attachés and emissaries, positions had been clarified, and draft treaties had been prepared, all driven on by Hitler's desire to have an agreement in place in time for his invasion of Poland, which he had earmarked to begin on August 26. Nonetheless, for some of the senior personnel of the Third Reich, arriving in the Soviet capital was a curious experience. As one of them noted, "There was a feeling of ambivalence that fate should lead us to Moscow, which we had previously fought bitterly as the enemy of European culture."[40]

After a welcoming ceremony at Khodynka airfield outside Moscow—for which swastika banners had to be requisitioned from a Soviet film studio, where they had recently been used for making anti-Nazi propaganda films—Ribbentrop and his entourage were whisked to the Kremlin for the first of their meetings with their Soviet counterparts. After the pleasantries were out of the way, they got down to business. The relatively simple task before them was to agree on the draft of a Soviet–German nonaggression pact. Initially, a 10-year term had been suggested, but Ribbentrop rashly suggested a 100-year term. Stalin was unimpressed, replying that "people will laugh at us for not being serious."[41] They then agreed to the text of a rather anodyne document with a preamble and seven articles, barely 300 words in total. It stressed the objective of "strengthening the cause of peace between Germany and the USSR" and declared that both parties would "desist from any act of violence, any aggressive action, and any attack on each other."[42]

That done, discussion moved to the more ticklish question of the "Secret Protocol"—which Stalin announced "we will not publish anywhere else"[43]—in which the spoils of their collaboration, "in the event of a territorial and political rearrangement," would be delineated. Ribbentrop told Stalin that Hitler accepted that eastern Poland, Bessarabia, Finland, Estonia, and Latvia up to the river Dvina would all fall "within the Soviet sphere of influence." Without flinching, Stalin demanded all of Latvia. Ribbentrop was obliged to put a call in to Hitler, who was anxiously waiting at the Berghof for news of the negotiations. Within half an hour, Hitler returned the call and tersely agreed to the change. With that, the fate of some 23 million people across Central Europe was sealed.[44]

Underpinning the "territorial rearrangements" promised by the Secret Protocol was a trade deal, signed three days earlier, allowing for the exchange of 180 million Reichsmarks of Soviet raw materials for 120 million Reichsmarks of German finished goods. An additional credit facility of 200 million Reichsmarks was extended to Moscow that was to be repaid in raw-material shipments after 1946. Pointedly, Molotov claimed that "we have never had any equally advantageous economic agreement with Great Britain, France, or any other country."[45]

After the Secret Protocol had been agreed, the two sides sat down to a *tour d'horizon* of current affairs, ranging from Japan and Turkey to France and Britain, while a draft communiqué was drawn up in an anteroom. The hard work done, the signatories and their respective entourages then gathered for an impromptu reception where caviar, sandwiches, vodka, and Crimean champagne were served. Interminable toasts followed, in the Russian manner. At one point, Stalin raised his glass to toast Hitler: "I know how much the German nation loves its Führer. I should therefore like to drink to his health."[46]

Both sides would have declared themselves well satisfied with the proceedings. Hitler had his carte blanche over Poland and was free to turn his armies eastward, safe in the knowledge that the Red Army would not intervene. Less immediately important to him, but no less significant, was the trade agreement, which promised Germany access to the Soviet Union's vast resources of raw materials—a huge boon if, in the event of war, the British were to impose their time-worn strategy of blockading Germany. However, it was Hitler's firm belief that the British and the French would back down. His opponents were "worms," he said, predicting that the invasion of Poland "would *never, never, never*" provoke a wider war.[47]

Stalin, too, would have been delighted. Within the space of a few short weeks, he had secured a nonaggression pact with his primary ideological opponent and signed off on a trade agreement that would potentially spur on the next phase of Soviet industrialization. In addition, while the continent of Europe was still mired in crisis, the Soviet Union could remain nominally removed. More than that, in the event of an outbreak of war, it would not only secure the return of almost all of the lands lost by the Russian Empire at the end of the First World War, but would also, in all likelihood, see its enemies fighting against one another. Little wonder, perhaps, that as the signatories gathered for the commemorative photograph beneath Lenin's stern gaze, Stalin was beaming widely.

News of the Nazi–Soviet Pact broke upon the outside world, in Churchill's words, "like an explosion." Certainly no one in Britain had expected the move; that very week, a Foreign Office briefing had declared such an arrangement "unlikely."[48] For many in and around Whitehall, the pact appeared to presage something like an apocalypse: Member of Parliament (MP) Henry "Chips" Channon wrote in his diary that "the Nazis and the Bolsheviks have combined to destroy civilisation, and the outlook for the world looks ghastly."[49] In the world beyond Westminster, the outlook was slightly rosier, with some even contriving to excuse Soviet actions as defensive and precautionary, but the consensus was that it appeared to make war inevitable. In the circumstances, it fell to *The Times* to sum up the mood. In an editorial, the London newspaper expressed doubt that the pact would "make any material difference," though it conceded that the full details were yet to emerge. Britain's position was clear, it said—its obligations to Poland were unaffected.[50]

In Poland, news of the Nazi–Soviet Pact was received with a combination of resignation and numb horror. Here, few were under any illusion about what the pact implied: Poland's recent history of occupation and partition was too raw and too fresh for that. One Warsaw diarist noted pessimistically that "nothing good" would come of Hitler's negotiation with the Soviets, adding that when the Germans and the Soviets found a common language, "what could that language be if not the partition of our country?"[51] The head of the British military mission to Poland, the redoubtable Lieutenant-General Sir Adrian Carton de Wiart, found himself urgently recalled to Warsaw from his country estate at Prostyń in the far east of the country, where he was shooting snipe. Briefed on his arrival by the British ambassador the next morning, he realized that "war was not a question of weeks but of days."[52] He visited the Polish commander-in-chief, Edward Śmigły-Rydz, the following day, and was dismayed to learn that the Polish defensive plan envisaged engaging the Germans as soon as they crossed the frontier, in terrain admirably suited to the use of tanks. If Śmigły-Rydz was a favorite of Piłsudski, Carton de Wiart noted in his memoir, it must be "for his loyalty and integrity, for I cannot think it was for his capabilities."[53]

Meanwhile, the Polish Foreign Office was looking for solid commitments from the country's allies. The foreign minister, Colonel Józef Beck, wrote to his ambassadors in London and Paris to declare that the announcement of the pact had merely demonstrated that the Soviets had "for a long time been playing a double game." The only possible response, he wrote, was "to reiterate the firm position of England, France and Poland," and to that end, he urged his ambassadors to seek consultations with the British and French governments.[54]

Two days after that, on the afternoon of August 25, Hitler summoned the British ambassador, Nevile Henderson, to a meeting in the Reich Chancellery in Berlin. Concerned at the news from London that his signature of a nonaggression pact with Stalin had left the Anglo-Polish guarantee unaffected, he sought to make a similarly "decisive step" in his relations with Britain. Consequently, in a long lecture to the ambassador, he declared that the "Macedonian conditions" on Germany's eastern frontier had to be rectified. The problem of the Corridor and of Danzig had to be solved, and he intended to solve it, by force if necessary.[55]

In return for British acquiescence in that policy, Hitler made a startling offer. He had always wanted an "Anglo-German understanding," he told Henderson, and in order to achieve it he was willing "to pledge himself personally" for the continued existence of the British Empire, and "to place the power of the German Reich at its disposal." A positive response from London, he said, would be "a blessing for Germany, and also for the British Empire"—but he warned that this would be his "last offer."[56] Though Henderson raised the objection that his government would consider the offer only as part of a wider, peaceful settlement of the Polish crisis, Hitler was adamant and suggested that the ambassador fly back to London immediately to present it to the British government.[57] Ribbentrop even put a shoulder to the wheel, telephoning Henderson upon his return to his office to inform him of yet another confected Polish "atrocity."[58]

Hitler's sense of urgency was down to his timetable. Facing Poland, he had some 1.5 million men poised to strike, divided into two army groups. Army Group North, with around 650,000 men, consisted of the 4th Army, facing east across the Polish Corridor, and the 3rd Army, which would move southward from East Prussia. Army Group South contained the 8th, 10th, and 14th Armies, the last bolstered by the addition of some 50,000 Slovak troops—in all nearly 900,000 men, who would strike northeastward and eastward from their starting positions in Silesia and Slovakia.[59]

Hitler had given the order to prepare the invasion of Poland two days previously, with operations to start at dawn the following morning, August 26. If he were to stick to that schedule, he would have to give the final order not much later than three o'clock that very afternoon; otherwise German troops would have to stand down, and a new timetable for action would need to be drawn up. Hitler was hoping that his offer to the British would suffice at least to keep London confused and uncommitted while Poland was destroyed. Determined not to delay his plans, he summoned the chief of the German High Command, Field Marshal Wilhelm Keitel, and shortly after 3:00 p.m. gave the instruction for the invasion of Poland to begin.[60] With that, orders began to be transmitted down the chain of command to the countless German units in the field that were poised close to the Polish frontier and awaiting final instructions. German consulates in Poland were directed, with immediate effect, to send all German citizens to Germany or to neutral countries.[61] The invasion of Poland—*Fall Weiss*, or "Case White," in German code—was scheduled to begin at 4:30 the following morning.

That very afternoon, while those orders were being transmitted, the Polish ambassador in London, Count Edward Raczyński, met with the British foreign secretary, Viscount Halifax, in the Foreign Office on Whitehall. Unlike Hitler's attempt to browbeat Henderson a few hours earlier, their discussion was short, cordial, and entirely lacking in histrionics. Before them was the draft of an "Agreement of Mutual Assistance" that had been drawn up over the previous two days. It was intended to cement the existing Anglo-Polish collaboration and restate Britain's resolve to stand by Poland in the event of German aggression. A short document—consisting of some 8 articles containing around 500 words—it contained a significant commitment: that if either signatory were to "become engaged in hostilities with a European power in consequence of aggression by the latter," the other party would lend "all the support and assistance" possible.[62] After reading the text through, Halifax and Raczyński added their signatures to the foot of the page. The "war of nerves," Raczyński would later recall, appeared to be drawing to an end.[63]

Hitler might have disagreed. Having given his order that afternoon, he was pacing his Reich Chancellery office "even more agitated," according to Keitel, than he had been earlier in the day. The reason for his nervous excitement was twofold. First, word had reached him late that afternoon that the Anglo-Polish Agreement had been signed, confirming that the British, far from being bullied and bribed, were determined to stand by their Polish ally. Second, receiving the Italian ambassador, Bernardo Attolico, Hitler learned that Mussolini would not be joining his adventure, as Italy was unready for war.[64] Momentarily crushed by what he saw as a gross betrayal, Hitler cut a sorry figure, staring blankly into the distance. Pulling himself together, he summoned Keitel again and demanded that "Case White" be called off, so that he might once again attempt to isolate Poland from its allies. After a lengthy discussion, Hitler issued recall orders at 7:30 that evening. As Keitel recalled, "D-Day was postponed."[65]

AT NINE O'CLOCK THAT NIGHT, AUGUST 25, LIEUTENANT DR. Hans-Albrecht Herzner called his men together for a final briefing in the barracks at Čadca, on the Slovak side of the Polish border. Herzner was a tall, thin-lipped, thirty-two-year-old reservist seconded to the Abwehr who had arrived earlier that evening from Breslau under false papers. He had orders to lead a clandestine operation across the frontier that would commence Germany's war against Poland.

After a brief roll call, Herzner supervised the final preparations. His group consisted of twenty-four men: ethnic Germans from the region who were dressed in civilian clothes, with just a swastika armband to show their allegiance. Only Herzner and his driver were wearing Wehrmacht uniforms. Each man was given a machine gun, four magazines, and a pistol.[66] The group was then split into two assault parties and loaded onto trucks for the short drive northwest. Disembarking at the hamlet of Dejovka, they continued on foot, and after waiting for reinforcements, which failed to arrive, they crossed the Polish frontier at half past midnight. Acutely aware of the historical significance of the moment, Herzner paused in the darkness to scribble a spidery note on a Wehrmacht message pad:

Generalkommando VIII. AK. Ic AO II, Breslau.
    Crossing Polish border with KOJ at 00.30 hours near point 627 north-northwest of Cadca.
    [signed] Herzner[67]

Herzner's "KOJ," or "Combat Group Jablunka," was one of a number of units established by the Abwehr just before the outbreak of war for

Herzner's irregulars: invading Poland single-handedly.
Ian Sayer Archive

the purposes of infiltration and sabotage. As has been shown, other such groups had been tasked with capturing or destroying strategically vital bridges, securing power plants, or sowing confusion.[68] Herzner's task was simple, but no less crucial. He was to cross the frontier in advance of the German invasion and capture the railway station at Mosty, 5 kilometers (3 miles) inside Polish territory. Then he was to hold it until the arrival of German forces, expected a few hours later. The strategic significance of Mosty was that it was the closest station to the rail tunnel beneath the Jablunkov Pass, the shortest route between Warsaw and Vienna. For the German invasion in this sector to be successful, it was vital that the tunnel be captured intact—and it was the Abwehr's belief that the Poles' sabotage charges in the tunnel were controlled from the station building at Mosty.

At 2:45 a.m. on August 26, Herzner's group arrived on the hillside overlooking their target. They had not had an easy journey. While skirting Polish sentries on the frontier and around the tunnel, the second unit had become lost in the forest, so the KOJ was now down to a mere dozen men. After waiting in vain for support, Herzner decided that the approaching dawn forced his hand. Shortly before sunrise, his men surrounded the station building, disarmed the station staff, and secured the area. Their mission, it seemed, had been accomplished. It was 4:00 a.m. The German invasion was expected to commence within the hour.[69]

Herzner faced two problems, however. The first was that his lockdown of the station building at Mosty was not as complete as he might have hoped: one of the staff members had managed to alert the local Polish garrison, using a telephone in the basement of the station. More seriously for Herzner, however, was that the German invasion he was spearheading was not going to materialize.

Hitler's recall order had reached front-line units between nine and ten o'clock the night before. In the circumstances, with many units already preparing their forward positions, the success of the order was remarkable. Even diversionary and sabotage units were recalled: in one case, a group was already 200 meters (about 650 feet) inside Polish territory when a breathless messenger in a German uniform caught up with them.[70] Not everyone could be reached in time, however. Herzner and his men had set out before the halt order had arrived, and—as ordered—were maintaining radio silence. Even regimental messengers sent to bring them back had been unable to locate them in the darkness.[71] Though he didn't yet know it, Herzner and his twelve men had invaded Poland single-handedly. They were on their own.

While Herzner was waiting in vain for the German advance, he soon faced more immediate problems. At dawn, the Polish guard detail from the north end of the tunnel attacked the station building. After fighting them off, and with no relief in sight, Herzner attempted to make telephone contact with his superiors, but couldn't negotiate his way past the Polish operator.[72] Desperate for information, at around 5:00 a.m. he sent one of his men to commandeer a locomotive, waiting nearby under steam, and take it south through the tunnel to deliver a message to division headquarters at Čadca.[73] Soon thereafter, Herzner received a telephone call from his superiors tersely instructing him to "release his prisoners, vacate the station building and return by the quickest route." Leading his men back, pursued by the tunnel guards and Polish police units, he would cross the Slovak border at 1:30 p.m. His "invasion" of Poland had lasted precisely thirteen hours.[74]

THE DAY AFTER THE DEBACLE AT THE JABLUNKOV PASS—AS Herzner caught his breath, and Polish generals angrily demanded of their German counterparts whether the result was "peace or war"[75]— Hitler attempted to carry on as usual. He wrote to Mussolini expressing his regret over the Duce's decision not to join his adventure, and asking that his ally at least support him in an "active propaganda campaign."[76]

The Poles, for their part, continued the secret, partial mobilization that had been in progress since mid-August. By the last week of that month, the process had been stepped up. As well as individual divisions and brigades, all state police, air force, and air defense units were recalled, the eastern districts of Lwów and Przemyśl were mobilized, and reservists were evacuated from Poznań and Pomerania east of the Vistula. In all, around three-quarters of Poland's combat forces were mobilized—the most that could be achieved while keeping the matter under wraps.[77] Jan Karski, then a lieutenant in the artillery, recalled the confusion at Warsaw's main station, where he realized that the mobilization had been "secret" only in the sense that there had been no public announcements. Nonetheless, he noted, the mood was still bullish. Discussing the ongoing crisis that night, his major told him, "England and France are not needed this time. We can finish this on our own."[78]

While the Poles secretly mobilized and Hitler chided his would-be ally, the British and the French continued their vain efforts at negotiation. Henderson returned to Berlin to inform Hitler of the final rejection of his offer, but he expressed the British government's desire for a lasting understanding with Germany once an amicable settlement with Poland had been reached.[79] Meanwhile, the French prime minister, Édouard Daladier, wrote to Hitler to ask that he rejoin efforts to find a peaceful solution to the crisis, and reminded him that a return to war in Europe would mean a victory only for destruction and barbarism.[80] Hitler, however, was unmoved. He had made up his mind, and any delay that he permitted was merely a ruse to wrong-foot his opponents. As General Walter Warlimont discovered on arriving at the Reich Chancellery that afternoon, any feeling of relief that war had been averted was wholly misplaced. Hitler's Wehrmacht adjutant, Colonel Rudolf Schmundt, told him, "Don't start celebrating too soon—it's only a question of a few days' postponement!"[81]

Tiring of the charade of negotiation, the Poles finally ordered a general mobilization on August 29—only to be browbeaten by the British and French into canceling the order, wary as they were of taking any steps that Berlin might choose to interpret as "provocative."[82] The result was more chaos at the railheads as travel orders were issued and countermanded and troops were left stranded. The Polish army would field around a million men across thirty-seven infantry divisions, eleven cavalry brigades, a dozen National Guard battalions, and three divisions of the Border Protection Corps (Korpus Ochrony Pogranicza, or KOP). Although some of those units were complete, many were lacking cadres and equipment and had now been prevented from reaching their positions. Of the thirty-four cavalry squadrons earmarked for the Poznań Army, for instance, only nineteen were already in situ; and of the fifty-four infantry battalions assigned to the Łódź Army, only thirty-four were in position. The Kraków Army had barely half of its allocation of heavy artillery.[83] Allied attempts at mediation had done little except hamstring Poland's defense.

Finally, the tension was broken by its instigator. At 12:40 p.m. on August 31, Hitler again gave the order for "Case White" to begin, at dawn the following day. "Since the situation on Germany's eastern frontier has become intolerable and all political possibilities of peaceful settlement have been exhausted," he wrote, "I have decided upon a solution by force."[84] Though Hitler was hoping, indeed expecting, that the British and the French would waver in their commitment to Poland, he can have been under few illusions about the willingness of the Polish government and people to fight. Hitler prided himself on being an avid reader of history, and a glance at Poland's long tradition of opposition to foreign occupation would surely have convinced him of that. He also had the correspondence of his ambassador in Warsaw, Hans-Adolf von Moltke, to remind him of Polish resistance. In one report, from early August 1939, Moltke had sought to counter the German assumption that Polish morale was fragile and that their will to resist was declining: "The old hatred of everything German and the conviction that it is Poland's destiny to cross swords with Germany," he wrote, "was too deep for passions to abate easily." Moreover, he added, the weeks of crisis had "so far failed to make any decisive breach in Polish morale and material powers of resistance." He concluded that a "decisive collapse . . . cannot be expected."[85] One way or another, it seemed, Hitler would have his war.

– Chapter Three –

A FRIGHTFUL FUTILITY

The morning of Friday, September 1, was oppressively warm, the result of a heatwave that summer. As most Britons still slumbered, the first news arrived of the German invasion of Poland when the Reuters News Agency reported what a German radio announcement had said.[1] A telegram from the British embassy in Warsaw to the Foreign Office in London confirmed the account, stating that the Germans had indeed crossed the Polish frontier and that widespread bombing was already under way. The daily papers carried nothing of the latest events; instead, they were full of details of the civilian evacuation from London and other cities due to begin that day, along with reports of Hitler's latest terms to ease the crisis over Poland.

For most people, then, word came by radio, with the first news bulletin at 10:30 a.m. A listener would have had to struggle to keep pace with the rush of words—"invasion . . . general mobilization . . . Parliament summoned . . . cabinet meeting . . . air raids . . . military objectives." Even newspaper audiences would have been hard pressed to follow the flow of events: not for the last time, newsreaders would mangle Polish place-names in discussing the locations that had already been bombed: "Tczew, Toruń, Jasło . . ."[2]

Given that the Polish–German crisis had been brewing for much of the summer, people were scarcely surprised; indeed, the ongoing evacuation showed that both the government and the people were quite well prepared for the exigencies of war. The news was primarily met with a sense of disappointment. As one diarist put it, "Surely a nation has never gone to war so grim and disillusioned and coldly resentful as we are now."[3] An imaginative housewife in Bolton had a clear target for her ire. "I would just like to get Hitler on this field at the top of our street just to give him some punishment," she was recorded as saying. "First thing I would do, saw his feet at the ankles, sharpen the shin bones and force him down into the earth, down to his shoulders, then I would just hammer the top of his head with my big saucepan until I'd driven him down out of sight."[4]

Britain's politicians were no less angered and no less resigned. Prime Minister Neville Chamberlain called a cabinet meeting for 11:30 that morning, which took place, he later intoned, "under the gravest possible conditions": "The event against which we had fought so long and so earnestly had come upon us." But, he said, "our consciences were clear, and there should be no possible question now where our duty lay."[5] Despite that expression of determination and clarity, what followed was a rather agonized discussion in which the cabinet tried to catch up with the ongoing gallop of events. They were not aided in their task by the disinformation still emanating from Berlin—and relayed by the German chargé d'affaires in London—that German forces were merely "returning fire" and that Polish cities had not been bombed. Italian offers of help, plus the brokering of a peace conference, did little to ease the growing confusion, and French concerns about the prospect of immediate military action provided another source of hesitation.

At the same time, the Poles were nudging the British government toward a position of active support. That morning, the Polish Foreign Ministry had cabled its embassies in London and Paris providing clarification on the German attack; the cable expressed the conviction that "in accordance with the existing treaties of alliance, [Poland] will receive immediate help from its Allies."[6] The Polish ambassador in London, Count

Edward Raczyński, then declared in his conversations with Foreign Secretary Viscount Halifax that, in his opinion, "the circumstances had arisen which called for the implementation of [the British] guarantee."[7] That afternoon the Polish foreign minister, Colonel Józef Beck, sent a telegram to the British ambassador in Warsaw requesting the involvement of the RAF forthwith.[8]

In the cabinet meeting, meanwhile, it was the minister for defense, Lord Chatfield, who took the lead, reporting the opinion of the Chiefs of Staff that if the guarantee was going to be implemented, then an ultimatum should be dispatched to Germany "without undue delay." Chamberlain concurred, and a draft was prepared warning Germany that "unless the German Government are prepared to give . . . satisfactory assurances that all aggressive action against Poland has been suspended and are prepared promptly to withdraw their forces from Polish territory, His Majesty's Government in the United Kingdom will without hesitation fulfil their obligations to Poland." The telegram was sent en clair to the British embassy in Berlin at 5:45 that evening.[9]

At 6:15 p.m., Chamberlain appeared in a packed and expectant House of Commons chamber. His personal agony was clear. "Eighteen months ago in this House," he said, "I prayed that the responsibility might not fall upon me to ask this country to accept the awful arbitrament of war. I fear that I may not be able to avoid that responsibility." But, he went on, it was clear as to where his duty lay. "No man can say that the government could have done more to try to keep open the way for an honourable and equitable settlement of the dispute between Germany and Poland," he said, adding, "We shall stand at the bar of history knowing that the responsibility for this terrible catastrophe lies on the shoulders of one man—the German chancellor, who has not hesitated to plunge the world into misery in order to serve his own senseless ambitions." Under the circumstances, he explained, there was "only one course open to us," and that was the delivery—in concert with the French—of what he called a "last warning." He then read the telegram aloud to the House.

In closing, Chamberlain struck a strong moral tone, stating that there would be "no peace in Europe" as long as the Nazi regime existed.

He ended on a defiant note: "Now it only remains for us to set our teeth and to enter upon this struggle, which we have so earnestly endeavoured to avoid, with determination to see it through to the end. We shall enter it with a clear conscience, with the support of the Dominions and the British Empire, and with the moral approval of the greater part of the world."[10] It had been a strong performance, in which the normally reserved Chamberlain had reportedly struck the dispatch box with his fist for emphasis.[11] But crucially, his last warning had not included a time limit, and many of the more belligerent MPs in the House of Commons feared that the British and French governments were still looking for a way to evade their commitments.

That evening, as the House broke for the night, Nevile Henderson finally succeeded in meeting with his German counterpart, Joachim von Ribbentrop.[12] On arrival at Wilhelmstrasse, he was met by Hitler's interpreter, Paul Schmidt, and ushered into Ribbentrop's presence, where Chamberlain's note was duly translated. Throughout, Schmidt recalled, Ribbentrop remained calm.[13] Evidently under instructions not to give any response, the minister reacted "as though he understood no English." He gave the same reaction when he learned of the French ambassador's note half an hour later.[14] When he subsequently took both missives to Hitler for his response, the Führer accepted them with derision, saying, "We will now see if they come to Poland's aid."[15]

THE FOLLOWING DAY, SEPTEMBER 2, HAD THE SAME FEBRILE, expectant mood; for Henderson in Berlin it was "a day of suspense."[16] But in place of the speculation and rumor, there was at least a little more concrete information about events in Poland. The *Daily Telegraph* provided readers with a full-page map and extensive details of the German attack, as well as an editorial praising Parliament for its stand "for Freedom against Brutal Oppression."[17] Only the Communist *Daily Worker* sounded a rather discordant note, criticizing the government for "doing nothing" to support Spain and Czechoslovakia, and portraying the new conflict as a "two-front war" that would deliver "victory against Fascism" and "victory over Chamberlain and the enemies of democracy."[18]

Conservative MP "Chips" Channon, a prominent supporter of Chamberlain, noted in his diary that "we are on the very verge of war." He declared himself "dejected, despondent, despairing."[19] But the public mood was, if anything, more positive, and certainly more phlegmatic than it had been the day before. One contributor to the new Mass Observation social research survey noted that though his customers "realised things were as bad as could be," there was nonetheless a determination that "Hitler must be taught a lesson." Another correspondent discerned an "improvement in public morale" and a "quieting effect" thanks to what she called "the certainty of war."[20] Of course, such sentiments were not universal. One Briton confessed to a "dose of the jitters" after listening to the news, others reported "feeling sick" or "upset" at the prospect of war. But there were also the eternal optimists who opined that "we are certain to win . . . we always do."[21]

Aside from such bravado, there were some reasons for optimism on the British and French side. Britain, of course, was primarily a naval power in 1939. Its empire had been built on international trade, and its global reach traditionally required a navy to police sea lanes and protect its far-flung interests. With over 1,400 vessels of all types, including 15 battleships, 184 destroyers, and 60 submarines, Britain boasted the largest navy in the world.[22] It also had the world's largest merchant fleet, amounting to fully one in three of all merchant vessels.[23] And though Britain's land forces were limited—numbering a little over 200,000 men in September 1939—they were mainly professional soldiers, with only a minority having been brought in by partial conscription earlier that year. In addition, they could call on 200,000 reservists and an additional 450,000 territorials.[24]

British equipment, meanwhile, was certainly not inferior to that of its would-be opponent. As well as the venerable, standard-issue Lee-Enfield rifle, British army units were armed with the Bren light machine gun—modified from an original Czech design—which had entered service the previous year; it was durable, accurate, and effective.

Armored units, however, were rather less well prepared. Though the Matilda Mark II—which had the thickest armor of any tank at the time, and boasted a potent 2-pounder gun—was already in production, only a handful had been delivered by September 1939, so British forces had to rely on the Mark I model, armed with only a heavy machine gun, and the lightly armored Mark I Cruiser tank.

In the air, the RAF had a total complement of front-line aircraft of 1,660 machines in September 1939.[25] Of its 155 squadrons, 16 were flying the redoubtable Hawker Hurricane, as well as 26 in the Blenheim light bomber and 10 in the twin-engine Handley Page Hampden. Over 300 Mark I examples of the Supermarine Spitfire had already been received, with a further 2,000 on order.[26] Though the RAF was not yet the formidable force it would later become, it certainly did not lack firepower.

French forces, too, were considerable. Essentially a mirror image of Britain's military, they boasted a large standing army, but with a smaller navy and air force. The army, raised via conscription, numbered around 900,000 men in the autumn of 1939, with a further 5 million trained reservists. Well armed and equipped across some 91 infantry divisions and 39 armored divisions, it was the second-largest army in the world—behind Stalin's USSR—and boasted much state-of-the-art equipment, such as the Char B1 heavy tank, widely considered to be the best tank available.

Away from land forces, the French were less well equipped. In the air, they had around 1,000 operational aircraft divided across 24 front-line fighter and 34 bomber squadrons, comprising primarily the sturdy but underpowered Morane-Saulnier 406 fighter and the unreliable Breguet 691 twin-engine light bomber.[27] The French navy, meanwhile, was much smaller than that of Britain, numbering some 70 destroyers, 19 cruisers, and 7 battleships crewed by a total of 160,000 personnel.[28]

British and French forces complemented each other well; one's shortcomings in one sphere were compensated by the other's preponderance in that area. As such, Anglo-French forces were a good match for their German opponents; arguably, they held the upper hand. Yet despite this apparent strength, there were several issues that precluded the effective deployment of that power.

The first was that Britain was effectively dependent on French co-operation. Separated from the continent by the English Channel, the British army needed the French as comrades-in-arms to launch any effective action against Germany. So, while Britain could rage over German aggression against Poland, the key to any effective counter-measures lay in French hands. For its part, meanwhile, France was divided. Though the cabinet had committed the country to meeting its alliance obligations toward Poland the previous week,[29] there were some who did not share that principled defiance, not least among them the foreign minister, Georges Bonnet. For one thing, huge French losses—human and material—in the First World War, coupled with political turmoil thereafter, had nurtured a faith in the policy of ap-peasing Germany, which endured long after it had been shown to be counterproductive. For another, French society labored under what has become known as the "Maginot mentality"—named after the extensive line of fortifications stretching along the Franco-German frontier—which engendered a false sense of security and an insularity that would inevitably cast doubt on France's foreign commitments. As the minister of war, General Louis Maurin, had asked the Chamber of Deputies in 1935, "How can anyone believe that we continue to think of offensives when we have spent billions of francs to establish a fortified barrier?"[30]

In addition, when the crisis of September 1939 broke, a number of more practical concerns hampered decisive action. The first was the un-derstandable French desire to complete the evacuation of Paris and the frontier areas, in the expectation that a German attack would follow swiftly from any declaration of war.[31] Moreover, both the French and (to a lesser extent) the British wished to give the Italian government a last chance to salvage peace via mediation—a trick that Mussolini had pulled off the previous autumn in Munich. With the French, and Bon-net especially, desperate for a solution to the crisis that stopped short of war, the Italians were happy to play along, though Mussolini's foreign minister, Count Galeazzo Ciano, knew well that—given the British demand for a German withdrawal as a prerequisite to talks—the approach would find little traction in Berlin. "It isn't my business," Ciano wrote in his diary, "to give Hitler advice that he would reject decisively, and maybe with contempt."[32]

In the circumstances, it was reasonable that some grew increasingly nervous on September 2, as no news arrived that the British and the French governments would be honoring their treaty commitments. Churchill spoke for many when he wrote to Chamberlain that morning to express his concern that "a further note" was being discussed in Paris. "The Poles have now been under heavy attack for thirty hours," he reminded the prime minister. "I trust you will be able to announce our Joint Declaration of War at latest when Parliament meets this afternoon."[33]

The Poles, too, were growing restive. That afternoon, the Polish ambassador in London had approached Chamberlain directly, requesting "the immediate fulfilment of British obligations to Poland." He was also reported to have been buttonholing cabinet members in the House of Commons with the same demand.[34] In due course, a cable would be drawn up by the Polish foreign minister, Colonel Józef Beck, which sought to stiffen British resolve further by giving a summary of events. "We are already fighting along the entire front with the bulk of the German forces," it read, "fighting for every metre, [and] even the garrison at Westerplatte is defending itself. The intervention of the entire air force is taking on an increasingly brutal form. Today we have extensive civilian casualties." He tartly referenced the Polish–British alliance, signed the previous week in London, and ended with, "Please inform [us] of the British government's decision without delay."[35]

When the cabinet met that afternoon, therefore, the mood was tense. While Chamberlain and Halifax were pressing for a further delay of any decision—or, indeed, ultimatum—mindful of the French desire for an extension of forty-eight hours to sound out Italian proposals and evacuate Paris, there were others who strongly argued against delay. The secretary of state for air, Sir Kingsley Wood, opposed delay because the "moral effect" of Britain "redeeming her pledge to Poland" would thereby be diminished. The secretary of state for war, Leslie Hore-Belisha, agreed, stating that public opinion was "strongly against our yielding an inch," and reminding his cabinet colleagues that "the Dictators had made demand after demand." Others concurred. By the conclusion of the meeting, Chamberlain believed he had agreement on "two main points": first, that there should be no negotiation with Germany unless it was prepared to withdraw its troops from Poland; and second, that any delay beyond midnight that night was "undesirable," and a communication to that effect to Germany therefore "clearly constituted an ultimatum."[36]

When he stood up in the House of Commons that evening, however, Chamberlain appeared to have forgotten what he and his cabinet had decided. In a brief, lackluster event, he spoke of the reasons for the delay, of the necessity of communication and coordination with the French, and of the British government's refusal to recognize Germany's unilateral annexation of Danzig. But there was no mention of an ultimatum or of any putative military defense of Poland.[37] When he sat down, it was to a deafening silence. "Members sat," one parliamentarian recalled, "as if turned to stone."[38]

It was the Labour deputy leader, Arthur Greenwood, standing in for the convalescing Clement Attlee, who rose to reply, and as he did so he drew a shout of "Speak for England, Arthur!" from the Conservative MP—and prominent opponent of appeasement—Leo Amery. Speaking extemporaneously of "what is in my heart," Greenwood exhibited the defiance that many thought had been missing from Chamberlain's bloodless speech. He talked of the gravity of the moment, and though sympathetic to the prime minister's predicament, wondered aloud "how long we are prepared to vacillate at a time when Britain and all that Britain stands for, and human civilisation, are in peril." He hoped that Chamberlain would have a final decision for the House when it reconvened the following morning, but warned that "every minute's delay [meant] imperilling the very foundations of our national honour."[39] Shortly thereafter, amid insults, recriminations, and confusion, the House broke up.

For a time that evening, it appeared that a cabinet revolt might be in the offing. After the Commons session was adjourned, much of Chamberlain's cabinet—twelve out of twenty-two members, including the chancellor, Sir John Simon, and Hore-Belisha—met in Simon's room in the House of Commons. Incensed by what they saw as Chamberlain's unilateral reversal of the decisions the cabinet had agreed upon that afternoon, and fearing that Poland was being abandoned, they demanded that the Commons be told the following day that Britain was fulfilling its treaty guarantee. If not, they said, the Chamberlain government would not survive. That night, Simon delivered a handwritten note to the prime minister:

> The statement tonight will throw the Poles into dejection. German propaganda will see to that. We assume that Warsaw is getting a reassuring telephone message at once. Nothing will repair the injury but an announcement of our fixed decision as soon as possible.
>
> We all feel that 12 o'clock tomorrow is too late, and think that we ought to adhere to the Cabinet timetable of midnight. The only thing that could justify 12 noon tomorrow for the expiry of the ultimatum would be an announcement that this had definitely been agreed with the French.
>
> Your colleagues here feel that if the French will not agree to expiry by 12 noon at the latest we are bound to act ourselves at once.[40]

The rebels were clear that Britain's sense of honor must not be made a hostage to French delay.

France, of course, was enduring agonies of its own. Prime Minister Édouard Daladier had, like Chamberlain, been one of the architects of appeasement and a cosignatory of the Munich Agreement the previous autumn. And, like his British counterpart, he knew appeasement had failed: negotiation with Hitler had run its course, and robust determination was the new order of the day. Consequently, he had issued a general mobilization and recalled Parliament to vote on war credits and an ultimatum to Germany. "Poland is our ally," he declared to the Chamber on

September 2, with a flair and élan that Chamberlain had so grievously lacked. If France should allow this aggression to be carried out, it would very soon find itself "despised, isolated and discredited, without allies and without support." Standing by Poland was a matter not only of vital interest, he said, but of the highest principle: "At the cost of our honor we should purchase only a precarious, revocable peace . . . and, when we have to fight tomorrow, having lost the esteem of our allies and of other nations, we would be nothing but an abject people, doomed to defeat and servitude."[41] At the end of his address, the deputies rose as one and applauded.

Yet for all that bellicose applause, other voices were making themselves heard. One was that of the socialist deputy and former minister Marcel Déat, whose pacifism and noninterventionism had famously found expression in an article entitled "Mourir pour Dantzig?" (Die for Danzig?) published earlier in 1939. In it, Déat had answered his own question with a resounding *Non*, arguing instead in favor of a continuation of appeasement. He suggested that Hitler would be sated with the cession of Danzig and that Polish intransigence was dragging all of Europe into war. By September, Déat's question had become the primary slogan of those in France who were in favor of nonintervention.

Another voice raised in protest—albeit not on ideological grounds—was that of France's commander-in-chief, General Maurice Gamelin. Already of retirement age in 1939, and with a distinguished record in the First World War to his name, Gamelin was widely respected and considered something of an intellectual. Yet his handling of the Polish crisis would be less than glorious. Despite having committed his army, earlier that summer, to assist Poland in the event of attack, he had no intention of—nor, consequently, had the French military any plans for—launching an immediate assault on Germany. Moreover, he had convinced himself that even though the bulk of German forces were engaged in Poland, Germany was nonetheless poised ready to attack in the West upon any declaration of war, and that he would target French railways and barracks to hamstring France's military mobilization. As a result, he petitioned Daladier for a delay of up to forty-eight hours in the submission of any ultimatum to Germany.[42]

While Gamelin moved military minds, the most influential political voice espousing delay was that of Daladier's foreign minister, Georges Bonnet. Bonnet had long been an advocate of France's time-honored strategy of containing Germany via an alliance with Russia and had given vociferous encouragement to the Anglo-French party sent to negotiate with Moscow the previous month. However, now that Stalin had opted for an arrangement with Hitler, Bonnet considered Poland as an unworthy alternative and actively sought to detach France from its treaty commitments toward Warsaw, using Poland's supposed stubbornness over Danzig as the pretext. Bonnet now espoused taking up the Italian offer of mediation and holding back—if not abandoning altogether—any declaration of war. His position had earned him a noisy rebuke from the Polish ambassador in Paris, Juliusz Łukasziewicz, who stormed into Bonnet's office on the afternoon of September 2 and accused him, with no little justification, of preparing a "new Munich" behind Poland's back.[43] As the head of the "peace party," it was Bonnet, lobbying Daladier against going to war, who was most responsible for the resulting French prevarication.

It was against this background, then, that Chamberlain called an urgent cabinet meeting at 10 Downing Street later that night, during a raging thunderstorm. He explained to his colleagues why he had gone "off script" in the Commons, citing the French concern that any early declaration of war would render them liable to surprise attack, and the resulting wrangle with Paris over the timing of the British and French ultimatums. However, stung by the criticisms he had received and mindful of the evident "strength of feeling" in the House, he proposed that Britain should act alone and send an ultimatum to Berlin—in the firm expectation that France would follow shortly afterward. After much discussion of the details and precise timings, it was agreed that the British ambassador in Berlin would be instructed "to seek an interview with Herr von Ribbentrop at 9 a.m., and to deliver an ultimatum to expire at 11 a.m."[44] When Chamberlain asked if any of those present dissented, no one spoke. "Right, gentlemen," he said, "this means war." At that moment, a clap of thunder burst over Whitehall and the cabinet room was illuminated by a blinding flash of lightning.[45]

That night, Churchill added his considerable weight to the cause, calling the French ambassador in London, Charles Corbin, to tell him that if France were to betray the Poles as it had the Czechs, then he—despite being a life-long Francophile—would be wholly indifferent to France's fate. When Corbin tried to remonstrate with him, arguing that there were "technical difficulties" in declaring war, Churchill was blunt: "I suppose you would call it a technical difficulty for a Pole if a German bomb fell on his head!"[46]

It is often suggested that Chamberlain was less than entirely committed to honoring the treaty obligations to Poland; that his apparent vacillations in the first days of September were evidence of a desire to avoid a military entanglement. Certainly, the British prime minister had become synonymous with appeasement, and that inevitably colored the view his contemporaries had of him, even after that policy had been abandoned. As he later wrote, he had found it hard to explain his policy to a House of Commons that was seemingly eager to believe his government "guilty of any cowardice and treachery."[47] Yet a sober reading of the original accounts of the period yields no evidence that the commitment to Poland was ever in serious doubt. When Chamberlain received the cabinet rebels, for instance, he agreed with them and promised to do his best to twist the arm of the French government. Chamberlain and Halifax were certainly rather cold and uninspiring—the latter was described by one historian as having an "almost inhuman inability to rise to an occasion"[48]—but beyond that infelicity, both men knew that Poland would not, and could not, be abandoned to its fate.[49] There was, Halifax wrote in his memoir, "no room for misunderstanding" of the British position: "We intended to maintain our obligation to Poland."[50]

Moreover, behind the scenes of Chamberlain's uninspiring public performance in those fevered days of early September, much had already been achieved. Civilian evacuation had been set in train, and military mobilization begun; even the French had been (temporarily) galvanized.

Contacts had also been made with some of the more hawkish anti-appeasers, such as Churchill, with a view to including them in a future war cabinet.[51] Chamberlain bore the responsibility of taking his nation to war with a heavy heart, not least because it marked a final repudiation of his own desperate efforts to preserve the peace in Europe. But his commitment to the Polish treaty never seriously wavered. It was a point that was confirmed by the Polish ambassador, Count Edward Raczyński, as quoted in *The Times* on September 4: "Never, during the negotiations, were we given the slightest reason to doubt British determination to stand by Poland."[52]

SO IT WAS THAT ON SEPTEMBER 3, AT 9:00 A.M. SHARP, AMBASsador Nevile Henderson was announced outside Ribbentrop's office in the German Foreign Ministry in Berlin. Ribbentrop had declined to receive him in person, as his visit presaged "nothing agreeable," and had again delegated responsibility to the Foreign Ministry's interpreter, Paul Schmidt, who had overslept and only just appeared. Henderson, Schmidt recalled, was ushered in "looking very serious," declined the offer of a seat, and remained "solemnly standing" in the center of the room. After expressing his regrets, Henderson read out the ultimatum he had been sent to deliver:

> More than twenty-four hours have elapsed since an immediate reply was requested to the warning of September 1st, and since then the attacks on Poland have been intensified. If His Majesty's Government has not received satisfactory assurances of the cessation of all aggressive action against Poland, and the withdrawal of German troops from that country, by 11 o'clock British Summer Time, from that time a state of war will exist between Great Britain and Germany.[53]

When he finished, Henderson handed the note to Schmidt, saying, "I am sincerely sorry that I must hand such a document to you in particular, as you have always been most anxious to help." Schmidt gave a few heartfelt words of his own before departing for the Reich Chancellery. On arriving there, Schmidt had to fight his way through a throng of officials, all eager to know what message had been delivered. Entering Hitler's vast office, he saw the Führer seated at his desk. Ribbentrop was standing close to the window, overlooking the Chancellery garden. The two were deep in conversation and looked up expectantly as he advanced. Stopping before the desk, Schmidt slowly translated the ultimatum. When he finished, he recalled, "there was complete silence. Hitler sat immobile, gazing before him. He was not at a loss, as was afterwards stated, nor did he rage as others allege. He sat completely silent and unmoving." After a time, Hitler finally turned to Ribbentrop, still standing at the window, and—with a "savage look"—asked, "What now?"[54]

Two hours later, London was awaiting the German response. Halifax arrived in Whitehall at 10:00 a.m., to be told that the ultimatum had been delivered as agreed, but that no reply had yet been forthcoming. An hour later, he went across to Downing Street, where the BBC had installed a makeshift studio in the cabinet room for Chamberlain to broadcast to the nation. At 11:12 a.m., a telephone call from the British embassy in Berlin confirmed that there had been no response from the German side. Three minutes after that, at 11:15, Chamberlain—looking "crumpled, despondent and old"[55]—made the most difficult speech of his career:

> This morning the British ambassador in Berlin handed the German government a final note stating that unless we heard from them by eleven o'clock that they were prepared at once to withdraw their troops from Poland, a state of war would exist between us.
>
> I have to tell you now that no such undertaking has been received, and that consequently this country is at war with Germany.

He went on to state what a "bitter blow" it was to see that his "long struggle to win peace" had failed, yet he consoled himself with the belief that there was nothing he could have done to bring about a more successful outcome. "In fulfilment of our obligations," he explained, Britain and France were going to the aid of Poland, which was "bravely resisting this wicked and unprovoked attack." Britain would be combating "brute force, bad faith, injustice, oppression and persecution," and in that struggle, he was certain that right would prevail.[56]

Beyond Whitehall, Chamberlain's solemn words were received with stoicism. Noted and vocal pacifist Vera Brittain listened to the prime minister with her children and found that tears were running down her cheeks.[57] Another listener recalled: "We all sat around the wireless set in silence. Even the children were quiet, and after the Prime Minister had made his affectingly simple statement, no one said a word. We all sat there for some moments until the national anthem was played, then, still in silence, each got up and went up to their own rooms."[58] After Chamberlain had finished, and several other official announcements had been made, the new realities of wartime quickly became apparent. As Churchill recalled, Chamberlain "had scarcely ceased speaking when a strange, prolonged, wailing noise, afterwards to become familiar, broke upon the ear."[59] It was the air-raid siren, calling Londoners—some still mute with shock—down into the shelters. For a time, there was a genuine concern that the declaration of war had had an immediate and catastrophic result. In Paddington, one man wondered whether London would share the grim fate of Warsaw and be turned into "blazing rubble."[60] But when the all-clear sounded, a nervous normality resumed. Sitting at an empty desk in the newly established Ministry of Economic Warfare, John Colville was told there was nothing more to be done that day. Opting to play a round of golf, he mused that Britain seemed "remarkably ill-prepared for Armageddon."[61]

While Britons pondered the immensity of the morning's events, in Berlin Ribbentrop summoned Ambassador Henderson to the Foreign Ministry to present the German government's response. In the intervening two hours, Hitler and his foreign minister had received the Soviet ambassador and scripted a lengthy "Rejection of the British Ultimatum,"

Hitler before the Reichstag, playing the innocent.
Heinrich Hoffmann / Library of Congress

which Ribbentrop now handed to Henderson. The document explicitly rejected the British demand for a German withdrawal before blaming the Poles, the British, and the Versailles Treaty for the unfolding crisis.

The British, it claimed, had given the intransigent Poles a "blank check" and had rejected Mussolini's overtures for peace. It closed by warning that Germany would "answer every British military action with the same weapons and in the same manner."[62] Henderson was undaunted, and when he had finished reading he merely told Ribbentrop, "It will be left to history to judge where the blame really lies."[63] With that, he left the Foreign Ministry, only minutes before his French counterpart, Robert Coulondre, arrived to deliver the ultimatum from Paris, which was due to expire that evening at 5:00. By the time it did—again without eliciting any formal response—the phone lines to both embassies had been cut and preparations were under way for the departure of their staffs. The time for diplomacy was over.

To many ordinary Germans, that realization came as a cold shock. Hitler's popularity—and his success—had been built on his peaceful (and piecemeal) revision of the Treaty of Versailles, and most people believed that, though he might indulge in some noisy saber-rattling, he would stop short of war. One Berlin taxi driver summed up the popular mind, suggesting to his fare that none of the German forces already in Poland "will have to fire a single shot." The whole thing, he believed, was little more than negotiation by other means. "This time there won't be any dead lists in the papers and we'll have plenty to eat. No sir," he went on, "Hitler won't get us into a war."[64]

When war was declared, there was consternation. "We were depressed," one Berliner recalled. "We had the feeling that something quite terrible was coming."[65] For many among the older generation, memories of the First World War loomed large; one cursed his fate and asked, "Wasn't one war enough in our lifetime?"[66] In Dresden, the diarist Victor Klemperer noted how the troop trains carried only gloomy faces—"different from 1914"—adding that the German press actively suppressed news of the British and French declarations of war, stressing instead Germany's "successes on all fronts."[67] In Berlin, the journalist Ruth Andreas-Friedrich was similarly horrified by the slide into war, but she fervently hoped that the eruption of open conflict might at least foreshadow the defeat of the Hitler regime. As she wrote in her diary: "A state of war . . . yet neither the French nor the English are marching across our frontiers. Why don't they march? Why don't they cross whatever river it is and bring the madness of war to an end, before the best of all nations have bled to death? From hour to hour, we wait on the intervention of the Great Powers."[68]

Hitler, too, it seems, was expecting some immediate response from his new enemies. That afternoon, he telephoned his home on the Obersalzberg and asked to speak to the Berghof's house manager, Herbert Döhring. He told Döhring that he should expect to be "one of the first to get a hit on the head" in the event of Allied bombing, and therefore advised that the house's valuables and works of art should be taken down into the cellar for safe-keeping.[69] In the days that followed, similar measures were undertaken by museums and galleries all over the Reich:

many of them not only dispersed their collections to safety, but closed their doors for the duration of the war. In Berlin, the equestrian statue of Frederick the Great on Unter den Linden was shuttered and enclosed in concrete; the bust of Nefertiti was carefully crated and sent to the cellar of the Reichsbank. Germany's civilians enjoyed no such protection. Although blackout and rationing regimes were announced with immediate effect, a general evacuation of children from the cities would not be considered for another year.[70]

In Warsaw, meanwhile, bombing was already a daily reality. Sporadic aerial attacks over the previous two days had culminated in more intensive raids on the morning of September 3—primarily on aviation and industrial targets in the suburbs, including Rakowiec, Siekierki, and Grochów—and cost ten lives.[71] "Constant air-raid alarms—our life is now a constant journey between the basement and the apartment," one diarist noted.[72] Another mused, "Now it is clear to all that, although we are not on the front line, the front is actually above us—the war is being fought overhead."[73] Already, Varsovians were growing accustomed to the new realities of warfare. Trams and buses were illuminated only with a dim blue light, and windows were crisscrossed with strips of paper to minimize injuries from flying glass. The city also had to accommodate the many refugees who were pouring in from the provinces seeking safety, their carts and wagons piled high with belongings. In addition, Warsaw's radio stations had called upon the city's inhabitants that very morning to join labor details, as slit trenches needed to be dug in the city's parks and open spaces to provide a modicum of protection from air attack.[74]

Nonetheless, Poland's public mood on September 3, spurred by the rather rosy reports of the Polish press, was upbeat. As one eyewitness recalled, "Varsovians were not anticipating defeat[;] . . . there was great combat spirit."[75] The previous day, Polish cavalry troops backed by infantry had carried out a raid that penetrated 8 kilometers (5 miles) across the German frontier into Silesia, capturing the towns of Geyersdorf (Dębowa Łęka) and Fraustadt (Wschowa) and forcing the Germans into a temporary retreat.[76] Moreover, that very morning six Karaś bombers of the Polish 2nd Air Regiment had successfully attacked a column of German tanks advancing toward Jordanów, causing numerous casualties.[77] One Polish diarist recorded how thrilled people were when German aircraft were shot down, especially when they witnessed the event. In one incident, he noted, "boys were mad with joy when they saw the bomber falling in flames." "So, we were really bringing down German planes. There was no doubt about it," he mused. "It makes you believe in your own success."[78]

There was also an expectation that help would be forthcoming. Władysław Szpilman recalled listening to the radio with his parents that morning when the program was suddenly interrupted by news of an important announcement, followed by the playing of military marches. "We could hardly stand the nervous tension," he wrote. But when the Polish national anthem was played, followed by that of the United Kingdom, "we learned that we no longer faced our enemy alone; we had a powerful ally and the war was certain to be won." The emotion was hard to contain: "Mother had tears in her eyes, Father was sobbing unashamedly."[79] Others recorded similar sentiments. A housewife, Maria Komornicka, was at home in Mokotów when she heard enthusiastic cheers from the street: "I thought I heard 'Long Live the Army' and looked out the window expecting to see an army march past, but I saw people running toward Krucza St. What they were shouting was 'Long live Britain'—'Niech żyje Anglia'—and people were running to the British embassy, because the radio had announced that Britain had declared war. In the blinking of an eye, flags were hoisted."[80]

A crowd stretching "for miles" down Warsaw's most elegant street, Nowy Świat, then converged outside the British embassy, lustily singing their own renditions of "God Save the King" and "Tipperary," throwing flowers, and hoisting anyone thought to be British shoulder-high. The ambassador, Sir Howard Kennard, was obliged to show himself on the small balcony of the embassy to acknowledge the crowds, and each time he did so, he was met with wild cheering and shouts of "Long live Britain!" In time, the Polish foreign minister, Józef Beck, arrived, his

More in expectation than hope: crowds in Warsaw
cheer the British declaration of war.
Osródek Karta, Warsaw

car scarcely able to push its way through the throng. For a while, he
and a bemused Kennard were obliged to salute one another across the
street, before Beck was finally able to force his way into the building
and join the ambassador to shake hands on the balcony. Beck was offered a glass of champagne, but refused, replying that the moment was
"too sad" for his country. The two then addressed the crowd. "Long
live Poland!" Kennard proclaimed, in Polish, before adding in English,
"We will fight side by side against aggression and injustice." Beck then
raised his hand to quiet the tumultuous cheering and declared, "We
never doubted that England would fight with Poland." He went on:
"Britain and Poland have locked hands in a fight for freedom and justice. Britain will not let Poland down and Poland will not let Britain
down. If anyone is disappointed, it will surely not be one of us." Later
that afternoon, such joyous scenes would repeat in front of the French
embassy, with a hearty version of "La Marseillaise" and cheers of "Vive
la France!"[81]

THE QUESTION REMAINED ABOUT WHAT MILITARY ASSISTANCE Poland might reasonably expect from its new allies. France had already agreed—via the Kasprzycki–Gamelin Convention of May 1939—the extent of the military support it would offer to Poland in the event of conflict. However, little had been done in the interim to enable the timely realization of those promises. Worse still, though the French held the trump cards in military matters, they had left the British to take the political lead, thereby making themselves willing hostages to London's hesitation. Chamberlain's government, though serious about drawing a line in the sand to halt Hitler's territorial ambitions, had hoped that merely by raising its voice, Hitler would be cowed into submission. Consequently, the bold political gesture of guarantees and alliances had not been translated into any concrete plans for military action. The active defense of Poland against German aggression that autumn was simply not part of British strategy.[82] As Chamberlain himself lamented to Britain's US ambassador, Joseph Kennedy, in August, "The futility of it all is the thing that's frightful; after all [we] cannot save the Poles."[83] He knew that Britain could offer Poland little beyond vague expressions of moral support.

Warsaw's perspective on what might legitimately be expected from Poland's allies was different. Naturally, the Polish General Staff anticipated that which Gamelin had promised in May: a large-scale offensive against Germany in the west. So, when Edward Śmigły-Rydz briefed the chief of the Polish military mission to France, Lieutenant-General Stanisław Burhardt-Bukacki, on September 1, he explicitly instructed him to press for the opening of a "French front" on land and for immediate help from the French air force.[84] This, after all, was the very minimum of what the Poles felt they had been promised.

Under the circumstances, it should come as no surprise that some Poles had rather inflated expectations of what the Anglo-French declaration of war might achieve. One Varsovian noted the popular belief that British bombers would arrive over Poland at "any moment" to help in the fight against the Germans.[85] Such attitudes were not confined to the ranks of the ill informed. As Ambassador Kennard and Polish Foreign

Minister Beck were speaking on the balcony of the British embassy in Warsaw, Beck's personal secretary was talking with the second secretary at the embassy, Robert Hankey, who expressed the "certainty" that the RAF would "launch raids on Germany before the end of the day."[86]

Ten-year-old Niusia Szewczykówna confided her hopes to her diary. "Papa says that Great Britain is a mighty power with a strong Navy and Air Force," she wrote. "I shall have to learn English because I know only one word 'Goodbye,' and that's hardly enough to carry on a conversation with English soldiers. Papa said that in three or four weeks they'll be here. When they come, I should like to thank them for helping us to beat Hitler but if I haven't learnt sufficient English to say so, I'll just have to hug them and they'll know what I mean."[87]

CHAPTER FOUR

THE TEMERITY TO RESIST

IRONICALLY, PERHAPS, JUST AS THE DECLARATION OF WAR BY the British and French was stiffening Polish resolve in Warsaw, Poland's defense on its frontiers began to falter. Over the previous days, Polish armies had bravely resisted the invasion in a series of engagements that would collectively come to be known as the Battle of the Borders. At Mokra, Węgierska Górka, Mława, and elsewhere—and particularly where they occupied fortified positions—they had given the invaders a bloody nose, but now the German preponderance in men and materiel began to make itself felt. It was a predicament summed up by a Polish peasant standing at the roadside near Kłobuck, not far from Poland's southwestern frontier, as he watched the German troops pass by in their trucks and armored cars. "So many Germans," he repeated over and over, "so many Germans, and none of them on foot!"[1]

At Mława, north of Warsaw, Polish defense lines reinforced with bunkers and antitank ditches initially checked the southward advance of the German 3rd Army. However, stretching for over 30 kilometers (18 miles), those lines were always at risk of being penetrated, as German forces were probing in search of weak points. One such point was found toward the eastern end of the Mława defenses, where a section of the line north of Rzęgnowo was held by a single Polish infantry regiment supported only by two artillery squadrons and the Masovian Cavalry Brigade. There, on the evening of September 2, the German 1st and 12th Infantry Divisions broke through, forcing the Poles to withdraw to a makeshift secondary line. More seriously, however, the collapse of the Rzęgnowo defenses meant the entire Mława line was jeopardized, as those units still holding the German advance farther west were threatened with an attack from the rear. On September 3, the defenders of Mława were ordered to withdraw.

One witness to the withdrawal was Brigadier-General Władysław Anders, the charismatic commander of the Nowogródek Cavalry Brigade, whose unit had been belatedly brought in to strengthen the eastern section of the line. "When I finally reached the 20th Infantry Division," he later recalled, "I found it already in retreat. It had fought the enemy in excellent spirit and, when it could hold its positions no longer, had begun to retire in good order. But when I came up with it, the retreat had ceased to be orderly. Hundreds of German aircraft bombed the retiring columns, and even made attacks on soldiers moving in small groups across country."[2] The retreat was in danger of turning into a rout.

Such was the speed of the German advance that chaos ensued as the line fractured. In Przasnysz, a barracks of the 11th Uhlan Regiment was overrun by German advance forces on September 3, with the guards still at the gate, sabers drawn, and others eating in the mess.[3] The town of Ciechanów, 30 kilometers (18.5 miles) south of Mława, fell later the same day after a short battle in which a Polish armored train spearheaded a forlorn defense.[4] Colonel Stanisław Sosabowski, holding part of the line with his 21st Infantry Regiment ("Children of Warsaw"), found himself and his men abandoned by their fleeing comrades; they realized to their dismay that they were now behind the German advance. Concealing themselves in forests and woods, and moving by night, they began to make their way south, hoping to escape their predicament. In the process they witnessed the aftermath of a frenzied Polish retreat:

Not far from my headquarters I was horrified to notice a battery of abandoned guns, with boxes of untouched ammunition lying around them. . . . Everywhere were the signs of panic. Horses with cut harnesses wandered in the fields. Wagons blocked the way, their contents strewn on the roads and in the ditches. Official papers, maps and military orders festooned the hedges and wire fences, guns lay abandoned, many of them still with breech blocks in position.[5]

It was little wonder, he mused, that his messages to neighboring units had gone unanswered.

Sosabowski was wise to move by night, as the Luftwaffe was wreaking havoc by day, targeting civilians and soldiers alike. Brigadier-General Anders saw their work when he passed through burning villages, recently raided from the air, where the bodies of civilians still littered the streets. He then witnessed the horror of an air attack with his own eyes: "I saw a group of small children being led by their teacher to the shelter of the woods. Suddenly there was the roar of an aeroplane. The pilot circled round, descending to a height of 50 metres [164 feet]. As he dropped his bombs and fired his machine guns, the children scattered like sparrows. The aeroplane disappeared as quickly as it had come, but on the field some crumpled and lifeless bundles of bright clothing remained."[6]

Just to the west of the Mława positions, similar scenes were playing out. At Wąbrzeźno, Konstanty Peszyński, a major in the 4th Army, saw "throngs of people" heading south, away from the German advance. "It's hard to forget those terrified faces," he wrote. "Prams with infants pushed down the roads by terrified mothers, the elderly with their heads down straining to keep up with the young. The fathers and sons, hauling their property or whatever fell into their hands on overloaded bicycles. The poor wretches! Many barefoot without coats, having grabbed their crying children by the hands, ran without thought or hope." Moments later, Peszyński recalled, "the sky seemed to freeze with terror" as German bombers, flying so low they "almost touched the ground," strafed and bombed the crowd, sending the panicked civilians "scattering in

Hitler's Wehrmacht: the harbingers of race war.
akg-images / ullstein bild / Pressefoto Kindermann

every direction." Peszyński was in no doubt that the pilots knew their targets were refugees. "What barbarians, what beasts!" he wrote. "My heart ached, tears filled my eyes."[7]

Peszyński's experiences in those few days were typical. Not only did he witness the cruelty of the invaders, but he saw very clearly their technological advantage and the grim novelty of the Blitzkrieg. Though his men fought bravely, and not without success against the initial German assault, they found themselves under constant threat of air attack, and were ultimately outflanked by fast-moving motorcycle troops. With that, he wrote, "the men buckled," and the next frontal tank assault finally sapped their will to resist. Without air cover or adequate armor, outnumbered and outgunned, Peszyński mused that it was exactly awareness of what they lacked that depressed his men. "Nothing demoralizes as powerfully as fighting with nothing but heroism," he said.[8]

Once the line had broken, moreover, it was almost impossible to halt the flight. "The retreating troops," Peszyński wrote, "mixed in with the reserves, forming scattered chaotic groups, without any combat value. I spent the next few hours on the road, stopping the withdrawing troops, setting them in order, and sending them back to their regiments." However, on arriving at the next town, he found its authorities and police already preparing to leave. Rounding up a few hundred stragglers, he sought to establish a defensive line on the river Drwęca, where he was "convinced we would stop the enemy." But, again, he received the order to fall back a farther 40 kilometers (25 miles). "It really was a retreat," Peszyński recalled, "and we, as it turned out, were withdrawing last."[9]

Far to the south, a similar narrative was playing out. Initially, prepared positions—such as the network of bunkers at Węgierska Górka or the wetlands around Pszczyna, west of Kraków—had held up the German advance. At Orzesze, east of Rybnik, for instance, advancing German forces were drawn into a trap consisting of numerous interlocking machine-gun posts: "Without knowing it," Lieutenant Erich Mende recalled, "we found ourselves close to well-camouflaged field fortifications of the Polish infantry, which opened up on us from many positions. Progress was unthinkable; just a few steps and one was hit. In a flash, the cry went up: 'Medic! Medic!'" That action alone would cost fourteen German lives.[10]

Farther east, the attack of the German 18th Corps, sweeping north and east down the valleys from the Tatra Mountains, was initially halted by a valiant Polish defense near Nowy Targ. When here, too, a breakthrough was threatened, reinforcements arrived in the shape of the 10th Motorized Cavalry Brigade—the so-called Black Brigade—under Colonel Stanisław Maczek, the only fully operational motorized unit then available to the Polish High Command. Maczek, a veteran of the Isonzo Front and the Polish–Soviet War, was a gifted tactician and a pioneer in the use of small, mobile, well-equipped units, similar to the German Stormtroopers of the First World War. Facing the numerical superiority of the Germans in 1939, his tactical thinking was deceptively simple:

Engage the enemy in terrain with only close-range horizons, drawing the enemy into ravines and defiles, where he will not be able to open up his ranks without wasting too much valuable time; into narrows where he will be forced to fight with his fingers rather than his fist. To gain additional time and force his respect, continually seek opportunities to "bite back" with brief forays or counterstrikes, thus forcing the enemy into time-consuming cautiousness or exposing him repeatedly to surprises that will not expedite his advance.[11]

Maczek's delaying tactics would serve him and his Black Brigade well. Holding the area close to Jordanów and Wysoka Hill for two days, they frustrated the advance of a force that Maczek reckoned was ten times greater than their own before carrying out a fighting withdrawal, engaging the Germans in guerrilla attacks to continually slow their pursuit.[12] In the end, Jordanów was a German victory, but a costly one: more than sixty of the tanks the 18th Corps had brought into the battle had been destroyed.[13]

Such Polish tactics, coupled with the imaginative use of terrain and fixed defenses, could prove remarkably effective. Once those positions were lost, however, or abandoned for fear of being outflanked and encircled, the resulting withdrawal quickly turned into a headlong flight. Efforts to regroup were then constantly endangered by the speed of the German advance and by the threat of air attack. Such attacks could be devastating, not only bringing a high cost in lives and materiel, but also fatally compromising morale. Jan Karski recalled how his unit was loaded onto a train in Oświęcim and endured a fitful journey eastward while being targeted by German aircraft that "bombed and strafed the train for nearly an hour." Those who survived the ordeal, he wrote, were "no longer an army, a detachment, or a battery, but individuals wandering collectively toward some wholly indefinite goal. We found the highways jammed with hundreds of thousands of refugees, soldiers looking for their commands and others just drifting with the tide."[14]

In the Polish Corridor, it was the same story. Here the Polish defenders—mainly the 9th and 27th Infantry Divisions and the Pomeranian Cavalry Brigade—had initially contained the German advance in places with a spirited defense along the line of the river Brda, as well as in several other engagements, such as at Tuszyny and Chojnice. Given the overwhelming numerical superiority of the German forces invading the Corridor—the German 4th Army comprised six infantry divisions, two motorized divisions, and one armored division, ranged against two Polish infantry divisions and a cavalry brigade—and the strategic vulnerability of the area, the plan for the Polish forces was for a fighting retreat southeastward, to the line of the river Vistula, which, it was hoped, could be more effectively defended.

At first, that fighting retreat was quite effective. At Gostycyn, the Polish 34th Infantry Regiment gamely engaged the German armored spearhead of the 3rd Panzer Division in a battle that lasted for several hours and temporarily slowed the advance.[15] Farther east near Błądzim, meanwhile, Polish forces adopted a different tactic, engaging forward units of the German 5th Infantry Regiment with artillery and rifle fire before swiftly withdrawing. "Hardly had they seen us," one frustrated German infantryman wrote, "before they galloped off on their horses, leaving their artillery, and took up positions 600 meters (2,000 feet) farther away."[16]

Elsewhere, Polish forces used ambushes or surprise attacks to keep their enemy at bay. At Klonowo, a Polish counterattack threw the German advance into momentary chaos, as a Wehrmacht officer recalled: "A quick about turn to retreat through an abandoned village! But this village is not nearly as deserted as it looks from the outside. There is an immediate banging and crashing against the armour. With a jerk, the [armored] car stops; it has lost a wheel. The next second, my driver slumps noiselessly sideways over the gearstick."[17] One of those killed in that same engagement was a young lieutenant, Heinrich von Weizsäcker, serving with the prestigious 9th Infantry Regiment, who was shot in the throat during the Polish counterattack. His body, which could not be recovered for some time, was watched over that night by his younger brother Richard (later president of Germany) prior to burial the next day. "The war had hardly begun," Richard would later write, "and it had already changed my life forever."[18]

Despite such delaying actions, however, German forces would not be halted. General Heinz Guderian, long an advocate of mobile, tank-led warfare, led his 19th Army Corps on relentlessly, at times personally spearheading the advance. At Sokole-Kuźnica on the Brda, he galvanized German forces, putting a stop to their "idiotic firing," and sent assault teams across the river in rubber boats to outflank the Polish defenders. "Casualties were negligible," he noted in his memoirs. By the end of the day, the bridgehead was secured and the 3rd Panzer Division was once again moving eastward toward Świecie on the Vistula.[19] Polish forces still in the Corridor were in danger of being cut off.

According to the Italian journalist Indro Montanelli, who accompanied the German advance, the Poles fought with "admirable stubbornness." The Germans had scored notable successes, he acknowledged, but "don't imagine that it was painless. The Poles hung on tenaciously until the ground beneath their feet began to burn. And even then the retreat wasn't a flight—without once turning their backs, the stubborn Poles opposed the enemy fire."[20] As a Wehrmacht infantryman remembered, it certainly wasn't the easy fight German troops had expected: "We reached the cemetery and jumped like rabbits between the gravestones. One salvo after another rained down. . . . The first moans from the wounded were heard. Whoever entered into this war with enthusiasm would at this moment get goosebumps. I will never forget how I found a comrade by the side of the road with his chest torn open. He was still conscious, and one could see his heart beating. He didn't last the day."[21] Nonetheless, as at Mława, once the line broke, the speed of the German advance meant that the Polish withdrawal from the Corridor quickly came to resemble a rout. At Błądzim, Adam Zakrzewski, a colonel in the Pomorska Cavalry Brigade, witnessed shattered elements of the Polish 27th Infantry Division trickling back, away from the front line. "It was then that I first heard the words 'We've been crushed,'" he wrote. "I would unfortunately hear them too often in the future."[22] That trickle soon became a flood. Those who did not surrender formed long columns of men, horses, and machinery, all streaming southeastward toward the Vistula.[23]

The German response was to send the 20th Infantry Division on a headlong advance toward the river in order to cut off that southward retreat. Farther north, the eastward progress of the 3rd Panzer Division was so swift that it outran its supply column and soon complained of a lack of fuel and ammunition.[24] Within those closing pincers, Polish forces—primarily the remains of the 9th and 27th Divisions and the Pomorska Cavalry Brigade—fought an increasingly desperate and splintered rear-guard action, some attempting to break out, others fighting to the end, others still opting to lay down their weapons. In addition to being corralled on the ground, they were constantly attacked from the air. As one eyewitness recalled:

> The bombing lasted about an hour and it was so intense that the sky was clouded with smoke and the bright autumn sun was no longer visible. When the squadrons flew away, the bombing was over, and the smoke dispersed, a blood-chilling sight appeared in front of us. Bodies were strewn across the road, and the horses that were killed were still in harness. The remnants of equipment and wagons were scattered about us. The trenches were full of slain soldiers; those that survived emerged but there were so few of them that in reality the 34th and 50th Infantry Regiments had ceased to exist.[25]

Accounts of the grim fate of Polish forces are often brief, but no less tragic for that. Guderian—though no stranger to hyperbole—recalled a Polish artillery regiment that was overrun and destroyed by German tanks, writing in his memoir that "only two of its guns managed to fire at all."[26] In another engagement, the Koronowo National Defense Battalion was all but wiped out when, after withstanding the assault of the German 3rd Infantry Division, it opted to make a bayonet charge rather than surrender when its ammunition ran out; few would survive.[27] The 2nd Squadron of the 2nd Polish Light Cavalry Regiment, meanwhile, fought to the death at Kosowo, almost within reach of the Vistula and the safety of the far bank. Even those who made the crossing were sometimes overcome with the gravity of their collective defeat.

One captain was so distraught by the bloody fate of his cavalry squadron, which was ambushed as they crossed the river near Chełmno, that he took his own life.[28]

Among those who successfully escaped was Adam Zakrzewski, as well as surviving units of the Pomorska Cavalry Brigade. He recorded his group's progress south through abandoned villages hugging the western bank of the Vistula. At Topolno, he recalled, their route was blocked by heavy machine-gun fire, and they were forced to dismount to engage an unseen enemy. The resulting firefight was "the bloodiest battle" he had yet fought, with enemy fire "coming from every direction." Though they prevailed in pressing through, his group would pay a high price for their escape, with many officers and men wounded or killed. The casualties included horses, especially, which, he said, "could not hide from the enemy fire."[29] For an experienced cavalryman, it was heartbreaking.

Throughout the Corridor, many small towns and villages bore witness to the desperate plight of Polish forces. At Plewno, a little over 10 kilometers (6 miles) west of Świecie, one German soldier described "a chaotic litter of baggage waggons, motor vehicles and numerous guns," which gave "powerful testimony" to the Poles' "wild flight."[30] Another noted: "There are graves by the side of the road—many Polish, topped with the Polish helmet, and a few German. On both sides, there is Polish equipment: machinery, ammunition, hundreds—if not thousands—of steel helmets, gas masks, kitbags, coats, rifle and artillery shells, some still packed. . . . Horse corpses give off a terrible stink."[31] Shortly after midday on September 4, the German "ring" in the Corridor was closed when the spearheads of the two encircling armies met near Świecie. In that pocket, according to German estimates, up to 6,000 men were taken prisoner. There was also a considerable haul of materiel, including 350 horses and "heavy and light artillery and countless waggons."[32]

Polish sources noted the loss of, among others, the 16th and 18th Uhlan Regiments, the 2nd Light Cavalry Regiment, and the 9th Infantry Division. General Władysław Bortnowski, who had commanded the Pomeranian Army, was brutally honest in his assessment. In his telegram to Edward Śmigły-Rydz, he wrote:

The situation is that all the troops that have been cut off can now be considered lost. All that is left of the 27th Division is the division commander, about 3 infantry battalions and 5 batteries. . . . Of the 9th Division—only the incomplete 22nd Regiment and one battery. . . . Something might still come up, but the bridgehead was destroyed at half six this morning and . . . in the current situation it seems to me impossible. This is the state of things.[33]

Looking pale and exhausted, Bortnowski blamed himself for the debacle, confessing to a fellow general, "It's either a bullet in the head or resignation."[34] In the event, it would be neither. Bortnowski would fight again, but the battle for the Polish Corridor was over. It was, according to one contemporary commentator, the first encirclement battle of the modern era.[35]

ALREADY THAT DAY, AS THE POLISH FORCES IN THE CORRIDOR were laying down their arms, Hitler was touring the front with his entourage. He had left Berlin the previous night, not long after the French ambassador had announced Paris's declaration of war, intending not only to encourage the troops but also to make some public demonstration of his own will to continue the fight. Escorting the German dictator to an active battlefront was no easy feat. The Führer left the German capital aboard his armored train—codenamed *Amerika*—which now became the traveling headquarters of the Third Reich, replete with adjutants, doctors, bodyguards, liaison officers, photographers, valets, secretaries, catering staff, cleaners, maids, and drivers. He was also trailed by two convoys of cars and a squadron of aircraft.[36]

This traveling circus arrived in Bad Polzin (Połczyn-Zdrój), in Pomerania, in the early hours of September 4, and soon after nine o'clock set off for the front in a convoy of five Mercedes cars, containing Hitler, Martin Bormann, and General Wilhelm Keitel, alongside a host of adjutants and bodyguards. After taking a briefing from the commander of the 4th Army, General Günther von Kluge, and mingling with star-struck soldiers, Hitler traveled on to Topolno on the Vistula, the command post of the 3rd Infantry Division, where he watched German troops crossing the river. "What this means to me!" he enthused as he took in the scene through field glasses.[37] When he was finished gazing across the Vistula, he was driven to the village of Plietnitz (Płytnica), where he was met by his train. Photographer Heinrich Hoffmann, for one, was delighted to return to the creature comforts of the *Amerika*. He recalled that "we were so filthy and covered with the yellow dust of the Polish roads, that we were unrecognizable. Fortunately, however, the special train was well-equipped with baths and a handsome barber's shop, and by midnight we were transformed once more into civilised human beings."[38]

Two days later, on the morning of Wednesday, September 6, after visiting the wounded at Gross Born military camp, Hitler once again set off on a tour of the front. His convoy snaked its way through the countryside of the Corridor to Grudziądz, once the Prussian citadel of Graudenz. En route, Hitler stopped at the village of Plewno, west of Świecie, where he was met by Heinz Guderian, who gave him a tour of the nearby battlefields, taking in the remains of some Polish positions. Hoffmann thought it all a "terrible and ghastly sight" that robbed the victory "of all its glamour," but Hitler was enormously impressed, asking whether the destruction had been wrought by tanks or aircraft.[39] That afternoon, the Führer also inspected some of Guderian's troops, men of the 3rd Panzer Division, who were excitedly drawn up in the sunshine. When he arrived, he hailed their achievements, promising that "what has been won at the cost of German blood will stay forever German."[40] The soldiers pressed closely in toward his Mercedes, reaching out to shake his hand, a few snapping away eagerly with their cameras. "We are delighted beyond words . . . our hearts swell in his presence," one of them enthused.[41] Hitler's bodyguards indulged the throng, evidently convinced that the Führer was not at any risk. The only casualty from Hitler's entourage that day would be Karl Krause, Hitler's valet, who was peremptorily dismissed by his master for serving him Polish spring water over lunch, instead of his favored—German—Fachinger mineral water.[42]

That evening, after completing the journey to Grudziądz to take in the view across the nearby Vistula, Hitler was driven back to Gross Born (Borne Sulinowo). In all, over two days, his convoy had traveled some 600 kilometers (370 miles) along dusty, often unpaved roads choked with soldiers and military materiel, all of which had been meticulously reported by the German press. Even Italian reporters joined in the chorus of praise, the account of Indro Montanelli positively brimming with adulation. "We met the Führer," he wrote:

Germany's first soldier. Simply dressed, in his iron-gray uniform, the only decoration a small Iron Cross, very modest. He had come to be with his men at the moment of the passage across the Vistula, a sacred moment in Germany's history. He didn't want honors, salutes, fanfare. He appeared and disappeared. One soldier among the many we saw. His face expressed no joy, no emotion, no satisfaction. You know Hitler's face: inscrutable, pale, his gaze far off. So it was today.[43]

Hitler's visit, it seems, was something like a propaganda Blitzkrieg.

Away from the journalists and the newsreel cameras, however, the bleak realities of Hitler's war were already becoming clear. Bydgoszcz—the former German Bromberg—was a city with a rich history, having been part of the medieval Polish Kingdom (and later Commonwealth) before being annexed by Prussia in the partitions of the eighteenth century. By the time it was returned to Poland in 1918, the city had a large German-majority population, and it would develop into a bastion of German cultural and political life in the Polish Republic. In less fraught times, it might have emerged as an exemplar of Polish–German coexistence and cooperation—and for a time in the 1930s relations were indeed relatively cordial. But by 1939, with the German minority marginalized and disadvantaged within the Polish state, the climate had deteriorated into one of tension and mutual suspicion, ably stoked by Nazi propaganda.[44] Now, "Bromberg" would become a byword for ethnic cleansing.

The Nazi regime was already experienced in using the ethnic Germans of Central Europe—the so-called *Volksdeutsche*—as the tools of German policy. In the Sudeten crisis of 1938, ethnic Germans had expertly played the role of the perennially persecuted and disgruntled, spurring Western intervention and the eventual dismemberment of Czechoslovakia. In September 1939, it was clearly anticipated by the Polish government that Poland's *Volksdeutsche* might assist incoming German troops, conduct guerrilla warfare, or desert from the Polish military. A secret order, discovered on a Luftwaffe airman downed near Poznań on September 2, appeared to confirm that assumption, as it instructed *Volksdeutsche* how they were to best make contact with their "liberators."[45] Unsurprisingly, then, Polish accounts of the opening days of the war are littered with the real or imagined misdeeds of the German "fifth column," ranging from covert signaling to the Luftwaffe to murder and acts of sabotage. In the febrile circumstances, acts of violence—even lynchings—were not uncommon. One Polish army major recalled some *Volksdeutsche* being brought to him "beaten up and half-conscious"; they were suspected of espionage for supposedly having communicated to a German pilot with the motions of a whip. Their accusers, he wrote, were "embittered to madness" by the war, and "grabbed the Germans at the slightest suspicion." He placed them under arrest, but—after examining his conscience—released them with no further action. He refused to take their lives out of simple revenge.[46]

The events at Bydgoszcz would provide the crowning example of this phenomenon. There, on the morning of September 3, Polish troops in the process of withdrawing southeastward through the city were fired on at several locations. One Polish officer spoke of witnessing a "real Hitlerite rising" in Bydgoszcz when ethnic German irregulars, "with a lot of machine guns and grenades[,] . . . managed to destroy our retreating supply trains."[47] Another eyewitness recalled the "violent racket of rapid gunfire" coming from a German-owned bakery close to his home.[48] Other accounts described gunfire coming from church spires, factories, and the houses of German families. Some spoke of running battles on Gdańska Street and Piastowski Square. As one Polish inhabitant put it, "It was clear beyond doubt that numerous groups of organised assailants were taking part in the action throughout the town."[49]

The Polish response to the uprising was swift. With Wehrmacht forces still some 20 kilometers (12.5 miles) distant, a counterattack was organized utilizing the army and reservists. It was coordinated from the town's police headquarters, where a long list had been compiled of the many addresses where shooting had been reported; it was some forty pages long. Armed with these addresses, small groups of police, gendarmes, and members of the Polish Scouting Association set out across the city to search the suspect properties and engage the possible insurgents. In many cases, the city's German inhabitants were simply rounded up, and those found with weapons were usually shot out of hand. In one case, Polish soldiers apprehended a German who had fired into the apartment of a local priest, dragged him out of his apartment, and executed him.[50]

Those *Volksdeutsche* who could not explain their presence in the city—many had arrived from neighboring towns and villages—were arrested and taken to the barracks of the 61st Regiment on Pomorska Street for interrogation, often hurried along with kicks and blows from rifle butts. By early evening, the German revolt had been quelled. The death toll is disputed. Contemporary eyewitnesses spoke of some 150 Germans dead, with a dozen or so more executed the following day after a court martial.[51] Later scholarship has raised the total figure to as high as 400, which includes some 16 Polish soldiers killed in the insurgency.[52]

Bydgoszcz had witnessed a brief, bloody skirmish in which the German element of its population—in anticipation of the imminent arrival of the Wehrmacht—had risen against their former neighbors and had been ruthlessly crushed. Ordinarily, perhaps, that would have been the end of the episode, but these were not ordinary times. The needs of

Germany's propaganda machine and its racist ideology had to be fed—and the events in Bydgoszcz would have to be avenged.

Just as at Bydgoszcz to the north, the province of Upper Silesia in the southwest also saw diversionary activity from an ethnic German fifth column. That province, which had been subjected to an uneasy partition in 1921 between Germans and Poles, contained unhappy minorities on both sides of the border. With the outbreak of war, some of the ethnic Germans on the Polish side saw the opportunity to avenge themselves on their Polish neighbors and engage Polish forces to aid the German invasion. The results, in some cases, were running battles and bitter ethnic violence.

Jan Karski, an officer in the Kraków Cavalry Brigade, described how his unit's orderly withdrawal from Oświęcim was attacked by insurgents: "As we marched through the streets . . . towards the railroad, to our complete astonishment and dismay, the inhabitants began firing at us from the windows. They were Polish citizens of German descent . . . who were, in this fashion, announcing their new allegiance."[53] Such violence often peaked after regular Polish forces had been withdrawn. In Katowice, the retreat prompted clashes between Polish and German irregulars that "resembled a civil war," with neighbors, friends, even family members facing off against one another.[54] In one instance, a skirmish close to the Deutsche Bank building supposedly saw a 150-strong Polish "self-defense force" defeat a large group of German militants.[55] The British journalist Clare Hollingworth, who witnessed the aftermath as captured Nazi sympathizers were brought to the main square, wrote, "Thirty or forty young men, the oldest not above twenty, were marched by under double guard. All wore swastika armbands. Hearing the guns and alarm, they had assumed that the German forces were through [and] had catapulted onto the streets yelling 'Heil Hitler!' Instead of a popular rising, they had found [Polish] troops to surround and disarm them." A short while later, Hollingworth heard the volley of gunfire as the young men were executed.[56]

Of course, once Polish forces had left Katowice, the Germans were not slow to avenge themselves. One of their reprisal actions, on September 4, was recorded by a young eyewitness named Rafał Kieslowski, a boy scout who had participated in the defense of the city before changing out of his uniform and attempting to pose as a noncombatant. Caught in a German roundup, Kieslowski was taken to a walled courtyard, where he was held with a large group of soldiers and civilians, including women and children, and subjected to a rudimentary interrogation. Soon after, he and a group of around forty others were separated out and marched—under the insults and blows of their guards—to another courtyard. Once they arrived, the gate was bolted behind them and an execution squad opened fire on the group. Kieslowski was lucky to survive, feigning death among the bodies of his fellows. He listened as the German executioners delivered the coup de grâce to the wounded before a second group of prisoners was brought in and dispatched in the same manner. He wriggled free of the corpses some time later and was the only survivor. He later estimated that some 100 civilians had been killed, including old men, women, and children as well as around 40 Polish soldiers.[57]

On that same day, some of Katowice's defenders were still bravely holding out. In the south of the city, in Kościuszko Park, a steel tower 50 meters (165 feet) high was being used as a lookout post by a small group of boy scouts. Though they had been abandoned by the Polish withdrawal, and were armed only with a machine gun, they had vowed to continue the fight. That morning, it is said, they fired on arriving units of the German 239th Infantry Division and were duly shelled by artillery and killed. Their story—embellished by the postwar novel *The Parachute Tower* by Kazimierz Gołba—would become one of Poland's most enduring heroic myths of 1939.[58]

After the fall of Katowice, Kraków was threatened. The ancient Polish capital, the former seat of Polish kings and the cultural heart of the nation, faced the prospect of war on its doorstep with profound unease. Air raids over the previous few days had damaged the airfield at Rakowice as well as the train station and St. Florian's Church, just beyond the last remaining city gate. "The explosions were so terrifying," one eyewitness recalled, "that after a few hours the long howl of sirens sent people instantly to their cellars." Already on September 3, Kraków's iconic *hejnał*—the interrupted trumpet melody played every hour from the tower of St. Mary's Cathedral—was suspended. There were even rumors that the Germans would enter the city the very next day.[59]

Despite the imminent danger, at the local military headquarters Clare Hollingworth heard a strangely optimistic assessment from a Polish officer. "You will understand, Mademoiselle," he explained, "that we must yield ground in order to straighten our line. Our real defense must lie along the rivers San and Vistula." Hollingworth asked if they were willing to sacrifice the entire Kraków region. "We are prepared for that," the officer replied. "It's for the ultimate victory. Poland will lose territory during the war, but she will gain more, much more, afterwards." At once Hollingworth saw the fundamental flaw in Polish strategy: "They do not realise that they would never be able to fall back fast enough, never unify their front on the Vistula or anywhere else." She concluded, more presciently perhaps than many of the military men around her, that "the war was moving too fast for the Poles."[60] That afternoon, Kraków's mayor was evacuated to the east, alongside government officials and the military command. Hollingworth, too, soon followed—with a gnawing sense of guilt that neither Britain nor France would be able to prevent what was to come.

With the departure of its civil and military authorities, Kraków was left defenseless. The deputy mayor, Dr. Stanisław Klimecki, stepped into the breach, telling the residents, "The most important commandment at the present time is to maintain courage and remain calm. Cold blood, self-control, and physical and spiritual endurance are indispensable to maintaining security and order among civilians. Work and life should go on as before."[61] On the afternoon of September 5, the remaining city fathers declared Kraków an open city, in the hope that that might save it from destruction. The following morning, Klimecki set off to the suburbs by car, where huge white sheets were to be placed on the city's two prominent tumuli—Krakus Mound and Kościuszko Mound, 16 meters (52 feet) and 34 meters (111 feet) high, respectively—as a symbol of Kraków's surrender.

But when Klimecki approached the Piłsudski Bridge over the Vistula, he was halted by a pistol shot. He waved a white handkerchief at his assailants, and a German soldier asked his business. "I'm the city mayor," Klimecki replied. He assured the soldier that there were no military units left in the city and that Kraków would not be defended. The soldier then instructed him to return to city hall and await a German delegation, which would be arriving at 9:00 a.m. Shortly thereafter, a green flare was shot into the sky to tell the invaders that their attack had been canceled.[62]

Later that morning, German troops entered the city. "Enemy units make their way through the streets," one resident wrote, "mighty tanks, motorised units, huge guns pulled by splendid horses and proud, ramrod-stiff German soldiers—victors! Karmelicka Street now reverberates with a dull, terrifying thud, while groups of people silently watch these 'invincible' Germans in mute horror. Our hearts are heavy, we feel so small, so meaningless, so despondent."[63]

As Kraków fell on September 6, the Polish defense of the Westerplatte, far to the north, was also nearing its end. The fortified customs post outside Danzig had witnessed the opening shots of the war, and in the days that followed it had become synonymous with Poland's brave resistance—so much so that, every day, Polish radio had proudly declared that "Westerplatte broni się nadal!" (Westerplatte still fights on!)

That fight, however, was a very unequal one. The 200-strong Westerplatte garrison had fought off repeated German assaults, and though it had endured the *Schleswig-Holstein*'s spectacular but sporadic shelling, the relentless attacks of the *Stuka* dive-bombers made continued resistance difficult. On September 2, an evening attack by two *Stuka* squadrons had delivered over 250 high-explosive bombs on the defenders, destroying barracks, guardhouses, and ammunition stores. A direct hit on one building—Guardhouse No. 5—killed at least seven soldiers. Observing the action from the safety of the *Schleswig-Holstein*, marine bandmaster Willi Aurich believed he was witnessing the final act of the battle. "The heavens darken with rising smoke," he wrote. "On board, everyone is full of confidence that this must be the end for the Westerplatte."[64]

Such was the havoc caused among the defenders, indeed, that the garrison commander, Major Henryk Sucharski, ordered the codes and classified documents destroyed, in anticipation of an imminent ground assault. What happened next is the subject of some controversy. According to some accounts, Sucharski ordered that a white flag be raised above the command post, prompting a heated argument with his deputy, Captain Franciszek Dąbrowski, during which Sucharski collapsed, either with exhaustion or in a fit of epilepsy.[65] Others suggest that the two men briefly fought with each other.[66] Whatever the circumstances, the result was that Dąbrowski effectively took command. After having Sucharski sedated and isolated from the rest of the garrison, he countermanded the order to surrender.[67]

In the days that followed, as the Germans girded themselves for a renewed land assault along the spit, the Westerplatte's defenders, though buoyed by news of the Anglo-French declaration of war, were aware of Poland's difficult situation. They constantly discussed whether they should surrender, with Sucharski in favor and Dąbrowski against. Meanwhile the Germans continued their attacks. A renewed artillery assault on the morning of September 5 was followed the next day by a less conventional approach—the detonation of train tanker wagons filled with fuel close to the depot's perimeter, in an effort to destroy Polish defenses. Yet the Poles held firm. Though only a dozen or so of the defenders had been killed, there were many wounded languishing in the stale air of the mess cellar, and the garrison's only doctor, lacking adequate medical supplies, struggled to provide even the most basic care. In one instance, he was forced to use his own nail scissors to clamp a stomach wound, leaving them inside the patient.[68] The destruction wrought on the ground, meanwhile, was considerable. "Enemy artillery fire literally ploughed the land," one Polish officer recalled, uprooting trees and smashing the concrete outposts to rubble.[69] It was little wonder that many of the defenders—like Major Sucharski—showed symptoms of nervous collapse.

When the tanker assault failed, the Germans planned a new attack for the morning of September 7. It mirrored exactly that of the opening day of the war, with the guns of the *Schleswig-Holstein* softening up Polish positions with a predawn artillery assault, followed by an infantry attack. This time, however, the Germans were better apprised of what they were up against, and, crucially, Polish morale was failing. After making good progress with their ground assault, destroying a number of guardhouses and outposts, the German troops withdrew to regroup, leaving another tanker of fuel to detonate as they left.[70] The lull gave the Polish garrison time to reconsider their position. The Poles knew they could expect no relief, and there was every reason to assume that the next ground assault would end with desperate hand-to-hand fighting in the heart of the depot complex. In such circumstances, the decision was made to surrender. Around 9:30 a.m., a white flag was raised from a shattered window on the first floor of the barrack block. Sucharski thanked his men for their service and honored the fallen with a prayer. The garrison then sang "Śpij, kolego" (Sleep, my friend), the traditional hymn for military funerals, and were ordered to stand down.[71]

With that, Sucharski led his men toward the German line, officers in the vanguard and wounded to the rear. At first, they were treated brusquely by the SA and SS men present, who searched them and stripped them of their possessions. But their treatment improved when, at around 11:00 a.m., Sucharski met with Captain Kleikamp of the *Schleswig-Holstein* and offered the surrender of the Westerplatte. While Sucharski waited for the operation's commander, Major-General Friedrich Eberhardt, to formally accept the surrender, both sides had pause for thought. A German propaganda unit photographed Sucharski in his full dress uniform, his Virtuti Militari medal hanging at his breast, a scowl of resignation on his face. Contrary to his own instincts, he and his men had held out against German air and ground attacks for seven days, in the process becoming synonymous with Poland's brave defiance. Indeed, within weeks, the Westerplatte story would be entwined with its own mythology, as in the famous poem by Konstanty Gałczyński describing the men of the garrison ascending to the "heavenly fields" of immortality:

> When their days came to an end
> and it was time to die in the summer,
> They marched in fours straight to heaven
> the soldiers of Westerplatte.[72]

For the Germans, meanwhile, there was consternation. Not only had they expected many more defenders to emerge from the ruins of the Westerplatte complex, but they also searched the site in vain for the bunkers and fortifications they imagined were there. After a brief interrogation, Eberhardt granted Sucharski the honor of keeping his officer's saber on his person, a mark of his respect. With that, the officers and men of the garrison were marched into captivity past the jeers and curses of a civilian mob that had been whipped into a righteous fury by German propaganda.[73]

THOUGH THE LOSS OF KRAKÓW AND THE FALL OF THE WESTERplatte dealt a heavy blow to Poland's pride, it was not there that the decisive campaigns were being fought. In Poland's southwest, close to the frontier with Silesia, the German 10th Army was aiming unerringly toward Warsaw with the instruction—from Hitler himself—to "look neither left nor right, but only forwards towards its goal."[74]

Despite the mauling that it had received at Mokra on the opening day of the war, the 10th Army had expected the first organized Polish resistance to focus on the river Warta, the most serious natural obstacle to its advance on the capital. In some places, the Polish defense was indeed determined. One Wehrmacht lieutenant recalled that over the first two days of combat on the southwest frontier, "the fighting had been hard, at times damned hard. In some locations, the enemy did not want to give way. Constantly, our progress was impeded by forests, swamps, and rivers, which gave the enemy the opportunity to defend himself with skill, guile, and deviousness. Constantly, our infantry was forced to the ground by intense fire."[75] When encountering such obdurate defense, however, German forces had what one diarist called a "special recipe" to deal with their opponents: "We simply stay so hot on the heels of the enemy that they cannot entrench themselves and give us any resistance."[76] Lieutenant Heinz-Günther Guderian, son of the illustrious father, would have concurred. In September 1939, he was commanding a tank in the 35th Panzer Regiment, part of the 10th Army. In his account of the campaign, he described the doctrine in simple terms: "The enemy must be allowed no rest, we must go on fighting, pushing on with all possible speed."[77] It was the essence of Blitzkrieg.

Contrary to later German propaganda, Blitzkrieg was a tactic that, at this time, was only being imperfectly applied. Of course, the swift advance had the beneficial effect of disrupting the formation of a coherent Polish defense, but it could also leave attacking units isolated. Guderian *fils* recalled how he and his unit found themselves some 10 kilometers (6 miles) ahead of the remainder of the regiment. Feeling "uncomfortable," they were obliged to adopt a defensive posture "with hulls touching" until they were relieved the following morning.[78] Another officer recalled that, while racing for the Warta bridges, he was alarmed to discover that he was dangerously exposed, with neighboring units still bogged down in combat some 25 kilometers (15 miles) to his rear.[79] Driving eastward toward Lublin, Clare Hollingworth stopped to ask for directions and wondered aloud if the Germans had already passed by. "No Germans, only the machines," a Polish peasant replied. "You mean the tanks?" asked Hollingworth. The man replied in the affirmative, quickly adding, "But we've seen no Germans."[80] Despite such shortcomings, the tactic was nonetheless successful. As one Polish staff officer ruefully admitted, Polish planning had been "based on a speedy retreat, but German divisions—Panzer, light, motorized and infantry—proved to be faster."[81]

Such was the speed of the German advance in the southwestern theater, in fact, that the planned Polish defense on the Warta scarcely materialized.

German forces captured the bridges over the river at Sieradz, Mnichów, and Warta and swiftly set about establishing bridgeheads on the eastern bank.[82] Arriving near Działoszyn on the afternoon of September 3, infantryman Walther Krappe described the desolate scene that greeted his eyes as his division waited to cross the half-demolished bridge: "Women and children stood in front of their burnt-out houses and collected together their last possessions that were mostly already charred. Our artillery and flyers had done all they could to ensure that no stone in this small town was left atop another."[83]

Upstream, the ancient city of Częstochowa also fell to the Germans that afternoon after the withdrawal of the 7th Infantry Division, which had fought a bitter and prolonged battle with the invaders on the city's western outskirts the previous day, destroying (according to one estimate) as many as forty enemy tanks and vehicles.[84] Once the city was occupied, there were fears for the safety of its famed icon, the Black Madonna, housed in the Jasna Góra monastery, which—Polish propaganda stated—was being used by the Germans as a stable. "Hitler has no respect," one Warsaw diarist noted. "The world is outraged."[85] In Paris, Archbishop Cardinal Jean Verdier reacted to reports that the Germans had bombed the monastery by proclaiming, "For 700 years this image of the Mother of God has been the very heart of Poland. The Poles will never forget that the enemy has dared to lay a hand on their Holy Mother!"[86] (In fact, the Black Madonna had already been hidden by Jasna Góra's friars and replaced with a copy. It would survive the war unscathed.[87])

The fate of the Black Madonna was the least of the city's immediate worries, however. On the first night of the war, Polish troops had ambushed a German staff car at Gnaszyn, just west of Częstochowa, taking a lieutenant-colonel captive and killing three soldiers. The arriving Germans were therefore keen to avenge themselves and quickly began rounding up thousands of the city's Polish and Jewish inhabitants before marching them to the cathedral square, where they had to lie face down on the ground.[88] On the afternoon of September 4, the prisoners were searched, and those who appeared to be Jewish, or were armed with

Led away to an unknown fate: Polish prisoners of the Wehrmacht.
Muzeum II Wojny Światowej, Gdańsk

even a pocketknife, were led away to an unknown fate. In the chaos that followed, nervous soldiers fired machine guns into a column of prisoners and killed over 100 of them. The official German war diary summarizing the event said that "the partisan war" in Częstochowa had been "quelled." The reality was more brutally prosaic: as one Wehrmacht soldier recalled, "We were ordered to fire on anything that moved."[89]

Once they had crossed the Warta, German forces advanced swiftly northeastward, encountering little opposition. Lieutenant Wiktor Jackiewicz of the 23rd Grodno Uhlan Regiment, who had been sent by his superiors to establish the whereabouts of the enemy, watched the advance. Observing the road east of Radomsko, he was astonished at what he saw. "What a view spread out before my eyes," he later recalled. "Tanks, lorries with infantry and mechanised artillery were roaring down the Piotrków road full steam ahead. Another column was marching from Radomsko to Przedbórz, which I estimated to be a division of motorised infantry. The column heading for Piotrków consisted without the slightest doubt of at least one armoured division."[90] Fortunately for him, Jackiewicz and his detachment of cavalry had orders not to engage.

Other Polish forces, however, were already en route to meet the invaders. According to the German propaganda version of the campaign, the Polish air force was completely destroyed on the ground in the opening days of the war, those few brave souls who dared venture into the air being swiftly dispatched by the Messerschmitts and Junkerses of the Luftwaffe. The truth, however, was rather more complex. The Polish air force was largely outdated and was most definitely outnumbered by the Germans; it had suffered considerable losses in the opening days of the war, but it was far from spent as a combat unit. Indeed, according to Count Johann von Kielmansegg—a major on the staff of the 1st Panzer Division—September 3 would be known to his men as the Day of the Polish Air Force.[91]

On that day, official statistics registered some 330 sorties by Polish aircraft, around a third of them over the southwestern front, where Kielmansegg noted around fifteen raids on his sector alone, targeting those seemingly endless columns of German vehicles and armor. Many of those raids were carried out by Polish Karaś (PZL.23) light bombers, comparatively modern aircraft with an all-metal airframe and a crew of three. According to the official record, the bombers enjoyed "considerable success" in engaging the German spearheads in the Radomsko region, registering sixty-one sorties for the loss of nine aircraft.[92] One Polish soldier who witnessed the attacks recalled them with glee, describing "the blast of bombs, flames of burning vehicles and infantry scattering in panic."[93]

Kielmansegg was much less enthusiastic. While critical of the accuracy of Polish bombing, he nonetheless stated that "you have to hand it to these Poles, they carried out their missions with tremendous guts and considerable skill." He was also most impressed by a downed Polish airman who, despite his injuries, refused to say anything under interrogation. In all, however, he noted that though his troops were forced off the roads and into the forests to escape the raids, their progress was otherwise scarcely affected.[94]

As Kielmansegg was evaluating the air attacks, a few kilometers to the north Polish forces of the Łódź Army were digging in on Borowska Góra (Borowa Heights), three modest but strategically important hills west of Piotrków Trybunalski. There, two divisions of infantry and a battalion of forty-seven 7TP light tanks were hoping to exploit the terrain to hold the advance of the German 4th Panzer Division, and thereby finally stabilize the line. Tank-on-tank engagements had taken place before—notably at the Battle of Jordanów, west of Kraków—but those at Borowska Góra would be among the most significant.

The Polish 7TP tanks of the 301st Light Tank Battalion were not the most advanced machines available. But, based on the British Vickers 6-Ton model, they were sturdy and serviceable, and a good match for the lighter, and more lightly armored, German workhorses, the Panzer Is and IIs.[95] Unsurprisingly, then, they won some successes against the invaders on September 4, destroying fifteen tanks and armored cars of the 4th Panzer near the village of Wola Krzysztoporska in exchange for the loss of seven of their own. However, in the fierce hand-to-hand fighting that followed, the hills of Borowska Góra changed hands a number of times before they were finally secured by the Germans. One diarist wrote that the German infantry triumphed "after a hard battle of many hours," and the Poles were "chased to the Devil."[96] Afterward, the remnants of the smashed 7th Polish Infantry Division were rounded up in Janów and many prisoners were taken, including the divisional commander, General Janusz Gąsiorowski, who had the dubious honor of being the first general to be taken captive in the war. Nonetheless, the Wehrmacht's daily report for the following day, September 5, was less than loquacious, noting simply that "extensive enemy positions have been broken" and "the Borowa Heights have been captured."[97]

If Borowska Góra marked one of the first tank battles of the war, a short distance to the south, older methods of warfare were still very much in use. At Lesiopole, Wiktor Jackiewicz and his cavalry unit found themselves cut off after observing the rapid German advance. "What I so feared now happened," he later recalled:

> Before me was a battalion of German infantry, dispersed—luckily—not entrenched. I had only two options: to surrender to captivity, or to charge through. Only one decision was possible: to charge through at a run.
>
> I shall never forget the moment when I gave the signal with a whirl of my sabre and we set out at a gallop in dead silence, not a single "hurrah," just the sound of galloping horses and their snorting. The Germans dispersed before us, tried to set up their machine guns; loose shots were fired and—strangest of all—there was total panic among the Germans. I had hardly any losses.[98]

Far from being an object of ridicule, a Polish cavalry charge could clearly still provoke terror in the enemy.

Nonetheless, there would be no respite for the Poles. German forces drove on relentlessly toward Warsaw, exploiting the growing gap between the sectors held by the Łódź and Kraków Armies, and advanced into the district of Piotrków Trybunalski, which was held by the understrength Prusy Army. Initially, the German attack—led by the elite 1st Panzer Division—was repulsed, denied progress by an "organized and effective" network of defenses, artillery positions, and minefields on the western and southern outskirts of Piotrków. As Count von Kielmansegg noted with evident surprise, "The enemy seems determined on defense."[99] Yet after a spirited Polish counterattack by a battalion of 7TP tanks was halted, the 1st Panzer regained the initiative and quickly found an opening in the Polish defenses. By early evening on September 5, Piotrków was being outflanked, and after a further two hours of house-to-house fighting in the city itself, the battle was over.[100]

As Piotrków fell, the nearby town of Sulejów was also suffering. The previous afternoon, though undefended and choked with refugees from the south and west, it had been exposed to the full force of a Luftwaffe air assault. As one eyewitness remembered, the raid was heralded by "a terrifying whistle" followed by a cacophony of explosions in which it seemed "the walls were about to crumble." Escaping the town to the potato fields beyond, she found herself surrounded by the wounded and dying: "All around me . . . I could hear moans, prayers, and desperate cries for help. Next to me was a soldier torn up by shrapnel, bleeding and begging for someone to end his suffering." Looking back, she saw Sulejów "burning like a torch." The town was almost entirely destroyed and as many as 700 lives were lost.[101]

The collapse of the front around Łódź highlighted one of the main problems the Poles faced. Aside from the acute military challenge, Polish forces struggled with failing communications. Not only were wired field telephones and radio networks severely impacted by the German bombing campaign of the opening days of the war, but a culture of military secrecy—inherited from Józef Piłsudski—compounded the resulting difficulties, meaning that neighboring armies were not permitted to know what their compatriots were doing. Indeed, all communications had to be routed via the High Command in Warsaw. Astonishingly, the Polish defense plan was strictly confidential, and even senior army commanders were not informed of their respective tasks beyond the first days of the war.[102] As a result, the High Command often had only a tenuous grip on realities at the front—and at times even relied on German command reports for information. Field commanders, meanwhile, were constantly forced to improvise, unaware of the progress of battle in the adjacent sector, and in only halting contact even with their own subordinates. So when the commander of the Łódź Army, General Juliusz Rómmel, needed to coordinate operations with the neighboring Prusy Army during the defense of Piotrków, his request had to be directed via the commander-in-chief, Edward Śmigły-Rydz himself.[103]

Such problems made fighting against a superior enemy even more difficult, but in one instance they were to prove especially critical. With the fall of Piotrków Trybunalski, the "road to Warsaw" was effectively blocked only by those remaining elements of the Łódź Army that were defending their eponymous city, 120 kilometers (75 miles) southwest of the capital. However, under determined attack from the German 4th

Panzer Division, including elements of the SS-Leibstandarte, the Łódź Army began to fall back in an increasingly disorderly retreat. In the vanguard of that retreat, it appeared, was the army's commander, General Rómmel, who had abandoned his headquarters at Julianów, west of Łódź, on the morning of September 6, following a German air raid.[104]

Without effective command, the Łódź Army's withdrawal quickly degenerated into headlong flight. As one German account put it, "Everywhere, there were discarded weapons, ammunition, equipment, and abandoned vehicles. Hundreds of Polish soldiers surrendered without a fight."[105] Łódź, too, was abandoned. A diarist noted that the authorities had already left the city the previous night, and freed prisoners now wandered through the streets in their prison uniforms.[106] A resident described the crowds of refugees streaming into Łódź, among them many army deserters. "These men," Samuel Goldberg wrote, "their faces filled with the terror of death and annihilation, were discarding their uniforms and their weapons to don civilian attire. Even their underclothing, which bore military markings, was removed and thrown into latrines or burned. . . . It began to look to me as though the entire Polish Army had simply given up."[107]

In the ensuing maelstrom, General Wiktor Thommée, commanding the Piotrków Operational Group, sent an adjutant to Julianów to ascertain the whereabouts of the Łódź Army's headquarters. The adjutant, Major Cezary Niewęgłowski, arrived to find only the evidence of a hurried departure. He was so shocked by what he saw as profound dereliction of duty by his superiors that, after reporting back to General Thommée, he took his own life. "I was a soldier for the passion, not for a piece of bread," he wrote in his last testament:

I was a patriot, perhaps impetuous in my ambition, but sincere. I believed in my leaders, but I have been disappointed. For a country of 34 million to lose a war in five days—is not a military disaster, but a moral one. This disaster has shown our organizational incompetence, lack of foresight, and with it, conceit and a bottomless self-assurance of some of the "great" men. This crushed me because the chaos and confusion which followed has brought unbearable humiliation upon us. Over these few days, I have witnessed the heroism and valor of our soldiers, and the incompetence of our commanders.[108]

Poland's High Command, it seemed, was not only failing its soldiers, but losing whatever tenuous grip it had on events. As the Łódź front disintegrated, and the High Command in Warsaw found itself unable to make contact with the itinerant Łódź Army Headquarters, Śmigły-Rydz concluded that the time had come for decisive action. Bowing to the inevitable, he issued an order for the withdrawal of the Polish armies beyond the line formed by the rivers Vistula, Narew, and San, thereby effectively ceding the western half of the country to the enemy.[109] In truth, such a move had always been part of Śmigły Rydz's planning: a withdrawal to defensible lines, in anticipation of the relief that would come from an Anglo-French offensive against Germany in the west.[110] But he would not have expected the time for that withdrawal to arrive so soon.

With a general withdrawal finally sanctioned, the Polish retreat accelerated. As one Łódź inhabitant, Fryderyk Winnykamień, recalled, military personnel mixed with civilian refugees in a "tide of humanity" sweeping toward Warsaw. The twenty-year-old had left Łódź the night before with his parents and two sisters; as a Jew, he was anxious not to test the Germans' reputation for anti-Semitism. By dawn they had found themselves in an "uninterrupted convoy" containing wagons, military vehicles, and countless pedestrians, including "visibly exhausted and hungry soldiers, mercilessly driving on their horses, which looked just as exhausted and miserable as they did." They were surrounded by civilians: "Whole families, like us, on foot carrying all that they could in cases, rucksacks, and bundles. . . . Mothers carried infants and small children in their arms, men packed like camels with all their possessions. . . . They were driven forward by the specters of war, of plunder, and of murder, which pushed them ever onward, regardless of the lack of food, the heat of the day, or their own exhaustion."[111] Of course, such unfortunates elicited little sympathy from their German pursuers.

Johann von Kielmansegg considered them simply as an obstacle to the forward progress of his unit; he even found humor in the situation when he caught sight of an old farmer's wife with her last remaining possessions, "a clucking chicken under her arm and a huge alarm clock in the other hand."[112] Neither were columns of fleeing civilians spared aerial attack. One such group was strafed by German aircraft east of Łódź. An eyewitness recalled a "shower of bullets" in which countless civilians were killed, "dead bodies covering the highways" while the injured tried to crawl away to safety "amidst moans and shrieks."[113]

Polish prisoners of war were likewise shown little mercy by the Germans. At Ciepielów, south of Warsaw, on September 8, the advance of the German 15th Motorized Infantry Regiment was halted by the Polish 74th Infantry in a brief but bloody engagement in which a popular German company commander, Captain Mark von Lewinski, was killed by a Polish sniper. The regimental commander, Colonel Walter Wessel, was enraged, mourning the loss of his captain and cursing the "cheek" of the Poles for wanting to halt his advance.[114] In response, he ordered that some 300 Polish prisoners of war were to be treated as partisans. They were stripped of their papers and their uniform jackets and ordered to march in single file to the rear. Some minutes later, an eyewitness heard the chatter of machine guns: "I hurry in that direction and see . . . the Polish prisoners shot, lying in the ditch by the side of the road."[115] Astonishingly, but for the postwar discovery of this anonymous testimony, and a few grainy photographs, the killings at Ciepielów might have slipped from the historical record completely.

Actions such as these—euphemistically called "reprisals" or "pacifications" by the Germans—would become commonplace. In part, of course, they were a consequence of the nature of the Blitzkrieg, in which mobile, fast-moving troops, disrupting and isolating a more static defense, caused many of the defenders to be left behind the front line, where any continued resistance could easily be interpreted as the work of "irregulars" or partisans.[116] The result was "partisan psychosis": the fear, actively stoked by some Wehrmacht commanders, that Polish

Polish prisoners of war, murdered near Ciepielów.
akg-images

snipers and "bandits" were lurking behind every hedgerow and in every building, waiting to launch an ambush or an attack from the rear.[117]

This psychosis extended to Polish civilians as well, with the distinction between combatants and noncombatants growing ever more blurred. As one trigger-happy German infantryman wrote home, "As we're in enemy territory I trust no one! The pistol should talk before I believe someone."[118] This phenomenon was certainly recognized at the time. The war diary of the German 31st Infantry Division, for instance, noted that "the first days of the war have already shown that the men and the inexperienced officers were made insufficiently aware in their training of the typical conditions in warfare." The result, it said, was a "nervousness, anxiety and disorientation" that led to "shootings and arson."[119] In countless instances, German troops behaved with wanton, murderous cruelty toward Polish civilian populations, targeting ordinary people as hostages, or murdering them as "bandits." At Sulejówek, for instance, fifty civilians were murdered in retaliation for the death of a single German officer.[120] The burning of villages was similarly routine; indeed, it was becoming standard practice when German units came under fire.[121] In this way, local civilians were targeted in revenge for the legitimate defensive actions of the Polish army.

In addition, the convention that civilians were executed if they were found in possession of a weapon gave carte blanche to some of the most brutal impulses of German soldiers. As many eyewitnesses recalled, a weapon could be interpreted in myriad ways and could include such innocuous items as flintlocks, pocket knives, razors, or rusty bayonets.[122] Farmers were particularly at risk, as even the most routine search of their properties could often yield a shotgun or a pitchfork. Consequently, they regularly found themselves victims of German massacres: eighteen were shot after the defense of Uniejów, for example, twenty-four were murdered at Wylazłów, thirty were killed in Chechło, and thirty-two were executed near Łowicz.[123] The list goes on.

Of course, there were several factors driving this brutal behavior. It has been suggested, for instance, that one reason for the murderous impetuosity among German troops was perhaps their use of Pervitin—a methamphetamine in pill form that produced improvements in energy, concentration, and libido and had become very popular in Germany. Tests carried out by the Wehrmacht, which issued the drug, in particular, to drivers during the invasion of Poland, discovered among the subjects heightened alertness, increased self-confidence, reduced inhibitions, and a greater willingness to take risks. Of course, Pervitin was also readily available to ordinary soldiers, and though the level of consumption is unclear, it can be assumed that a proportion of them had their own supply. When the author Heinrich Böll wrote to his parents and siblings from Poland that autumn, he asked them to "send Pervitin."[124]

The military benefits of the drug are obvious. Soldiers who were alert, willing to take risks, and able to stay awake for three days on end made for highly effective fighters in the new age of mobile warfare. Indeed, the guidelines issued the following year for the drug's safe use stated that "the experience of the Polish campaign" showed that military success in 1939 had been "crucially influenced" by Pervitin.[125] It is very probable that those advertised effects would have lowered inhibition and made German soldiers more likely to commit atrocities against civilian populations, particularly when combined with "partisan psychosis." Just as Pervitin turned them into more efficient fighters, it almost certainly also made them into more efficient killers.

Yet, whatever the roles played by Pervitin or by "partisan psychosis," there can be no doubt that the primary driver of German atrocities in Poland in 1939 was simple racism. As at Ciepielów, the very act of Polish resistance was often seen through a racist lens. Harrying and ambushing a superior enemy, German soldiers told themselves, was the sort of cowardly warfare that was waged by the racially inferior—and by Nazi logic, it deserved the most brutal punishment. As one soldier wrote at the time, the Poles "behave in an un-European way and indeed an un-human way. . . . The civilians go to prayer, hiding themselves behind holy pictures and crosses, but then fire at our people again whenever they can. Who can blame us for feeling bitter and using harsher methods?"[126] German soldiers did not treat Polish civilians or prisoners of war with respect because they did not consider them to deserve it. To the German mind, these people were "uncivilised," "filthy," "a rabble"— in short, as one soldier confessed he believed, barely human.[127] German soldiers were engaged in a race war, and the Polish people—whether soldiers or civilians—were the enemy.

Atrocities, then, were by no means exceptional. Among countless examples, the experiences of a few Polish villages must serve to demonstrate the wider slaughter. At Złoczew, near Sieradz, units of the 95th Infantry Regiment and SS-Leibstandarte murdered around 200 Poles, including refugees, women, and children, in a frenzy of nocturnal violence. One survivor recalled the Germans shooting "not only at those fleeing, but at anyone they saw on the lane, on the street, or in the courtyard."[128] The fires in Złoczew would burn for days, consuming most of the village. A later investigation by the German military found no explanation for the killings.[129] At Kajetanowice, meanwhile, seventy-two Polish civilians were shot or burned alive after the death of two German horses in a "friendly fire" incident. Of the dead, only fifteen could be identified; they included three children, the youngest of them barely six months old.[130]

Brutal as they were, such actions would pale into near insignificance in comparison to the events witnessed at Bydgoszcz. When German forces entered the city on the morning of September 5, they were primed to avenge the Polish suppression of the earlier insurrection by ethnic Germans. Ominously, the war diary of the German 122nd Infantry Regiment, then entering Bydgoszcz from the north, suggested that no quarter would be given to the city's remaining defenders, a makeshift 2,000-strong militia composed of laborers, railway workers, students, and boy scouts: "Those who resist," it proclaimed, "will be shot."[131]

By the time resistance had been quelled that afternoon, those dire predictions were already being realized. When sporadic violence continued, the town's new commander, Brigadier-General Eccard Freiherr von Gablentz, ordered a full-scale "pacification." The following day, September 6, units of the Wehrmacht, along with the Order Police and Security Police—assisted by *Volksdeutsche* informants—began a systematic search of the town. They were looking for weapons as well as for anyone who might be responsible for the earlier executions of German insurgents. As one witness recalled, they were "dragging people out of their homes, making them stand for hours with their arms in the air, arresting adults and boy scouts alike." "Filled with fear," he went on, "we listened to the screams coming from the street, wondering if we would be next."[132]

"Pacification" quickly became indistinguishable from a general targeting of the Polish elite and intelligentsia along with revenge executions in response to spasms of continued Polish resistance. Those identified by the *Volksdeutsche* as perpetrators were generally executed on the spot, as were those discovered in possession of any sort of weapon.[133] In addition, countless others deemed in any way suspect were arrested and taken to empty buildings, such as the former army barracks on Gdańska

Street, where they would be interrogated. One of those arrested, Franciszek Derezinski, later recounted his experience: "I was picked up on the street by German police and led to the artillery barracks, along with around 500 other Poles. Ethnic Germans there identified people who had allegedly murdered *Volksdeutsche*. These persons were immediately shot and local Jews were forced to dig a grave for them in the courtyard of the barracks."[134]

Elsewhere in the town, continued outbreaks of sniping from Polish militiamen provoked ever more draconian countermeasures. On September 7, the command of the 4th Army ordered the military and police units in Bydgoszcz to take hostages from among the civilian population and publicly execute them in response to further attacks. When a sniper shot and wounded a German soldier the following day, that threat was carried out: some forty Polish hostages were shot in the market square.[135] Among them was a group of boy scouts between the ages of twelve and sixteen. "Unaware of what awaited them," one bystander recalled, "these poor children joked and even played games amongst themselves. They realised the truth only when they were made to line up . . . and the machine guns were brought. Some of the little ones began to cry, but the others gave proof of the most admirable courage. They intoned the Polish national anthem and fell like heroes."[136] A priest who rushed to give them the last rites was shot as well.

Within a couple of days, the German media began to provide a "spin" on events, remaining silent about the brutal reprisals being carried out by their own troops while loudly proclaiming the barbarism and subhumanity of the Poles, fostering a further clamor for revenge. On September 9, the Nazi Party newspaper, the *Völkischer Beobachter* (National Observer), led the chorus, describing the "Gruesome Crimes in Bromberg" in the most harrowing terms. Men, women, and children had been beaten to death, tongues had been cut out, and eyes gouged by the "Polish vermin," it said. "In streets and gardens," it added, "lie the mutilated bodies of countless ethnic Germans, the victims of a cruel Polish slaughter."[137] The evocative term *Bromberger Blutsonntag* (Bromberg's Bloody Sunday) was coined by Berlin's propagandists for the earlier killing of *Volksdeutsche* insurgents, with the instruction that it "must enter as a permanent term in the dictionary and circumnavigate the globe."[138] In response to these real and imagined crimes, German actions in Bydgoszcz would provide a grim foretaste—for Poland and the world beyond—of the horrors that were to come.

GIVEN THE ACCELERATING GERMAN ADVANCE AND THE REPORTS of the horrific atrocities being committed in its wake, the mood in Warsaw grew increasingly anxious. Having ordered the general military withdrawal behind the Vistula on the evening of September 6, the following day Edward Śmigły-Rydz gave instructions for the evacuation of the Polish High Command itself from Warsaw to Brest, about 200 kilometers (125 miles) to the east. Writing in his diary that evening, the Polish prime minister, Felicjan Sławoj Składkowski, pondered whether it might be possible to "hold on" to the capital. However, after being summoned to see Śmigły-Rydz, he learned that the Germans were less than 20 kilometers (12 miles) away. Conditions were such that it was now "impossible either to govern or to command the army."[139] Evacuation of both the government and the High Command, it seemed, was the only option left.

Such a move would have been difficult enough to achieve in peacetime, but during a war, with the enemy on the doorstep, it was inviting catastrophe. Two days earlier, most of the official bodies and ministries had already been ordered to leave the capital. Among them was the British military mission, headed by Lieutenant-General Adrian Carton de Wiart, which had found its progress eastward hampered by a "slowly moving mass of heart-rending humanity, pushing and pedalling their incongruous forms of transport, clutching their children and their pitiful bundles, and trudging no one knew where."[140]

Once the order for a government evacuation had been given, those conditions deteriorated still further, with many ordinary Varsovians also abandoning the city despite appeals from the police for volunteers to help dig trenches in the western suburbs. One eyewitness described joining a stream of human traffic that was crossing Warsaw's Poniatowski Bridge. "This was a real Exodus," he wrote. "The trams were plastered with people and soldiers like fly papers; the big horse wagons were packed; there were large lorries, small delivery vans, military convoys, and masses and masses of pedestrians all moving out towards the suburbs of Praga on the right bank of the river. They thronged every road leading away from Warsaw."[141] Another refugee recalled the crush on the bridge. It was "an innumerable multitude," Zofia Chomętowska wrote, "confusion, horses, wagons, soldiers, and civilians. We finally move on, we have priority as 'evacuees.' But still, it took us five hours to cross the Vistula!"[142]

Once beyond the city center, the caravans of refugees were exposed to the full fury of the Luftwaffe, and they were bombed and strafed at will by the *Stukas*. The road to Wawer in the southeastern suburbs presented a vision of horror, one refugee recalled: "Now and then the rhythmical and characteristic humming sound of the aeroplane motors could be heard. These steely monsters dived on their chosen aims and without any hindrance threw down their loads, spreading death and destruction." Nonetheless, in the aftermath of each attack, the scattered mass of people would re-form and continue its desperate journey. It was "like a rolling sea of humanity, steadily increasing and continually moving forward."[143]

One prominent Warsaw citizen was thoroughly unimpressed by the headlong flight of so many of his compatriots. Wacław Lipiński was a historian and veteran of the First World War; he had been brought out of retirement with the German invasion and made head of propaganda for the Warsaw Command. Broadcasting daily to the people of the capital, he must have felt the decision of so many of the city's inhabitants to leave as a personal blow. "Thousands of people continue leaving the city," he wrote in his diary:

> The evacuation of the government, carried out in such an indecent hurry, created in Warsaw an atmosphere of panic which has been spreading like an epidemic. Everyone who holds any public office is

racing across the Vistula, sped on by some kind of psychosis of fear and terror. I cannot understand this, it is beyond my comprehension. Weren't they all, only a few days ago, so heroic and willing to fight and endure? A few bombs, a few explosions, the proximity of the Germans has turned those people into a pack of cowards. Are we really worth so little?[144]

Aside from the human consequences, the result was confusion. Whereas in Warsaw Śmigły-Rydz had at least enjoyed a tenuous grip on events, beyond the capital he and his staff were effectively blind and deaf, unable to lead the continued defense of Poland. If field commanders received any orders at all now, they rarely reflected the reality on the ground. The situation was no better in Warsaw itself. On September 8, the decision was taken to defend the capital by establishing an improvised "Warsaw Army Group" under the command of General Juliusz Rómmel. Rómmel was fresh from his failure as commander of the Łódź Army and was accused of having abandoned his troops on the battlefield. Worse still, in the abject chaos that now typified the Polish High Command, his precise position in Warsaw remained undefined: no one seemed to know what role he was to take or what forces he had at his disposal. When the head of Warsaw's Defense Command, General Walerian Czuma, was asked what Rómmel was doing, he replied that he didn't know. "He has visited my headquarters," he said, "but that's all."[145]

Though Rómmel might not have been an inspired appointment, that of Warsaw's mayor, Stefan Starzyński, as civilian commissar to the Warsaw Military Command, certainly was. Starzyński, who had been a hugely popular and effective mayor of the capital through much of the 1930s, took over de facto control of the defense of the city. From the start, he brought a fresh dynamism to the task, his actions characterized by a contemporary as "noble tenacity."[146] He made daily radio speeches to maintain morale and organized a Civil Guard to replace the evacuated police force. The American photographer Julien Bryan described his stoicism. "Neither danger nor hunger nor loss of sleep," Bryan wrote admiringly, "seemed to have much effect on this man. For two weeks he never left the building, snatching what sleep he could on an office couch or on the floor." Even during an air raid, the mayor remained at his desk, working throughout.[147] Starzyński's lieutenants, not least among them his propaganda chief, Wacław Lipiński, wholeheartedly echoed his defiant mood. "Warsaw will be defended to the last breath," Lipiński declared in one of his radio addresses. "If it falls, it will mean that a German tank has rolled over the last Polish soldier left."[148]

Some took that defiance to heart, with mixed results. The head of the High Command's propaganda department, Colonel Roman Umiastowski, panicked by the arrival of German troops in the southwestern suburbs, made a radio announcement in which he pled for all the residents of Warsaw to devote their energy to building barricades, starting immediately.[149] Quickly, countless makeshift barriers and obstacles were raised across the city, utilizing buses, trams, paving stones, and earth, all of which seriously hampered the flow of traffic, and with that, the city's effective defense. Marta Korwin discovered "rocks, upset street cars and automobiles, and piles of rubbish" strewn across her street and wondered which fool had asked the people to erect barricades. Her displeasure stemmed from the fact that, after having spent two days trying to establish a makeshift medical center, her field hospital was now effectively inaccessible.[150]

Such medical facilities were sorely needed. Not only was Warsaw attempting to cope with the tens of thousands of displaced soldiers and civilian refugees who had poured into the city from the provinces, but it was under almost constant attack from the air. For one diarist, the warning procedure was already grimly familiar:

> The wireless was interrupted by a voice announcing the approach of enemy machines and a minute or two later long blasts from sirens and hooters all over Warsaw sounded the alarm. At the same time, the familiar stern voice of the announcer was heard: "Air-raid alarm for the town of Warsaw, for the town of Warsaw . . ." followed again by the continuous warbling of sirens. Didn't we know that sound! It was the music which accompanied the destruction of so many lives.[151]

Traveling across the city during an air raid, Korwin found it completely deserted. "Not a soul was on the streets," she wrote. "Warsaw seemed a city without people." Hurrying to pick up wounded servicemen, she soon found herself a target for the enemy pilots and jumped into a ditch by the roadside. "The bombers were flying so low that we could see the faces of the airmen distinctly," she recalled. "They were encountering no opposition. They were masters of the sky, out for a joy ride. One of the pilots was laughing as he pointed to the destruction beneath him. The bombing went on. . . . Why were they bombing, I wondered? No one and nothing lay below; there was only devastation."[152]

The effects were harrowing: "Here lay a shoe and a hat, over there a coat. A pool of fresh blood told a tale of horror." Korwin remembered seeing what she thought was a discarded overcoat after a raid, but rushing to investigate, discovered that it was a Jewish boy. He had a gaping shrapnel wound and was already beyond help. "He could no longer speak," she wrote. "When he saw me, he lifted his hand and opened it. In his palm was a tiny, one-ounce package of tea he had been carrying to the hospital." Korwin took the package and told the boy that his mission would be completed: she would take it to the hospital for him, where it would give comfort to an injured soldier. With that, she recalled, "the boy relaxed and died in peace." She never discovered his name.[153]

Yet, whatever the cost, it seemed that Warsaw would be defended. On September 8, General Czuma issued his first order of the day to the city's garrison. "The commander-in-chief has entrusted you with the defense of the capital," he announced:

He demands that the enemy's attack be defeated at the gates of Warsaw, that the rape of Polish soil be brought to an end, and that those comrades fallen in battle—soldiers, women, and children—be avenged. We shall reach out a hand to the fighting troops to support them in the coming battles. We have taken our positions, from which there will be no retreat. The enemy will receive only one answer: "Enough! Not a step farther!" And we have only one order: "The commander-in-chief's order will be carried out."[154]

That evening, as the first German spearheads entered the suburb of Wola in the southwest of Warsaw, the housewife Maria Komornicka confided her fears to her diary. "I suppose the fate of Warsaw has been sealed," she wrote. "We should be prepared to sit in the cellars. What a nightmare. We might be buried under the rubble. Warsaw might be turned to ruins. . . . Good God, have mercy on us."[155]

– CHAPTER FIVE –

"POLAND IS NOT YET LOST"

THOSE VARSOVIANS ABLE TO CONSULT THE NEWSPAPERS ON the morning of September 9 might have found some grounds for cautious optimism. In fact, only one newspaper was still printing in the capital that day, the socialist *Robotnik* (Worker), but the tone of its front page was upbeat: "Franco-British Forces," it proclaimed, were "marching on the Rhine."[1]

Two days earlier, French forces had indeed launched an invasion of the Saarland, probing across the German frontier into the Warndt Forest south of Saarlouis and the area south and southeast of Saarbrücken. The action was undertaken ostensibly in support of France's Polish allies and in partial fulfillment of the undertaking, given to the Poles by General Gamelin in May 1939, to throw "the bulk" of French forces against Germany. In truth, however, the eleven divisions of the French 2nd Army Group carried out only a limited incursion, advancing some 13 kilometers (8 miles) toward the town of Hornbach. In all, twelve small towns and villages were taken unopposed, with French tanks and infantry inching nervously forward, while the German defenders mostly melted away, leaving daubed slogans in their wake that proclaimed the Wehrmacht's pacific intentions. The German commander in the west,

General Wilhelm Ritter von Leeb, recalled the rather ridiculous nature of events: "Placards on the French side say 'Please don't shoot. We will not shoot.' We answer with 'If you don't shoot, neither will we.'"[2] Where battle was actually joined, it was scarcely less farcical. On one occasion, a French platoon was stopped in its tracks for an entire day by the fire from a single automatic weapon.[3]

Though the French did not know it, at that time they enjoyed a huge advantage over their German enemy. Not only did they have a numerical superiority of three to one, but those Wehrmacht forces facing them had been cut to the bone in the expectation of a swift defeat of Poland before any possible Anglo-French intervention could be made to count. Consequently, German ground forces were completely lacking in armor; machine guns and artillery were in short supply; and the Luftwaffe presence over the Saar was restricted to only a few obsolete biplanes. The German army in the west had been effectively hollowed out.[4] Leeb did not wholly understand why the French did not attack with more vigor. "Evidently they are not ready," he concluded, "or they don't want to pick the chestnuts out of the fire, and are waiting for the British." To a German officer of the old school, a veteran of the First World War, French timidity was simply baffling.[5]

Moreover, the area into which the French were cautiously advancing was not as well fortified as it at first appeared. Dominated by the Siegfried Line—the complex of layered German defenses that stretched from Holland to the Swiss border—the Saarland was certainly dotted with minefields, bunkers, and tank obstacles. But the defenses were not complete: there were gaps, and many of the bunkers themselves were not finished. Indeed, speaking after the war, General Alfred Jodl would describe the area at the time as "little better than a building site."[6]

Had the French attacked the Saarland with force in 1939, therefore, they would have quickly discovered that their opponents were under strength and that those seemingly formidable defenses were little more than a Potemkin village. But they rarely displayed any vigor at all, cautiously inching forward and halting at the slightest whiff of resistance. Though General Gamelin spoke of doing "all we can to help the Poles,"[7] he was clearly not prepared to sacrifice any French lives in doing so. Indeed, the French seemed to resent that they had been put in the firing line. Arriving in Paris in the first week of September, the former head of the British military mission in Warsaw, Adrian Carton de Wiart, noted that his French colleagues and friends "were all equally bitter and disgruntled with Britain for having stuck to her word to declare war on Germany if Poland was invaded." The French, he would complain in his memoirs, "with their usual realism," had failed to understand why the British had allied themselves to the Poles; indeed, they harbored the impression that "the Poles wouldn't have fought . . . if Britain hadn't declared war."[8] In such circumstances, it was perhaps fortunate for Gamelin that casualties were light, with only a couple of hundred dead on both sides. The French Saar offensive was little more than an Allied propaganda exercise.

Nonetheless, following the tone of the rather breathless French communiqués of the time, the incursion was reported in the most dramatic terms. Though *The Times* of London cautioned that French accounts should not be interpreted "in a fashion which may cause disappointment later," the *Daily Mail* had no such qualms, writing that the French army was "pouring over the German border" and that Germany was rushing troops west to meet the invaders.[9]

In Poland, meanwhile, where people were desperate to believe in Allied determination and vigor, the French communiqués were reproduced verbatim in the press and often embellished with rumor, hearsay, and no little wishful thinking. One Lwów newspaper spoke of the Germans fleeing "in panic" as "enormous French motorized forces" broke through the Siegfried Line and sent crowds of refugees to flood Berlin. Later reports claimed that German forces were retreating in chaos, that the bridges on the Rhine had been captured, and that Aachen, Mainz, Frankfurt, and Stuttgart were being evacuated. Very quickly, the Saar operation appeared, from a Polish perspective, to take on the character of a liberation. "We are being relieved, a little more each day," a *Robotnik* editorial opined on September 9: "Several German divisions, a significant portion of their air force and tanks, have been of necessity transferred to the French front." The Wilno paper *Słowo* (Word) went further: "The moment is nigh when the German General Staff will be forced to throw all of their forces to the west."[10] Ordinary Poles took their lead from such fantastic prognostications. One especially imaginative diarist near Lwów brimmed with enthusiasm for the actions of Poland's allies, writing that "Britain rules the seas and the skies," that the German battleship *Gneisenau* had been sunk, that Berlin's industrial areas had been "bombed to rubble," and that the French had captured Frankfurt.[11] In Warsaw, meanwhile, housewife Maria Komornicka rejoiced about what she called "the Allied advance" in the west. "Today is one week since the declaration of war by Britain and France," she wrote in her diary. "We can already feel that Germany is becoming weaker."[12]

In truth, there was very little to rejoice about. Poland's western allies were only reluctantly inching toward war, and the Saar offensive was symbolic of their collective timidity and lack of resolve. The Polish military attaché in Paris was under few illusions. On September 11, he wrote to his superiors in Warsaw to outline French inaction hitherto. He explained that he had urged Gamelin, in writing, to speed things up.[13] The head of the Polish military mission in London pithily summed up the French action as "fighting a war without a war."[14]

The arrival of the British Expeditionary Force did little to improve matters. The first five divisions were already arriving in France, but lacking transport, training, and even maps, they were described by one of their corps commanders as "quite unfit for war, practically in every respect."[15] Moreover, subordinated to French command, they were incapable of independent action, even if they had had the capacity or the will. It seemed that they were little more than a token bolstering of French morale. The chief of the Imperial General Staff, General Edmund Ironside, noted the French mood after his attaché returned from a visit to the front. "The French believe," he wrote, "that this struggle with Germany must happen in every century and probably more often. Their one desire is to emerge from the war with something of their manhood left. They are therefore going to do nothing until we are more in line. They do not want to fight in front of the Maginot Line and therefore they are not going to put too many men there." His conclusion: "The more I look into our strategical position, the more serious does it seem."[16]

There was hardly any good news in the air, either. Though Polish newspapers excitedly proclaimed that Germany's industrial districts had been "turned to rubble" by the RAF, and that the iconic Krupp factory in Essen had already been destroyed, here, too, the reality was much more pedestrian.[17] The RAF had gone into action, and on September 4, twenty-nine Wellington and Blenheim aircraft had raided German warships and naval installations at Wilhelmshaven and Brunsbüttel, where five of the twenty-nine were lost to antiaircraft fire and little serious damage was caused. There had been even less damage the previous night, when a force of ten Whitleys from 51st and 58th Squadrons dropped 5.4 million leaflets over "targets" such as Hamburg, Bremen, and the Ruhr.[18] The leaflets, entitled "Warning! A Message from Great Britain," gave the reasons for Britain's declaration of war and stressed the British government's "desire for peace." The idea of bombing nonmilitary targets in Germany—as the Luftwaffe was already ruthlessly doing in Poland—had been dismissed by Prime Minister Chamberlain out of hand, largely for fear that it might lead to retaliatory raids on London and Paris.[19] Moreover, when on September 5 it was proposed that munitions stores in the Black Forest might be set alight by an incendiary raid, the secretary for air, Sir Kingsley Wood, was horrified. He replied in disbelief, "Are you aware it is private property?"[20]

Meanwhile, the head of the Polish military mission in London, Major-General Mieczysław Norwid-Neugebauer, was holding talks with senior members of the British military establishment, keeping them abreast of developments in Poland and seeking to realize Allied promises of help. Throughout the conversations, he was complimented about the valor of the Polish army and assured that everything would be done to assist in the fight, but his attempts to pin down specifics were met only with evasions and deference to higher authority. In one of his reports to Warsaw that September, Norwid-Neugebauer wrote that General Ironside "assures me that he will do everything he can to pressure the political decision makers in our favor."[21] However, as Ironside himself noted in his diary, that pressure bore little fruit. When it was suggested to Chamberlain that a "gloves off" approach should be adopted in the air war against Germany, for instance, the prime minister "shook his head in a dull way as if it were too much to consider."[22]

Despite their public protestations that the defense of Poland was a matter of national honor, both the British and the French governments were brutally sanguine in private about the extent to which they were prepared to assist their ally. In justifying their inactivity, Britain's military and political leaders appeared to be willing to delude themselves about the murderous nature of Germany's aerial campaign over Poland. At the same time as the British ambassador in Warsaw was outlining the Germans' "tactics of deliberate and indiscriminate bombing of open towns," and relaying the desperate pleas of the Polish foreign minister for "retaliation on German military objectives," a war cabinet memorandum on the "German Observance of International Law" cleared the enemy of any transgression.[23] It suggested that those instances where civilian targets had been hit were a succession of accidents and the result of "normal inaccuracy."[24] As if this moral myopia were not enough to justify inaction, the argument was aired that Allied forces should be preserved for future battles. The private secretary to Viscount Halifax, the British foreign minister, noted that it would be wrong to "dash off against the Germans, either by land or air, merely to relieve the Poles, when by conserving our effort we should be able to deal a much shrewder blow later." General Gamelin concurred that preserving Allied force was the preferable option. On September 4, he stated that "to break or discourage the French Army, Navy or Air Force would in no way advance matters."[25]

The apogee of Allied inertia was apparent at the Supreme War Council, which met at Abbeville on the morning of September 12 with Neville Chamberlain, General Gamelin, and French prime minister Édouard Daladier in attendance. In their discussions, Daladier and Chamberlain stressed their "unity of will" and their desire "to live in peace and quiet without a constant menace." When asked his view of the military situation, Daladier replied that it had developed "as had been anticipated, and hoped for, by the French General Staff," adding that though French forces were "approaching the Siegfried Line . . . no spectacular success was anticipated." Indeed, the objective underlying operations in the Saarland "was to help Poland by distracting the attention of Germany," and Daladier had "no intention of throwing his army against German main defenses." Chamberlain described the French decision to avoid large-scale operations as "wise," claiming that "there was no hurry, as time was on our side." In any case, it was clear that "nothing the Allies could do would save Poland from being overrun." When asked whether any change of plan was contemplated, in the event of Poland holding on longer than expected, Gamelin bluntly said no, adding that such a turn of events would merely give the Allies more time to prepare their own defenses.[26] It was, as one historian has memorably summarized it, "a veritable orgy of mutual congratulation at not having succumbed to the temptation of attacking Germany."[27]

After a swift discussion of other matters, ranging from Spain to Syria, the two prime ministers penned a joint communiqué to be issued to the world's press. It read: "This meeting has fully confirmed the strength of the resolve of Great Britain and France to devote their entire strength and resources to the waging of the conflict which has been forced upon them, and to give all possible assistance to their Polish ally, who is resisting with so much gallantry the ruthless invasion of her territory."[28] Impressive words, no doubt, but the truth was that Britain and France were planning to defend Poland using vowels and consonants alone.

When Chamberlain addressed the House of Commons the next day to report on the proceedings of the Supreme War Council meeting, he once again declared the determination of the British and French peoples to put an end to the perpetual threat of Nazi aggression and "to honour to the full their obligations to Poland." Beyond that principle, he was deliberately vague, claiming that he did not want to give away any information to the enemy.[29]

Chamberlain also gave nothing away to his allies. The Polish ambassador's note to Halifax that same day, asking for clarification of Allied intentions, went unanswered.[30] Meanwhile, in Paris, the head of the Polish mission was no longer permitted to see General Gamelin, and was reduced to begging his superiors in Poland for information on the wider strategic situation: "I am getting nothing," he said, from the French.[31] The Poles, it seemed, were being frozen out. In London, Major-General Norwid-Neugebauer perceived the Polish predicament with absolute clarity. In a message to Warsaw on September 14, he explained that the British were planning for the long term, aiming to fight until Hitler was defeated, instead of pursuing the short-term aim of liberating Poland. Consequently, he wrote, "at this time we are left to ourselves."[32]

WHILE BRITISH AND FRENCH POLITICIANS AGONIZED, POLAND was enduring very real agonies of its own. Though military operations in the former Corridor had ceased, Polish civilians there were obliged to deal with the aftermath: the murderous persecution that came with German rule. It was most obvious in Bydgoszcz, where—as we have seen—reprisals for the earlier Polish killing of ethnic German insurgents merged with a brutal attempt to suppress Polish resistance. The killing reached a bloody climax on September 10 with the "pacification" of the southern suburb of Szwederowo (Schwedenhöhe in German), where the town militia had made a determined stand when the Wehrmacht had first arrived. It had been a focus of violence ever since. *Aktion Schwedenhöhe* would be spearheaded by a new type of unit— the *Einsatzgruppe*, or "deployment group"—tasked specifically with the "neutralization" of resistance behind the front line. Formed primarily of SS men and police, the Einsatzgruppen had been established the previous year to secure important sites during the annexation of Austria. In 1939, they were reestablished, albeit with a rather different task, that of eliminating "oppositional elements" encountered in the wake of the German advance into Poland. Initially there were six Einsatzgruppen with around 500 men each. Though they had seen isolated action during the invasion, the "pacification" of Bydgoszcz was to be one of their most important—and formative—engagements.

According to the rather euphemistic language of the Einsatzgruppe's own report, the operation in Szwederowo was to be a "cleansing action" in which "entire suburbs of Bromberg" were to be "systematically searched." Where weapons were found, or resistance encountered, "harsh measures" were to be employed.[33] At 6:30 a.m., when the men of Einsatzgruppe IV mustered for a pep talk from their commander, SS-*Sturmbannführer* Major Helmut Bischoff, they were informed that they were to avenge their fellow Germans who had been murdered by the Poles on Bloody Sunday, and that they now had an opportunity to "prove themselves as men." In case those listening did not grasp the subtext of his speech, Bischoff told them they would not be reprimanded if they "shot unarmed Poles who looked somehow suspicious."[34]

What followed was a thorough sweep of Szwederowo in which the men of the Einsatzgruppe, supported by Order Police and *Volksdeutsche*, purported to identify those who had targeted Germans earlier that week and searched for weapons. By midafternoon, around 60 Poles had already been shot and a further 900 taken prisoner, to be held—as SS chief Heinrich Himmler had ordered—as hostages, "to be shot in case of the slightest insurrection or resistance."[35] In one instance, 18 Poles—including one woman—were shot in the local cemetery. In another, an eighteen-year-old youth was shot in front of his mother because an axe was found in a pigsty.[36] By the end of the day, some 120 Poles had been executed. Of those taken as hostages, a further 150 or so were identified as "suspect" by the *Volksdeutsche* and murdered in the forests outside the town.[37]

In total, between the German entry into Bydgoszcz on September 5 and the departure of the Einsatzgruppen a week later on the 12th, at least 1,306 Poles are thought to have been murdered.[38] In the weeks and months that followed, a further 545 would be tried in the town's new German *Sondergericht* (Special Court), of whom around 200 would be sentenced to death and executed in the grounds of the town prison.[39]

Farther to the east, more conventional methods of warfare still prevailed. There, German forces were advancing southward from East Prussia toward the line of the river Narew, where bridgeheads had already been secured at Pułtusk and Różan, north of Warsaw.[40] At the suggestion of General Guderian, the operational plan for the 3rd Army had been altered, however, and now a more eastward crossing of the Narew was foreseen, aiming not to the immediate east of Warsaw, but in the direction of Brest (200 kilometers [125 miles] east of the capital). The intention was to outflank the Polish forces northeast of Warsaw and deny the opponent the chance of establishing a new defensive line on the river Bug.[41]

Standing in Guderian's way along the southern bank of the eastern Narew were extensive defenses—bunkers and field fortifications—that had been hastily begun earlier that year and were complete in their essentials. More than twenty bunkers had been constructed in the sector around the town of Nowogród, mainly along the river bank; to the east, near Wizna, there were a further nine, perched on higher ground and dominating the wide Narew valley. In the valley itself, the wetlands and numerous channels of the river made for a formidable natural obstacle. If the German 3rd Army wanted to cross the valley, it would have to deal with the fortifications and the men who crewed them.

Among the latter was Władysław Raginis, a slight, soft-spoken, thirty-one-year-old captain in the Border Protection Corps, who was in command of the Wizna Fortified Area. Facing the German advance across the valley beneath him—and some 20 kilometers (12 miles) away from the nearest Polish garrison—Raginis sought to galvanize the 700 or so men under his command. He and his deputy, Lieutenant Stanisław Brykalski, swore an oath that they would not give up their positions alive.

The German attack progressed agonizingly slowly. First, Polish sappers destroyed the bridge at Wizna on September 7, just as the vanguard of the 10th Panzer Division arrived. As a result, the infantry was able to cross the river, but was now without armored support. The men soon discovered that, as one Wehrmacht colonel noticed, "on the far side of the wide, marshy Narew valley, there [were] Polish defensive bunkers. We [were] now forced to stand idly by, until the division [had] secured the crossing."[42] So, while pioneers and pontoon-building detachments were brought up, the infantry attack on the Wizna defenses proceeded in a rather haphazard and piecemeal fashion. When Guderian arrived on the morning of September 9, he was told that the Polish positions had already been taken, but later that day he discovered, to his dismay, that the report had been mistaken. Crossing the river, he found that "nothing was happening" on the south side of the Narew, and "the troops knew nothing about any order to attack." "I cannot pretend," he wrote, "that I was anything but disappointed by what had so far happened."[43] To make matters worse, the pontoon bridge ordered for Wizna had been commandeered by another unit, so the task of getting German armor across the Narew was further delayed.

Once the German assault got under way in earnest, however, on the morning of September 10, the defenders quickly felt the effects. After an hour of "softening up" with artillery fire and air attack, the infantry assault began. By evening, the bunkers—too far apart to provide mutual fire support—had begun to fall to the Germans. "At about 3:00 p.m. I lost the first heavy machine gun and was blinded," one defender recalled:

By 6:00 the enemy had destroyed all the machine guns in our bunker and seriously wounded myself and 5 men. As conditions in the single pitch-dark room were deteriorating, we no longer had heavy machine guns or antitank rifles to defend ourselves, and because we were running out of air . . . I decided to surrender the bunker. Every soldier who exited through the emergency exit, including the wounded, was severely kicked and beaten by the German soldiers. As for me, while leaving the bunker second to last, I was shot in the head with a pistol.[44]

Unsurprisingly, perhaps, some of the defenders refused to surrender even when they were surrounded. As one German account recalled:

The Polish defenders would not give up the fight for anything. Our detachment was again pelted with machine-gun fire. Still, another sapper crawled up to the machine-gun position, the explosive charge was detonated, and the gun fell silent. The attempt to enter the shelter, however, came to nothing, because the dome was still undamaged, and from it the Polish machine gun kept us under fire. . . . Two machine guns, which had until then maintained savage fire, were destroyed. But the Poles still would not surrender.[45]

When the ammunition was finally exhausted and the last of the Polish positions could no longer be held, Raginis ordered his men to leave the remaining bunker. The last out was rifleman Seweryn Biegański. "Captain Raginis ordered us to take off our webbing and to lay down our arms," he recalled. "In a few words he thanked us for the defense, for carrying out our soldierly duty so well and then . . . opened the door." As Biegański was about to leave, he looked back expecting to see Raginis behind him, but from the darkness of the bunker came the blast of an exploding grenade. True to his word, Raginis had not given up his post alive; he had "chosen death over captivity."[46]

Downstream from Wizna, engagements at Łomża and Nowogród also served to hold up Guderian's advance. At Łomża, a bitter Polish defense, led by elements of the 33rd Infantry Regiment, centered on the former tsarist forts on the north bank of the river. Here, a complex of earthen embankments and barrack blocks, reinforced with trenches and barbed wire, was vigorously defended. As the local commander, Lieutenant-Colonel Lucjan Stanek, recalled, the Poles made up in martial spirit what they lacked in materiel: "Deprived of practically everything—help, ammunition, food, and rest—the only thing we do not lose is our tenacity. Tenacity that will last as long as the task continues. To guard the crossings, to guard them at all costs. To keep the Germans from breaking through to the south—this is what fills the mind of every soldier, and this relentless thought keeps the regiment fighting."[47] On the night of September 10, after enduring some three days of frontal infantry assault as well as air attacks and flanking assaults across the river itself, the men of the Polish garrison withdrew, wary that the fall of Wizna might leave them cut off.

Farther west, at Nowogród, it was a similar story. There, the Germans faced eight newly constructed bunkers that were strung along the southern bank of the river amid a network of slit trenches and barbed-wire entanglements. After their first attempts to cross the Narew on September 5 and 6 were rebuffed with heavy losses, the German 21st Infantry Division attempted to force a crossing under cover of darkness, deploying anti-aircraft guns—the famed 88s—in an effort to destroy the Polish bunkers. When this failed, too, and after a Polish counterattack, the focus of the assault changed, and the Germans were finally able to cross the river in the town itself, supported by intense artillery fire and aerial bombing. As at Łomża, the Polish garrison executed a fighting withdrawal that night after finding itself surrounded. One company commander recalled, "We flanked the German detachment . . . and moved to attack. They had not expected us to come from that direction and ran off, allowing us to break through. By the time they opened fire on us, we were already 300 meters [985 feet] away."[48]

Though the engagements on the Narew were intertwined and all equally effective, it is often only the defense of Wizna that receives any popular attention. Perhaps because of the circumstances of Władysław Raginis's death, it is portrayed as a heroic last stand—Poland's Thermopylae. The memorial at the bunker site—with the words, "Go tell the Fatherland, passerby, that we fought to the end, obedient to our duty"— even consciously echoes the Greek epitaph.[49] The bravery of Raginis and his men, their determination and self-sacrifice, is undoubted, particularly as they were effectively abandoned to their fate by their superiors.[50] Whether the commanders appreciated it or not, the crossings on the upper Narew were crucial to the success of Guderian's plan to drive farther east toward Brest, and the few days' delay inflicted upon the Germans there were of vital assistance to the wider Polish withdrawal southward.

However, the more breathless claims attached to the Wizna story are harder to validate. Wizna alone did not—as some accounts suggest[51]—halt the 40,000 men of the German 3rd Army in their tracks; that accolade must be shared with the men who defended Łomża and Nowogród farther west. Neither did the battle last for three days. Though the Germans first arrived at the river on the 7th, there was evidently little genuine combat in the sector until the morning of the 10th, when the assault on the fortifications began in earnest. It is perhaps telling in this regard that contemporary German sources give Wizna very little mention beyond complaining of the "weak bridgehead" there, and the resulting slow progress.[52] To them, it seems, it was little more than a skirmish during the frustrating wait to cross the river.

The death toll in the Narew battles is unknown, but it would have run to hundreds on each side. Many more Poles than that were taken prisoner by the Germans. If they were lucky, they would be treated as prisoners of war. However, that did not necessarily mean that their problems were over. The Polish army doctor Walerian Terajewicz, who was taken prisoner south of Łomża, and was held with other POWs at a former barracks in Zambrów, recalled the ordeal:

> On the night of September 13, I was awakened by rifle shots and machine-gun fire. As it turned out, when some commotion arose among the prisoners . . . the guards opened fire on them without warning and kept on firing for several minutes. I went to take care of the freshly wounded—there were a few dozen of them. They told me they hadn't been trying to escape—some were asking for water, others needed to relieve themselves—and the Germans responded by opening fire on those who lay on the ground.[53]

Such atrocities were fast becoming the norm. A few days before the Zambrów massacre, the town of Kłecko, west of Warsaw, had felt the full force of a German "reprisal." There, a local priest, Father Mateusz Zabłocki, had taken the lead in organizing a civil guard, armed with rifles and shotguns, to oppose the invasion. When the town surrendered, on September 11, German retribution was swift. Zabłocki was taken away by the Gestapo (an experience he would not survive), and soldiers went from house to house to round up the town's menfolk, who were then corralled in the market square. They were divided into those deemed innocent and those considered racially or politically suspect, meaning Jews and anyone who put up resistance or had been found armed. The suspects were then marched off in small groups to the town's sports stadium, where they were shot. In all, more than 300 men and boys were murdered in Kłecko over two days. Many of them were teenagers; the youngest was eleven years old.[54]

At the same time that the men and boys of Kłecko were being slaughtered, at Końskie, south of Warsaw, another atrocity took place, which, unusually, left a mark in the photographic record. As chance would have it, Leni Riefenstahl, one of Hitler's most famous propagandists, had arrived at Końskie with a film crew. Riefenstahl, who had made the propaganda films *The Triumph of the Will* and *Olympia* before the war, had been granted war correspondent status in 1939 and had put together a film unit that was subordinated to Joseph Goebbels's Propaganda Ministry. She had come to Końskie, a small town 90 kilometers (56 miles) southeast of Łódź, on September 10 to visit the nearby headquarters of the German 10th Army and its commander, Walther von Reichenau. Instead of glad-handing the Nazi elite, however, she would witness some disturbing events.

On September 12, Końskie saw the funeral of four German soldiers who had been killed in combat some days earlier. Rumor had it that their bodies had been mutilated, so tempers among German troops were running unusually high. Groups of soldiers began combing the town for Jews, forty of whom would be set to work digging graves for the soldiers. Only a few of them were given shovels, however; the remainder had to dig with their bare hands while they were beaten and abused by the German mob. A Wehrmacht officer attempted in vain to maintain order.

Watching the scene, Riefenstahl was doubtless horrified by the yawning chasm between Nazism's pristine propaganda image, which she had helped create, and the bloody reality. When the officer departed, the violence increased, with the Jews being kicked and punched. According to her own account, Riefenstahl attempted to intervene, berating the men and imploring them to follow the order to disperse. In response, she claimed, she was herself abused and had a rifle pointed at her. It was at that moment that her distress was captured in a photograph taken by one of the soldiers: it showed tears staining her cheeks, an anguished grimace on her face.[55] Soon after that shot was taken, a brutal attempt to restore order triggered a wholesale massacre: an officer fired at fleeing

Jews, and soldiers started shooting blindly into the crowd. Twenty-two Jews were killed.[56] Riefenstahl was so upset that she asked that her war reporting engagement be canceled and returned to Berlin.[57]

As the massacre at Końskie showed, racism was one of the primary motivating factors in the German army's slide into barbarism. Memoirs and letters of Wehrmacht personnel from 1939 are full of sneering contempt for the country they were invading, many of them describing Poland as "Asiatic," "primitive," and "uncivilized." Typical, perhaps, was this soldier's description of the villages and civilians he encountered during the German advance northwest of Częstochowa: "The houses in these villages are crammed with filth, outside and inside. Tiled roofs are apparently unknown in Poland; one sees nothing but thatched cottages. The people who stand outside their huts and gape at us appear never to have heard of the word 'culture'; they all look dirty and bedraggled, the women as well as the men. It seems to me that these 'representatives of civilization' are in a competition to be the dirtiest."[58]

Some commentators allowed their anti-Semitic conditioning full expression. Passing close to Łódź, one soldier mockingly noted, among the refugees clogging the roads, "members of the Chosen People, of all, mostly revolting, shades." Referring to the crude cartoons of Jewish stereotypes often shown in the Nazi newspaper *Der Stürmer* (The Stormtrooper), he commented that such images, "which once appeared to us to be exaggerated, were eclipsed by the reality that we saw and smelled."[59] Another soldier, noting the Jews' "dirty, grease-smeared kaftans" and "lice-ridden hats," suggested that "those who do not know of the Jewish Question, or don't want to know about it, should be sent here. Here they can study it thoroughly and they will be converted."[60] Even Claus Schenk von Stauffenberg, the later hero of the German resistance—and Hitler's attempted assassin—appeared to share the racist zeitgeist. Serving with the 1st Light Division, part of the German 10th Army, he wrote home on September 14 from Kozienice on the Vistula, having fought his way through much of western Poland, describing the country as "desolate, all sand and dust," displaying "infinite poverty, clutter and shabbiness." The population was little better, in his view. He called

Open season: Jewish prisoners.
Muzeum II Wojny Światowej, Gdańsk

it "an unbelievable rabble," noting there were "very many Jews and [a] very much mixed population. A people which is surely only comfortable under the knout."[61]

Inevitably, petty humiliations and brutal persecutions followed on from such assessments. Where Jews were not shot outright, they could be forced to clean the streets on their hands and knees, or paraded around in market squares while being abused or beaten with rifle butts. They could be forced to have their beards publicly clipped, in violation of Orthodox Jewish prohibitions against shaving facial hair. One example must stand for the numberless instances of everyday tyranny. When, west of Bełchatów, two German infantrymen confronted a Jewish shopkeeper,

> he dug out all his old German vocabulary and stressed to us both that he was just an honest merchant and that we Germans were good people. He gesticulated with his hands and feet, but all his playacting left us with a sour taste in the mouth. . . . I said to Alfred that we should

make him disappear. He nodded, and we accompanied him into the kitchen. Alfred opened the cellar hatch—the cellar was three-quarters full with water—I gave "Isidor" a kick and he splattered into the water. The hatch was slammed down and we swiftly pushed heavy furniture on top of it. . . . As we left the house, on the other side of the road we saw a thickset Jewess crying like a little baby. . . . We warned "Rebecca" not to try and let "Isidor" out of his hopeless situation[;] otherwise she would find herself sharing the same fate.[62]

Events such as these were not anomalies or isolated occurrences; they were commonplace, witnessed in almost every village and town. The statistics speak for themselves: on the day of the Końskie massacre alone—September 12—there were 29 other massacres and executions around the region with nearly 300 victims. And that day was far from exceptional. Throughout September, the German campaign in Poland saw at least 615 such mass killings costing over 12,000 lives.[63]

Barbarism penetrated every sphere of the war. From the outset, the strafing of civilians from the air was routine, and columns of refugees were regular targets for German pilots. As the Polish air force disappeared from the skies, the Luftwaffe was left unchallenged and was able to bomb at will, hitting towns and villages with no air defenses and no military significance. One of the most egregious examples of this occurred on the afternoon of September 13, when German bombers of the Luftwaffe's 8th Air Corps appeared in the skies above Frampol, a small town in southern Poland west of Zamość. Far from the front lines, Frampol had already been bombed a couple of times, but that afternoon observers saw, "at high altitude, four threes of German bombers . . . moving across the sky, symmetrically, evenly suspended in the air, more like a fly-past than an attack," as one eyewitness later recalled. Within moments, the center of the town was consumed in a flash of explosions: "Flames shoot into the sky and the hell on earth is crowned with a black cloud of smoke," he said.[64] Then, as soon as they had arrived, the bombers departed, leaving Frampol "a sea of fire."

Although casualties on the ground were few, little of the town itself survived the inferno.

The bombing of Frampol, which had no military presence or strategic significance, is thought to have been purely experimental. The town was built on a perfect geometric grid that converged on a central square with a town hall and church—a layout that allowed Luftwaffe observers to photograph and measure the bombing's results. The town was destroyed, it appears, simply to give German pilots and bombardiers a chance to practice their nefarious art.[65] Barbarism had become the new normal.

Facing this threat, the Poles did everything they could to defend themselves. They even launched a counteroffensive. Though German advance formations had already reached the suburbs of Warsaw, owing to their swift progress, they had left considerable Polish forces in their wake—forces that might still constitute a threat. German intelligence about Polish forces was "truly wretched," as one German staff officer lamented.[66] Between Warsaw and Łódź, eight Polish divisions were unaccounted for; some, certainly, had ceased to exist—their shattered remnants clogging the routes to the capital—but others were still very much present. Among the latter was the entire Poznań Army, which had been outflanked by the German invasion and was yet to see serious action. Its commander, General Tadeusz Kutrzeba, was a fifty-three-year-old veteran who had already had an eventful career. He had witnessed the assassination of Archduke Franz Ferdinand in Sarajevo in 1914, while serving as an officer in the Austro-Hungarian Army, and thereafter, during the First World War, he had seen action on the Balkan and Russian fronts. Considered something of an intellectual, he had been appointed commander of the Polish Military Academy in 1928, where he had overseen a number of strategic studies and had become an advocate of mechanization.

Yet Kutrzeba had been bypassed by the German invasion of 1939. Commanding the Poznań Army, his had been the most westerly of Polish military districts, centered in the natural salient of Wielkopolska,

Major-General Tadeusz Kutrzeba,
Polish commander on the Bzura.
public domain

around the cities of Poznań and Gniezno. And when the German advance focused on a swift assault on Warsaw, with the main thrusts coming from Silesia and East Prussia, his Poznań Army had found itself sidelined, largely unengaged, and seemingly doomed to a dispiriting retreat eastward toward the capital.

The Poznań Army did not meekly accept its fate, however. "We were raging with the frustration of impotence," one of its senior officers wrote, and in this situation, they "preferred to plunge into a deadly battle."[67] Echoing those sentiments, Kutrzeba petitioned the Polish commander-in-chief, Edward Śmigły-Rydz, to permit him to launch a flanking attack on the German 8th Army to his south.

As he later wrote, his logic was simple: "Further marches with their physical and psychological burdens would weaken us without bringing any tactical advantages. We left [Wielkopolska] voluntarily, apparently without any desire to fight. Now battle was generally desired." He thought that attacking the German flank, where the 30th Infantry Division was spread out over some 25 kilometers (15 miles)—and was not expecting an attack from the north—promised "a real chance of success."[68]

Initially, then, Śmigły-Rydz was unimpressed by Kutrzeba's proposal to attack—believing that his general harbored some overly optimistic assumptions about Polish martial spirit—and reiterated that his forces were ordered to march toward Warsaw.[69] But in the chaos of the High Command's evacuation, communications temporarily broke down, and Kutrzeba, seeing an opportunity to relieve the capital and enable some of those forces still west of Warsaw to withdraw eastward, decided to go it alone. On the afternoon of September 9, his forces—including the 14th, 17th, and 25th Infantry Divisions—struck southward on a broad 20-kilometer (12-mile) front across the river Bzura and into the German flank.

The first target that day was Łęczyca, a historic little town astride the Bzura, which had been captured by the Germans a few days before. In his zeal, the local Polish commander—Brigadier-General Edmund Knoll-Kownacki—launched the assault earlier than ordered, thereby alerting the Germans to the Polish threat. Nonetheless, Knoll-Kownacki's men were successful, spurred by the desire to prove themselves. As one artilleryman recalled, the men of his battery, "tired of the nine-day retreat, at last began shelling the enemy. And you should have seen them bustle about their guns!" The cavalry, too, had their tails up. "When we reached Łęczyca," an officer of the Pomeranian Cavalry Brigade wrote, "I experienced a very happy moment for the first time in the September campaign: we were no longer retreating."[70]

Roles were being reversed: it was the Germans now who were fleeing in disarray. Łęczyca erupted in a popular uprising. "Suddenly the town is full of people, emerging from cellars and tunnels," one chronicler wrote. "They are armed, they attack retreating wounded and individual combat vehicles, destroy telephone lines and light signals close to the command post." That night the commanding officer of the German 46th Infantry Regiment made desperate appeals to his superiors for reinforcements, describing their situation as "hopeless."[71] German losses in Łęczyca were indeed substantial. As a Polish cavalryman recalled, "That night, the streets were strewn with the corpses of so many men that we had great difficulty getting through the bloodstained town. Even our mounts snorted with displeasure as they stepped over the dead."[72]

A similar story unfolded the next day near Piątek, 10 kilometers (6.2 miles) to the east, where Polish forces again demonstrated their mettle. A soldier in an SA detachment who was defending the town against repeated Polish attacks described the brutal engagement, recalling that the fourth assault was the most determined:

> From all directions came machine-gun fire. And . . . while the machine guns strafed our foxholes from both flanks and close in front . . . hand grenades and mortars crashed into our positions every few minutes. Our sector was being pounded systematically, and with astounding accuracy, from both the left and right sides. The men could neither move nor establish the enemy's firing positions. Already in the first volley, two men in their foxhole were thoroughly peppered by shrapnel. They were killed outright.[73]

A Polish officer with the 58th Infantry Regiment witnessed what happened next:

> The men were quickened with new energy and strength when—what we could not hear, but could guess—an order ran along the lines: "Fix bayonets, grenades at the ready.". . . The whole advance line throws grenades, then drops to the ground for a moment and after five to seven seconds the German positions are engulfed in a powerful rumble of explosions. At the same time, under the cover of dust and smoke from the grenades, our infantrymen fall on the Germans, stabbing with their bayonets those who had not escaped, clubbing them with the butts of their rifles, wreaking havoc and terror in the German lines.[74]

Farther east, at Łowicz, the fighting was just as intense. The town was initially liberated by units of the 64th Infantry Division at dawn on

September 12. As a reconnaissance officer recalled, the Germans did not give up easily, instead fighting for every inch, but the Poles prevailed. "The town is now quiet," he wrote:

> Enemy survivors, lost and marauding in our rear, have been eliminated. German troops who had been trying to hold the southeast end of the town have retreated. The morning, sunny after a misty dawn, floods the liberated town with happy sunlight. The townspeople fill the streets, expressing their joy in every way they can. There are flowers, buckets of hot and cold drinks, bread, sweets, fruit, and no end of joyful cheers.[75]

The Polish offensive was bringing some genuine success. All along the line south of the Bzura, German forces were in retreat, and countless villages and towns were being liberated. For the Germans, after the rapid advances of the previous ten days, such setbacks came as a shock. As one staff officer recalled, "There was bad news followed by more bad news, raining down on us like blows from a club."[76] For the Poles, however, these were heady days. "We stayed hard on their heels reclaiming one town after another," one cavalryman wrote. "We pursued the enemy for almost three days and villagers we met along the way greeted us affectionately as their deliverers, weeping and kissing our boots. I will never forget the feelings that I experienced then."[77] Such enthusiasm proved infectious. When Śmigły-Rydz belatedly made contact with Kutrzeba to give the Bzura operations his retrospective blessing, he advised the general to continue his advance in the direction of Radom, over 100 kilometers (62 miles) from his current position.[78] In New York, meanwhile, the Associated Press reported, erroneously, that Łódź had been liberated.[79]

The thrill of liberation would not last. Already on September 10, with the Bzura campaign barely under way, Army Group South was preparing a German counterattack concentrating on the area immediately west of Warsaw, so as to cut off any Polish attempt to withdraw

"Quickened with new energy and strength": Polish cavalry advance
through Sochaczew during the Battle on the Bzura.
Wikimedia; public domain

to the capital.[80] Moreover, the Poznań Army's successes on the Bzura
had largely been attained by exploiting the element of surprise, as well
as by moving troops at night, so as to negate German air superiority. It
remained to be seen whether such tactics would continue to be effective.
Most crucially, while the German line on the Bzura had buckled, and
the Wehrmacht had been forced to cede territory, it had not broken.
Polish victories there had been dearly won—paid for, as Kutrzeba put
it, "with too much blood"[81]—and some units were already at the end of
their strength. The inevitable German counterattack would test their
resolve and morale all over again.

It was at the height of the Polish offensive on the Bzura that Hitler
decided to visit his commanders in nearby Łódź. Arriving by air on the
morning of September 13, he proceeded to a briefing with General Kurt
von Briesen, commander of the 30th Infantry Division, which had been

so mauled by the Poles over the preceding days. Briesen greeted Hitler at his field headquarters, a schoolhouse well within range of Polish artillery. With his right arm plastered and suspended in a sling, owing to shrapnel injuries he had sustained during the defense of Piątek three days earlier, the general evidently made a favorable impression. Asked about his injury, Briesen informed his commander-in-chief that he had led his last reserve battalion into action in spite of his wounds. Turning to his liaison officer, Hitler swooned, "That's how I imagined a Prussian general to be when I was a child."[82] Later, Hitler was even more effusive in his admiration when talking to Field Marshal Wilhelm Keitel: "You can't have enough soldiers like that. He's a man after my own heart."[83]

When it came, the German counterattack was ferocious. Despite pushing back all along the line, its focus was the eastern end of the front, around Łowicz and Sochaczew, which would become a pinch-point in the Polish attempt to withdraw toward Warsaw. If the Germans could cut off that line of retreat, they would encircle all the Polish forces fighting on the Bzura. As Count Johann von Kielmansegg noted, "The Pole must realize what is at stake. If he is defeated, then his fate will finally be sealed."[84]

Anticipating this bottleneck on the eastern Bzura, Kutrzeba ordered his forces there to advance southward toward the town of Skierniewice, to relieve the pressure. Because of Polish exhaustion and German reinforcements, however, that advance was stillborn. Worse still, rather than hold their bridgehead on the southern bank of the Bzura, the local commander, General Władysław Bortnowski—seemingly fearful of approaching German armor—ordered his men to withdraw to the north bank of the river. Bortnowski, whose Pomeranian Army had been largely destroyed in the battles for the Polish Corridor, may well have been psychologically scarred by his experiences, leaving his decision-making fatally impaired. One of his colleagues, Brigadier-General Mikołaj Bołtuć, certainly thought so. He told General Wiktor Thommée that he had found Bortnowski on the road north of Sochaczew, and that he seemed to have suffered a "complete nervous breakdown." Bortnowski, refusing to believe that the Bzura offensive could bring any success, ordered his men not to fire on the Germans, lest they provoke retaliation, Bołtuć said. Bołtuć was understandably furious at this evident dereliction of soldierly duty. "If I die, let everyone know that I died because of that son of a bitch," he told Thommée.[85] Two days later, Bołtuć was killed in battle outside Warsaw.

If Bortnowski was indeed suffering from shell-shock, the days that followed would not have helped his mental state. Despite his defeatist instructions, his men fought valiantly at Łowicz and Sochaczew, holding out against German forces that had been reinforced by units drawn from the western suburbs of Warsaw, including elements of the 4th Panzer Division and Hitler's elite SS-Leibstandarte. After three days of intense fighting, however, the Polish line finally gave way. At Sochaczew, the remaining Polish forces withdrew northward across the river early on September 15. "The Germans were close," a Polish sergeant recalled. "We could see the flashes of heavy machine guns firing. Just before we reached the river, [a lieutenant] fell mortally wounded. Not one officer was left in our company."[86] Kurt Meyer, a *Brigadeführer* in the SS-Leibstandarte, had nothing but admiration for his opponents. "The Poles . . . proved repeatedly that they knew how to die," he later wrote. "It would be unjust to deny the courage of these Polish units. The fighting on the Bzura was desperate and intense. The best Polish blood was mixed with the river water. The Poles' losses were terrifying."[87] At Łowicz, the scene was similar. There, Janusz Bardziński, a lieutenant in the 17th Wielkopolska Cavalry Brigade, which had been holding the bridge during the Polish withdrawal, sent a final message as the Germans approached: "Enemy infantry at assault range. I am under mortar and machine gun barrage. Most lancers killed or injured. I am lightly wounded. Still doing my duty, but it is too late for help. That's all, Colonel. For Country and Regiment. This is my last report."[88]

Though the German ground assault was harrowing enough, attacks from the air were even more devastating. The Poles had largely avoided the attentions of the Luftwaffe during their advance, but once they lost the initiative on the battlefield, they began to feel the full might of German air superiority, with wave after wave of enemy aircraft bombing and

The chaos of defeat: a Polish supply train.
Muzeum II Wojny Światowej, Gdańsk

strafing the fleeing columns at will. "No one dared to part with Mother Earth!" one Polish officer wrote in his diary. "Whoever raised his head was hit with a burst of bullets from the planes, which, having completed their task of destroying fighting formations, went after individual people, wagons, riders, and even horses."[89] General Kutrzeba himself experienced the power of the Luftwaffe while crossing the Bzura at Witkowice: "Every movement, every grouping, all the routes of advance were subjected to a pounding from the air," he wrote. "Hell on earth had begun. The bridges were destroyed, the fords jammed, the columns waiting to cross destroyed by bombs." In a grimly symbolic scene, the commander of the Bzura offensive was forced to lie low in a copse, unable to cross the river until the air attack ceased.[90]

Polish morale plummeted after the bombardments. One officer bemoaned the fact that his men had no antiaircraft equipment, and so were "left with nothing but helpless anger" at the resulting slaughter.[91] Count von Kielmansegg recalled that, even after they had been taken prisoner, some Poles were "half mad with fear, and throw themselves to the ground when even the sound of aircraft engines can be heard." The Polish officers, he noted, were "visibly shattered and constantly expressing the opinion, somewhat apologetically, that no one can withstand tanks and *Stukas.*"[92]

As the Germans pushed north toward the Vistula in an attempt to cut Polish forces off from an eastward retreat toward Warsaw, the battle degenerated into a slaughter. The remaining Polish units desperately tried to hold the line to enable their fellows to escape. For some, it was an ignominious flight. One officer with the Pomeranian Cavalry Brigade, Roman Bąkowski, was crushed by the order that his unit was to ford the Bzura on foot and leave its horses behind. He wrote, "We bid a sad farewell to our mounts. To me personally, it was very difficult, leaving my racehorse, the mare Cysterna, whom I had ridden at the Polish Army Championship in Lwów in 1938, and who was like a second fiancée to me. I unsaddled and unbridled her, kissed her, and let her loose with hundreds of other horses. She was free from her faithful service."[93]

Though Bąkowski would escape the German noose, navigating his way on foot through the German lines to Warsaw, others were not so lucky. Czesław Szczepaniak, an artillery lieutenant, witnessed the aftermath of a German assault on the village of Budy Iłowskie, close to the Vistula, on September 16. There, enemy tanks had destroyed a horse-drawn artillery battery unit while soldiers were attempting to maneuver to new positions. "A terrible sight!" he wrote. "Some of the riders' bodies seemed frozen on the backs of their dead horses, with a gun or whip still in their hands, with fear in their eyes or a mouth grimaced with pain, with faces covered with dried sweat and blood. Other bodies, fallen or kneeling at the guns, lying next to their faithful horses, next to wagons and ammunition, and farther on, bodies mangled by tanks, the ground mixed with blood."[94]

Such images would have been familiar to the Italian war correspondent Indro Montanelli. Accompanying German forces, he was brought to the Bzura battlefields and shown the corpses of Polish cavalrymen and their horses as they were being cleared. He duly penned an article for the *Corriere della Sera* titled "Cavalli contro autoblindo" (Horses against armored cars) in which he wrote of war's "cruel grimacing face." He specifically described the streets where "dead horses marked the senseless route of the Polish cavalry," which, he said, had been "launched in desperation against the wall of armored German units." He went on to imagine—quite inaccurately—how the scene might have unfolded, waxing lyrical about "four furious charges" by the Polish cavalrymen, "with heads down and lance in hand, like a tournament of centuries ago": "Wild charges of horses launched themselves into the blockade of German fire, dashing into this line of fire, wave after wave of horses falling and rotting in a chaotic, bloody tangle, reminiscent of the ditches of Waterloo, of bullfights, of seething nets of tuna. Then, as the dust and earth torn up by the bombing settled, horses without riders and riders without horses could be seen wandering the arid wasteland."

"Horses against armored vehicles," Montanelli concluded, was "the leitmotiv of this war."[95] Some days later, his words were duly reported by the German magazine *Die Wehrmacht*, and from there—mixed with stories of the engagement at Krojanty on the opening day of the war—they became a staple ingredient of German propaganda. Even the otherwise sensible American radio correspondent William Shirer was taken in by the story. Visiting the former Polish Corridor on September 18, he wrote in his diary, "In the woods in the Corridor, the sickening sweet smell of dead horses and the sweeter smell of dead men. Here, the Germans say, a whole division of Polish cavalry charged against hundreds of tanks and was annihilated." "Against tanks the Poles used cavalry," he told listeners in a broadcast two days later, "and the result was terrible—for the cavalry."[96] With that, a myth was born, which persists even today.[97]

Of the many lies and inaccuracies of Montanelli's article, perhaps the most egregious was the contention that the Germans fought their enemy in a chivalrous manner, aiming their guns low to avoid unnecessary casualties. This was so far from the truth that one must wonder whether Montanelli visited the front lines at all. Chivalry was little in evidence on the German side. Instead, there were numerous atrocities affecting Polish soldiers and civilians alike. Already at the very beginning of the fighting on the Bzura, German soldiers in the villages, threatened by the Polish advance north of Zgierz, began rounding up male civilians. As they withdrew, their captives were corralled into barns, which were then set on fire. Those who tried to escape the inferno were machine-gunned. Similar actions occurred all along the front line. At Łowicz, men of the 31st Infantry Division moved from street to street blindly throwing hand grenades into houses.[98] At Piątek, 70 Poles were rounded up and shot on September 14. Three days later a further 76 were slaughtered at Henryków, northwest of Sochaczew.[99]

Such actions cannot be excused by the "heat of battle," as many of these massacres occurred long after the fighting had ceased. At Jasieniec on September 16, for example, German tanks shelled a Polish field hospital that was clearly marked with the Red Cross sign, killing 50 wounded soldiers.[100] After the fall of Kutno, around 6,000 men were rounded up in the town center; among them were soldiers and other "suspicious elements," many of whom were shot.[101] As ever, Jews were especially targeted. At Błonie, for instance, on September 18, members of the SS-Leibstandarte massacred some 50 Jews who had been detained earlier by the Wehrmacht.[102]

Amid this catalog of barbarism, one of the worst examples occurred at Śladów, close to the Vistula, on September 18. There, advancing German armored units used civilians as "human shields" to face down remaining elements of Polish cavalry. When the fighting was finished, they were ordered to bury the dead and told they would be freed afterward. Events soon took an even more sinister turn. As a survivor remembered:

> The officer gave an order to lead us over to the embankment, and assembled us at the edge of the river, along with all the seriously wounded soldiers. Unable to walk, they had been carried there. Some soldiers hidden in the reeds came out of hiding and . . . were shot on the spot. At the sight of this, all of those arrested began to plead for mercy. The Germans laughed and called us "Polish dogs." They lined us up in two rows, on the right flank about 150 Polish soldiers, on the

One of many: a German massacre of civilians.
akg-images

left civilians between 15 and 75 years old, also around 150 in number. There was one man who had his 4-year-old son with him; the Germans took the boy away, but he kept crying for his father, so they got angry and brought the child back.

When the machine guns began firing, the Poles jumped into the river to escape the slaughter, but were shot by the soldiers "like wild ducks." There were only two survivors: men who managed to hide under the river bank before swimming away to safety under cover of darkness.[103] The massacre claimed 358 lives.

The more fortunate Poles managed to surrender and survive. Once their positions were overrun, or escape became impossible, most laid down their weapons and hoped they would be treated decently. Count von Kielmansegg found it remarkable "how quickly and completely the Polish attack . . . collapsed." "The enemy does not withdraw," he recalled with a whiff of contempt. "He doesn't flee. No, he surrenders, on the spot, where he meets the counterattack. They surrender in their thousands."[104] In the village of Sanniki, advancing Germans approached the church—the only building left standing—and were surprised to find a company of Polish soldiers inside, praying by candlelight. As the Germans entered, the Poles simply stood up, laid their guns on the floor, and silently surrendered.[105]

In due course, these prisoners would be taken to a *Dulag*—a *Durchgangslager*, or "transit camp," often a Polish army barracks or similar site, where they would be registered and sorted by rank, place of residence, and usefulness for physical labor. Thereafter, privates and noncommissioned officers (NCOs) would be sent to a *Stalag*, where they would be employed as laborers, while officers would be dispatched to an *Oflag*, where they were not required to work.[106] Unsurprisingly, perhaps, large numbers of Polish prisoners were unenthusiastic about the prospect of a life of hard labor in a prisoner-of-war camp, and many tried to abscond before their fates were sealed. Mixing into Polish society, such fugitives would form the vanguard of the Polish Underground.

Others avoided surrender altogether, slipping through German lines as the ring closed around the remnants of the Poznań and Pomeranian Armies in the Bzura pocket. One officer later recalled running with his men past German positions at night, with wild firing chasing their progress. Regrouping at sunrise, he ordered his men to split up: "Knowing that we could no longer move as a unit, I told the men to make their way to Warsaw on their own," he said. "Through fields and pastures, keeping away from the roads, the last soldiers of the 8th Mounted Rifles Regiment headed in toward the capital."[107]

They were joining a ragged mass: the remnants of armies that—if not already defeated—were exhausted and gravely damaged by their experiences. As Colonel Ludwik Czyżewski noted, the tide of traveling troops was "moving at a pace of no more than 2 kilometers (1.2 miles) per hour." Indeed, they presented an easy target to the enemy: "Had an organized and disciplined German unit appeared at that time and opened fire on this packed mass of soldiers, a devastating panic would have broken out. For nobody was thinking of any kind of reconnaissance or protection for the marching troops. All anyone had on their mind was to reach Warsaw as fast as possible."[108] Such were the ravages of war, however, that the city to which they were heading was already scarcely recognizable.

Chapter Six

OF "LIBERATORS" AND ABSENT FRIENDS

W ARSAW IN 1939 WAS ONE OF THE MOST IMPRESSIVE CAPI-
tals of Central Europe. Perched on an escarpment on the left
bank of the Vistula, the city center—clustered around a beautiful old
medieval town often painted by Canaletto[1]—had all the accoutrements
of a modern metropolis: a university, an opera house, and a concert hall
as well as numerous ministries and palaces, avenues and parks, and
churches and patrician residences. Little wonder, perhaps, that it was
once known as the "Paris of the North."

By the third week of the war, however, battered Warsaw had already
become a shadow of its former self, bearing the scars not only of aerial
assault but also of artillery attack. Many of the city's landmarks had
been hit by now, including the nineteenth-century Citadel, the main
railway station, and the bridges spanning the Vistula. Arriving in the
capital from the fortress at Modlin that week, Colonel Stanisław Sosabowski quickly became aware of "a cloud of dark smoke hanging lazily
over the city." He would soon see the wounds of war. As they "breast[ed]
a small rise," he wrote, "the silhouette of Warsaw was suddenly spread
out before us. At once, we could see something was different—something was missing. Apart from the clouds of smoke, the smell of burning

and the flickering orange flames, the outline of the town had changed. The towers and spires of the churches, the well-known landmarks, had toppled into piles of rubble."[2]

The city Sosabowski was entering was not yet under siege. Though German troops had arrived in the southwestern suburbs on the evening of September 8, their advance had been halted and then stalled thanks to the Polish counterattack on the Bzura, which had necessitated the westward transfer of some of the German troops then close to Warsaw. Once the threat of a breakthrough on the Bzura had abated, however, the German pressure on the capital again increased. There were more air raids, more probing attacks in the southwest, and, crucially, a fast-moving pincer advance deep into the city's eastern hinterland. As one diarist noted with alarm on September 15, "The Germans are attempting to surround Warsaw."[3]

Since the breakthrough on the Narew, General Guderian's forces had raced southward, aiming not only to cut off Warsaw, but also to block a possible Polish retreat toward Brest and prevent the Poles from sabotaging vital infrastructure. Guderian himself was setting the fast pace of the advance. Colonel Hans-Karl von Esebeck encountered the general by the roadside and was asked for his map:

> On my map-board I always have my map folded so that it displays the area we might cover in a good day's march. "No, no," says the general, "unfold the whole map." Then, pointing at the map, now hanging down to the ground: "Can you see the bridge over the Bug down there? That's the one I've got to have—by early tomorrow morning." I cannot believe my ears. A hundred kilometres as the crow flies . . . and it is already beginning to get dark.[4]

Esebeck and his men achieved their objective, securing the crucial crossing over the river Bug east of Sokołów by dawn the next day. It was a perfect demonstration of the new art of war.

The Germans did not have everything their own way. At Kałuszyn, 50 kilometers (30 miles) east of Warsaw, the southward advance of the

44th Infantry Regiment was halted dramatically on the night of September 11–12. German forces had taken the town the previous day, dug in, and herded the civilian population into the cemetery, so that no one could inform the nearby Polish troops of their presence. But those Polish units, including the 11th Uhlan Regiment, were well aware of the Germans' arrival, and they were determined to strike back before German reinforcements could secure the position. A plan was devised whereby a frontal cavalry assault would drive the Germans into an ambush set up along their likely line of retreat, the road east to Siedlce. The counterattack began when the 4th Squadron of the 11th Uhlans thundered into the town under cover of darkness, scattering German infantrymen as they went. As their commander, Lieutenant Andrzej Żyliński, recalled:

> We entered the first gardens of Kałuszyn. There were more Germans here, they fled like rabbits over the fences, into the gardens and orchards. We couldn't follow them, so we kept on, still shouting "Hurrah!" We emerged into a road crossing. . . . We kept on galloping toward the center of Kałuszyn. The Germans fired flares: the place was as bright as day. In front of us a large group of Germans was running away, several dozen of them. A German officer tried to stop them, shouting.[5]

Żyliński's cavalry charge may have been carried out in error, following a misunderstanding with his superior officer.[6] Nonetheless, the Polish cavalry seized the initiative, unseated the occupiers, and enabled infantry detachments, among them elements of the 6th Legions Regiment, to rout the Germans. By dawn, Kałuszyn was again in Polish hands. An armored counterattack had been beaten back and the ambush on the Siedlce road had harassed the German retreat. But victory came at a heavy cost. Losses on both sides were considerable, numbering well into the hundreds, and included some 50 of Żyliński's horses. A German battalion commander, Major Krawutschke, was thought to have committed suicide.[7] When the fighting was over, only 62 of the town's 645 buildings were still standing. As one eyewitness recalled, "The market square was covered with corpses in field-gray uniforms, ripped by cannons and mortars."[8]

The respite gained by the Polish victory at Kałuszyn could only be temporary, however. Just to the west, Brigadier-General Władysław Anders, one of the Polish army's most gifted commanders, was ordered to attack with his Nowogródek Cavalry Brigade near Mińsk-Mazowiecki. Despite making good progress, he was driven back and forced to disengage. It is testament to the chaos that engulfed the Polish High Command in the early weeks of September that Anders and his men were initially ordered to hold the line to the west of Warsaw before being moved 50 kilometers (30 miles) eastward, across the Vistula, to engage German forces east of the capital. Withdrawing after the engagement, he passed through the town of Garwolin, where "there was nothing left but dying embers, for on the eve of our passage through the town, the German air force had burned it down," Anders later wrote. "The many human corpses and dead horses on the streets bore witness to their visit."[9] With that, Anders continued southeast, heading for Lublin.

Warsaw was being surrounded, and after the Polish counteroffensive faltered in the marshes of the Bzura, it found itself at the heart of a narrowing core of territory ranging from the fortress of Modlin, 25 kilometers (15 miles) north of the capital, to the town of Otwock, a similar distance to the south. Modlin itself represented a formidable obstacle to the German advance. Here a vast complex of fortifications, some dating to Napoleonic times, guarded the confluence of the Vistula and the Narew, and with that, the northern approaches to Warsaw. In September 1939, it already contained huge amounts of men and military materiel, including 4 infantry divisions—totaling some 15,000 men—plus 96 artillery pieces, 7 tanks, and Armored Train No. 15, christened *Śmierć*, or "Death."[10] Any army seeking to take Warsaw first had to neutralize Modlin.

West of the capital, Polish-held territory included most of Kampinos Forest, where the remnants of General Kutrzeba's Pomeranian and Poznań Armies had found refuge. Yet, as Kutrzeba himself explained, the forest was under constant German attack, particularly from the air. "It's dreadful what's happening in the Kampinos," he told General Wiktor Thommée. "I have never been through anything like that. It's a nightmare. Hundreds killed and wounded, incessant fire, panic-stricken troops running in all directions without a purpose, always under enemy bombs. I don't know how I got out of that hell."[11] As Thommée recalled, it took a long time for Kutrzeba to recover his composure.

Some of the inhabitants of Warsaw would doubtless have shared Kutrzeba's mental and physical exhaustion. Yet the two weeks of air attack had not yet dampened the upbeat mood. Returning to the city on September 14, one Varsovian noted that despite the many elaborate barricades that had been hastily erected on the streets, "life seemed more or less normal." While soldiers were ever present, and civilians had to endure air raids and make do with dwindling supplies, "the general impression was one of restrained hope and optimism," according to one who was present.[12] A sense of solidarity emerged, with countless volunteers assisting in preparing the city for the coming onslaught. Some of them helped the many refugees already clogging the streets; others answered the call for assistance in digging defenses, though there were not enough spades to go around.[13] Soldiers exhausted by their days-long march to the capital would have their feet washed at the roadside in a "simple, humble contribution" by Warsaw's womenfolk.[14] The pianist Władysław Szpilman, who had joined in the labor gangs digging trenches in the suburbs, described an elderly Jewish man—"a black whirlwind of kaftan and beard"—working alongside him, hacking at the baked earth with "Biblical fervour." When Szpilman tried to persuade the man to go home and rest, he was told, "I have a shop." The man then gave an anguished sob and continued digging. It seemed everyone had something to defend. Szpilman dug for two days straight.[15]

Many Varsovians were acutely aware that they were fighting for a higher cause. For the new civilian commissar of Warsaw, Stefan Starzyński, it was a fight for an eternal Poland: a nation that once again stood as a bulwark of humanity and culture. "The people of Warsaw will endure all tempests, all storms, all raids, all bombs," he announced in one of his radio addresses. "They will not flinch, for they know that the Hitlerite plague shall be destroyed, that Germany's disgrace will forever bury that nation and that nothing will ever wipe away this shame, and Poland will emerge from this war victorious, strong and powerful . . . to the glory of the country and to the glory of the whole world, whose culture and civilization she has protected many times from barbaric hordes."[16] For others, their resistance was also aiding Poland's British and French allies, who they imagined were fighting the Germans on the western front. "The radio announced that the German attack on Warsaw has been stopped," one housewife noted. "Of course, they are not far away, but thank you God even for this, because every day's delay is crucial for the Allied advance from the west."[17]

But for all the defiance of its inhabitants, Warsaw was in dire peril. One diarist noted how the German aerial attack over the city was stepped up, often defeating the city's efforts to defend itself. "No air-raid warnings were given now," he wrote. "They had crippled the city and its defense preparations." The bombers loomed high above the city, silhouetted against the blue September sky. "We had to hurry down into the cellars," he recalled. "If a bomb fell on the building beneath which you were hiding, it meant certain death; it was the bullet in this deadly game of Russian roulette."[18] Marta Korwin witnessed a German air raid as she passed a market square: "I stopped . . . to let [the crowd] pass. At that moment a bomb dropped on the pavement; it stood upright and then exploded. I had not heard the plane. I had seen bombs dropping from a plane's belly before, but only this time did I see a bomb touch the ground and then explode. A number of people fell down like bags of sand; the rest vanished. My driver and I jumped out of the truck to see if we could help, but they had all been killed outright."[19]

By now, heavy artillery shells were landing on the city at a rate of forty every hour—one every ninety seconds. "One never knew," one diarist wrote, "from which direction a shell would come; it would come without warning, and seemingly without purpose."[20] Władysław Szpilman recalled how the roads were quickly choked with rubble as well as with the corpses of horses and civilians, making it difficult for him to reach the radio station where his piano recitals were intended to raise the city's mood. "More and more buildings lost their window panes," he wrote. "There were round holes in the walls where they suffered a hit, and corners of masonry were knocked off. By night the sky was red with the glow of firelight and the air full of the smell of burning."[21]

The lack of food in the city began to make life hard for Varsovians. Bread lines became commonplace, and people scavenged. "If a horse was killed in the street, people queued to go at it with kitchen knives," one memoirist wrote. The bombing offered one positive: "After each raid, thousands of stunned fish floated to the surface of the Vistula, some of them enormous. The men collected the fish into buckets and we had excellent feasts."[22]

One of the most clear-eyed observers of Warsaw's suffering during the German siege was the American photographer Julien Bryan, who arrived in the city on September 7, just after most of the foreigners and government officials had left. Though he momentarily questioned his own sanity, he swiftly recognized the opportunity that had landed in his lap: this was, he said, "the kind of scoop that every photographer and newspaperman dreams about." Meeting with Stefan Starzyński, he was left in no doubt about the significance of his presence. "Your pictures may prove to be of real importance," Warsaw's former mayor told him, "so that the world may know what has happened here." Bryan was duly provided with a guide, an interpreter, a car—a battered 1936 Adler Trumpf—and a permit to photograph whatever he liked.[23] He would become the primary visual chronicler of the siege of Warsaw.

Bryan crisscrossed the city that September photographing the bread lines, the barricades, the aftermath of the bombing, and—most memorably—the human cost of war. He visited recently bombed hospitals, which were full of hysterical patients and stoic staff; and he saw the effects of a direct hit on a residential block on a street named Na Skarpie. It "looked as if a giant with an ice-cream scoop had taken out the entire central section," he later wrote. Inside, the bodies of fourteen women and children would be recovered. But it is Bryan's photographic portraits of ordinary Varsovians that are most striking: the young boy

Kazimiera Mika bends over the body of her sister, killed in a German air raid. *Julien Bryan; public domain*

sitting, his chin in his hand, amid the rubble of his former home; the pained, pinched faces of the housewives in the bread line, who knew that a similar queue had been attacked by German aircraft the day before, but were loath to give up their place; the elderly woman standing dazed before the remains of her house, clutching two silver spoons and a pair of scissors—all she had left.

Bryan took his most memorable images when he came across the aftermath of a German strafing raid on September 13. In a small field close to Powązki Cemetery west of the city, a group of women had been digging for potatoes when a Luftwaffe plane raked the area with machine-gun fire, killing two of them. When he arrived, Bryan began photographing the bloody scene, but was interrupted by ten-year-old Kazimiera Mika, the younger sister of one of the dead, who seemingly couldn't understand why her sister would not speak to her:

"What has happened?" she cried. Then she leaned down, touched the dead girl's face, and drew back in horror. "Oh, my beautiful sister!" she wailed. "What have they done to you?" Then, after a few seconds:

"Please talk to me! Please, oh, please! What will become of me without you!" The child looked at us in bewilderment. I threw my arm about her and held her tightly, trying to comfort her. She cried. So did I and the two Polish officers who were with me. What could we, or anyone else, say to this child?[24]

Bryan's picture of Kazimiera pleading and bending over her sister's dead body would become one of the most iconic images of the war.

At the same time, the atmosphere in the capital was febrile—full of panic, conspiracy theories, and rumors of German spies and "diversants" (saboteurs). According to Wacław Lipiński, Polish propaganda—of which he was a primary exponent—was partly to blame by circulating wild stories of the Germans dropping poisoned sweets or gas-filled balloons. By fostering anxiety and mutual suspicion, Lipiński believed, such stories were "nothing short of criminal."[25] They also produced some unintended consequences. Władysław Szpilman recalled an elderly spinster in his apartment block with a German-sounding surname who refused to go down to the air-raid shelter; instead, she remained in her apartment stoically playing the piano. Concluding that she must be a spy, signaling to the Germans via her piano-playing, the building's staff decided to tie her up and confine her to the basement. In so doing, they inadvertently saved the old lady's life, as her flat was destroyed a few hours later by an artillery strike.[26]

As well as wrestling with their own paranoia, the capital's defenders were outnumbered and outgunned. One sergeant recalled how the arrival of some thirty-five volunteers cheered his men, but then he noted that the new arrivals were armed only with old French rifles; moreover, they had only about "60 rounds each . . . as well as one hand grenade each." Though they lacked equipment, they had "full and fervent hearts" and a "desire to fight the ancient barbaric enemy."[27] Commanding the 21st Infantry Regiment in the defense of Praga, on the east bank of the Vistula, Colonel Stanisław Sosabowski told a similar tale, recalling that his men had so little artillery ammunition that for every hundred shells the Germans fired, "we could return only one." Often, enemy patrols would be allowed to advance right up to his positions before his men opened fire, and where possible they would engage the Germans with bayonets rather than waste bullets.[28] Faced with enemy superiority, his men had to use every advantage they possessed. Thus, while lying low during the day, the soldiers would come to life at night, with patrols sweeping the area to "keep the Germans awake and guessing." "We knew every street, every back alley, every garden," Sosabowski wrote. "We had maps showing plans of the drains and underground cables; we knew every entry and every exit; my men could go where they pleased. The Germans never knew where we would strike next."[29]

In truth, the German forces were biding their time. They had expected Warsaw to be surrendered without a fight, and now, though the air assault continued unabated, many of the armored spearheads had been withdrawn to meet the Polish threat on the Bzura, leaving mostly infantry troops to hold the line around the capital. As General Franz Halder noted in his diary on September 15, with the city almost surrounded, his preference was to force a surrender through starvation rather than an all-out assault. After all, he wrote, "we are in no hurry, and we don't need the forces now outside Warsaw anywhere else."[30]

Despite Halder's brutal plan, efforts were made to induce the Warsaw garrison to surrender. On the morning of September 16, a German staff car appeared in the Praga suburbs flanked by two tanks and flying a large white flag. Under a ceasefire, a German officer approached the Polish lines brandishing a letter containing a demand for the city's surrender, which he asked be taken to the "Officer Commanding, Warsaw." Colonel Sosabowski received him, sent the note on to General Juliusz Rómmel's headquarters, and blindfolded the German messenger until the reply arrived. When it did, some ninety minutes later, it was in the negative. "General [Walerian] Czuma," Sosabowski recalled, "would neither talk with, nor see, the enemy emissary." With that, the German officer saluted and took his leave.[31] Warsaw would fight on.

That evening and into the following day, Warsaw was subjected to a determined bombardment specifically targeting the city's infrastructure—

gas, electricity, and water works—as well as the General Military Inspectorate, the War Ministry, the Royal Castle and Citadel, the barracks, the artillery positions, and Polish command centers.[32] In the process, much of the city found itself under a sustained aerial and artillery attack that seemed to exceed all that had gone before. Marta Korwin recorded bad news arriving from the city center: part of the Royal Castle had been destroyed, fires were burning in the parliament building, and the vaulting of St. John's Cathedral had collapsed. "It seemed," she wrote, "as if every third house was in flames." Maria Komornicka's concerns were more immediate. She and her family were huddled in the stairwell of their apartment block in Mokotów when "suddenly there was a terrible noise, the rattle of broken glass, and the smell of rotten eggs. I was sure that our building was hit, but as we found out, No. 18 across the street took a large hole in the front wall; glass was shattered in our windows and our window frames were damaged."[33] One Varsovian's diary was darkly laconic: "Sunday. God's day, yet more shells have fallen on Warsaw today than on any other. Gradually everything is being destroyed."[34] That day, Sunday, September 17, would bring momentous news, but nothing to cheer the defenders of Warsaw.

EVENTS IN THE POLISH CAPITAL RECEIVED VARYING DEGREES OF scrutiny abroad. Though the British and French governments were busy concerning themselves with the sham offensive on the Saar, and with the inevitable problems of rationing, evacuation, and mobilization, there was strangely little focus on Poland's agony. The press was distracted by the domestic implications of the war, and privately one British MP even sought to blame the victims, complaining in his diary that Poland's resistance against the Germans had amounted to "nothing at all."[35] In Berlin and Moscow, in contrast, the progress of the war was being watched very closely, with both sides wary of one another and watching for any sign of backsliding on the territorial arrangement authorized by the Secret Protocol to the Nazi–Soviet Pact.

Already on September 3, Joachim von Ribbentrop had written to the German ambassador in Moscow, Count Friedrich-Werner von der Schulenburg, to ask when Soviet forces might be expected to occupy their "sphere of influence" in Poland, as had been agreed in the treaty discussions. As Ribbentrop explained, the defeat of the Polish army was expected "within a few weeks," and it was in everybody's interest for the Red Army to "move against Polish forces" at the proper time.[36] The Soviets, however, though keen to lay claim to the territories promised to them under the Secret Protocol, were wary of undermining their dubious claim to neutrality in the ongoing conflict, and so were unwilling to openly ally themselves to the German cause. As Vyacheslav Molotov told the German ambassador, "We are of the view that the time to start concrete action has not yet come. . . . [I]t seems to us that through excessive haste we might injure our cause and promote unity among our opponents."[37] For the time being, it seemed, Germany would fight Poland alone.

The Red Army had not been idle in the interim, however. Already on September 2, a state of alert had been declared on the Polish frontier and the border detachments present in the area had been brought up to battle readiness. Then, on September 6, a partial mobilization of the Red Army was ordered covering all the western military districts; the order, however, requested what was euphemistically called a "large-scale training drill." Five days later, the military districts contiguous with the Polish border were ordered to concentrate their forces close to the frontier—again, on the pretext of a drill. The following day, the Soviet Union's western rail network was effectively put at the disposal of the Red Army: civilian traffic was reduced, engines and rolling stock were requisitioned, and coal reserves were secured.[38]

Despite that partial mobilization, the Kremlin was evidently alarmed by the speed of the German advance.[39] Molotov expressed his concern that the Soviet Union would not be able to "start a new war" if an armistice with the Poles were to come too quickly. Nonetheless, the Soviet foreign minister outlined to his German counterpart the political justification that would be used for the Soviet invasion, explaining that "the

Soviet Government intended to take the occasion of the further advance of German troops to declare that Poland was falling apart and that it was necessary for the Soviet Union, in consequence, to come to the aid of the Ukrainians and the White Russians." This argument, the Kremlin believed, would "make the intervention of the Soviet Union plausible to the masses and at the same time avoid giving the Soviet Union the appearance of an aggressor."[40] Like clockwork, an article appeared in *Pravda* shortly thereafter, on September 14, written by the Politburo's propaganda chief, Andrei Zhdanov. Zhdanov explained the reason for Poland's looming defeat as the result of the Warsaw government's oppression of its Byelorussian and Ukrainian minorities.[41]

In fact, it is doubtful whether the Soviet masses found this argument at all plausible. The Soviet authorities had struggled over the previous three weeks or so to explain the political volte-face of the Nazi–Soviet Pact to its citizens, and those who attempted the feat were often met with incomprehension or even hostility.[42] Some days before the Soviet invasion of Poland, the Polish military attaché in Moscow, Stefan Brzeszczyński, witnessed one such speaker address a crowd in Gorky Park. After expressing hostility toward the Poles, which Brzeszczyński thought the crowd received "rather coolly," the agitator ended by asking whether the Soviet Union should "stand by and watch our Byelorussian and Ukrainian brethren suffer." In response, the crowd—having clearly failed to understand the thrust of the argument—began loudly demanding that the Red Army march westward to engage "the evil Germans."[43]

More important than persuading the Soviet people were the wider geostrategic concerns, which were also assuaged around this time. The French action in the Saarland, which had been half-hearted at best, finally fizzled out, and the Soviets signed an armistice with the Japanese, with hostilities in eastern Mongolia scheduled to cease in the coming days. Then, on September 14, Molotov told Schulenburg that the Red Army was mobilized, and the Soviet invasion of Poland could now take place. However, to confirm the "political motivation" for the invasion, it was essential for the Red Army "not to take action until the government center of Poland, the city of Warsaw, had fallen." Consequently,

Molotov asked to be informed "as nearly as possible . . . when the capture of Warsaw could be counted on."[44]

The following day, September 15, Ribbentrop telegrammed Schulenburg again, requesting that he "formally communicate" to Molotov that the occupation of Warsaw was expected "in the next few days." He went on to reiterate the agreement reached in Moscow regarding "spheres of interest," and to welcome the prospect of the Soviet Union now "[taking] a hand militarily," as it relieved the Wehrmacht of "the necessity of annihilating the remainder of the Polish Army." He appended the draft text of a joint communiqué explaining that Moscow and Berlin saw it as their "joint task to restore peace and order in . . . their natural spheres of influence." A day later, Molotov confirmed that the "military intervention by the Soviet Union" was imminent, and in the early hours of September 17, Schulenburg was summoned to the Kremlin to be informed by Stalin himself that the Red Army would cross the Polish frontier at dawn.[45]

With his de facto ally thus apprised of the imminent Red Army invasion, Stalin now informed the Poles of his intentions. Thus, the Polish ambassador in Moscow, Wacław Grzybowski, was also summoned to the Kremlin in the early hours of September 17, where he was met by the Soviet deputy foreign minister, Vladimir Potemkin. Though he had served in Moscow for three years, and must have been well versed in the Kremlin's machinations, Grzybowski was nonetheless surprised by what followed—not least as he had only recently been speculating on the apparent readiness of the Soviet Union to assist in Poland's defense.[46] That night, he was presented with a note from the Soviet government signed by Molotov outlining the reasons for the Red Army's intended intervention. "The Polish government has disintegrated," it read, and with the end of the Polish state, "all agreements concluded between the USSR and Poland ceased to be in effect." Given this collapse, and the threat that it posed to the USSR, the Soviet government was unable to "remain indifferent" to the fate of its "brothers of the same blood, the Ukrainians and Byelorussians, residing on Polish territory." Consequently, the Red Army had been instructed to "cross the border and take under their protection the lives and property of the inhabitants of western Ukraine and western Byelorussia."[47] "Western Ukraine" and "western Byelorussia," of course, meant eastern Poland.

Grzybowski gamely fought his corner, refusing to accept the note and protesting the Soviet Union's unilateral actions. He explained desperately that the Polish government was still present in the country and that the Polish army was still fighting. He argued that Poland's difficulties had no bearing on its sovereignty. Did anyone question Russia's existence, he asked, when Napoleon occupied Moscow? According to Potemkin, Grzybowski became so agitated that he "could hardly pronounce his words."[48] But it was all in vain. When Grzybowski refused to accept the note, Potemkin ordered one of his aides to take it directly to the Polish embassy. Hurrying back to his office, Grzybowski composed a telegram to the Polish Foreign Ministry—sent via Bucharest—explaining the sinister turn of events and declaring that he was "awaiting instructions."[49] By the time that dispatch had been sent, the Red Army was already advancing on Poland's eastern frontier.

The Soviet forces that moved off that morning had been organized into two fronts arranged to the north and south of the river Pripyat: the Byelorussian Front, under General Mikhail Kovalev, and the Ukrainian Front, under General Semyon Timoshenko. Together, they comprised nearly 500,000 combat troops divided into 28 rifle divisions, 7 cavalry divisions, 7 artillery regiments, and 10 armored brigades and assisted by 4,850 tanks, 5,500 armored vehicles, and 2,000 aircraft.[50] Each front also boasted three mobile spearheads made up of cavalry and tank brigades. These forces were instructed to lead a swift advance into Poland, capturing Wilno, Grodno, and Lwów within forty-eight hours.[51] These were ambitious targets. Clearly, speed was of the essence—the Soviet commissar for defense, Kliment Voroshilov, even referred to the Soviet advance, without irony, as a "lightning strike."[52] The task of the invading armies, their battle orders informed them, was "to destroy and capture the armed forces of Poland," with the forward units moving to cut off the Wilno district in the north and to interrupt a general Polish retreat toward the southeast, through the so-called Romanian bridgehead.[53]

"An army of beggars":
Stalin's soldiers invade.
Laski Diffusion

So much for the theory. In truth, the Soviet advance was rather more chaotic. Having been eviscerated by Stalin's purges of the late 1930s, in which a huge proportion of the officer corps had been liquidated, the Red Army was far from fighting fit. Moreover, given that its mobilization had been hurried by the urgent need to claim the territories promised to Stalin, its advance was characterized by logistical chaos and disorganization. Initially, at least, the two fronts lacked many of their component units, with many more units lacking personnel or equipment. According to Soviet records, the mobilization had revealed a lack of uniforms and equipment, with supplies often having to be borrowed from reserve units.[54] Others were not so lucky.

The 21st Rifle Division, for instance, contained "400 men in its ranks who were not fully kitted out, of whom many were in bast [fabric] shoes, barefoot, in civilian trousers and caps."[55] Such shortcomings did not go unnoticed. Observers in Poland would later recall the Red Army's stunted ponies, dirty boots, and shabby uniforms with dismay—it was all so very different from the Polish image of the immaculate Uhlan, or even the elegant Wehrmacht officer.[56] One eyewitness described how Soviet soldiers would buy out the shops wherever they stopped; and that they were astonished that they could have as much as they wanted—especially sweets and chocolate—without ration cards.[57] Another described the Red Army as "an army of beggars . . . an emaciated ravenous crowd." "This was Asia," he concluded. "Asia had invaded us."[58]

Soviet military hardware could also be less than impressive. Tanks, though numerous, were primarily of two types: the BT-7, a lightly armored "cruiser tank," intended for swift advances, and the T-26, an older, slower infantry tank. Neither of them was especially modern, reliable, or effective.[59] In 1939, more Soviet tanks were lost to mechanical breakdown than to combat, and supply and maintenance crews often lagged far behind the advance columns, causing forward units to wait, or else take fuel or spare parts from other battalions.[60] Arguably it was only the lack of adequate antitank weapons among the Polish forces facing them that prevented a more even fight. A similar situation pertained in the air, where many of the 2,000 or so aircraft available to support the Red Army advance were outdated types of biplanes, such as the Polikarpov Po-2 or the Polikarpov I-15. As one Polish eyewitness recalled, "The planes were easy to recognize because they moved very slowly, compared to German Messerschmitts and even Polish PZLs. You could tell right away it was a different army."[61] Accidents, too, were common. The Soviet air ace Sergei Gritsevets, twice winner of the Hero of the Soviet Union award, was killed on September 16, when his I-15 collided with another aircraft outside Orsha, preventing him from being deployed to the Polish front.[62]

Facing the Red Army along the 1,400-kilometer (870-mile) frontier were disparate Polish forces, consisting primarily of the Border Protection Corps (Korpus Ochrony Pogranicza, or KOP). Lightly armed, with little artillery or armor, they were spread across some 18 battalions and numbered around 12,000 men. In addition, eastern Poland contained around 300,000 regular troops in varying states of readiness: either reserve units that were still being formed and trained, or units that had withdrawn eastward after facing the Germans.[63] Though largely lacking air support and sufficient artillery, these Polish forces nonetheless possessed some advantages. One was the static network of defenses that had been constructed around Sarny, north of Równe (Rivne). The Sarny Fortified Area, though incomplete, still encompassed a swath of some 170 kilometers (100 miles) along either side of the river Słucz (Sluch) with bunkers, trenches, and earthworks. In addition, two Polish armored trains were stationed in the eastern provinces: the *Pierwszy Marszałek*, close to Sarny itself, and, defending the fortress at Brest, the *Bartosz Głowacki*, which, incidentally, was named after the peasant hero of the Battle of Racławice of 1794, a rare Polish victory against the Russians.

Yet it would be the border guards of the KOP that would face the brunt of the initial Soviet advance. Formed in 1924, the KOP's task had been to control the long and somewhat lawless frontier with the Soviet Union and prevent communist infiltration. The prospect of a full-scale Red Army invasion was rather beyond its remit, however, and the Polish commander-in-chief, Edward Śmigły-Rydz, would in due course give the order that the KOP was not to engage the Soviets "except in the event of attack." In truth, many border guard units did not have the luxury of a choice.

The chaos of those first hours of the Soviet invasion was typified by an exchange between the KOP regiment commander in Czortków (Chortkiv), Colonel Marceli Kotarba, and the General Staff. When he was asked to send an emissary to the Soviets to discover their intentions, Kotarba replied, "All my battalions are fighting and two Soviet tanks have been destroyed. I doubt whether I will be able to fulfill the order regarding the envoy." Undeterred, the General Staff officer insisted that an emissary be sent, to which Kotarba responded curtly, "Soviet planes over Czortków." A further demand that talks with the Soviets be opened was met with the answer "Air raid. I must go." The next question neatly encapsulated Poland's predicament: "Is this raid by German or Soviet planes?" the staff officer asked.[64]

For all the confusion, the men of the KOP did not lack determination. As one commander instructed his men, they were to stand their ground, "turn their faces to the east, and fight."[65] At Dzisna, in the far northeastern corner of Poland close to the border with Latvia, soldiers of the KOP Głębokie Regiment teamed up with local police and volunteers, including students, to defend their district from attack by a combination of local irregulars and Red Army forces. The fact that one KOP battalion lost fully 50 percent of its men is proof of the ferocity of the fighting. In another engagement, near Husiatyn, a KOP regiment accounted for over 200 Soviet dead in a firefight with the invaders.[66]

One of the most remarkable KOP actions in the opening days of the Soviet invasion was the defense of the fortifications at Sarny, where border guards held off the hugely superior Soviet 60th Rifle Division, despite the risk of being surrounded. One of those KOP commanders was Lieutenant Jan Bołbott, whose fifty or so men held their positions against strong enemy forces—including tanks, sappers, and infantry with flamethrowers—for more than two days. At one point, Bołbott pleaded with his superiors, "Please send a counterstrike or we will all die." But they were powerless to oblige. On the morning of September 21, his position was finally overwhelmed after the Red Army managed to get close enough to block the outside of the bunkers with flammable material and ignite it. Bołbott and his comrades were burned alive.[67]

For all these sacrifices, many KOP units, acutely aware of their own military shortcomings, followed their orders not to engage the Soviets. On the Ukrainian Front, the Soviet 5th Army reported that "the enemy has not rendered significant resistance at the state border and is retreating westward."[68] To the north of the Ukrainian Front, much of the Sarny garrison was evacuated westward early on in the invasion to avoid being encircled.[69] Some border guards saw little military logic in resisting against such insuperable odds. "I wondered about the sense of taking up arms in a doomed fight when we had no antitank weapons," one officer recalled. "Should we provide the tanks with cannon-fodder just to make a statement? Wouldn't that be madness? Should we not instead avoid unnecessary losses?" Petitioning his captain, and then the regimental command, he received permission to withdraw: "Secret documents were destroyed. Border posts were recalled. . . . We set off for the nearest forest in a long column."[70] Far from disappearing, however, many of those men would later resurface alongside Polish army units, or join one of the many nascent Polish resistance organizations.

Behind the frontier, many Poles were simply baffled by unfolding events. "Various most fantastic rumors became facts for us, around which we spun interpretations and forecast the future," a woman recalled. "When, one misty September morning on the Moscow–Warsaw road, tanks, armoured cars, cavalry and infantry in combat gear appeared moving westward, we suddenly faced a number of questions for which we had no answers. Where was this grey army decorated with stars going? Was it bringing us assistance or final defeat? What was the meaning of all of this?"[71] For some, it was immediately clear what was afoot. At Niżniów (Nyzhniv), east of Stanisławów (Ivano-Frankivsk), retreating Polish troops urged the civilian population to flee with them. "Run! Run for your lives, good people!" they shouted. "Hide anywhere you can for they are showing no mercy. Hurry! The Russians are coming!"[72] As another eyewitness recalled, the result was panic. "People ran in all directions, unable to find time or places in which to hide. I stood aghast as one small boy, frightened and confused, stopped to stare at an approaching tank. They simply machine-gunned him down."[73]

Elsewhere, local populations believed that the Soviets came in peace— that they were "fellow Slavs" who would do them no harm.[74] One Pole remembered the Soviet soldiers as being "very friendly, very peaceful . . . they had such an excellent attitude. They came as friends, they embraced us, they kept saying that they had come to liberate us, liberate us from capitalism, from the bourgeoisie."[75] In Tarnopol (Ternopil), the city authorities urged the population to welcome the invaders, and in Równe local officials rode to meet the Red Army, thanking Soviet officers for bringing help in the fight against the Germans. Even where they were welcomed, however, Red Army units sometimes could not conceal their belligerent intentions. At Złoczów (Zolochiv), east of Lwów, the mayor greeted a Soviet cavalry unit with bread and salt only to be kicked to the ground by the Red Army commander. Not long after, he was executed.[76]

The resulting disarray was not aided by the contradictory messages emanating from the Soviet forces themselves. It may have been Polish wishful thinking to imagine that the Red Army was coming to help them fight the Germans, but it was also quite evident that some Soviet soldiers themselves were confused as to the purpose of their march into Poland. As the Red Army's own records show, despite the propaganda offensive, some "incorrect opinions" were still very much in evidence. "We haven't been attacked. We don't want an inch of someone else's land, so why are we on the march?" asked a soldier from the 13th Rifle Corps. Another wondered, "Don't we pursue a policy of peace? So why have we crossed the Polish border?" A soldier of the 4th Tank Brigade went further, complaining that they had not been informed who they were going to fight against. He added disapprovingly that "this is against the teachings of Lenin and Stalin." Another aired the heretical idea that the USSR was little better than Hitler's Third Reich: "Germany is seizing Poland's land," he said, "and we are doing the same."[77] In such circumstances, it was perhaps not surprising that the Polish experience of encountering the Red Army in 1939 varied so widely, from amicable to murderous.

Moreover, it is clear that there was a policy of deliberate disinformation on the part of the invading army, which was masking its real intentions by proclaiming that it was indeed riding to Poland's aid. Jan Karski, who was retreating eastward toward Tarnopol when news of the Soviet invasion broke, described the scene when his men came across a Red Army truck equipped with a loudspeaker. The voice addressed the Polish soldiers in a thick Russian accent as they milled around the truck in confusion: "Hey you, are you with us or are you not? We aren't going to stand here in the middle of the road the whole day waiting for you to make up your minds. There's nothing to be frightened about. We are Slavs like yourselves, not Germans. We are not your enemies."[78] Such disinformation—a time-worn Soviet strategy—paid dividends. When Red Army forces crossed the Polish frontier east of Równe that morning, men of the KOP "Hoszcza" Battalion assumed—as others did—that they were coming to their aid. This assumption was reinforced by a call from headquarters requesting that a formal reception should be prepared for their new allies. But when the KOP officers, in full dress uniform, greeted their Soviet counterparts outside their barracks later that day, they were shocked to be ordered to surrender their weapons.[79]

Official Red Army leaflets carried the same lie. Though some contained such mangled Polish as to be scarcely legible, others were eloquently mendacious. An example carrying the signature of General Timoshenko announced, "Only the Red Army will deliver the Polish nation from this unhappy war and give you a chance to begin a peaceful life. Trust us—the Red Army and the Soviet Union—we are your only friend."[80] Official announcements were abetted by local ruses. Near Ostróg (Ostroh), in a deliberate attempt to fool the Poles into quiescence, arriving Soviet forces were accompanied by a military band playing the patriotic Polish song "March of the First Brigade."[81]

It is unsurprising, therefore, that the rumor that the Soviets were arriving as allies would spread so swiftly across what remained of Poland. Some Polish military units evidently attempted to counter the growing bafflement by announcing that the Red Army was coming to assist the Germans, and that it was disarming and interning Polish troops.[82] As it so often does, however, hope trumped truth.

Despite the chaos, the Polish army, alongside disbanded elements of the KOP, was still able to offer sustained resistance to the Soviet invasion. In the northern city of Wilno, for instance, a garrison augmented by thousands of volunteers awaited the Soviet advance. As elsewhere, the defense was marked by a degree of disorganization. The garrison's commander, Colonel Jarosław Okulicz-Kozaryn, who had fought in the Russian army during the First World War, initially foresaw a fighting retreat toward the Lithuanian frontier, but after the first Soviet units arrived, he changed his mind and ordered a more determined defense, despite the fact that few preparations had been made. The reaction of Konstanty Peszyński, a major in an antitank unit, was perhaps typical. He received the news of the Soviet invasion "like a thunderbolt" and

New foes: a Soviet tank in eastern Poland.
akg-images / Universal Images Group / Sovfoto

joined a makeshift defense corps. Armed with just his rifle, he vowed that he would never surrender "to those Bolshevik scoundrels."[83]

The makeshift defense of Wilno comprised around 7,000 soldiers, ranging from volunteers to trained cadres, as well as some 15 artillery pieces and several dozen machine guns. Lacking mortars or antitank rifles, the defenders would be forced to improvise, deploying gasoline bombs and exploiting the urban environment. Firing positions on the Hill of Three Crosses, in the heart of the city, were manned by a group of student volunteers. Elsewhere, the men of the Polish 1st Light Artillery Regiment were in the thick of the fight. "Suddenly we found ourselves in the line of fire," Warrant Officer Adolf Koc wrote. "We had our guns set on the road . . . and we walked straight into the Russians, like a dumb ox. Thankfully they didn't see us. We went through a yard, aimed our guns at the Russians . . . and fired." After initially withdrawing, the Soviet troops soon reappeared. Koc's men opened fire again before adopting an ingenious method to deal with the tanks: "One of my chaps from Lwów said: 'Let me have those hand grenades. I'll go up there, what's there to fear?'" Koc recalled. "He took them, walked up to the tanks through a narrow ditch, and threw them. One of the tanks exploded. The crew were stunned. The other withdrew."[84] The men of the 6th Legions Infantry Regiment were equally effective. As one eyewitness recalled, "The tanks were followed by infantry. They cried 'Hurrah! For Stalin! For the Motherland! Hurrah!' I will never forget those cries. But we took them with flanking fire."

Yet the defenders were impressed by the determination of the Red Army troops. "One falls, another comes after him, is hit, and another comes. A whole heap of corpses grew—and not a small one. . . . We fought until evening, and I saw the tanks catch fire one after another, our chaps throwing bottles with gasoline."[85] Officially, the Red Army registered twenty-four of its soldiers killed in the capture of Wilno.[86] It is almost certainly an underestimate.

Despite these successes, by midday on September 19 the sheer numbers of Soviet troops forced the Polish garrison to execute a fighting withdrawal toward the Lithuanian border 20 kilometers (12 miles) away. "I stopped at the hospital to fetch my things," Konstanty Peszyński recalled. "Soldiers and patients asked me to stay and promised to hide me. I thanked them for their good intentions, but I could not stay behind, for I would be disobeying orders, if for no other reason."[87] Peszyński, who had vowed to defy the "Bolshevik scoundrels," would not escape them, however. Captured by the Soviet authorities in Lithuania, he disappeared; he is thought to have been among the Polish officers murdered in the Katyń massacres. Those who remained behind in Wilno faced an uncertain future. One of them recalled waking up "in a different world" on the first morning of the Soviet occupation, with the streets full of Red Army soldiers and armored vehicles in a determined show of strength. "The city itself had changed," he wrote. "People in normal clothing disappeared. People wore the oldest rags they could find. The shops were shut and all goods were hoarded."[88]

If the garrison at Wilno was guilty of being unprepared for the city's defense, the same could not be said of Grodno (Hrodna), 120 kilometers (75 miles) to the southwest. After a brief, aborted uprising by pro-communist elements—spurred by Soviet leaflets declaring that the Red Army was coming to the aid of the working class—the defense of the town was well organized, using scouts, firemen, and civilian volunteers to bolster numbers to over 2,000 fighting men. The will to fight, one soldier recalled, was strong. When his commanding officer announced, with tears in his eyes, that the Soviet Union had invaded, he "declared the situation hopeless, without any chance of victory, and so allowed the men to lay down their arms." Those who did not want to surrender, "but chose to fight for the honor of the city, and the honor of the Polish army, were to step to the right." The entire platoon, the soldier remembered, stepped to the right.[89] Beyond that martial spirit, however, supplies of arms were painfully short. The garrison possessed a total of twenty-four heavy machine guns and two antiaircraft guns. One cavalry squadron commander noted that his 107 men were armed with only "rifles, sabers, and lances."[90]

Grodno resisted the first Soviet assault on the morning of September 20. A dozen or so Red Army tanks drove into the center of town, emboldened, it seemed, by the army's success in overrunning outlying villages. Here, however, they ran into organized resistance. Though their armor could not be pierced by the defenders' antiaircraft guns, other ways were soon found to destroy them, such as firing at their tracks or throwing gasoline bombs.[91] The town's defiance, very much a communal effort, included schoolchildren, older students, and refugees and soldiers from beyond the region who had fled the Germans. One schoolteacher recalled:

> A stray police unit is fighting. They are Poznanians, 30 men. They fight as long as they have ammunition in their rucksacks, as long as grenades hang at their belts, as long as the machine gun they had pulled up the barricade spits bullets. The boy runners bring them more ammunition

from the barracks and gasoline-filled bottles from the people. Women bring them jugs of hot coffee, bread, [and] *bigos* [soup], and take away the wounded.[92]

Boy scouts, too, played a prominent role, darting between the Soviet tanks armed with gasoline bombs. As one of the defenders recalled, "The tanks didn't stand a chance in the narrow streets."[93] But success came at a terrible cost. One of the scouts, a thirteen-year-old named Tadeusz Jasiński, was caught by Soviet soldiers, and as punishment they tied him to the front of a tank to serve as a human shield. Mortally wounded, he was later taken back to his mother, who sought to ease his final moments with news of the Polish success. "Tadzik, rejoice!" she told him. "The Polish Army is coming back! Uhlans with banners! They are singing!" Tadzik died in her arms.[94]

When the Soviets returned later that day, battle was concentrated on the river Niemen, which flows through the town, with Soviet armored columns attempting to blast their way through Polish strongholds. One of the defenders, who recalled seeing a Soviet tank drive onto one of the bridges over the river, said, "It was soon hit from a gun that was on the first floor of the 81st Infantry Regiment barracks. Bam! It span round, and that was it. It was stuck. Another tank came, trying to push it aside, but it was hit too. One was on fire and the other soon caught fire too. They must have been clever, those chaps from the barracks."[95] Clever or not, the Polish defense was broken on the night of September 21, and orders were given for a general evacuation northward to Lithuania. Those who were unable or unwilling to leave the city disappeared into Soviet captivity or into the nascent Polish underground.

According to Soviet sources, 57 Red Army personnel were killed in the battle for Grodno; unofficially, the death toll is estimated at some 500. Soviet records also claim that around 600 Poles were killed, but this figure most likely does not include those who fell victim to mass executions at the hands of the Red Army after the surrender, including students, prisoners of war, and scouts, among others.[96] In one instance, some 29 Polish officers were executed after being marched out of town

The grim reality of Soviet occupation: General Olszyna-Wilczyński, murdered by a Red Army patrol. *public domain*

on the pretense that they were going to be set free.[97] Another of those killed was the commander of the Grodno garrison, Brigadier-General Józef Olszyna-Wilczyński, who was stopped by a Red Army patrol while heading toward Lithuania in a staff car. Pulled from the vehicle, he was taken to the side of the road along with his adjutant and summarily shot.[98] The general's wife, who had traveled to Grodno to "share his fate," was presented with his briefcase by Soviet soldiers after the execution; it was spattered with his blood.[99]

Atrocities such as those accompanying the fall of Grodno were sadly commonplace during the Soviet invasion. Massacres and maltreatment were seen as justified—of officers, in particular, because, in Soviet eyes, most were trebly damned: as Catholics, Poles, and noblemen. At Hrubieszów, one officer was shot because he had failed to hand over his pistol when surrendering.[100] In another case, a platoon commander of the 45th Red Army Rifle Division took two captured Polish officers into a forest, relieved them of their money, and executed them.[101] Further examples are legion, but one of the most telling is that of the KOP captain who, just before his execution by a Red Army soldier, was told, "That will teach you to be a professional officer."[102]

Naturally, both officers and ordinary soldiers attempted to evade detection by discarding their uniforms or their markers of rank. As a local priest noted, Polish uniforms put soldiers in danger, so they did everything they could to shed them, begging for civilian clothes in return.[103] But the Soviets had their methods. One sinister account reports that fugitive Polish soldiers were rounded up by officers with peculiar accents and odd uniforms, who asked if they wanted to "fight the Russians." Those who volunteered were led away and never seen again.[104] Elsewhere, prisoners would be lined up to have their hands checked: those with soft, white palms—*beloruchki*—were clearly not working class, and so could expect to be beaten or shot.[105] Any soldier who was well dressed or well equipped was viewed with suspicion by the Soviets. Dariusz Dąbrowski, who recalled being taken prisoner by the Red Army at Orany (Varėna) on the Polish–Lithuanian frontier, later said, "I took off my distinctions, but I had my whistle, you see. And they said, 'You are the commanding officer, because you've got a whistle.' A friend of mine took off his distinctions as well, but he had a tailor-made uniform, so he was arrested. And we had a young chap with us who had binoculars, and they thought he must be something special for that reason. So . . . the three of us were taken for special interrogation."[106] Dąbrowski would subsequently be released after pretending to be a humble tram driver.

Others tried similar tricks. Henryk Meszczyński had been a battalion commander in the KOP and understood the danger he was in. "Everyone wanted to shoot us," he recalled. After taking off his insignia and then dumping his uniform entirely, he had donned shabby civilian clothes and a railway worker's cap. Then he was picked up by a passing Soviet convoy. Invited to ride in the cab with the major, he was offered alcohol before being told that the back of the truck contained Polish officers en route to an unknown fate.[107] While the Germans were unleashing a race war in the west of Poland, the Soviets imported class war to the east in the Red Army's baggage train.

The major believed Meszczyński—his ingenuity saved his life. But like those in the back of the truck, thousands of his fellows were not so fortunate and disappeared into the Soviet penal system. Józef Bartoszewicz recalled being taken prisoner near Słonim (Slonim), east of

Białystok: "They put us in prison. The prison was battered and covered in blood. I don't know who they'd killed there." After a day or so, he and the other Poles were ordered to line up in the yard and stripped of everything they had: belts, watches, razors, even shoelaces. They were then herded to the station and driven into cattle cars at gunpoint. "We didn't know where they were taking us," Bartoszewicz later said.[108] After a two-week journey, he arrived in the notorious prison camp of Starobelsk (Starobilsk), near Voroshilovgrad (Luhansk). Bartoszewicz was lucky: he was sent from there to a slave labor camp in Ukraine. Those who had remained in Starobelsk would later be among the 22,000 Poles murdered in the Katyń massacres.[109]

For the Poles in eastern Poland, the arrival of the Red Army prefaced a seismic shift, as Soviet occupation soon made itself felt. It was, as one observer recalled, "like a gigantic ant-hill that [had] been violently shaken."[110] Just as the officer class quickly found itself persecuted in the new constellation, so Polishness became a potentially life-threatening condition. Identified by Soviet propaganda as the oppressors of the Byelorussian and Ukrainian populations of the region, Poles suddenly found themselves living in hostile territory. The first indication of this sinister new climate was the welcome that some Ukrainians, Byelorussians, and Jews extended to the arriving Red Army in response to the Soviet narrative of "liberation." It could range from groups of villagers greeting the soldiers with bread and salt—the traditional Slavic welcome—to the erection of makeshift triumphal arches bearing the hammer and sickle. One Red Army major-general recalled the reception that he and his men received when they entered the town of Nowogródek (Navahrudak): "A strange sight opened up to us," he wrote: "As soon as they saw the Soviet tanks . . . a spontaneous demonstration took place. Women and girls began handing out flowers. Initially sparsely, but then more and more frequently, people began cheering. As we went down the street, we were welcomed by 'Long Live the Red Army!' and 'Long Live the Soviet Union!' shouted from every direction."[111]

Soon after the Red Army's arrival, another novelty arose: the establishment of local militias seeking to keep order and speed up the

The myth of the Red Army as liberator.
akg-images / Universal Images Group / Tass

communist transformation of society. In the village of Wiśniowczyk (Vyshnivchyk), near Tarnopol, the local priest noted disapprovingly that "local governments are forming spontaneously. The worst scum floats to the surface. All kinds of the lowest vermin, hoodlums, rogues, thieves, drunks, loafers, and stinkers take power. They are all over the place, shouting, clamoring, bawling, and uttering threats. . . . This kind of thing makes one shudder."[112] Near Brest, another Polish resident recalled that the new authorities were "composed of Byelorussian and Jewish volunteers. They wore red armbands on their sleeve. . . . And our people, the Poles, had to sneak around carefully. When the Soviets arrived we became second-class citizens."[113]

In the turmoil that followed, national and social tensions quickly resurfaced. Zofia Chomętowska observed the breakdown of society at first hand as she trekked westward through Polesie with countless other Polish refugees in the wake of the Soviet invasion. Everywhere, she recalled, they were eyed with suspicion, and often barely concealed hatred, by local, non-Polish populations. "The Jews are the worst," she wrote. "They cheerfully shout 'The Bolsheviks are coming!' [*Bolsheviki idut*].

They have forgotten that the Russians hate them, yet they await them impatiently. . . . They look at us with malice and rejoice in our misfortunes."[114] It was not an isolated example. According to a local policeman, some of the Jews of Borysław (Boryslav) organized a symbolic funeral for Poland: a procession following a coffin draped in the Polish flag.[115]

Targeting the property of the local Polish aristocracy, the Red Army urged the local Byelorussian and Ukrainian populations to rise up against their class enemies and "oppressors." In the village of Maszów (Mashiv), near Kowel (Kovel'), a Soviet lieutenant made a speech in the main square in which he called upon the people to take what rightfully belonged to them. He urged them to avenge the pain of twenty years of exploitation, proclaiming that they should "kill and take the property of those who filled their pockets and barns with your blood."[116] It was open season on the Poles. Andrzej Ramułt, from an aristocratic family near Stryj (Stryi), saw the local Ukrainian population plunder their estate. "People at first just came and looked at everything but wouldn't go inside," he recalled. "But eventually they all pounced on it, all of them, even those who had been rather friendly toward us. . . . The manor house was completely stripped of everything." Whatever could not be moved was destroyed, such as the bookcases and their contents: "Children sat in front of the house and diligently tore out page after page," Ramułt said.[117]

Elsewhere, things took a far nastier turn. In the Tarnopol region, where Ukrainian villagers attacked their Polish neighbors, one local landowner was tied to a pole and had strips of flesh torn from his body; his wounds were then dressed with salt. He was forced to watch the execution of his family. In Pińsk (Pinsk), the president of the district court was attacked by a local militia, who tied his feet to a wagon and drove the horses around the cobbled streets until he breathed his last.[118] In one village near Kobryń (Kobryn), a mob brought a group of Poles out to the surrounding fields and shot everyone. As one eyewitness remembered, "They threw them into pits, still alive. My father was alive when they threw him into the pit, and when he stood up and shouted at them 'Even if you murder us, Poland will still be here!' they smashed his skull with spades."[119]

In such circumstances, many Poles trying to escape from the eastern territories went to great lengths to avoid their former neighbors. Near Stanisławów, a woman observed young soldiers still in uniform sneaking through the woods near her home. "They ask if we are Polish," she wrote. "They are trying to avoid Ukrainian villages. Our 'cousins' [the Ukrainians] let them sleep in their barns then take away their guns and murder them in their sleep. It's hard to believe what's beginning to happen. Fear and helplessness must be the lot of all Poles."[120]

Panic was a common reaction, particularly among those who remembered the last Soviet invasion, in 1920. "Many people started to run away, even though there was nowhere to escape to; they left everything, including children and wives," recalled a teacher.[121] An infantry major summed up the fatalistic attitude of many when they heard the news of this second invasion. In his diary on September 21, he noted, "Tonight the news was confirmed: the war declared by the Soviets. In a way, it dispels all doubt. . . . All that is left for us is to die an honorable death. Twenty days ago, we had to get used to the thought of war; now we must get used to the thought of total annihilation."[122] For some, it was too much to bear. Jan Karski recalled a "rasping, desperate sobbing" spreading through his men as the realization dawned that they were now the prisoners of the Soviets. The tension was broken by a hysterical voice: "Brothers, this is the fourth partition of Poland! May God have mercy on me!" With that, the sound of a revolver shot rang out. The man had taken his own life. "No one knew his name," Karski wrote, "his company, or anything about him."[123]

The writer and philosopher Stanisław Witkiewicz was also driven to extremes. Witkiewicz—or "Witkacy," as he was known—understood Soviet communism better than most. He had witnessed the outbreak of the Bolshevik revolution in Petrograd in 1917, and a decade later had written the dystopian novel *Insatiability*, a darkly pessimistic parody of a future Poland overrun by an unscrupulous demagogue with a seductive ideology. In September 1939, Witkiewicz sought sanctuary in the estate of a friend at Jeziory (Velyki Ozera), near Sarny and east of Brest. But when he heard of the Soviet invasion and the horrors that it had brought to the region, he took an overdose of barbiturates and slit his carotid artery, committing suicide. He had no desire to live in the world that he had so accurately foreseen.[124]

WHILE POLAND WAS FIGHTING FOR ITS LIFE, ITS ALLIES WERE pondering their responses. For the British, the Soviet invasion came as an unpleasant surprise, even after the profound shock engendered by the Nazi–Soviet Pact itself. Churchill complained of Moscow's gross "bad faith," and the civil servant John Colville described the Kremlin's communiqué justifying its actions as "without doubt the most revolting document that modern history has produced."[125] The MP Harold Nicolson was "dumbfounded" by the news, seeing it as a "terrific blow" that made an Allied victory all the more uncertain. "Within a few days," he mused, "we shall have Germany, Russia and Japan against us." Before long, "the Axis will rule Europe," and France would make terms. Even the time-worn British tactic of blockading Germany was out of the question, Nicolson wrote in his diary; rather, "it is a question of them encircling and blockading us." "In a few days our whole position might collapse," he concluded. "Nothing could be more black."[126]

For those on the political left, the invasion was particularly discomfiting, as it damaged the credibility and moral standing of the Soviet Union. The veteran socialist Beatrice Webb—who had once described the USSR as "a new civilisation"—was horrified. "Satan has won," she wrote in her diary. "Stalin and Molotov have become the villains of the piece," and their invasion of Poland was "a monument to international immorality." The Kremlin had squandered what she called its "moral prestige," and it was "the blackest tragedy in human history."[127] For the socialist writer Naomi Mitchison, the Soviet Union's actions were "knocking the bottom out of what one has been working for all these years."[128] She was right. It was difficult to sell the idea of the USSR as a bastion of antifascism when it was so publicly colluding with fascists.

The British Communist Party was completely wrong-footed by the invasion. Dutifully following the Comintern line at the time, the party leader, Harry Pollitt, had published a pamphlet on September 14 titled *How to Win the War*. In it, he had stressed that the Polish people were "right to fight against the Nazi invasion," and argued that for the United Kingdom to "stand aside from this conflict . . . would be a betrayal of everything our forebears have fought to achieve in the . . . struggle against capitalism."[129] However, even as his pamphlet hit the streets, Pollitt learned that the Kremlin's instructions had changed. Now, all "fraternal" Communist parties were to "correct" their policies. "Tactics must be changed," the Kremlin proclaimed. "Under no circumstances may the international working class defend fascist Poland." Not only had the Soviets stopped referring to Nazi Germany as "fascist," but it appeared that their use of the term had taken on an elasticity that few would previously have believed. Humiliated and isolated by the shift, Pollitt was forced to resign; Rajani Palme Dutt—a rather arid, Oxford-educated Leninist, who had previously lauded the "clarity" of the old position—succeeded him as party general secretary.[130]

For those bemused by such contortions, an editorial in *The Times* on September 18 provided a clear-eyed assessment. It juxtaposed Poland's twin aggressors and suggested that the only people to be disappointed by Soviet actions were those who had clung to the naïve belief that the USSR was in some way distinct from "her Nazi neighbour." "Public opinion here," it went on, "is revolted . . . by these cynical exercises in lower diplomacy. Sympathy for Poland, which was warm and eager yesterday, is aflame today."[131]

Sadly for Poland, that sympathy barely flickered in the Portland stone courtyards of Whitehall. To some in the Foreign Office, the Red Army's attack on Poland was not unexpected, but neither did it do much to change the general, lethargic thrust of Allied policy. Certainly, questions were asked as to whether the Soviet invasion would provoke a declaration of war—in accordance with the Anglo-Polish

Agreement—just as the German invasion had some two weeks previously. The Polish ambassador, Count Edward Raczyński, was certainly keen to push this line: he delivered a note to the Foreign Office stating that "the Polish government reserves the right to invoke the obligations of its allies arising out of the treaties now in force."[132] In response, both to the ambassador and to the British politicians and civil servants raising the same question, Viscount Halifax was clear: though the Anglo-Polish Agreement had only spoken vaguely of aggression by "a European power," the Secret Protocol to the agreement had specified that it meant Germany. Moreover, the foreign secretary declared, both the British and the French felt that it would be "a mistake" to declare war on the USSR. Instead, the British government offered a rather insipid statement to the effect that, despite the Soviet invasion, Britain's "obligations to Poland" would remain unaffected.[133]

Britain's understanding of those obligations might have been surmised from listening to an official radio broadcast sent from London to Warsaw on September 19: "This is a message from the people of Britain to the city of Warsaw. All the world is admiring your courage. Once again, Poland has fallen victim to the aggressive designs of her neighbours. Once again, she has by her heroic defiance of the invader become the standard-bearer of liberty in Europe. We, your allies, intend to continue the struggle for the restoration of your liberties."[134] For Varsovians, suffering a third week of German air raids and artillery shelling, it was thin gruel.

In fact, the thinking of those in and around the British government was still remarkably muddled, in part in those early days because the precise nature and intention of the Soviet invasion was still far from clear. Some perceived in the Kremlin's actions an anti-German motive: a preemptive move to face down a potential opponent. It was a sentiment encouraged by Moscow's strenuous profession of neutrality toward the war's other combatant nations. Churchill was among those thus misled. In his famed "Enigma" speech, broadcast on October 1, 1939, he praised Poland's "indestructible soul" and rightly noted that the Kremlin was motivated primarily by Russian national interest. But he was wrong when he described the new German–Soviet frontier through Poland as an "eastern front" that Hitler "does not dare assail."[135] His erroneous assumption—which was shared by many—was that it had been German–Soviet tensions that had brought the Red Army into Poland. In truth, it was the opposite. It was merely the first manifestation of the cozy division of spoils agreed to in the Secret Protocol to the Nazi–Soviet Pact.

Others argued that the presence of a new German–Soviet frontier, and the removal of the "buffer" of Poland, would do a good job of fostering a "desirable friction," which would sooner or later lead to a confrontation between the two totalitarian states. In such circumstances, they asked, was it not better to refrain from any precipitate action and instead cautiously observe events? In both schools of thought, Poland was effectively abandoned. As one historian of the period glumly concluded, many British politicians of the time seemed to feel "they had a God-given right to dispose of Poland as circumstances dictated."[136]

That final disposal took place in the English seaside town of Hove on September 22, at the second meeting of the Anglo-French Supreme War Council. There, Chamberlain and Halifax again met with Prime Minister Édouard Daladier and the commander-in-chief of the French armed forces, General Maurice Gamelin. The visit owed something to British farce. According to Alexander Cadogan, the permanent under-secretary of state for foreign affairs, who traveled with the British party from London that morning, their arrival in Hove was a surprise to the locals, who had been told only to expect a meeting of "government officials." Consequently, Cadogan recalled, they wandered around the "passages of an awful Victorian building, hung with the Victorian pictures of dead aldermen," until a functionary asked Halifax if he was a government official. Answering in the affirmative, he and his companions were then ushered around to the front door, where the prime minister was duly recognized with a cry of "Chamberlain! Cor Blimey!" Then, while waiting for the French delegation to arrive, the group was greeted by the town mayor, "the local butcher," Cadogan assumed, "but quite nice."[137]

The discussions that followed were thorough and wide-ranging. Daladier espoused the idea of sending a "token force" to the eastern

Mediterranean—either Salonika or Istanbul—to strengthen the resolve of the Balkan nations to resist further German expansion. The positions of Italy and Romania were raised, and Chamberlain wondered whether either one might be persuaded to resist joining Germany in its nefarious endeavor. Turkey, too, would be sounded out, and a Balkan federation was mooted.[138] After lunch—"not too bad," according to Cadogan[139]— the talks resumed, concentrating on the desirability of Anglo-French collaboration in armaments production before moving on to a discussion of German and Allied dispositions on the "Western Front." Both sides declared themselves satisfied with the progress made and approved a joint communiqué to be released to the press that was as anodyne as it was brief.[140]

Poland—the cause for which both countries had declared war barely two weeks before—was mentioned twice in the two and a half hours of talks: once to bemoan the fact that "the front in Poland no longer existed," and again in reference to that country's "defeat." The communiqué did not mention Poland once. In Allied eyes, it seemed, Poland was already a lost cause.

The people of Warsaw, suffering the horrors of a German siege, had no idea they had been abandoned. Many wondered about the whereabouts of the promised British and French assistance, but most Varsovians reacted with stoic faith in their foreign saviors. "You know the British," one air-raid warden told the diarist Alexander Polonius. "They are slow in making up their minds, but they are definitely coming. They can easily land their planes in the fortress at Modlin where there are considerable supplies of petrol, and we shall soon see them over Warsaw." As Polonius recalled, there was a temporary outpouring of optimism, with rumors that Polish antiaircraft gunners had been warned to avoid "friendly fire" against Allied aircraft. Even Polonius himself was cheered: "We are not forgotten," he wrote in his diary. "On the contrary, effective help is on the way."[141] He could not have been more wrong.

Chapter Seven

"INTO THE ARMS OF DEATH"

W HILE POLAND WAS FIGHTING FOR ITS LIFE, AND ITS WEST-ern allies were sitting on their hands, Hitler was busy consolidating his gains. On September 19, he had arrived in the Pomeranian resort of Zoppot, just along the coast from Gdynia in the Bay of Danzig, where the elegant Kasino Hotel had been cleared to serve as his headquarters.

That afternoon, Hitler climbed into his Mercedes once again for the journey to the center of Danzig, where he arrived around 5:00 p.m. Heading into the old town, he drove through the elaborate Golden Gate, which was festooned with swastika flags, and was mobbed by flag-waving Danzigers, who were barely restrained by a thin cordon of police. Banners strung across the Long Market declared "Danzig Greets Its Führer!" and "One People, One Reich, One Führer!" in Gothic script. According to his valet, Heinz Linge, the welcome that Hitler received in Danzig that day "exceeded everything he had ever known previously, including the triumphant entries into Linz and Vienna." Linge recalled Hitler standing in his car and saluting the population thronging the streets and pavements, and the people, "drunk with joy, bombard[ing]

Hitler arrives to claim Danzig.
Muzeum II Wojny Światowej, Gdańsk

him with bouquets of flowers and posies." The emotion of the moment was palpable, Linge wrote. "Everybody—except Hitler—was fighting back his tears."[1]

When he finally arrived at his destination, the elegant seventeenth-century Artushof (Artus Court), Hitler was met by his most senior lieutenants: foreign minister Joachim von Ribbentrop, SS chief Heinrich Himmler, party secretary Martin Bormann, commander-in-chief Field Marshal Wilhelm Keitel, and the *Gauleiter* for the Danzig region, Albert Forster. As that guest list suggests, this was an important visit. Indeed, it was highly symbolic. Just as Hitler had addressed the German people by radio on the first day of the campaign, so he spoke to them now from Danzig: a city that, for many Germans, symbolized German suffering, and whose conquest provided justification for the war.

He began rather quietly and hesitantly, declaring that he was well aware of "the greatness of the hour," and stressing that Danzig had always been German. He repeated his now well-practiced account of the circumstances that had led to this point: the iniquities of the Treaty of

Versailles, the martyrdom of the German minority, and the foolishness of the Poles—whom he damned as culturally inferior and dictatorially ruled by a "consumptive upper class"—in rejecting his reasonable suggestions for a solution.[2] Instead, he said, the Poles "chose struggle," goaded by the perfidious British. In the battles that followed, he conceded, the lower ranks had "fought courageously," but "the middle-rank leadership lacked intelligence and the upper-echelon leadership was bad beyond criticism." In its organization, he quipped, the army was "Polish," using the pejorative German synonym for chaos, and drawing a prolonged round of laughter and applause from his audience. He boasted:

> As I am speaking to you now, our troops are arrayed along a long line stretching from Lemberg [Lwów] to Brest and northwards. Since yesterday afternoon, endless columns of the badly beaten Polish army have been marching from the Kutno area as prisoners of war. Yesterday morning, they numbered 20,000; there were 50,000 last night; 70,000 this morning. I do not know how great their numbers are at present, but there is one thing I do know: whatever remains of this Polish army west of this line will capitulate within a few days and lay down its arms, or it will be smashed![3]

Hitler went on to contrast the "humane manner" in which his forces had conducted the war with the bestiality of the Poles—the "dirtiest deeds committed throughout the past centuries," the "thousands of slaughtered ethnic Germans, the brutishly butchered women, girls and children . . . massacred, mutilated, with their eyes gouged out." Speaking of his new ally, Stalin, he told his audience that the Red Army's invasion had been motivated by the need to "safeguard the interests" of Poland's Byelorussian and Ukrainian minorities. Moreover, he suggested that the Red Army's actions had had no military significance, and that German forces alone had defeated the Poles "in scarcely eighteen days."[4] Stalin would have been delighted.

Contrary to his claim that the Polish campaign was over, however, Hitler knew well that fighting was still raging within earshot of the center of Danzig. When Heinz Linge later questioned him about it, "when he was in a good mood," Hitler told him that, "for political and propaganda purposes," the Soviets did not wish to "bask in any of the glory of victory," so the fiction was proclaimed that the war had already been brought to a successful end.[5] The truth was that, even within the district of Danzig itself, pockets of Polish resistance were still holding out.

At Oksywie, for instance, north of the port of Gdynia and barely 15 kilometers (9 miles) from Danzig, the Polish defense of an area of forested high ground—the Oksywie Heights—had degenerated into a conflict resembling the conditions of the Great War. The defenders were manning hastily dug trenches, while the Germans were forced to attack across flooded marshland. To those engaged in the fighting, that sense of anachronism would only have been heightened by the presence, on the Polish side, of a volunteer company of scythemen, raised from a local workers' union, who fought in one of the initial skirmishes before being withdrawn and armed with captured rifles.[6]

By the time the local Polish commander, Colonel Stanisław Dąbek, withdrew the remainder of his forces to the Oksywie Heights on September 12, the garrison—a mélange of militia, marines, and artillerymen—numbered around 9,000 men; armed with 140 heavy machine guns and two dozen pieces of artillery, they occupied an area of less than 4 square kilometers (1.5 square miles).[7] Dąbek was said to have steeled his men by proclaiming, "I will show you how a Pole fights and dies"—words that would later be emblazoned upon his grave.[8] The German forces facing him, under the command of Luftwaffe general Leonhard Kaupisch, included elements of the SS-Heimwehr Danzig, which had brutally ended the siege at the Polish Post Office on the first day of the war, and had committed the massacre of some 33 Poles in the village of Książki just a few days before.[9] According to one Polish account, the men of the SS unit were clearly better suited to "combat" with unarmed civilians than to engagement with a trained army. Now, assailed by flanking fire during their advance, one German battalion was all but wiped out: "The swamps resounded with screams, as was always the case with defeated Germans. Surprised in open terrain, they fled in panic across the marsh, leaving behind their wounded and killed," the Polish account said.[10] It was the second time the men of the SS-Heimwehr Danzig had been forced into an ignominious retreat, as they had been involved at the Westerplatte. Nonetheless, they were later cheered in the streets of Danzig, their pockets stuffed with candy and cigarettes by grateful civilians.[11]

Over the week that followed, the battle for Oksywie would develop into one of the bitterest and most costly of the entire campaign. Surrounded on three sides, with their backs to the Bay of Danzig, the Polish defenders would endure incessant skirmishing as well as air raids and artillery fire from the *Schleswig-Holstein*, which was moored close to the Westerplatte. As an account by one *Stuka* pilot relates, the raids spared nothing and no one: "Our goal was to carry out an attack on batteries and bunkers, signal lights, trenches and artillery positions. . . . I flew in combat order and dived. The bombs fell right next to the houses, blowing off the roofs. After a while I saw people running out and, as I pulled up, another plane came down, strafing the scattering Poles. The third strike was aimed at the roads leading down to the water, where we caught up with the fleeing Poles again."[12] As the Oksywie pocket was gradually reduced, casualty rates soared; some 2,000 of the defenders were killed. On September 18, Dąbek sent a telegram to his superior, Rear-Admiral Józef Unrug, outlining how the territory they defended had shrunk, how the guns had been destroyed by air raids, and how the garrison was running dangerously short of ammunition and food. He asked for a decision on whether the defense should be continued, expressing his willingness to do so if ordered. In reply, Unrug wrote, "I leave that decision to you, Colonel, but please know that I want no massacres." He repeated, "I want no massacres."[13]

Realizing that he could not hold the positions for much longer, on the afternoon of September 19 Colonel Dąbek evacuated some of his remaining troops to the Hel Peninsula, across the bay. He then gathered his staff officers. "Our role as commanders is over," he told them, "but we have not ceased to be soldiers, and our duty as soldiers we will fulfill until the end."[14] Soon thereafter, he led his men on a last foray toward

The guns of Oksywie, barely silenced by Hitler's arrival.
Muzeum II Wojny Światowej, Gdańsk

the Germans, engaging the enemy with a crackle of gunfire and inviting a hail of artillery shells in response. Later that evening, just as Hitler was beginning his address to the German people in nearby Danzig, Colonel Dąbek recognized the insuperable odds that his men faced and gave an order to end the fight. He then took out his service pistol and shot himself.[15] As a mark of respect for the defenders, the Germans allowed Dąbek to be buried with military honors, with four Wehrmacht officers in attendance.[16]

Soon after that, the Polish headquarters in Oksywie was finally overrun. A signals officer on Hel listened in as the switchboard room fell: "I heard the sounds of a struggle, gunshots, and the operator said: 'The Germans are here! Long Live Poland!' [Niemcy wchodzą! Niech żyje Polska!]," he later wrote. "A second later, another voice spoke in Polish, but with a strong guttural German accent."[17] With that, the connection to Oksywie was lost. Hel now held out alone.

Two days later, Hitler—who was still quartered in Zoppot—was doing a good impression of the "first soldier of the Reich," just as he had promised in his speech before the Reichstag on the first day of the war.[18] According to Heinz Linge, he "behaved as though he were on manoeuvres in the field," traveling to the front almost daily, inspecting the aftermath of battle, and meeting his generals. In Danzig, on September 21, he was ferried by minesweeper to the city harbor, where he boarded the *Schleswig-Holstein* to congratulate her crew on the role they had played in crushing Polish resistance on the Westerplatte. He then visited the battlefield itself, pacing pensively amid the shell holes and broken trees. According to Linge, Hitler was most interested in assessing the damage that the *Schleswig-Holstein*'s guns and the *Stuka* attacks had wrought.[19]

In the afternoon, he was returned to Gdynia and Oksywie to see the aftermath of the fighting there. According to the account of General Walter Warlimont, who was part of Hitler's staff, the journey to Oksywie was to be the cause of some considerable friction. Unusually, given the large number of top brass present for Hitler's speech, the Führer's convoy—excluding his own six-wheeled Mercedes-Benz G4—comprised as many as thirty limousines, which contained senior personnel as well as their adjutants and bodyguards. As it set off for Oksywie, this traveling circus aroused Warlimont's indignation when he noticed that the various vehicles were forming up two abreast, so as to best satisfy the precise requirements of protocol. Aghast at such vanity, Warlimont then witnessed Martin Bormann fly into a rage, cursing those present "in outrageous language," as he felt that he had been slighted.[20] In the dog-eat-dog world of Nazi politics, such petty matters took on huge significance.

While senior Nazis jostled for position, farther along the coast, on the Hel Peninsula, real fighting was still raging. In order to defend the Hel naval base at the eastern tip of the spit, a "fortified area" had been established in the mid-1930s, which, though incomplete by September 1939, nonetheless consisted of four heavy artillery emplacements as well as three antiaircraft batteries, an independent power supply, and a garrison of over 3,000 men.[21] This "Hel Fortified Area" was under the command of Rear-Admiral Józef Unrug, who, despite having been born in Germany, having commanded a U-boat in the Imperial German Navy during the Great War, and speaking better German than he did Polish, remained true to his Polish roots: he reportedly "forgot how to speak German" on September 1, 1939.[22]

The battle for Hel was one of the longest of the campaign. It began in earnest on September 11, when elements of the German 207th Infantry Division took the town of Władysławowo at the neck of the peninsula, leaving remaining Polish forces cut off from the mainland. What followed was a land offensive, with German units pushing their foes into a slow fighting retreat along the 35-kilometer (22-mile) peninsula. In this effort the Germans on the ground were aided by an aerial assault employing dive-bombers as well as naval artillery to soften up the defenders. After Hitler's arrival in Zoppot, his entourage could enjoy watching the spectacle of Hel being shelled from the hotel terrace, the *Schleswig-Holstein* having been joined in the Bay of Danzig by the *Schlesien* on September 20. Hitler's interpreter, Paul Schmidt, recalled that "with their high funnels and superstructure," the old German cruisers "made the whole scene look like some old picture of a naval engagement, especially when the Polish artillery retaliated and waterspouts shot up round the ships."[23]

On Hel, the effects of the bombardments were not as great as the gentlemen in Zoppot might have hoped. The raids were certainly impressive. One Polish naval officer describing an attack by the *Schleswig-Holstein* noted: "First, a flash, then after a few seconds came the sound of an incoming shell, and then two detonations in quick succession; the delayed report of the discharge, followed by the louder blast of the exploding shell. The earth seemed to sway under my feet. Next a pillar of smoke 30–50 meters [18–30 feet] high." Given the slim target the peninsula presented, however, many of the shells fell in the water, and those that hit the beach and foreshore were largely ineffective. Even on land, the sandy ground tended to nullify the full explosive effects, with many shells failing to detonate. As the naval officer noted, "In spite of the terrific detonations, they caused no significant damage." Even the psychological effect, he suggested, was minimal: "The men," he said, "have grown accustomed to the bombardment."[24]

Morale was more of a problem for the defenders. A lack of food sapped the will to resist. By September 23, potatoes had already run out, and there was no meat to be found except for whatever could be scavenged from horse carcasses. Moreover, with no prospect of victory, there was little will to continue the unequal fight, particularly when rumors spread of Poland's plight beyond the bay and beyond the horizon. One eyewitness explained the problem with brutal honesty. The defense of Hel, he said, was more "a show of despair" than a practical proposition, and they could not "expect every soldier to die a hero's death for an idea."[25] Nonetheless, Hel would fight on.

WHILE THE KASINO HOTEL IN ZOPPOT OFFERED ITS GUESTS WAR as a spectacle, farther along the coast the German "New World Order" was proving anything but entertaining for the Polish inhabitants of Danzig. Many of the city's Poles had already been rounded up in the first days of the war and brought to collecting points, such as Victoria School, where they would be "processed." They included priests, teachers, lawyers, politicians: all those who might feasibly provide a focus for resistance to the German occupation. Already upon arrival, the new regime was brutally clear. "The Poles entering the courtyard were pummeled with batons by a row of Stormtroopers," one prisoner recalled. Once inside, their identification cards and all valuables would be confiscated. "After registration," the prisoner said, "I was directed to a cellar so crowded that there was standing room only. Among the victims of the beating I noticed Father Komorowski. His mouth was a bloody pulp. Near him stood Mr. Tejowski with his face swollen from the blows. Nobody felt like talking. Silence reigned."[26]

According to the German newspapers in Danzig, such individuals were "unreliable elements"—"traitors, arsonists, looters, and enemies of the state"—and their internment was a necessary countermeasure against "Polish aggression." They would be "sieved" at Victoria School, as well as "deloused, debugged, and disinfected"; after all, one newspaper reminded its readers, "it is unimaginable how filthy these Poles are."[27] On September 15, the camp in the school was closed and the inmates were taken to a number of makeshift internment camps, where they would be made to pay for their supposed crimes with hard labor. On the way, they were forced to march through the streets of Danzig, where they were jeered and abused by the civilian population. The sight of the prisoners, bruised and limping, should have aroused pity, but, as one of their number recalled, it just generated more hatred: "Torn, beaten up, haggard, they staggered along . . . cursed by passersby," he said.[28]

Among the camps to which the unfortunate prisoners were sent, Stutthof (Sztutowo)—a former resort some 30 kilometers (18 miles) east of Danzig—would become the most enduring. There, conditions were brutal from the outset. Arriving prisoners were systematically broken with a barrage of blows and insults. When Ryszard Dudzik had the temerity to tell an SS officer that he had fought in the defense of the Westerplatte, he was beaten unconscious with a pistol, losing most of his teeth in the process.[29] "From now on," the camp commandant informed them, "you are no longer people, just numbers. You have lost all rights, you left them at the gate."[30] Stutthof was no place for the sick, or malingerers, they were told; there were only the living and the dead. Every inmate was expected to be able to recite their prisoner number, clearly, in German. Failure to do so would result in punishment, as one inmate discovered when she forgot her number during her first roll call: "I received a terrible beating," she later said. "When I fell, my friends helped me stand up in my spot. I was called out again and had to tell my number, but I couldn't. Another pummeling. Unconscious, I was thrown into the block."[31]

The new inmates were immediately set to work clearing trees from the swampy ground and constructing the wooden barrack blocks that would house the new arrivals. One prisoner from that first transport, Wacław Lewandowski, remembered that "the pace of the work was murderous. If one stopped to stretch for a moment, or worked slowly, one was immediately kicked, hit, or otherwise tormented."[32] Some inmates were taken to the Westerplatte, where, under the contemptuous eyes of their SS guards, they cleared the site of munitions and removed the debris from the earlier fighting. One prisoner, recalling the horrendous treatment they received, noted that it could lead to deteriorating health and even worse results: "We were served our first meal—coffee, bread. We had no cups. We drank from our caps, berets. That's how it went for a few days. We would sleep outside, in the ruins. They didn't even give us any tents or blankets. Most of us had only summer clothes, some were in their pajamas. And so, many of us got ill. One time a few guys reported sick to the Germans. Instead of medical help, they got a beating."[33]

For the prisoners that remained in Stutthof, conditions were little better. While the barracks were being built that autumn, the prisoners were housed in tents, with only a single tap for washing. One inmate recalled that "the water trickled so slowly that one had to wait a long time to get a handful. . . . But we only had limited time, as all the prisoners had to wash in an hour."[34] Unsurprisingly, perhaps, the exhausted prisoners would often forgo washing, hurrying instead to get some food, usually a thin, indeterminate soup and a piece of stale rye bread. One of them was dismayed to note that the dogs of the SS guards received better food than the inmates.[35]

Even when they lay down to rest, there was little comfort to be had. Ryszard Dudzik recalled that "there were no beds: we lay on straw that was soaked with urine, and sometimes with excrement. . . . We lay all on one side, like herrings in a barrel, and there was no possibility even to turn over, unless everyone turned over at the same time. If someone went to the toilet at night, he would have great difficulty retaking his place in the straw. Inside, there was the most incredible stink."[36] The prisoners were being systematically degraded, weakened to the point of collapse. "Even the mentally strong among us were broken," one inmate recalled, "crying from pain, humiliation, and exhaustion."[37]

By the time of Hitler's arrival in Danzig, Stutthof was already "home" to some 400 prisoners. It was fast emerging as the hub of a network of internment camps in the Danzig region that would soon contain thousands more people. The conditions demonstrated that the realities of German rule were brutally simple: Poles were to be reduced to the status of slaves, with no purpose except to serve their German masters—or die in the process.

HITLER NEVER VISITED STUTTHOF, JUST AS HE NEVER VISITED any of his concentration camps. The purpose of his visit to Danzig was primarily for propaganda. Beyond that, he was keen to visit the front lines, savor the whiff of cordite in his nostrils, and spur his troops on to new successes. After Danzig, his next logical destination was Warsaw, where Polish soldiers and civilians were still doggedly holding out in a living refutation of Hitler's claim that the war had already been won. Hitler boarded his private plane—a modified Focke-Wulf Fw-200 Condor—on the morning of September 22, landing some time later in a field outside the Polish capital. After a short visit to Łochów, east of Warsaw, to see the wreck of the Polish armored train *Generał Sosnkowski*, which had been derailed in an air attack and become something of a tourist attraction, Hitler was taken to a German command post in Praga, on the east bank of the Vistula.[38] As his pilot, Hans Baur, remembered, from there he wanted to witness "the final bombardment of Warsaw," believing that it would lead to the city's surrender.[39] He was to be disappointed.

As Hitler observed the Polish capital from a church tower on September 22, he would have been unaware that the city was not quite as stricken and defeated as he might have imagined. It was only on that day, for instance, that the Germans had finally succeeded in cutting Warsaw off from the fortress to its north, Modlin.[40] Despite the loss of the connection to Warsaw, the area defended around Modlin was still considerable, encompassing some 30 square kilometers (11 square miles), with the formidable red-brick fortress at its heart. It was defended by

15,000 soldiers, primarily of the 8th and 28th Infantry Divisions, and still held a similar number of civilians. In addition, around 100 artillery pieces were present, as well as nearly 5,000 horses, 62 heavy machine guns, and a small number of tankettes.[41] In a throwback to the days of the Polish–Soviet War of 1920, the defense of Modlin also relied on the armored train *Śmierć*, an agglomeration of artillery platforms and assault cars that was 70 meters (230 feet) long and had a crew of around 150. It was used to transport munitions within the Modlin sector and provided artillery support to Polish infantry at the eastern end of the sector. Remarkably, on September 19, the *Śmierć* also engaged in an artillery duel with a German counterpart—the *Panzerzug 7*—which was patrolling the line beyond the front.[42]

Modlin would be bitterly defended. Sporadic German ground assaults had gained some territory, but most of the offensive had been carried out by artillery and air attack, aiming primarily at the fortress complex and the bridges over the rivers by which the three areas held by the Poles maintained contact. German air attacks by *Stuka* bombers were not always guaranteed success, as one pilot recalled: "18 bombs of 500 kilograms [1,100 pounds] each, 12 bombs of 250 kilograms [550 pounds], and 48 bombs of 50 kilograms [110 pounds], in each sortie—and the bridge didn't even sway."[43] Elsewhere, however, they could be devastatingly effective. The garrison commander, Brigadier-General Wiktor Thommée, recalled that his unit "stopped trying to put out fires when the task became completely futile. The fortress was in flames, houses and barracks were collapsing. Rubble, unexploded bombs, shrapnel littered the streets and square, bomb craters were everywhere."[44] One of Modlin's defenders anticipated the fate of Zakroczym, a historic town once built to guard the crossings on the Vistula that was now facing destruction. "Perhaps in a few short days," he wrote, "it will fall victim to German bombs and artillery shells . . . not a house of it will be left standing."[45]

And yet the defenders fought on, bravely emerging from their shelters to meet the ground assault that inevitably followed every air raid. As one of them remembered:

After a few minutes the Germans attacked. We remained silent at first. The Germans must have thought that after such an intense artillery barrage and with a possible shortage of ammunition, our crew was ready to surrender. But they were sorely disappointed. At the first burst from our light artillery squadron, our machine guns—which had only been waiting for that moment—exploded into a powerful song. I noticed that the Germans instantly dropped to the ground, many of them likely never to get up again. Our accurate gunfire did not allow the enemy to move forward even in isolated leaps. The barrage proved to be impassable.[46]

After a series of such ineffective ground attacks, the Germans attempted negotiation. Rochus Misch, then an *Unterscharführer* (sergeant) in the SS-Leibstandarte Adolf Hitler—and later to become Hitler's personal bodyguard—was part of a four-man group that approached Polish lines to try to negotiate a surrender. As he was from Upper Silesia, he was thought to speak sufficient Polish for the task, though, as he confessed, his knowledge of the language extended only to "trying to make German words sound like Polish." For this reason, perhaps, the talks with the Poles failed. After spending "a few hours" wandering around the defenses, he and the group that accompanied him opted to return to their own side. However, just as they were negotiating some barbed-wire obstacles, some 80 meters (260 feet) from the Polish lines, the Poles opened fire. Misch was hit in the arm and the chest, with a bullet passing only 2 centimeters (0.8 inches) from his heart. Clearly, the Poles were in no mood to surrender.[47]

In the stalemate that followed, the Germans resorted to leafleting raids, as they did in Warsaw, hoping to break the defenders' spirits by stressing the pointlessness of the fight and their betrayal by Poland's "Western Friends." It was an approach that seemed to hold some promise of success, playing as it did on the Poles' gnawing sense that they had indeed been sacrificed by the British and the French. As one of the defenders lamented:

Lovely phrases broadcast by Western radio stations, such as "You are an inspiration to other nations" or "History will forever remember your heroism," are taken by the men as a bitter mockery of our current situation. We are not fighting for "inspired nations" to calmly watch our tragedy from a distance. We are fighting for the very existence of *our* nation. We have no use for lofty words from our allies, but need specific actions to prove that our allies deserve that name and are truly on our side.[48]

Sadly, in that demand, the Poles were to be disappointed.

Despite their dire strategic situation, the Poles were still capable of springing a surprise on their opponents. A few days before Hitler's arrival in Praga, Polish efforts to force a passage into Warsaw by some surviving elements of the Poznań Army had resulted in the Battle of Wólka Węglowa, to the north of the capital. It was a rare Polish victory, albeit a Pyrrhic one. Here, Polish cavalry repeatedly charged German positions near Mościska before being engaged by armor. One of the participants, Colonel Klemens Rudnicki, commander of the 9th Uhlan Regiment, described the engagement as "an assault on an enemy taken by surprise." Initially the Poles made good progress: "Both squadrons attacked in a series of rushes," Rudnicki later reported. "Several tanks and cars left behind by the enemy were captured, and small groups of Germans were quickly annihilated. After a few minutes the whole village had been occupied."[49] It was a skirmish that would be immortalized in the breathless account of an Italian war correspondent, Mario Appelius:

Suddenly, a heroic group of cavalrymen, about 500 horses, flew at full gallop out of the undergrowth. They advanced with an unfurled banner in their midst. . . . All German machine guns fell silent, only the cannons continued to fire. Their barrage created a wall of fire about 300 meters [985 feet] in front of the German lines. The Polish cavalry advanced at full speed: a sight straight out of a medieval painting!

They were led by their commander with a raised saber. The distance between the Polish cavalry and the wall of German fire was quickly shrinking. To continue this charge into the arms of death was madness. And yet the Poles broke through.[50]

In truth, after their initial success, the Poles had to endure an armored counterattack before disengaging later in the afternoon. They had sustained heavy losses. That evening, all surviving cavalrymen were ordered to dismount and proceed on foot, under cover of darkness, into Warsaw. Their horses were set loose. "It was a dreadful order," Rudnicki wrote, "smelling of 'sauve qui peut' [every man for himself]."[51] The departing Uhlans left over 100 dead comrades behind and a similar number of wounded. The remainder of the two cavalry regiments managed to break through to the capital.

One of those who made it through during those last days before the ring closed was General Tadeusz Kutrzeba, the architect of the Polish counterattack on the Bzura. Along with remnants of the Poznań and Pomeranian Armies, he made his way into the capital on September 20 and presented himself at the headquarters of General Juliusz Rómmel, the commander of Polish forces in Warsaw. "I have lost a battle," he told them forthrightly. Though he had expected a dressing down or even a confrontation—after all, Rómmel had neglected to send assistance to his men on the Bzura—he was to be pleasantly surprised. "I was received with chivalry, honor and understanding," Kutrzeba recalled, "no trace of displeasure, no complacency."[52] In time, he would be appointed Rómmel's deputy.

On September 22, with Hitler across the Vistula in Praga, Polish forces attempted to repeat the trick they had pulled at Wólka Węglowa at nearby Łomianki. Early that morning, around 5,000 soldiers—the last of the Poznań Army—set off under the command of General Mikołaj Bołtuć in an attempt to pierce German lines and break through to Warsaw. After they broke the first line of defense, their advance was halted by intense artillery fire at the railway embankment that ran parallel to the river. According to one German account, the Poles "did not even have a bravery born of desperation, rather [they] were moved by a fatalistic sense of futility."[53] Others disagreed. A soldier of the German 30th Infantry Regiment described the Polish attack as being so intense that some German positions became untenable; panic briefly reigned, he said, but then "officers, NCOs, and men fought back desperately with rifles and machine guns, finally pulling hand grenades and entrenching tools from their belts in the hand-to-hand fighting."[54] Dawn revealed a bloody scene. The dead littered the roadside, and horses, wagons, artillery pieces, cars, and trucks had all been thrown together in a "whirlwind of destruction."[55] By the afternoon, unable to break through, and having lost their commander in the battle, the Poles called off the attack. Their losses were estimated at around 800 dead.

One death that day would have special significance. Word reached Hitler on the afternoon of September 22 that Colonel-General Werner Freiherr von Fritsch, the monocled former commander-in-chief of the Wehrmacht, had been killed at the front outside Warsaw. Having been forced into retirement the previous year, after being disgraced in a spurious homosexual scandal, Fritsch had returned to command his former regiment, the 12th Artillery, and had been inspecting the front lines at Praga when he was caught by a bullet in the upper thigh. Whether it was from a ricochet or directly from a sniper's gun was unknown, but in any case, it severed his femoral artery. As his adjutant recalled, the general collapsed immediately, waving away his efforts to loosen his belt with a weary "Just leave it," and then lost consciousness. Before a tourniquet could be applied, Fritsch had bled to death.[56]

According to pilot Hans Baur, Hitler was informed of the death as he waited to board his aircraft that afternoon to leave for Danzig. He "briefly expressed his regret," Baur wrote, "then got back into the plane."[57] In the days that followed, Hitler would pen a short communiqué and order a state funeral, which he himself would not attend. Many of those who knew the general suspected that, depressed by his treatment the previous year, he had chosen to end his life by deliberately exposing himself to enemy fire.[58] The diarist Victor Klemperer would have summed up the thoughts of many Germans when he recorded the event: "Colonel-General Fritsch, until a few months ago Commander-in-Chief of the army, fell outside Warsaw on 22 September. A few lines of obituary, tiny picture, details merely in passing and trivialised. Independently of one another Eva [Klemperer's wife] and I placed the same question mark."[59]

Just as Polish units were trying to make it into Warsaw, so the city's many remaining foreign nationals were trying to get out. On September 21, they got their chance when it was announced that a temporary ceasefire would permit the evacuation of those foreigners holding passports from neutral countries. One of those leaving was the American photographer Julien Bryan, who had been chronicling the siege of the city and was now gathered with hundreds of others outside the Hotel Bristol, clutching only the one small piece of hand baggage that was permitted. In due course, a convoy of cars and army trucks arrived, and the evacuees were processed and loaded. Bryan's thoughts were with those who could not escape the maelstrom. One of the saddest sights, he later wrote, was the Polish staff of the US embassy, who "calmly rounded up the others to go to a place of safety, when they themselves must remain." Another who stayed behind was the US vice-consul, Thaddeus Chyliński, who refused to leave his Polish wife, though he possessed an American passport.[60]

Once the evacuees were all loaded into the trucks and cars, the convoy set off across the Vistula into Praga and then traveled northward, past the ruined houses and bemused civilians and toward the "no-man's-land" a few kilometers beyond. Crossing the Polish lines, Bryan recalled, they "could see shallow trenches and machine guns, crudely camouflaged with small branches, and infantry lying quietly with their rifles in shell holes and ditches. Barely five hundred yards behind them, in the workers' district of Praga, children were playing." Shortly thereafter, the evacuees climbed down from the vehicles, said their goodbyes to their Polish drivers, and continued their journey on foot. In due course, they were met by German soldiers, who helped them onto a fleet of spotless army trucks for their onward journey to

Königsberg (Kaliningrad) and safety. "The Germans made quite a show," one eyewitness noted. "Handsome officers in bright new-looking uniforms hastened to pick up the hand baggage of women and to carry their small children for them, smiling all the while."[61] "It was all smiles and courtesy," Bryan remembered. "Having shelled and bombed us for weeks, now they carried our bags, patted babies." He couldn't help but notice that a German propaganda film unit was on hand to record the event for posterity. Bryan smuggled out the fruit of his own efforts at counterpropaganda—the three small rolls of film containing his iconic images of the German siege—inside a souvenir gas mask.[62]

The city that Bryan had left was in turmoil. German infantry assaults continued and were met with a sometimes desperate response. A nurse in a field hospital recalled a Polish soldier rushing into the building to announce that the Germans had broken through and that tanks were on their street. She watched as the building was fortified: "I begin packing, they help barricade the windows. Hand grenades are being handed out, we get them too. The captain walks up to me: 'Can you use a gun? This is for your personal use.' A small 'Belgian' [pistol] falls in my pocket. Behind the barricades, soldiers with grenades, rifles, ammunition on hand. Machine guns upstairs. All eyes are focused. Without fear."[63]

Where the German attacks were successful, they were often followed by a level of brutality that had become sadly customary. One resident, Michalina Mazińska, experienced the new realities at first hand when her block, in Brzeziny on the east side of the Vistula, was taken by the enemy. When the Germans arrived, she told a postwar commission, she was in her flat with her husband and child. The Germans took her husband outside into the courtyard: "My child was crying desperately for its father, and I looked through the window. The Germans got three men, ordered them to put their hands up and shot all three of them. I couldn't stay in the flat due to the overwhelming noise and shooting, so I went to the basement. As I was going downstairs, I heard the last words of my husband, who said, 'Jesus, Mary, deliver my soul!' Germans yelling, a crack and a blood-curdling groan."[64] Three days later, when she dared to retrieve her husband's body, she found that he had taken six bullets and had also been stabbed in the side with a bayonet. His only fault was to have been unlucky.

The Wehrmacht kept up the pressure on the ground, but most of the danger for Warsaw came from the air. The bombing of the city had already been ramped up after September 17, in an effort to force a surrender and make good on Hitler's claim that the war was over. As one observer noted perceptively, "The Germans evidently realised our Allies would not create a second front, and that they could employ all their strength to crush our resistance. The advance of the Soviet Army seemingly had intensified the frenzy of their attack."[65] The Luftwaffe's targets included the Royal Castle, the Sejm (parliament building), the Cathedral of St. John, and the city's concert hall. "Nothing is sacred to the enemy," one diarist complained.[66] As one gleeful German account put it, Warsaw was the target of a number of successful aerial attacks, particularly against the power plants, water works, and gasworks, as well as road and rail junctions in the suburbs. The *Stukas* "fall like meteors, heavy and blindingly fast . . . flames erupt with wonderful precision, accurate hits on appointed targets throw up pillars of smoke. . . . A boiling red glow of fires glimmers over the city."[67]

In addition to the Luftwaffe raids, the Germans sent countless artillery shells—some estimated 25,000 in one day[68]—to bring chaos to the city's streets and suburbs. Władysław Szpilman recalled that "the street, red with the glow of fires, was empty, and there was no sound but the echo of bursting shells. . . . Heavy blood-red masses of smoke loomed over the buildings."[69] In the southern suburb of Mokotów, the bombs hit the house next door to Maria Komornicka, shattering all the windows. "As soon as I walked away from the window it hit," she wrote in her diary. "The ceiling over Mum's bed caved in. Good thing she was not in it. She was sitting on the toilet."[70]

For those beneath the hail of bombs, it could be a real test of nerves. One diarist testified to the emotional strain of an air raid: "Crowded together . . . everyone stands and listens. Hearts beat loudly. You can hear a continuous whine—that's an exploding bomb cutting through the air. Before you hear it actually explode, there is a terrible second of anticipation. During a fraction of a second, thousands of thoughts run through your mind and your heart misses a beat. . . . People curl up to make themselves smaller, as small as possible, anything to avoid the bomb."[71]

Some found it difficult to cope. In one instance, a fireman raged in despair at the destruction on a Warsaw street. "The town hall is burning," he yelled at no one in particular, "the castle is burning! Do you understand what it means to see all these beloved buildings burning and not be able to help? Warsaw is burning. The Germans are smashing everything we have!"[72] Having devoted his life to saving Warsaw's citizens and property, his impotence in the face of so much destruction was too much for him to take. Lack of rest exacerbated the nervous tension. An officer in an antiaircraft unit complained that it was hard to sleep when "every few minutes you heard the whizz of an artillery shell, followed by a flash like lightning, which illuminated the room." Just as frustrating for him was his anxious young deputy, who constantly shone a torch at his fiancée's photograph, saying over and over "Jeszcze żyję, jeszcze żyję" (I am still alive, I am still alive).[73]

Others were not so fortunate. One Warsaw resident recalled being caught in a raid in the Targówek district of Praga. After taking cover, she emerged to see 10 corpses on the street. "We collected the blood-stained bodies with spades," she said. "The remains were so mangled, it was impossible to tell them apart."[74] A report from September 19 noted that, on that day alone, the municipal authorities retrieved some 166 unclaimed corpses from the city's streets. These bodies would be buried in parkland and open ground, such as Krasiński Square or the Zoological Garden.[75] Alexander Polonius joined a burial party at the Frascati Gardens in central Warsaw, where some seventy corpses were taken the following day. "They were brought in wheelbarrows and carts, loaded one on top of the other like so many lumps of meat, their heads and limbs dangling and shaking as the carts jolted over the uneven ground," he later wrote. The most difficult part of the task, he recalled, was to search the bodies for identification, which meant rifling through blood-soaked coats and handbags. Most were impossible to identify, however: "Many of the bodies were those of women who had obviously been shopping and shot while they stood in the queue. They still clasped their handbags with their money, but had no identification on them whatsoever."[76]

Food was already an urgent priority for all Varsovians. Given that the city had been cut off by the Germans for around a week, and the population was swollen with refugees from the suburbs as well as soldiers from Kampinos Forest, the food situation was critical. Scavenging, even pilfering, were commonplace. Marta Korwin remembered agonizing over the moral implications of stealing from a nearby field of cabbages in order to feed the patients in her hospital. "It had not taken long—less than three weeks—to change our ethical values," she wrote.[77] Desperation bred ingenuity. Horsemeat soon found its way onto the kitchen table, and it was even praised by the authorities for its flavor. It did at least have the advantage of relative abundance: equine corpses had become common on Warsaw's streets, and many of them would scarcely be cold before they were butchered by hungry civilians. One eyewitness recalled visiting a restaurant on Nowy Świat, where he was treated to a soup made from red cabbage and horsemeat: "A horse's jawbone and a cannon bone protruded from the soup tureen," he darkly joked.[78]

In such trying circumstances, a little humor was invariably required, and some found it in the German leaflets that were dropped on the city on the morning of September 21. The leaflets were intended to intimidate: to demand the city's surrender, to reiterate Poland's predicament and the failings of its military and leadership, and to threaten further bombing if the city's defenders did not comply. But both the mangled Polish grammar and the empty promises of fair treatment for prisoners aroused little except a cynical smile. "We received leaflets like those, in broken Polish, every day, and we laughed at the spelling mistakes," one observer later wrote. "We did not believe in German 'chivalry,' as our experience provided evidence to the contrary." Another diarist added that "no one paid any attention to the German threats and promises. The leaflets were torn up or burned. Some people thought they were poisoned. One fell in our garden. . . . Father stuck his walking stick through it and brought it unostentatiously into the kitchen and burned it in the cooker."[79]

Such petty acts of defiance demonstrate that, for some at least, morale was solid and the will to resist unimpaired, despite the suffering. In fact, the secret situational reports of Warsaw's Defense Command would seem to confirm that conclusion. A "positive atmosphere" among the residents continued, it was reported on September 21, and though the news of the Soviet invasion had caused concern, the "will to fight and the faith in ultimate victory" were unaffected.[80] The anecdotal evidence from Warsaw's diarists lends further corroboration. One recalled a sergeant calmly addressing injured soldiers in a cellar during an air raid. "It is nothing, boys," he said, "if they destroy us, burn us, kill us. Death comes only once. And to lose a fortune, a hand, a leg, or life itself for what one believes, for a holy cause—one has to do it. If the whole of Poland is occupied—if it be completely destroyed—we shall rise again, so don't worry, boys."[81]

The mainstay of Warsaw's morale during the siege was Stefan Starzyński's daily radio broadcast. His defiant addresses lent a purpose to the suffering and gave Varsovians a vision for the future. "No news carried with it more authority," one man recalled, "than that broadcast every day by Mayor Starzyński, whose daily talks to the populace were listened to with religious attention. In them, he spoke about current events, he educated the people, he heartened them to resist, he interpreted and explained the situation and exposed the lies spread by the German wireless service."[82]

Starzyński's address on the afternoon of September 23 was a prime example. Looking back over his time as mayor, he told his listeners:

I wanted Warsaw to be great. I believed that it would be great. I and my colleagues drew up plans, sketched the great Warsaw of the future. And Warsaw is great. It happened sooner than we expected. Not in fifty years, not in a hundred, but today I see a great Warsaw. As I speak these words to you, I see her through the windows in all her glory and grandeur, surrounded by billows of smoke, reddened with flames of fire, magnificent, indestructible, grand, fighting Warsaw. And though the places where magnificent orphanages were to stand are filled with rubble, though barricades thickly covered with the bodies of the dead stand where parks used to be, though hospitals are in flames—not in fifty years, not in a hundred, but today Warsaw is at the height of her grandeur and glory, as she fights for the honor of Poland.[83]

These words would stay with the city's inhabitants. That afternoon, shortly after three o'clock, the main power station serving Warsaw was destroyed in a German air raid. With that, the electricity supply failed and the radio abruptly shut off during a broadcast of the second movement of Rachmaninov's Piano Concerto in C minor.[84] Starzyński was now condemned to silence, unable to air his inspiring addresses. And German forces stood poised for what Hitler hoped would be the final chapter in Polish defiance.

Chapter Eight

IMPENITENT THIEVES

O N THE SAME DAY THAT HITLER WAS PEERING AT WARSAW through field glasses, and the Western Allies were honing their platitudes in Hove, Poland suffered another existential blow: Lwów, the country's southeastern cultural and political center, the centerpiece of its defense in the region, surrendered to the Red Army.

Lwów had been bombed by the Germans on the very first day of the war and had duly begun to prepare itself for another attack, but the German forces, at that time at least, appeared to be targeting other sites. The city was a major Polish bastion in the eastern borderlands, home to over 300,000 people as well as a prestigious university, the famous Ossoliński Library, and a host of other political and cultural institutions. After being added to the Polish realm in 1349, Lwów had resisted invading Swedes, Cossacks, Hungarians, Turks, and Russians, earning the sobriquet of "Semper Fidelis" in 1658 in recognition of its vital role in defending Christian Europe's eastern approaches.

Restored to a reborn Poland in 1920, Lwów became the country's third-largest city and an important regional center. Its university, which had been founded in 1661, gained renown for its School of Mathematics; under Professor Stefan Banach, scholars meeting in the city's "Scottish

Café" to ponder theoretical issues could win prizes for solving the most challenging problems. The School of Law would later come to prominence for two of its alumni—Hersch Lauterpacht and Rafał Lemkin—who were instrumental in framing the legal concepts enshrined in the postwar International Military Tribunal at Nuremberg.[1] Lwów was culturally very mixed—a "city of blurred borders," as the journalist Joseph Roth had called it—with around a quarter of the population Jewish and a smaller minority of Ukrainians. But the vibrant melting pot of the nineteenth century had changed into something rather more sinister by the 1930s. Anti-Jewish riots erupted in 1932, and such tensions would rise again as the storm clouds of war gathered in the summer of 1939. Lwów would be forced to fight for its existence—and test its loyalty to Poland—once again.

By mid-September, Lwów was a shadow of its former self. The ravages of war had already taken their toll and, clogged with countless refugees, the city no longer looked like the proud eastern bastion of the nation. According to Stanisław Maczek, commander of the 10th Motorized Cavalry Brigade, who arrived in Lwów on September 15, it showed a rather different face: "lurking like someone anticipating an expected strike with resignation, dark, dirty . . . illuminated only by occasional dying fires from air raids." This was a far cry from the city that had earned the tag of eternal fidelity and had proudly resisted the Soviet onslaught in 1920. Now, Maczek noted mournfully, it was a "dying flicker of hope": a refuge approached from the west by "a crumbling Poland" that hoped "with its final breath for one last show of resistance, perhaps for nothing more than history's sake."[2]

For all the symbolism, Lwów's significance to Poland in 1939 was primarily strategic. As the gateway to the southeast, and the key to any possible withdrawal toward the Romanian frontier, it was crucial to Poland's fortunes, synonymous almost with the idea of a last-ditch defense. Consequently, Lwów would be vigorously defended, its forces marshaled by the garrison commander, General Władysław Langner. A native of the region, Langner had fought in the Polish Legions in the First World War and spent most of his subsequent career away from

Lwów; he had only returned to the city, as commander of the military district, early in 1938. His layered defense plan began with an outer line some 25 kilometers (15 miles) west of the city, running from Bełżec and Rawa Ruska (Rava-Rus'ka) in the north to Gródek Jagielloński (Horodok) and Komarno in the southwest. Within the city itself, prominent geographical features, such as Kortumowa Hill, were fortified as much as possible. Indeed, volunteers had constructed a new network of barricades and antitank ditches on the city's periphery. In addition, the garrison boasted two battalions of infantry, a volunteer battalion, a militia brigade, three artillery batteries, and assorted other elements, which were to be concentrated in strongpoints along the main approaches of any expected attack.[3]

Those preparations would be required sooner than had been expected. The Wehrmacht advanced swiftly into Galicia, and by September 10 German troops were at Jarosław battling the Polish rear guard—which contained the 10th Motorized Cavalry Brigade under the redoubtable Colonel Maczek. This campaign was part of the German effort to cross the river San, one of the last natural barriers to an eastward advance. Maczek would later remember the battle—the exhaustion, the lack of supplies, and the stress of constant combat—as "the most excruciating experience not only for me as brigade commander, but also for my soldiers right down to the last man."[4] Nonetheless, he and his brigade would ultimately withdraw in good order under cover of darkness, and they would remain undefeated. However, once the crossing of the San had been forced, German infantry made their way across the pontoon bridges and on toward Lwów.[5]

By that time, German spearheads were already well advanced. Starting from the Eastern Beskids in Slovakia, units of the 1st Gebirgs (Mountain) Division had bypassed Polish defenses, and after a vicious engagement on the Dukla Pass, they had advanced into southeastern Poland. Already on September 11, five days after the fall of Kraków, they had taken Sambor (Sambir), less than 70 kilometers (43 miles) southwest of Lwów. Driven on by the ruthless ambition and ideological conviction of one of the division's commanders, Ferdinand Schörner—a fanatical Nazi loyalist—the units were already forging ahead toward Lwów.[6] According to one German eyewitness account of the time, the Gebirgsjäger raced on through Galicia past the detritus of war: "discarded helmets, guns, ammunition, equipment lying behind, then more dead horses, gradually bloating in the heat, giving off a sweetish smell, some armoured cars with broken wheels and shafts. . . . We come across exhausted prisoners in long columns; they stare . . . with blank expressions."[7] When they reached the city's western outskirts the following day, September 12, they are said to have overtaken two busloads of Polish soldiers, who could only gaze at them in bewilderment.[8]

True to their order to take Lwów by storm, the Gebirgsjäger attempted a surprise assault on the city that same afternoon, advancing down the main western approach road, Gródecka Street (Horodotska Street). Assailed by sniper fire and artillery barrages, they reached the Church of St. Elizabeth not far from the city center, where they were forced to withdraw. As one of the artillerymen who met the German attack that day recalled, "When they saw us, they started jumping out, but they were too late. . . . [O]ur faithful field guns blared out with head-on fire. All that was left of that vehicle after that first salvo was a heap of iron and a wisp of smoke. The rest of the column soon met the same fate. Infantry tried to run into the nearby buildings, but the gates were locked and our heavy machine gun kept sweeping the street."[9]

The following day, as artillery duels raged, the probing attacks began again. A German assault on Kortumowa Hill, northwest of the city, was successful, and subsequent Polish counterattacks failed to dislodge the invaders. On September 14, a delegation from the city council went to speak with General Langner to suggest that military operations should be suspended, for fear the city would be destroyed. Already the power plant, the water supply, and the gasworks had been hit. In addition, the large numbers of refugees who had streamed into the city in previous weeks had swollen the population far beyond what could reasonably be sustained; food supplies were running low, and the city's makeshift hospitals were full.[10] To his dismay, Langner had also been forced to allow many of the local police and government staff to leave the city. As he recorded in his diary, "I am left alone without administrative authorities or security organs."[11]

For all their difficulties, however, if the inhabitants of Lwów needed any impetus to spur on the defense of the city, they would have found it in the fate of Przemyśl, 90 kilometers (56 miles) to the west. After it fell to the German 7th Infantry Division on September 15, Przemyśl had been exposed to the full force of Nazi barbarism, with the 20,000-strong Jewish community immediately singled out for abuse and persecution. That persecution quickly turned murderous when Einsatzgruppen units began carrying out roundups of the Jewish population. As one eyewitness recalled, the victims were herded through the streets pursued by a mob of soldiers, who beat and pistol-whipped those who fell behind. The brutal journey ended in the cemetery of the nearby village of Pikulice:

It was a scene out of Dante's hell. All the men driven through the streets in the morning lay there dead. Some men from the nearby houses told me what had happened. The Jews had been driven up to the side of the hill and ordered to turn around. A truck was already standing there. A canvas had been lifted off a heavy machine gun, and several bursts of fire rang out, sweeping back and forth. Then a few more shots were fired into the few bodies that were still writhing. All was still. The soldiers climbed into the truck, and drove away.

I went quietly up to the little hill. The corpses were lying on their backs or sides in the most contorted positions, some on top of others, with their arms outstretched, their heads shattered by the bullets. Here were pools of blood; there the earth was rust-coloured with blood; the grass glistened with blood; blood was drying on the corpses. Women with bloodied hands were hunting through the pile of bodies for their fathers, husbands, sons. A sickish sweet smell pervaded the air.[12]

It is thought that as many as 600 people were murdered in Przemyśl in a three-day killing spree, making it the largest single massacre of the Polish campaign. The city's Wehrmacht commander identified the perpetrators as members of the Einsatzgruppe von Woyrsch.[13] A Polish eyewitness, meanwhile, noted simply that they were "laughing young Germans, the proud representatives of Hitler's New Order."[14]

If the defenders of Lwów were not short on motivation, they were certainly lacking reinforcement. And, as Langner complained to his diary, his soldiers were often ill trained and unaccustomed to urban warfare. As a result, he wrote, "our losses are disproportionately high," with most casualties coming from gunfire and shrapnel.[15] Another problem he faced was that of the failing loyalty of the city's Ukrainian minority. Not only did they assist the German advance, he claimed, but they also fired on Polish troops. In nearby Stanisławów, it was reported that a rebellion of Ukrainian locals had resulted in Polish army units being disarmed and officers being murdered.[16]

Despite such challenges, the repeated probing attacks of the Germans within Lwów were beaten back. The speedy advance of the Gebirgsjäger had succeeded in penetrating the city's western suburbs, but it had proved unable to take the city in a coup de main, and—more seriously—it had outstripped the German supply column, leaving many soldiers to subsist on looted maize and captured ammunition.[17] Moreover, while the battle for Lwów continued, numerous Polish units were left behind in the wake of that German spearhead, their escape routes to the south and east now cut off. Three of these—the 11th, 24th, and 38th Infantry Divisions, together comprising the remains of the Małopolska Army—found themselves near Sądowa Wisznia (Sudova Vyshnya), 50 kilometers (30 miles) west of Lwów, and were resolved to fight their way into the city to assist in its defense. Under its commander, General Kazimierz Sosnkowski—who had refused a desk job on the outbreak of war to lead at the front—the Małopolska Army still numbered some 16,000 troops, albeit many of them exhausted and lacking artillery, armor, and transport.[18] The plan was a bold one: as his biographer would later write, Sosnkowski was now creating a front "where nothing but the maddest patriotism existed."[19] His men would fight their way northeast and break through the overstretched German flank in an attempt to reach the forest of Janów, and from there they would cut through the

German lines into Lwów. The action would come to be known as the Battle of Jaworów.

It began on the evening of September 15, when Polish forces moved off under cover of darkness to engage the German units that lay before them. Though they lacked artillery and transport, they made good progress, surprising a number of German detachments full of men still exhausted from their forced march across Galicia. According to a gunner in the German 79th Gebirgs Artillery Regiment, he and his comrades had marched some 60 kilometers (37 miles) that day alone and were begging for rest.[20] They would not get their wish. One by one, the villages west of Lwów were liberated—Tuczapy, Czarnokońce (Chornokuntsi), Rodatycze (Rodatychi)—as the Poles fought on, taking the German forces by surprise with a close-range infantry assault. "They barely managed to open fire," one veteran of the battle wrote, "when we pounced on them in their foxholes."[21] In Hartfeld, which had been founded by German colonists and retained an ethnic German presence, the fighting was especially bitter, with hand-to-hand combat resulting in heavy losses on both sides. When it was finally taken by the Poles in the early hours of the next morning, the village had been destroyed. According to one artilleryman, the fires of what remained lent the scene a "tragic ambience."[22]

Contemporary German propaganda accounts, and their modern echoes, tend to focus on the fighting at Hartfeld, but the most remarkable engagement of the Battle of Jaworów was undoubtedly that at Mużyłowice (Muzhylovychi), 4 kilometers (2.5 miles) to the northwest, where elements of the 11th and 38th Divisions met the 3rd Battalion of the elite SS division Germania. The SS-Germania was one of three divisions established to serve at the personal behest of Hitler, known as the SS-Verfügungstruppe, which had been raised from SS members and were, effectively, Hitler's private army. The invasion of Poland was intended to be the "blooding" of the SS: its chance to prove itself as a fighting force on the battlefield. The engagement at Mużyłowice, however, would show how far the SS still had to go. Despite being very well equipped and well armed, and facing Polish troops who lacked armor, artillery, and transport, the SS-Germania was caught at rest and spread out in woodland, where it was evidently not expecting to be attacked. In the fierce fighting that followed, men of the Polish 49th Hutsul Rifle Regiment stormed the German positions in a nighttime bayonet assault, "slashing and stabbing . . . at anything that moved." Arriving soon after the main attack, the commander of the 11th Infantry Division, Colonel Bronisław Prugar-Ketling, described the scene:

> Bursts of machine-gun fire started and fell silent. One could almost see the hand that pressed the trigger suddenly stiffen and lifelessly fall, paralyzed by the strike of a rifle stock or a bayonet. There were no screams. The fight went on in darkness and ominous silence. No one was directing it any longer, and no one pleaded for mercy. The whole thing made one shiver. And the horror that overcame the Germans must have exceeded everything they had experienced before. They certainly had never encountered such surprise and such an assault. The corpses we later saw looked ghastly. The terror in which they died still showed on their faces.[23]

When the battle was over, the commander of Germania's 3rd Battalion, SS-*Obersturmbannführer* (Lieutenant-Colonel) Heinrich Köppen—a portly, bespectacled, forty-eight-year-old Bavarian—had been killed, along with twenty-two of his men; the remainder had been forced to flee in ignominy. Alongside the dead, a foggy dawn revealed a rich material booty: "We rubbed our eyes to make sure it was not an illusion," Prugar-Ketling wrote. "It looked so unbelievable. A large, rich village . . . packed to the brim with equipment and war materiel."[24] Kazimierz Sosnkowski was similarly impressed:

> When we reached the high street running north–south through the whole spread-out village, an unforgettable sight opened before our eyes: as far as the eye could see, the broad street was piled with crammed motor cars, cannons and trailers, armored cars for the crews,

ammunition wagons, motorcycles. It was easy to guess the dramatic course of events. Here, the enemy had no longer fought: the proper battle had taken place on the western outskirts of the village. At the first attempt to move the column, the whole convoy jammed, and the Germans, thrown into panic, abandoned their gear and took to their heels. According to local eyewitnesses, some of them fled with nothing but their underpants.[25]

In the aftermath of the engagement, Sosnkowski counted some 400 abandoned vehicles.

With hard-fought successes such as these, the Polish Małopolska Army eventually reached Janów Forest; from there, it was hoped, a passage could be forced into Lwów. The men were exhausted, however, and wanted "only to pause in their march to slump to the ground and instantly fall asleep."[26] Moreover, given that they could no longer exploit the tactic of surprise, and the Germans now knew where they were, they had surrendered the initiative. Very quickly, therefore, they were subjected to a pulverizing air and artillery attack that took a heavy toll. Prugar-Ketling wrote:

> Even to eyes well accustomed to the horrors of war, it was a terrible picture. The horribly massacred bodies of men and horses, scattered in pieces across a large area on the ground and in the trees, gave the impression of some satanic revenge. Upturned cars, wagons, and cannon limbers blocked the passages between mutilated branches. Everywhere, scraps of uniforms, tents, blankets, and other equipment hung from the trees or lay scattered on the bloody, cratered earth. . . . I had seen many a battlefield, many a time witnessed heavy and bloody combat, but never had I seen such a dreadful harvest of war.[27]

After this "softening up" from the air, the Poles were subjected to a ground assault by troops of the 7th Infantry Division, whose men attempted to fight their way into the forest as dusk fell. But for the Germans, too, as the corps diarist recorded, the battle that ensued was the stuff of nightmares, with "the upturned tree trunks as our enemies, which creep around, move around, leap out, which are the front and the back. In a word the forest is the ally of the defenders. . . . It's as if the bushes themselves could fire—a horrible entanglement of machine gun nests and undergrowth."[28] Janów would become known to the Germans as the "Forest of Death."

After holding the German attack in the forest until the evening of the 17th, the Poles, in the vain hope that an attack from the city might help them penetrate the German lines, began to withdraw eastward in the direction of Lwów. In the end, encircled by enemy tanks at Hołosko (Holosko) on the northern edge of the city, the remnants of Prugar-Ketling's 11th Division were forced to capitulate, with only a few able to sneak through the German ring to enter Lwów. Sosnkowski, meanwhile, ordered his men to split into smaller groups and try to break into the city individually, or else make their way south to the Hungarian border.[29]

By that time, a new enemy was looming on the eastern horizon. General Langner was alerted to the Soviet threat by a message from the Border Protection Corps commander at Czortków, who reported hearing the sound of engines and the neighing of horses from across the frontier.[30] General Sosnkowski, then in Janów Forest, received the news from a Polish airman who had been shot down and tried to swallow the message he was to deliver. The document, "half chewed up" and "stuck together in several places," was scarcely legible, but its opening line was clear enough: "Today, Soviet forces crossed the border of Poland from Połock [Polatsk] to the Dniester . . ." As the line was read, Sosnkowski recalled, "dead silence fell."[31]

Other units were not so fortunate, and with radio communication at best intermittent, many were ignorant of developments on the eastern frontier, or were forced to rely instead on rumor and hearsay. In the confusion, Soviet agents and sympathizers already active in Lwów were able to exploit the information vacuum, spreading the lie that Soviet forces were coming to help them against the Germans.[32] A Soviet leaflet dropped on the city on September 17 blamed Poland's supposed collapse on its "incompetent government" and claimed that its ministers and generals had "fled like cowards," abandoning the country to its disastrous fate. Consequently, it went on, the Red Army was coming to deliver "working Poles . . . from enslavement, ruin, and defeat at the hands of the enemy." It ended by urging Polish soldiers to lay down their arms, reminding them that resistance against the Red Army was futile, and asking for their help in delivering Poland "from the shackles of the landlords and nobles." If they did so, the leaflet promised, "freedom and a happy life will be ensured."[33]

German propaganda delivered a different message. A leaflet from the Germans dropped on Lwów that same afternoon declared that the city had already been turned into a battlefield, that further resistance was senseless, and that the Red Army had crossed the Polish frontier "as Germany's allies." The note falsely claimed that Warsaw had capitulated and demanded that Lwów follow suit, stipulating that hostilities should cease by midday on September 18, with all Polish soldiers laying down their weapons by that time. If German demands were not met, the note went on, women, children, and men over the age of fifty would be permitted to leave the city by way of the Winniki (Vynnyky) road until 5:00 p.m. After that time, "an attack from land and air will be carried out with all ruthlessness."[34] Needless to say, the Polish defenders ignored the demand.

Later that day, General Langner received confirmation of what he had already suspected: the Red Army had crossed the border. A message from the High Command instructed him as to how he and his forces were to respond to the invasion: "We are only fighting the Germans," it read. "We are not at war with the Bolsheviks. On the frontier the KOP has fired warning shots to show that we are not allowing them in willingly. Do not engage them unless you are engaged."[35]

The following day, Langner consulted with his commanders. Hard information on Soviet intentions was still scarce. It seemed that the Red

Army had generally refrained from engaging Polish forces to the east of Lwów, and claimed to have arrived to fight the Germans. The general was under no illusions about Soviet "fraternity" and did not believe in their "friendly intentions,"[36] but he still had to make a decision. He considered ordering a nighttime withdrawal toward the southeast; however, bolstered by the presence of two armored trains—the *Śmiały* and the *Bartosz Głowacki*—that had arrived in the city, and anticipating the arrival of General Sosnkowski from Janów Forest, he decided to continue the city's defense.[37] The order was given for a volunteer defense corps to be raised, martial law was proclaimed, and makeshift defenses were erected. "There was no asphalt, they had pulled the cobblestones and pavement slabs to make barricades against tanks," one soldier recalled. "Not even a single German could get into Lwów that way. The young people made gasoline bombs; everything that lived fought for Lwów."[38] For some, however, the battle was already taking its toll. "It is hard to live," Alma Heczko wrote in her diary. "Life is neurotic. Continually listening for aircraft, the whistle of shells flying overhead, being thrown out of bed at night. All of this affects one's mood."[39]

On the morning of the 19th, another German envoy approached Polish lines on Gródecka Street to demand capitulation, stating that the city would be subjected to a massive bombardment if the garrison did not comply. Langner confirmed receipt of the note but was not prepared to capitulate.[40] That afternoon, though air-raiding was temporarily halted, there were concerted ground assaults from the southwest, the north, and the east that were only held off with heavy casualties. In truth, the Germans were already preparing their withdrawal, ceding the city and the wider region to Soviet rule, as prescribed by the Secret Protocol to the Nazi–Soviet Pact. It seemed that the 1,000 or so Gebirgsjäger killed in the attempt to take Lwów had given their lives in a fool's errand.

While the Germans made one last attempt to force the city's surrender by threats and brute force, the Soviets tried cunning. Early the next morning, the Red Army spearheads arrived in the eastern suburb of Łyczaków (Lychakiv), announcing themselves by driving toward Polish positions and then promptly withdrawing eastward without firing a shot. Other units would soon follow. A teenager who witnessed the odd comings and goings that morning east of the city, Janina Król, later wrote, "An army came on some tiny horses. Very strange, they looked like a band of ragamuffins. We were all terrified, because the Germans had been so elegant, so refined when they came, but these looked awful, like bandits. Will they murder us all? The village was struck with fear. . . . Where they'd come from or why, we did not know. We were bewildered."[41]

While the fighting continued in the west, a German envoy brought another surrender offer. In recognition of the heroic Polish defense of Lwów, the note read, the garrison would be honored and the officers would be permitted to keep their side arms. Again Langner refused.[42] To the east, meanwhile, a Polish delegation traveled to meet the Soviet vanguard. The resulting talks were baffling. "Why have you come?" the Polish colonel, Bronisław Rakowski, asked a Red Army colonel. "You must have read the papers," the Soviet officer replied. When Rakowski told him the city was besieged and no papers got through, his response was, "So maybe you've heard on the radio what has taken place?" Rakowski understood the sinister turn of events very well, and fully appreciated why his "wholly unintelligent" counterpart "could not muster the courage" to tell the truth: that the Red Army had come as invaders and allies of Hitler. Enjoying the moment, he toyed with the colonel, telling him that the radio was dead after the Germans had cut the power. Then he repeated his original question: "So, why are you here?" The Soviet colonel squirmed for a moment and then said they were there to fight the Germans. "Oh, that's good," Rakowski replied, pretending to believe him and immediately showing him the German positions on a map. The Red Army colonel interrupted him, saying, "But we wish to enter the city." Rakowski declared that this was impossible, and that he had no authority to discuss it. His counterpart now asked if they might be given "observation points" for artillery, but added that they would still like to enter Lwów. Rakowski was not fooled, however. "Something odd is taking place," he mused later that day. "But one thing is certain, both

"Queer allies": Wehrmacht and Red Army officers confer outside Lwów.
akg-images

enemies want to break into the city."[43] As if to confirm the strangeness
of events, German and Soviet forces briefly clashed that morning near
Winniki, east of Lwów, with both sides suffering losses of men and materiel before the Germans withdrew.[44]

The presence of two enemy armies outside the city did little for civilian morale. As the diarist Alma Heczko wrote, "It seems that we Poles
are doomed. I think the defense of Lwów is futile when we are surrounded by enemies on every side." Enemy propaganda was especially
wearing: "Both the Germans and the Soviets want to create a mood of
helplessness, and that's why they are threatening us when they write that
the Polish government has fled," wrote Heczko. "Nobody cares about us,
that Warsaw is in ruins. . . . But we will fight for our city."[45]

Langner was forced to face reality, however. Feeling obliged to limit
the human and material damage to which the city would be exposed
in the event of an all-out assault, he called another meeting with his
commanders to "determine the conditions of further resistance." Open-

ing the discussion, Langner explained that he was unable to fight two enemies and could not "go against tanks with his bare hands."[46] The conclusions that he reached were bleak. He had received no relief from outside the city, and he expected none to arrive. Ammunition and food reserves were low; water and electrical supplies had already failed. What was more, though morale among the army's Polish soldiers was good, the arrival of the Soviets had compromised the loyalty of its Byelorussian and Ukrainian minorities; mass desertion, it seemed, was now a very real prospect. So, despite some misgivings, and no little sorrow, Langner's commanders concurred with the general's view that there was no other option than to negotiate a capitulation with the Soviets. With that, a meeting was arranged for the following morning, September 22, in Winniki.[47]

Langner came well prepared. His legal advisers had drawn up a list of conditions to be presented to the Red Army's negotiators, including the right of Polish officers to choose their place of residence, the right of other ranks to be released and return home, and the right of military families and civilians to have their property respected.[48] While these conditions were accepted by the Soviets without demur, a wider set of terms suggested by the city's mayor, Stanisław Ostrowski—including continued autonomy for city institutions, the maintenance of Polish law and language, and freedom of religion—were all rejected.[49] With that, the surrender of Lwów was agreed, scheduled to take place that same afternoon at three o'clock.

Returning to his command, Langner heard the first objections of some of his soldiers when a group of officers and NCOs, led by a Captain Różycki, marched into the defense command, pistols drawn, and demanded that the city continue the fight. Intercepted by a colonel on his way to Langner's office, Różycki was finally persuaded of the argument for capitulation. But even that colonel was not convinced of his case. Later in life he would write, "Perhaps he was right, perhaps we should have fought to the end."[50]

That afternoon, Langner finalized the text of addresses to his men and to the city, announcing the surrender and giving instructions on the procedures to be followed: all equipment was to be abandoned, and while the other ranks were to march, four abreast, toward specified collection points, officers were to gather at the city command before being marched "to the east." Discipline was to be maintained throughout.[51] In his address to the garrison, Langner declared that the defense of Lwów had been a "glorious page in the history of warfare." The men had bravely withstood the technological superiority of the enemy, and as they left their posts, they were to know that they were not surrendering to the Germans; rather, he said, "we were handing over the city to the Soviet Army, with which we did not fight, and with which we were ordered not to fight." He closed by thanking his men for their blood and toil, and vowed that the country would not forget their heroism.[52] To the civilian population, he expressed his thanks for the sacrifices they had endured and gave voice to his belief that Lwów would "forever remain faithful and heroic, and . . . will remain Polish for ever."[53]

Then, Langner departed for Tarnopol, 110 kilometers (68 miles) to the east, where he met the Soviet front commander, Marshal Semyon Timoshenko, to ensure that the surrender terms were kept. From there, he traveled on to Moscow to discuss matters with Marshal Boris Shaposhnikov, the chief of staff of the Red Army.[54] Throughout, he was told that the conditions agreed would be adhered to and that his officers would be safe, because—as the then Communist Party chief in Ukraine, Nikita Khrushchev, reassured him—"Russia always kept her obligations."[55] Langner was not convinced. He had tried to do his best for his men, but already at the end of his time in Moscow, he felt that he had been duped. He suspected that his presence there had been engineered solely so that he could be pressed for information on the Germans. Moreover, he was dismayed to see that the map hanging on Shaposhnikov's office wall clearly showed that Poland was to be partitioned once again.[56]

While Langner was absent, the people of Lwów began to witness the dark reality of Soviet occupation. One eyewitness recalled the Red Army's entry into the city with a shudder. "I was walking across Akademicki Square," he wrote, "when loudly rattling *tachankas* [machine-gun

Red Army troops parade in captured Lwów, beneath Stalin's stern gaze.
private collection

wagons] and tanks rode by. Men . . . clasped their guns tightly and looked suspiciously at the crowd. . . . The despondent and dense multitude slowly trickled home. At the corner there stood a weeping janitor. They had killed his 12-year-old son for having smiled at the sight of the wretched *tachankas* and the grimy soldiers."[57] There were other reprisals. In one case, all the men in an apartment block were rounded up after the dead body of a Red Army soldier was found in the courtyard. Despite having tried to save the man, they were accused of murder and shot in front of their wives and children.[58]

Meanwhile, Mayor Ostrowski met some of the 2,000 or so Polish officers, who gathered outside the defense command and asked him what they should do. The mayor replied bluntly that they should make themselves scarce. He was right. As they spoke, Soviet tanks arrived, and Red Army infantry began occupying every building. The assembled officers and men were then marched out of the city, eastward, in long columns. Over the following days, countless others followed them into captivity, some bound, beaten, and stripped of their boots, their epaulettes, and their dignity.[59] For many of them it was a journey that would end in the burial pits of Katyń.

As the strange skirmish at Winniki had demonstrated, relations between the Red Army and the Wehrmacht were not always cordial. There were other clashes, whether by accident or design. According to Colonel Adam Epler of the Polish 60th Infantry Division, confrontations between the two were not uncommon, especially toward the end of the campaign. German tanks were engaged by Soviet bombers, he recalled; in one instance, he said, "we saw a German bomber shot down by two Soviet fighters. Our outposts fought Germans and Bolshevists at the same time." "Queer allies they were," he concluded.[60]

Crucially, the arrangement between the Germans and the Soviets was not an alliance. The Nazi–Soviet Pact had been a nonaggression treaty, which—though it opened up the opportunity for a collaborative strategic relationship—did not signify the start of a formal alliance between the two states. Even though Berlin and Moscow shared the aim of destroying Poland, they operated largely in isolation from one another that September, with the notable exception of the Soviet radio station in the Byelorussian capital, Minsk, which repeatedly introduced the city's name into its broadcasts to aid Luftwaffe navigation.[61] Beyond this assistance, the Soviet position in the ongoing conflict was officially one of neutrality, a fiction that Stalin was very keen to maintain. His commanders were therefore instructed that Soviet and German forces—however closely their objectives were aligned—were to maintain a 25-kilometer (15-mile) distance from one another.[62] Evidence of active collaboration would gravely compromise Stalin's cause.

Nonetheless, a degree of coordination between the two armies was essential, and instructions were duly distributed to Soviet army groups on procedures to be followed to avoid "friendly-fire" incidents. German troops were to display a spread white cloth to approaching Soviet units, and fire green and red flares to identify themselves. In addition, the German command requested that the Red Army avoid nighttime attacks, a tactic favored by the Poles. Given that the Germans had already advanced beyond the line stipulated in Moscow the previous month,

Best of enemies.
Laski Diffusion

a staged withdrawal was agreed; the German side promised to return any lost Red Army soldiers they encountered to the nearest Soviet unit, and to treat those who were wounded.[63] On occasions when the two sides met, German troops were instructed to send an officer to deliver the following rather plaintive message: "The German army welcomes the army of the Soviet Union. Both the officers and the soldiers of the German army would like to be on good terms with you. The Red Army is expected to maintain this friendliness in return."[64]

Given that the Nazi and Soviet regimes had spent much of the previous decade vilifying each other, such caution might have seemed justified. Old habits and mindsets could be difficult to change, and neither side made much effort on an official level to do so. Indeed, as Nikita Khrushchev would later confess, it had been "impossible to explain . . . the idea of joining forces with Germany . . . to the man on the street."[65] The same applied, it seemed, to the Red Army soldier. For some, it was not the Polish army that they worried about, but their ostensible allies, the Wehrmacht. One Red Army major-general later recalled his concerns about where and when his men might meet German forces, adding that despite the pact with Hitler, "we all understood—deep in our souls—that the German fascists were still the bitterest enemies of Soviet rule."[66] Such feelings were often reciprocated. In one example, a diarist in Białystok noted that the Germans were "terrified of the Bolsheviks" and kept telling the civilian population not to stay in the city, but to withdraw westward with them. When the time came to hand over the city to the Soviets, she wrote, the Germans "practically fled."[67]

One encounter where relations appeared—at first sight at least—to be rather more cordial took place at Brest, known in German as Brest-Litowsk, where in early 1918 the Germans had dictated a punitive peace treaty to the nascent Bolshevik state. There, as at Lwów, the Soviet invasion met with German forces that had advanced beyond the agreed demarcation line, so the city needed to be handed over to Soviet control. It was an event that would come to symbolize the German–Soviet relationship.

The Germans had appeared at the gates of Brest on the evening of September 14, after General Guderian's headlong drive southward from the bridgeheads on the Narew. He had intended to take the city in a coup de main the following day, and his men duly made good progress against the city itself and the outer defenses of its old Russian fortress, which sat at the confluence of the river Bug and its eastward tributary, the Muchawiec (Mukhavets). However, Guderian's initial attempt to take the fortress was hampered by a lack of fuel and poor weather, which prevented the deployment of the Luftwaffe, as well as by the simple Polish tactic of parking an obsolete Renault FT-17 tank across the main entry to the Citadel.[68]

In the two days that followed, the Germans launched a number of infantry assaults in an effort to take the fortress, but the Poles beat them back each time. According to the official German war diary, the Poles "defended the citadel with intelligence and determination," deploying snipers and often attacking German forces from the rear to reoccupy previously lost positions.[69] On the morning of September 16, the German corps command decided that frontal attack promised little success, and ordered that the fortress should instead be besieged. That night, however,

Polish forces withdrew, sneaking away through an unguarded gateway, leaving only their wounded. The fortress was occupied without resistance shortly after eight o'clock the following morning, September 17.[70]

By that time, the Red Army had crossed Poland's eastern frontier and the power dynamic in Brest was already shifting. That very morning, official German accounts noted that news of the Soviet approach had caused "great excitement" among the city's Byelorussian population, many of whom saw the Soviet Union as their protector against Polish oppression. In the days that followed, a celebratory atmosphere developed in the city's suburbs, with the traditional greeting of bread and salt being prepared for the arriving Red Army soldiers.[71] At the same time, Polish refugees from Polesie, fleeing the Soviet advance, began to arrive.[72]

Awaiting the arrival of the Red Army, the officers of the German command in the city prepared as best they could, issuing orders on how the Soviet troops were to be greeted and making ready for a withdrawal behind the temporary demarcation line of the river Bug. In addition, they composed a leaflet in Polish to inform the city's inhabitants of the Soviet decision to intervene, and it stated that they intended to "occupy the remaining parts of Poland."[73] Guderian, meanwhile, had other concerns, not least among them dealing with the former bishop of Danzig, Edward O'Rourke, and his entourage, who had fled Warsaw; now, finding themselves in Brest, they were understandably anxious not to fall into Soviet hands. Guderian's solution, which was gratefully accepted, was to send the former bishop back northward to Königsberg in a returning German supply column.[74]

First contact with the Red Army was made on the morning of September 20, when a Soviet BA-10 armored car approached units of the 10th Panzer Division near Turna, north of the city. The Red Army officer it carried was then taken to the corps command post, where Guderian greeted him. The discussion that followed, which was mainly concerned with how to draw up a demarcation line, was described as "friendly" and continued into lunch.[75] In his memoirs, Guderian was rather less enthusiastic, complaining that the deadline agreed for a German withdrawal from Brest, two days later, gave his men too little time to evacuate their own wounded or recover their damaged vehicles.[76] Nonetheless, they agreed to a formal hand-over of the city to Soviet control on the afternoon of September 22.

On the morning of the hand-over, events went smoothly. According to the agreement, which had been formalized the previous day, Soviet forces took sole control of the city and its fortress from 8:00 a.m. Two hours later, a joint commission met to clarify any remaining points of confusion or friction. Then Guderian met with his opposite number, Brigadier-General Semyon Krivoshein, the commander of the Soviet 29th Light Tank Brigade. A short, wiry man sporting a Hitler-esque toothbrush moustache, Krivoshein, like Guderian, had been a pioneer in the use of tanks. Conversing in French, the two discussed procedures for the formal hand-over ceremony. Guderian had been given no instructions on how it should be carried out, so he improvised and suggested a joint march-past of Wehrmacht and Red Army forces for that afternoon, followed by the raising of the Soviet flag. Though Krivoshein was less than entirely enthusiastic, stating that his men were weary after their long march, he nonetheless agreed.[77]

At four o'clock that afternoon, the two generals reconvened on a small wooden platform, which had been hastily constructed in front of the main entrance to the German command, the regional administration building on Union of Lublin Street (Lenin Street). Standing before a flagpole bearing the German war flag, Guderian grinned broadly, looking resplendent in his red-lined greatcoat and black leather jackboots. To his left stood Krivoshein, wearing a belted leather coat to keep out the autumn chill. Surrounding the platform, beyond a knot of senior German military personnel, a mixed crowd of Wehrmacht and Red Army soldiers thronged the route of the parade, pockets of German field gray mingling with the black leather coats of Soviet officers, the olive drab of the infantry, and the dark overalls of the tank crews.

On the street beyond, a large crowd of civilians had gathered to watch events. Among them was twenty-year-old Raisa Shirnyuk, who recalled how word of the parade had spread: "There was no official announcement, but the rumor mill had worked well. Already that morning

All smiles: Guderian and
Krivoschein enjoy their victory.
*BArch, Bild 1011-121-0011A-22 /
Gutjahr / CC-BY-SA 3.0*

everyone in the town knew that the troops would be marching there."[78]
According to one German account, the crowd, made up primarily of
Brest's non-Polish communities—Byelorussians and Jews—was enthu-
siastic, welcoming the Red Army with flowers and cheering.[79]

Then, to the blare of a military band, the parade began. German infantrymen led the way, their smart uniforms and precision goose-step
drawing admiring comments from the assembled crowds. Shirnyuk was
impressed by their military bearing, noting that their commanding officer kept the men in line by shouting, "Langsam, langsam, aber deutlich!"
(Slowly, slowly, but clearly!).[80] Motorized units followed: motorcycles
with sidecars, trucks, and half-tracks laden with soldiers and towing
artillery pieces. Tanks, too, clattered along the cobbled street. As each
group filed past the reviewing stand, they drew a crisp salute from both
Guderian and Krivoshein.

Inevitably, some of those watching drew comparisons between the
two forces on display. The somewhat primitive Soviet T-26 tanks, for

instance, contrasted rather obviously with more modern Wehrmacht examples, especially when one of the former slid off the road not far from the reviewing platform.[81] One local, Stanislav Miretski, noticed other differences: the Soviets' belts were canvas rather than leather, and while the Germans employed trucks to haul their artillery, the Red Army used "stunted and unsightly" horses with inferior harnesses.[82] Raisa Shirnyuk concurred, noting that the Red Army men, with their "dirty boots, dusty greatcoats, and stubble on their faces," compared rather unfavorably with their German counterparts. Another eyewitness drew a chilling conclusion from the poor appearance of the Soviet infantry. Boris Akimov was accustomed to seeing well-dressed Polish soldiers, so the "poverty and slovenliness" of the Red Army struck him, but their foul smell and dirty appearance prompted a more profound question: "What sort of a life will they bring to us?" he wondered.[83]

Wehrmacht and Red Army soldiers mixed awkwardly for the newsreel cameramen and photographers, sharing cigarettes and smiling, while Guderian and Krivoshein grinned from atop their platform. Only occasionally did the latent tensions show. Krivoshein reacted mischievously to Guderian's enthusiastic welcoming of a Luftwaffe fly-past, remarking, "We have better!" He was evidently determined not to be impressed by the display of German air power.[84] Elsewhere, an eyewitness saw a German soldier launch a playful kick at the backside of a Soviet soldier in front of him. But whether it was evidence of exuberance or underlying tension is impossible to discern.[85]

With the parade drawing to a close, Guderian, Krivoshein, and the senior personnel around them all turned to face the flagpole. As the military band struck up the German national anthem and the assembled officers and other men solemnly saluted, the blood-red German war flag was lowered, to be replaced by the deeper red of the Soviet hammer and sickle. As one of those present recalled, it was a searing moment: "I realized then," he said, "that the war was lost and we were under Soviet occupation." All the Poles in the crowd, he added, "had tears in their eyes."[86] With that, the band played "The Internationale"; Guderian and Krivoshein shook hands for the last time; and the German general joined his men as they departed to the west across the river Bug.

While the Germans and Soviets were congratulating one another at Brest, Polish forces farther west were engaged in a desperate fight to escape the maelstrom. Already on September 18, Polish radio had reported that the High Command and the government had escaped to Romania. The order was given that all military units were to attempt to follow suit, moving southeastward toward Lwów and thence to Kołomyja (Kolomyya) and the Romanian border. The problem, even for those Polish forces that were relatively intact and able to make a push for the frontier, was that between them and their sanctuary lay a rapidly shrinking space through which to escape, with the Germans on one side and the Red Army on the other.

Moreover, that space was rapidly filling with tens of thousands of ordinary Poles who had been displaced by the war and were fleeing the Germans and the Soviets. These refugees were clogging the roads as their caravans inched along, unsure where they might be able to find sanctuary. For many Poles, the decision of which side's occupation would be the less onerous was a difficult one. Deliberations naturally drew on Poland's long history of foreign oppression, and they would rage and rumble interminably as the refugees trudged along. One overheard exchange summed up the bleak choice that many refugees faced: "What will you do, sergeant, where will you go?" asked a voice. "I don't know, brother," came the reply. Weighing his options for a moment, the second speaker went on: "Go to the Germans and it's a bullet in the head. Go to the Soviets and your life is like a drop of dew that falls off a leaf and soaks into the ground. No one will ever hear from you again." After another pause he added: "I think I'll go to Hungary."[87]

For Zofia Chomętowska, a thirty-six-year-old aristocrat and socialite, there was little question of which way to head. Fleeing westward from her estate in Polesie, along with members of her family, she recorded

Polish refugees take to the road, for many the start of an odyssey.
Muzeum II Wojny Światowej, Gdańsk

the great migration that ensued as people tried to escape the Soviet invasion. She wrote of her fears: fear of the Soviets, fear of the Germans,
and fear of the hostile Byelorussian peasantry in whose midst they found
themselves. But she also included flashes of wry humor. At one point,
she came across Princess Izabella Radziwiłł, scion of one of Poland's
noblest families, nudging through the crowd in her Rolls-Royce. Seeing
Chomętowska, the princess called out, "What are you doing here?" to
which Chomętowska replied, "Same as you . . . escaping!"[88]

In her memoir, Chomętowska recalled the chaos, the sense that men
and women alike now had to fend for themselves, of civilization itself
having broken down. She encountered groups of soldiers who merged
with her caravan and then mysteriously diverged again—men who had
removed their insignia, had no commanding officers, and were now
"wandering wild," not knowing where they were. The roadsides were littered with the detritus of a world destroyed: "strewn with smashed cars,
all without tires . . . [g]reat lorries on their sides . . . pretty, brand new
limousines, sports cars, all covered with holes and without seats. They lie

there grim and helpless." And all the while, the "human wave" pushed onward; impossible to stop, it rolled across gardens and pavements, through farmers' fields and hedgerows, breaking fences and swamping rural villages:

> We see suitcases, trunks, and bundles, wives and mothers with children, and even a canary in a cage. But the road is terribly jammed and on the way a long line of people trudge along on foot. . . . Among the civilians one sees suffering and sick faces. The intelligentsia and townsfolk are not used to such physical strain. There are also railway workers in uniform, and almost everyone is unshaven, exhausted, and dirty, often limping. . . . We have the feeling that a storm has rolled over us, and keeps on rolling.[89]

Within that maelstrom, countless military units large and small were also looking for an escape, some in good order, others the remains of smashed and scattered units. Most, following their orders, if not their instincts, were heading southeast, toward the so-called Romanian bridgehead, where the surviving Polish forces—numbering some 120,000 men by the end of the campaign—hoped to regroup so as to carry on the fight elsewhere. The Polish government and High Command, which had endured a peripatetic and largely impotent existence since leaving Warsaw on September 7, traveling via Brest, Łuck (Lutsk), and Kołomyja, finally crossed the Romanian frontier in the early hours of September 18. It was said that Edward Śmigły-Rydz had to be persuaded to leave and that he contemplated suicide. He would later seek to justify his departure: "I was traveling for help. I believed in my authority abroad, I believed in the Allies, their honour and help. They betrayed me."[90]

However tragic and ignoble that escape may have been—and there are some who considered it a betrayal of the Polish soldiers who were left behind—a few chapters of the wider story deserve notice. On September 9, the decision was made in Warsaw to evacuate Poland's gold reserves, in all 80 metric tons (88 US tons) of bullion, to prevent them from falling into the hands of the Germans. Forty trucks, cars, and municipal buses were commandeered, including a fuel tanker to accompany the convoy. The drivers who were recruited included Halina Konopacka, a former Olympic discus champion and the wife of the man who organized the evacuation, the former treasury minister Ignacy Matuszewski. Alongside the gold bullion, it was decided to evacuate other valuables: artworks, state documents, and manuscripts. Traveling by night, with the Germans hard on their heels, the convoy first headed east, to Łuck, then to Lwów, and lastly to Śniatyń (Snyatyn) on the Romanian frontier, where it arrived on the evening of September 13.[91] For the gold, if not for its guardians, it was the beginning of an odyssey that would lead—via Turkey, Lebanon, France, and West Africa—to Britain, the United States, and Canada, where it finally arrived in 1944. Matuszewski, however, did not reap the rewards for a successful operation. Accused of embezzlement by the Polish government in exile, he escaped to the United States, where he died in 1946.[92]

Another vitally important evacuation was that of a small group of Polish mathematicians—Henryk Zygalski, Jerzy Różycki, and Marian Rejewski—who had been working to crack the German Enigma encryption machine for the Cypher Bureau of the Polish General Staff. The three left Warsaw by train on the evening of September 6, and after collisions, air raids, and numerous detours, reached Brest three days later. By that time, the city was already under air attack from the Germans; when the railway station was bombed the following day, the onward journey to safety was only possible by road. Given a car and ordered to drive to Romania as quickly as possible, the three then set off toward Kowel and Łuck. It would not be an easy journey. Zygalski's laconic diary entries convey some of the flavor of the disorganized escape: "September 13. We lose our superiors in Łuck. We race on to Włodzimierz [Volodymyr-Volynskyi]. Then turn back, then head once again for Włodzimierz. Meet the Major. He tells us to head back. We lose our way and go for Łuck. Not a pleasant day. We wait in Łuck."[93] After vehicle breakdowns, air raids, wrong turns, and constant fuel shortages, the group crossed the Romanian frontier on the night of September 17–18. Ten days later, Zygalski and the others would arrive in

"No one will ever hear from you again." Polish prisoners
of the Red Army, marching into oblivion.
Laski Diffusion

Paris. It was the start of a personal and technological adventure that
would lead to Bletchley Park and change the very course of the war. The
vital work that Rejewski, Zygalski, and Różycki did on the German
Enigma codes would, according to some estimates, shorten the war by
perhaps two years.[94]

For all the success stories, however, there were others who were not
so fortunate. The staff and families of the Polish Naval Command departed from Warsaw on September 5 and traveled first east to Brest,
then on to Pińsk and Brody, where they arrived on the night of September 13. Traveling predominantly by train, they were under regular attack
from the air. They had to abandon their journey south on September
16, when the tracks were damaged in a German air raid. Soon after
that, at Deraźne (Derazhne), near Rowno (Rivne), they encountered a
Soviet patrol and were forced to surrender. Though their families were
released, twenty-six Polish naval staff officers—including their commanding officer, Rear-Admiral Xawery Czernicki—disappeared into

Soviet captivity. They would later be murdered in the Katyń massacres.[95] Among the few officers to avoid capture that day was Rear-Admiral Jerzy Świrski, who had been traveling separately in a commandeered car, as he wanted to remain close to the General Staff. Sometimes it was on such tiny decisions that survival rested.[96]

In the circumstances, it is understandable that news of the Soviet invasion gave a new urgency to Polish escape efforts. The move was easiest, perhaps, for Poland's airmen, who could—theoretically at least—simply board their aircraft and take off southward. This is what happened in the case of Franciszek Kornicki's squadron, stationed near Lwów, which was able to depart quickly once the order to evacuate was given. Their fifty P.7 and P.11 aircraft landed some time later at Cernăuți airfield in Romania (today Chernivtsi, Ukraine). Kornicki was not among them, however. After an "enterprising pilot" had taken his plane, he was obliged to make his way to Romania over land.[97] A similar journey awaited the pilots of the 3rd Poznań Air Squadron. They had begun the war with twenty-one aircraft, but were down to just two when the order to evacuate came, meaning that most of them, along with their ground crew, were obliged to travel south in a column of trucks.[98]

For some Polish airmen, the real challenge was emotional rather than logistical. Not only did evacuation mean a final acknowledgment of defeat, but they would also have to abandon their families. As one pilot recalled, when he was ordered to evacuate he "understood that the show was over, and . . . felt strange. I couldn't believe that it was all over—Romania . . . dear God." On his last flight, he had time to ponder his situation: "I look at everything. I am flying over the river Dniester, thinking: It is guiding me for the last time. Time passes quickly. I turn my head back. . . . I can still see our land. Another moment and it is gone."[99] A few airmen took the evacuation particularly hard. Air force photographer Oswald Krydner, who crossed the Romanian border on September 18 on foot, over the river Prut, recalled the moment:

> I walked onto the bridge, no one stopped me, so I kept going. I stood on Romanian soil. Then I turned around. On the other side of the river

I saw the Polish flag was flying. Poland was there, Halinka [Krydner's wife] was there, our blood-stained land was there. Our people were being murdered by the enemy, our wives, our families. Dear God, have mercy. Tears poured down my face. I stood there, leaning on the railing, staring at the other side, half-conscious, numb.[100]

For some, the sense of capitulation was too much. "I have never seen so many people weeping," one bomber pilot remembered. "From time to time a shot would be heard, as someone who found the shame of defeat unbearable, and the future too horrible to contemplate, took his own life."[101]

If some of the airmen were at least able to reach safety with comparative ease, Poland's remaining ground forces were often obliged to fight their way southward. This was the strategic situation that provided the background to one of the largest engagements of the September campaign. Already on September 17, Polish forces north and west of the town of Tomaszów-Lubelski, 80 kilometers (50 miles) northwest of Lwów, found their route south blocked by the massed ranks of the Wehrmacht. On paper at least, those Polish forces were not inconsiderable, counting among their number elements of the Kraków and Lublin Armies, including 5 infantry divisions, the 1st Mountain Brigade, and the Kraków Cavalry Brigade. Most notably, they included the Warsaw Armored Motorized Brigade, which was equipped with around 80 armored vehicles, including 12 Vickers 6-Ton tanks and 22 of the heavier 7TP models. Under the command of Colonel Stefan Rowecki, one of the most talented commanders in the field, it was the largest remaining motorized unit in the Polish army. In reality, however, it was an army that was at the end of its endurance. Most units had been reduced to mere remnants of those that had mustered at the start of the war: the Kraków Army was down to about 3 divisions, half its original strength, and the 11th Infantry Regiment had been reduced by two-thirds to barely 1,000 men. Moreover, the soldiers that remained were exhausted, having marched hundreds of miles with little rest.[102]

To make matters worse, their hardware, too, was failing. Cut off from its supply train, the Polish force was running dangerously low on fuel, obliging Rowecki to employ desperate measures. On September 17 he ordered his own column to be dissolved and scavenged for gasoline. "I had several hundred of the brigade's cars abandoned, having drawn fuel from them," he wrote. "Beautiful limousines and other excellent cars were blown to smithereens. I kept only the combat vehicles, the rest were destroyed, even the pontoon column." Some of the men had tears in their eyes, he recalled, but "we had no choice." Tragically, even those measures yielded only 3,000 liters (about 800 gallons) of fuel, a third of what was required for a single day's travel.[103]

Rowecki was haunted by the thought that his engines would give up in the heat of battle. "Every time we have to tackle a harsher bit of the trail and I see our machines stagger and moan, I feel as if something is being torn out of my heart," he wrote. "If only we could have a chance to attack the enemy and do our soldierly duty, before we ultimately run out of gasoline."[104] He would get his wish. Between his brigade and the safety of Romania lay Tomaszów-Lubelski, which had already been occupied by the Germans on September 13; it was now home to elements of the German 8th Army Corps, consisting of two infantry divisions, and the 22nd Panzer Corps. Unsure what lay before him, and lacking maps with which to navigate, Rowecki was nonetheless optimistic. His brigade was to punch a path through the German lines to enable the remainder of Polish forces to escape encirclement. "We are to advance on Tomaszów on September 18," he wrote in his diary. "We fight at last."[105]

The attack, which began at dawn the following day, initially progressed well. Polish forces attempted to clear the villages on the northern approaches to Tomaszów, while an armored column entered the town from the west. The village of Tarnawatka, 6 kilometers (4 miles) north of Tomaszów, saw particularly bitter fighting, with the Poles battling to break through the defensive lines of the German 4th Light Division.[106] Inside the town, meanwhile, German artillery fire and air attacks were unable to prevent the Polish armored column from pressing forward. By the middle of the day, much of Tomaszów had been occupied by the attackers, and the main road to the south had been cut. Polish records would boast several hundred enemy soldiers killed, as well as dozens of prisoners taken and some twenty armored vehicles destroyed.[107] The damage to the town was considerable. As one German eyewitness noted that night, artillery fire, flares, and explosions illuminated a scene of desolation: "Everywhere new fires flicker. No village and no house seems undamaged anymore."[108]

Yet, having failed to take Tomaszów in a surprise attack, Polish forces now lacked the fuel, manpower, and will to fight on. Already on September 19, the Motorized Brigade was reporting that it had run out of fuel, was low on ammunition, and had been forced to requisition food from the locals.[109] When a determined German counterattack on the morning of September 20 slammed into the Poles' northern flank, hostilities were swiftly brought to an end. In the headquarters of the German 27th Infantry Division, a radio crackled into life with a message offering a Polish surrender. The Germans accepted and demanded that all surrendering units show a white flag and move—without their weapons—to the Tomaszów–Tarnawatka road.

That morning, the few remaining Polish tanks were destroyed—engine blocks were smashed, fuel tanks holed—before some 15,000 men laid down their arms north of Tomaszów. They included General Tadeusz Piskor, commander of the Lublin Army, and General Antoni Szylling, commander of the Kraków Army. Elsewhere around the town a further 45,000 men followed suit, and farther to the south, at Horyniec, the men of the Polish 55th Division also laid down their arms. The commander of the 55th summed up his own—and Poland's—predicament: "The division shared the tragic fate of the whole army. . . . [W]e received no help from anywhere, we were left to fend for ourselves against the world's most powerful forces."[110]

Colonel Rowecki was not among those who surrendered. After thanking his men for their service and dismissing them, he initially headed south toward Romania, but after a few hours of avoiding German patrols, he thought better of the idea and decided instead to make his way

A Wehrmacht soldier guards a pile of Polish helmets.
Szczecinski Archives / East News

to Warsaw. He would later be instrumental in the establishment of the Polish underground resistance.[111]

Soon after the surrender of the Kraków and Lublin Armies, a similar scenario played out northeast of Tomaszów-Lubelski. There, on September 21, the remnants of the Polish "Northern Front" appeared, largely comprising elements of the former Narew Independent Operational Group, which had been charged with holding the line of the river Narew in northeastern Poland. Under the command of General Stefan Dąb-Biernacki, these units were moving south; following the Soviet invasion of the previous week, they were aiming to reach the Romanian frontier. Like the Lublin and Kraków Armies before them, however, their passage was blocked by the German forces garrisoned in and around Tomaszów-Lubelski. They would not get through without a fight.

The first engagements followed on the morning of September 22, with Polish forces retaking several villages northeast of Tomaszów while a spearhead of the 13th Infantry Brigade attempted to take the town itself. The most success was enjoyed by the Nowogródek Cavalry Brigade, under the command of Brigadier-General Władysław Anders, which flanked Tomaszów to the north and attacked German forces in the town of Krasnobród, seeking a way around the impasse. At dawn on a foggy morning, a two-pronged cavalry charge at German positions on the outskirts of the town soon had the enemy in retreat, pursued by saber-wielding Uhlans. The Polish advance was temporarily checked by a countercharge by elements of the German 17th Cavalry Regiment, making it one of the last cavalry-on-cavalry engagements in history. By that night, however, the battle was over. The Polish victory was crowned by the freeing of some 100 prisoners who were being held in a church and the capture of General Rudolf Koch-Erpach, commander of the 8th Infantry Division, the first German general to be captured in the Second World War. Moreover, victory at Krasnobród allowed some Polish units to escape southward. As Anders himself recalled, "At 11 p.m. the enemy was defeated, the opening made and the exhausted troops began to pass through the gap." But success came at a high price. Having suffered some sixty casualties, Anders's cavalry brigade was now a spent force. "We had by now lost nearly all our motor transport and had no petrol for what was left," the general would later write in his memoir. "We hitched our guns to four pairs of weary horses, which, lathered in sweat, pulled them slowly forward."[112]

The Polish advance on Tomaszów itself was less successful, and the modest gains made were quickly reversed after a German counterattack. In the aftermath, most of the Polish units engaged in the area were disbanded or taken captive, with some 6,000 men surrendering to the Germans. Among them were the remnants of the prestigious 1st Legions Infantry Division, which had fought on the Narew and at Kałuszyn, but was finally destroyed by the German 8th Infantry Division east of Tarnawatka. The division's commander, Brigadier-General Wincenty Kowalski, who had been injured in that final battle, went with his men into captivity. The commander of the front, meanwhile, General Dąb-Biernacki, dismissed his staff and, dressed in civilian clothes, made good his escape via Hungary to France. According to his critics, it was the second time he had abandoned his troops.[113]

SLOWLY, INEXORABLY, THE GAP BETWEEN THE GERMAN AND So-viet lines was closing, with those Polish units caught in between obliged to surrender to one side or the other. Władysław Anders was minded to submit to neither. After his success at Krasnobród, he was pushing his dwindling band of lancers southward despite the exhaustion that many of them felt. "Soldiers slept in the saddle," he later wrote, "and the officers had to keep riding along the columns to wake them." He did not dare to halt to rest, he recalled, for fear that the men, once asleep, would be impossible to rouse.[114] The end for Anders, when it came, perfectly symbolized Poland's fate. After a chance encounter with a German patrol close to the village of Broszki (Brozhky), west of Lwów, he ordered a cavalry charge, which routed nearby elements of the German 28th Infantry Regiment, capturing an entire battalion. When messengers from the local German headquarters arrived to inform him that there could be no escape, he managed to persuade them to allow him a free passage in return for the release of the prisoners. Later that day, however, only 15 kilometers (9 miles) to the southeast, Anders discovered that the Red Army would not be quite so accommodating. Once he had tiptoed past Soviet advance units, the enormity of his task dawned on him: "Our artillery fired their last rounds, and our rifles their last shots. Our horses were starved and without water. There was no chance of breaking through."[115] Following a last, bloody skirmish with Soviet forces close to the village of Zastówka, barely 20 kilometers (12 miles) from the Hungarian frontier, he was injured and forced to surrender.

While the remnants of Polish forces at Tomaszów-Lubelski were being rounded up by the Germans, around 40 kilometers (25 miles) to the northeast, near the village of Husynne on the river Bug, another group of Polish forces escaping southward would meet their end at the hands of the Soviets. Numbering some 1,500 men, they, too, were a very mixed group: they included a mounted unit of the State Police from Warsaw, a squadron of the 14th Jazłowiecki Lancers Regiment, and the elite "Chemical Battalion," which was trained and equipped to counter the use of chemical weapons by the enemy.[116] On the afternoon of September 24, they stopped at Husynne to regroup, aware that they were being surrounded by overwhelming Soviet forces. The following day, after an artillery duel and clashes with Red Army infantry, they decided to try to break out of the closing ring.

The mounted State Police led the way. According to a corporal who was present, with their navy blue uniforms, their polished, patent leather helmets, and their horsehair crests, they seemed to recall cavalry's glory days: "Even in the anemic afternoon light," he wrote, "the emblems made the men seem like Napoleon's cuirassiers, raised from their graves to charge at the Emperor's command." They were not without effect, either, quickly scattering the enemy in panic. "The field through which the police charged," one cavalryman recalled, "was covered with the bodies of trampled and slashed Bolshevik infantry." A supporting charge by the Jazłowiecki Lancers then dealt with the survivors, leaving behind them a mass of "sprawling bloody corpses."[117] Improbably, cavalry had yet again proved its worth.

The success could not last, however. As at Krojanty at the very start of the campaign, cavalry's success proved fleeting when faced with an armored counterstrike. At Husynne, the Polish horsemen had barely mastered the field before a mass of Red Army tanks charged at them, their cannons blazing and machine guns chattering, forcing them into a costly retreat. By the time they reached their starting positions, they had no choice but to surrender, having lost over 140 men.[118] Surrounded by Soviet soldiers and ordered to lay down their weapons, the cavalrymen were separated from their horses before being berated by an uncomprehending Red Army colonel: "I should shoot you all to the last man! Dumb Poles!" he shouted. "We have come to liberate you from the bondage of your masters and you fire at us?"[119] The survivors, over a thousand men, went into Soviet captivity.

If the cavalry charge at Husynne was reminiscent of an earlier age in warfare, what followed was hideously modish. That same day, some twenty-five Polish prisoners were bayoneted in a nearby barn—murdered by their Red Army captors.[120]

Chapter Nine

"TO END ON A BATTLEFIELD"

A T DAWN ON SUNDAY, SEPTEMBER 24, WARSAW DIARIST AL-exander Polonius joined his local bread line. He had wanted to beat the crowd and arrived at 5:00 a.m., even though the bakery did not open until 6:00. Nonetheless, the line was already almost half a mile long, stretching so far along Puławska Street that he wondered dispirit-edly whether there would be any bread at the end of it at all.

The streets were quiet that morning, largely deserted except for the lines. In the city center, the damage from the German bombs was ubiq-uitous: "Scarcely a house that was not levelled or gutted," one observer wrote, "that was how all the main streets looked."[1] As Polonius waited, surveying the damaged buildings, some still wreathed in smoke, and watching a "blood-red dawn" spread over Praga to the east, he had a chance to observe his fellow Varsovians. They were a motley bunch: "Poor people, rich people, some in strange garments, skiing costumes, women enveloped in shawls to keep themselves warm, others with babies in their arms." As he watched, he noticed a small long-haired man, incon-gruously wearing a gray bowler hat and an old frock coat, who—"much to everybody's amusement"—began to relieve himself against a fence. "Some of the youngsters threw things at him, but he merely turned his head and continued." Polonius mused that the old man seemed to be "the personification of the abnormality of our lives."[2]

Inevitably, there were squabbles as the people in line jostled for position, some objecting that places were being saved for others. Since the city's power supply had failed the previous day, the lot of ordinary citizens had become infinitely more difficult. Without water, electricity, or gas, they were reduced to a primitive existence, and nerves were already fraying. As one diarist noted, it was the loss of the radio that pained them the most. Without the broadcasts, she wrote, "we were cut off from the world. That feeling was the worst of everything we had experienced."[3]

There was also gossip and news of the latest districts hit by the Germans: Praga, Powązki, and Żoliborz were said to be under almost constant artillery barrage. Some repeated the rumor that the Soviets were fighting the Germans, under the command of Edward Śmigły-Rydz, and that they had already reached Garwolin, 40 kilometers (25 miles) southeast of Warsaw.[4] Others claimed that the British had already landed at Danzig or Königsberg, and wondered how long it would take for their armored columns to reach the capital.[5] Some were in open despair at the unequal fight and the destruction being wrought. "If we haven't got the right arms," one housewife lamented, "why did we dare to stand up to them?"[6]

That morning, the most exciting rumor going around was that a German general—some said the commander-in-chief—had been killed in the fighting for Grochów, a suburb on the eastern side of the Vistula. "It sounded too good to be true," Polonius recalled. "The people did not believe the news."[7] As if to quash such scurrilous reports, discussion of General Werner Freiherr von Fritsch's death was interrupted by the arrival of German aircraft overhead; the planes wheeled and circled high in the sky before diving toward the street below, with wailing sirens and chattering guns. From the balconies of neighboring buildings, groups of soldiers fired impotently into the air with their rifles, desperate to provide some semblance of air defense. Nearby, a timber yard was already ablaze and burning fiercely.

According to Polonius, those in line were largely unmoved by the commotion around them, at least at first. Only when the aircraft returned did some of them leave the line to seek shelter, their places immediately filled by those behind, who "pressed as close to the wall as they could." People were afraid: "I could feel the trembling and shaking of human bodies as the aeroplanes dived straight at us, their machine guns spraying bullets," Polonius wrote in his diary. But, he noted, the line dared not disperse, because "bread was more valuable than safety."[8]

Ultimately, for all the drama of the morning, Polonius was to be disappointed. Soon after the German raiders had flown off to find fresh targets elsewhere, those remaining in line were told that there was no more bread that day. "I had got within a hundred yards of the gates of heaven: the bakery," he wrote, "and behind me stretched an endless crowd. Some did not even leave their places. They would wait patiently until the morning."[9]

By the last week of September, life amid the rubble of Warsaw consisted of little more than the constant search for food, the constant fear of bombing, and a constant diet of rumor and propaganda. Warsaw had endured German bombing since the first day of the war and had been under siege by German land forces for over two weeks. Much of the city center now lay in ruins, and almost without exception the prominent buildings and streets of the capital—the Royal Castle, the Old Town Square, the Saxon Garden—bore the scars of war, often smashed to rubble or burned out. Many streets were impassable, blocked by fallen masonry and navigable only by those able to pick a path through on foot. For all the exemplary valor and endurance of its inhabitants, Warsaw's resistance was approaching its end: that Sunday, September 24, marked the start of a concerted bombing campaign that would overshadow all that had gone before. Hitler wanted Warsaw's surrender within seven days.

The following day—"Black Monday," September 25—560 metric tons (620 US tons) of explosives and 72 metric tons (80 US tons) of incendiaries were dropped on the city.[10] This day's raiding was heavier than the most serious Luftwaffe raid on London during the Battle of Britain (350 metric tons [385 US tons]), heavier than the raid that destroyed Rotterdam in 1940 (97 metric tons [110 US tons]), and comparable to the 500 metric tons (550 US tons) of explosives dropped in the destruction of Coventry in November 1940.[11] As before, the bombing was concentrated not on the fronts, where German and Polish forces were still fighting, but on the city's central and residential districts. As one Polish colonel noted:

> The Germans had decided to take Warsaw by terror. It began around 7:00 a.m. and lasted without pause until around 5:00 p.m., [the Germans] intermittently using high-explosive and incendiary bombs. Within an hour the connection to our subordinate units was broken, smashed by explosions, destroyed by fire. Hell had opened up over Warsaw. Close to my shelter was that of the fire brigade officer who registered the reports of fires and ordered the response. He marked every fire with a little red flag on a large map of the city. By around 10:00 a.m., the map was covered with red, and he had run out of flags.[12]

One Praga resident caught in the bombing was walking down the street that morning, pondering why so many of Warsaw's civilians seemed to be drawn toward the city center, where "the hell was at its hottest." Just then, he heard the roar of approaching engines and turned to see a German dive-bomber heading straight for him. Throwing himself to the side of the road, he was deafened by the subsequent explosion and covered with earth and rubble. A 6-meter (20-foot) crater had been blown in the roadway. Dusting himself off, he struggled to make sense of the destruction. "Around the crater," he noted, "I counted thirteen disfigured corpses and several more torn to shreds, whose miserable remains hung from the maimed branches of poplar trees and fences. It was hard to tell how many."[13]

German artillery was also active, pounding the city's suburbs without mercy or respite. One German eyewitness thought the sound of German guns was becoming "the voice of Warsaw" and noted the mortars booming incessantly, "one battery after another." It was evidently quite a spectacle. "Watching by night," one artilleryman remembered, "we saw curves of coloured fire flashing gracefully toward Warsaw. The earth quivered and our eardrums seemed about to split. Looking to Warsaw we saw columns of smoke soaring languidly, as if from mighty cigars. In all directions long smoky tongues of fire spurted up every second. In the heavens the clouds were as red as blood."[14]

For many Varsovians, meanwhile, the raids were more harrowing than anything they had experienced over the previous weeks. Marta Korwin remembered that day as the worst of the whole siege, and another eyewitness described it as "a true hell": "Billows of smoke fill our eyes. Windows are shattered everywhere. . . . A bomb explodes in the courtyard. . . . [T]he wounded building shakes in its foundations. Masses of planes. The world seems to be caving in."[15]

In the aftermath, those emerging from their cellars and shelters were presented with a new vista of horror. So many fires were burning that the city looked like a single vast sea of fire and smoke. Ludwik Hirszfeld, a Warsaw doctor, wrote, "This is what the end of the world must look like . . . dark from the smoke of fires and soot, houses teetered and crumbled to the ground. People, as if gone mad, ran from house to house, from shelter to shelter. The streets were filled with the dead, wounded, horses next to men."[16] Like many, perhaps, Alexander Polonius struggled to find the "appropriate superlatives" to describe events. "To say merely that today was still worse than yesterday does not convey very much," he wrote. Instead, he offered a simple lament: "Too many bodies have perished in the fires, just burned; too many people have been buried in the public squares unidentified; too many lovely things have disappeared in the smoke. The rate of destruction has been so great that it is impossible to record the losses. . . . Everything that we possess, including life, is being annihilated."[17] Some 10,000 inhabitants of Warsaw were killed during the siege, many of them on that day.[18]

Unsurprisingly, morale was shaken. Colonel Tadeusz Tomaszewski, chief of staff to General Walerian Czuma, commander of the defense of Warsaw, wondered glumly whether the continuation of the fight for the city still had "any moral, political, or military purpose": "No water for three days. Food supplies close to exhausted, the population is beginning to starve. The hospitals are burnt down and bombed out. There are 43,000 wounded lying in the most primitive conditions, in cinemas, cafés, and cellars. . . . [T]housands of corpses are scattered across the city, with hardly a covering of earth."[19] That same day, the Citizens' Committee—an advisory body of prominent politicians—met in the Methodist community building on Mokotowska Street in the center of the city. The mood was downbeat: "It was clear to everyone," Senator Artur Sliwiński recalled, "that Warsaw's fate was sealed." Sliwiński, a former prime minister, dared to ask the question that hung over all their deliberations: What prospects could a continuation of the fight hold? He was met with silence. It was decided to seek the advice of the military and postpone further discussion until another meeting scheduled in the defense headquarters the following day.[20]

In the meantime, Warsaw burned. Wacław Lipiński, who ventured to the main thoroughfare of Marszałkowska Street that night, wrote, "It was bright out, horrifically bright, and on top of everything, a hot, dry wind has got up, carrying sparks, embers, and hot ashes. . . . Grenades explode one after another. They keep beating down on the wretched city, on the burning streets, on the people mad with terror. . . . No one to help, and fire spreads from place to place, from house to house. Some streets . . . are entirely engulfed in flames."[21] Within that Hades, Lipiński noted, the people of Warsaw struggled on, running "among streets aglow with fire," their voices barely audible above the crackling chaos, except for the "desperate wail of helpless children." Moved on by the spreading fire, they would find shelter where they could in the crumbling buildings.[22]

The morning would bring little respite. Soon after dawn the German artillery began firing again, now barely answered by the Polish side. Listening to the cacophony, Alexander Polonius was worried by the "thinness of our fire," but his greatest fear concerned the silences in between: at least the firing was proof of life, he explained. "It shows that we are defending our capital."[23] In addition, a German ground assault now began in the eastern suburbs, targeting the forts that ringed the city and had become the mainstays of the Polish defense.

According to a contemporary German account, the attack on the fort at Mokotów, in the south of Warsaw, proceeded so swiftly that the defenders were caught totally unawares. As a German lieutenant climbed down into the central courtyard that morning, he supposedly encountered a Polish soldier strolling across the quadrangle with a towel over his arm, en route to his morning ablutions. The Pole was so shocked, it was said, that he was unable to speak.[24] In truth, such nonchalance belongs to the fictional world of Joseph Goebbels's propaganda ministry. After the hammering they had received, the Poles were unlikely to be surprised by anything, except possibly a German surrender. The defense of Warsaw was as bitter and determined as ever. One account, from a Polish soldier on Opaczewska Street, in the western suburb of Ochota, is more reliable in describing the German attack, which was supported by tanks that advanced under a hail of artillery fire. "The battle went on despite our heavy losses," he wrote, explaining how his own howitzers were buried by the targeted incoming fire of the German artillery. The German attack stalled in that sector, but it came at a heavy cost to the defenders: "It would be hard to estimate how many soldiers fell in battle on that day," the soldier noted, but only 47 of the original 220 were present at a later roll call.[25]

For the civilians caught in the battle, the experience was the stuff of nightmares. Władysław Szpilman was amazed, in retrospect, that he managed to survive at all. After the person next to him was killed by shrapnel, he had squeezed into a restroom for safety with ten other people. They spent the following two nights there, listening to the constant noise of the guns and breathing the foul air, heavy with smoke and plaster dust. Some time later, he recalled, they "wondered how it had been possible," and they tried—unsuccessfully—to cram themselves into the same restroom again. They could only do so, he concluded, if they were in terror for their lives.[26]

It was against this background that the military commanders of Warsaw met again on the morning of September 26 and crowded into the defense command HQ in the basement of the city's Post Savings Bank. General Juliusz Rómmel opened proceedings by thanking the officers and men for their heroic defense of Warsaw and giving his assessment of the utility of continuing the fight.[27] Then, after hearing a similar presentation by the Citizens' Committee, he asked those present to answer with a simple yes or no as to whether the defense of the city should be continued. Though few of those present managed to restrict themselves to one-word answers, the consensus was that there was no point in carrying on. General Kutrzeba was one of those more loquacious than required, making plain his opposition to further sacrifice. The situation they faced was different from that of an army in the field, he explained, adding that "further resistance would mean a pointless suicide, the killing of the population and the destruction of the city." In such circumstances, he gave a bold and clear answer: "No."[28]

With that, Rómmel again took the floor. He told those present that both his conscience and his sense of soldierly duty had convinced him that further resistance was senseless, and that a continuation of the defense would only lead to a bloodbath. He called for a joint sitting of the Defense Council and the Citizens' Committee to take place that night, where he would inform them of his decision to surrender Warsaw. According to one eyewitness, Rómmel's decision was not put to a vote.[29]

Stefan Starzyński, the mayor, who had continued to voice his objection to any surrender, was overruled. One of his colleagues, Alexander Ivánka, recalled that it was the only time he ever saw Starzyński broken. In the aftermath, Starzyński called each of his coworkers to his office to inform them of the decision. "We must capitulate," he told Ivánka. "What do you plan to do?" he then asked. Ivánka replied that he did not know. "I don't know either," said Starzyński. "I think I will shoot myself."[30] Instead, Starzyński channeled his despair into another address to the people of Warsaw, this time to be distributed as a single sheet of paper. He expressed his continued defiance and the hope that—one day—Warsaw's suffering would be avenged. He wrote:

For the last time, I call upon our Allies. I no longer ask for help. It is too late. I demand vengeance. For the burnt churches, for the devastated antiquities, for the tears and the blood of the murdered innocents, for the agony of those torn by bombs, burnt by the fire of incendiary shells, suffocated in the collapsed shelters and cellars. And you, bandits, barbarians, who have attacked our country, carrying death and destruction—know this, that there is justice, that there is a judgment, before which we shall all stand to answer and be held responsible for our actions.[31]

Later that night, a messenger arrived from the Polish commander-in-chief, in remarkable fashion. Śmigły-Rydz had for much of the campaign been a peripheral figure, largely lacking in meaningful communication with his subordinates. He had escaped to Romania on September 18, where he was interned by the Romanian authorities, thereby making contact with Poland even more problematical. On September 22, General Rómmel, in Warsaw, had sent a courier in a repaired P.11a fighter to find the commander-in-chief, report on the situation in the capital, and ask how much longer they were to keep fighting. The courier seems to have landed by mistake in Hungary, but he passed the message on to the Polish envoy in Budapest, who sent it on to Romania, where Śmigły-Rydz received it on or around September 25.[32]

Śmigły-Rydz's reply, handwritten beneath the letterhead of the "General Inspectorate of the Armed Forces," instructed Rómmel that Warsaw was to fight on as long as food and ammunition lasted. It was transmitted by radio via Paris and handed to another airborne courier, who was instructed to return to Warsaw. The pilot entrusted with taking him, Stanisław Riess, was a test pilot from the PZL aircraft plant at Okęcie near Warsaw, and for this mission he commandeered a Polish plane—the last surviving prototype of the PZL.46, a single-engine light bomber—that was at the Bucharest airport. He took off on the afternoon of September 26 for the Polish capital, taking with him the courier, a Major Edmund Galinat, who had to lie flat in the fuselage.[33]

The journey was a difficult one, as Riess was obliged to fly above the clouds to avoid the attention of the enemy. Contending with malfunctioning instruments, however, he was repeatedly forced to dive down to take visual references. Approaching the fires of Warsaw some five hours later, he managed to land on the racecourse at Mokotów in the no-man's-land between German and Polish lines, where his human cargo disembarked and made his way into the city.

What followed was a mix of high drama and low farce. Galinat arrived at Defense Command HQ somewhat the worse for wear, having been given a restorative shot of vodka or two to recover from the flight. Rómmel was furious that a liaison officer on such an important mission should be someone who "could not even carry himself with propriety," and briefly considered having Galinat court-martialed for being drunk on duty. He relented, however, and allowed the major to relay his message. If he was carrying Śmigły-Rydz's assent to the capital's capitulation, Galinat must have forgotten about it, for Rómmel would later claim never to have received such an order.[34] But the courier seemingly brought another missive. He motioned toward the lining of his uniform, tore a section of it free, and handed it to the general. Rómmel read the message that was inscribed there and then burned the piece of silk in a candle flame.[35] It was the commander-in-chief's last executive order, instructing the military authorities to establish an underground organization—in the tradition of Poland's nineteenth-century *konspiracja* (conspiracy, or underground)—to continue the fight against the Germans.[36] Warsaw might capitulate, but Poland would not surrender.

IRONICALLY, PERHAPS, GIVEN THE DIRE STRAITS IN WHICH WARsaw found itself, there were some Polish units still at large in the east of the country who were trying to make their way to the capital. One such formation was the so-called Polesie Independent Operational Group, under the command of Brigadier-General Franciszek Kleeberg, which had initially intended to defend the area of Polesie, east of Brest, but

"All one can see is the chimneys of large bread ovens": the remains of a Polish town.
Muzeum II Wojny Światowej, Gdańsk

with the Soviet invasion had been forced to turn westward. Kleeberg, who was of Swedish and German heritage, had fought in the Austrian army in the First World War and taken part in the defense of Lwów in 1919. In 1939, he would be one of the few Polish commanders to lead his troops against both the Germans and the Soviets.

By the third week of September, Kleeberg's Operational Group was some 20,000 strong, a ragtag mixture of military remnants, units in good order, and desperate civilians. With them was Zofia Chomętowska, who was frantically trying to find her way west through a world seemingly turned upside down. There was little respite to be found from the horror of war. Crossing the river Bug, she encountered what remained of the town of Włodawa: "For the first time along our way, we see a completely destroyed and burnt-out town," she wrote. "All one can see is the chimneys of large bread ovens. All around us are charred dead trees. The ground is strewn with rubble, some hot, and the twisted remains of iron beds."[37]

For all the hardships, traveling in such a large group, with a substantial military component, did at least offer some semblance of security. Only a few kilometers away, two units that were struggling to catch up with Kleeberg would experience the new, dark realities. On September 26, the day that Chomętowska entered Włodawa, soldiers of the Pińsk Riverine Flotilla were taken captive by the Soviets some 20 kilometers (12 miles) to the northeast, near the village of Mokrany (Makrany). They had been marching westward since they had scuttled their river monitors on September 20. Some of their number had managed to find Kleeberg, and others had joined with a mixed 8,000-strong group made up mainly of KOP border troops, under the command of Brigadier-General Wilhelm Orlik-Rückemann. However, a third group had failed to keep pace with the others and, after being strafed by Soviet aircraft, found its progress blocked by Red Army tanks. "We realized that we had no ammunition," one of their number recalled. "An officer approached our group, asking if we wanted to continue fighting or surrender. We answered that we wanted to cross the Bug. The Soviet officer replied that our choice was only to fight on or surrender." The men complied, handing over their weapons and reporting for a roll call, at which the officers and NCOs—over 100 of them—were ordered to step out of the line, and were then stripped of their coats and equipment. As the ordinary ratings were marched away a while later, they heard the sound of gunshots. "We asked the Soviet officers if another Polish detachment was still fighting," one recalled. "In response, we were told, 'Those were your masters, shot dead in Mokrany Forest.'"[38] Some 30 Polish officers and NCOs are thought to have been murdered that day at Mokrany, though barely a dozen of them are named.

Two days later, the group headed by Orlik-Rückemann faced a similar situation outside the town of Szack (Shatsk), southeast of Włodawa. Sources differ as to the precise circumstances. Soviet accounts suggest that the Red Army moved forward expecting to accept a Polish surrender, while Polish accounts speak of Orlik-Rückemann's men finding their passage west blocked by Soviet troops.[39] Either way, battle was joined on the morning of September 28, and the Polish force quickly made progress, exploiting the apparent lack of combat experience of the Soviet 52nd Rifle Division facing them. Expertly utilizing the marshy ground, the Poles destroyed eight T-26 tanks before taking Szack with an infantry assault, and then held it against a sustained Red Army counterattack. It has been suggested that Orlik-Rückemann had wanted a confrontation to raise the morale of his men. If so, it seemed to have worked. As one officer recalled, "In every way, Szack was a memorable place for us."[40] Departing westward the following day, warily shadowed by the Soviets, the group left some 300 dead as they hurried to catch up with Kleeberg's Operational Group. Behind them, meanwhile, in the village of Mielniki (Melniki), 30 officers of the KOP were executed by their Red Army captors.[41]

Orlik-Rückemann's odyssey would come to an end two days later at Wytyczno, 30 kilometers (18 miles) to the west beyond the river Bug. Facing a superior Soviet force with tanks, artillery, and air support, the KOP group fought until they ran out of ammunition. Orlik-Rückemann then ordered his men to disperse; they should return home, find Kleeberg, or—like him—go underground and try to get to Warsaw. In the aftermath, the wounded were shown little mercy by their captors. As one eyewitness recalled, they were collected from the battlefield by locals and brought to the town hall of Wytyczno, where the Red Army locked the doors and refused them any medical assistance. By the time a medical unit arrived the following day, every one of them had bled to death.[42]

Yet, while Kleeberg's forces were still heading west toward Warsaw, the Polish leadership in the capital was already starting negotiations for the city's surrender. After Rómmel decided to capitulate, in the early afternoon of September 27, a ceasefire quieted the shattered streets of the city to allow terms to be negotiated. Following the cacophony of the preceding days, it was a peculiar experience, Marta Korwin recalled. "Two o'clock, suddenly—silence. . . . The planes are not seen any more; the artillery fire ceased. Our hearts stopped for a moment. What did it mean?"[43] Maria Komornicka had only rumors to report in her diary: "The news spread that a ceasefire has been announced for twenty-four hours," she wrote. "Some say it is to collect the wounded and bury the fallen, others that the Russians and the Germans are discussing who will get Warsaw. But nobody knows the truth."[44]

The truth was that General Kutrzeba traveled out to Sulejówek, a small town 15 kilometers (9 miles) east of Warsaw—now the headquarters of the German 1st Corps—that very afternoon. There, in a primary school building, the German commander, Lieutenant-General Walter Petzel, read him the surrender terms. In his memoir, Kutrzeba recalled his feelings as Petzel spoke the words "unconditional capitulation": "A stifled pain tears the soul. . . . I must clench my teeth, nail my thoughts to some secondary fact, dull my spirit, to swallow that burst of tears. . . . I'm choking on pain, I can barely contain the tears." Kutrzeba's second-in-command, Colonel Alexander Pragłowski, was unable to match his superior's stoicism, and fled the room in distress. After they agreed to terms, Petzel offered Kutrzeba his hand with the words, "The fortunes of war favored our side more. We were adversaries, but we are not personal enemies."[45]

Returning to Warsaw through the chaos of the front lines, Kutrzeba noted that the streets were already filling with civilians. People were out fetching water, or viewing the destruction around them. "I got the impression," he recalled, "that the state of morale in the city would deteriorate significantly if these impoverished and exhausted people were to be driven back into their cellars, or if the fighting flared up again."[46] He was right. Many of those emerging from their shelters that day were astonished at how low the city had sunk. When the guns fell silent that afternoon, Stanisław Sosabowski found only a world in which "everything was destroyed or damaged, dead or dying":

I had seen death and destruction in many forms, but never had I seen such mass destruction, which hit everyone, regardless of innocence or guilt. Gone were the proud buildings of churches, museums and art galleries; statues of famous men who had fought for our freedom lay smashed to pieces at the bases of their plinths, or stood decapitated and shell-scarred. The parks, created for their natural beauty, were empty and torn, the lawns dotted with the bare mounds of hurried graves. Trees, tossed in the air with the violence of the explosion, lay with exposed roots, as if they had been plucked by a giant hand and negligently thrown aside.[47]

Over it all, he recalled, hung the stench of putrefaction.

The following morning, Kutrzeba made his way to the suburb of Ra-kowiec, on the southwestern fringe of the city, where the command of the German 8th Army was situated in the remains of a Škoda factory. There, in the comparative comfort of an Opel Blitz bus, he met with General Johannes Blaskowitz and his staff, and they presented him with the terms he had agreed to the previous afternoon:

1. 29th September: all units to lay down their arms in specified area.
2. Disarmed units to gather in indicated sectors.
3. Barricades, road blocks, trenches, etc., on the main roads to be destroyed and mines removed.
4. Polish units to march out of Warsaw along certain routes according to a programme, under their own officers . . .
5. Privates and N.C.O.s to be released from camps and returned home after a few days.
6. Officers to go to Prisoner of War camps, but to retain their sabres.
7. Officers not surrendering would, on capture, be treated as criminals and not accorded rights under the Geneva Convention.
8. Troops to carry enough food for three days.[48]

After some perfunctory discussions, Kutrzeba signed the formal surrender of the Polish capital. "The end is painful—we did not deserve it," he remarked bitterly. When asked about the fate of the city, he answered simply: "Warsaw is no longer recognizable."[49]

With that, the fight for the Polish capital was over. Rómmel issued an address to its inhabitants, explaining that the city could no longer be

Kutrzeba surrendering an "unrecognizable" Warsaw to the Germans.
Heinrich Hoffmann / Library of Congress

defended, but that it had given an "example of endurance, fortitude, and a spirit of brave sacrifice," and had thereby won the respect of the free world. "Warsaw has fulfilled her duty," he said. "The war continues and I believe deeply that victory will be ours."[50] Meanwhile, military officers had the onerous task of relaying news of the surrender to their men. For Sosabowski, it was a dreadful responsibility. Some of the men, he recalled, were sunbathing on the top of their former positions, "smoking and washing and eating in the open for the first time in fourteen days." Each one of them, he explained, had greeted the end of the battle with thanks for his life. But what came next?[51] For some, it was despair. One eyewitness remembered an officer coming down the stairs of his command post, dancing and singing "Capitulation! Capitulation!," before drawing his pistol and shooting himself.[52]

Over the days that followed, some 140,000 Polish troops gathered at the designated assembly points and marched into captivity. They were marching as well into an uncertain future. In many cases, ordinary soldiers were duly released after being "processed"; they were returned—if possible—to their homes and families. Some were not so fortunate. The demands of the German Reich for forced labor meant that many would ultimately find themselves dragooned as slave laborers and deported to Hitler's Germany, where they would endure a punishing existence on farms and in factories in conditions that often mimicked those in the concentration camps.[53] The prominent among them could fall into the hands of the Einsatzgruppen, which were armed with a list—known as the *Sonderfahndungsbuch* (Special Investigation Book)—of those 61,000 eminent Poles who were considered detrimental to German interests, including priests, professors, activists, politicians, lawyers, and writers, and were slated for extermination.[54] With the surrender of Warsaw, the process of the decapitation of Polish society, which had been foreshadowed in the slaughter at Bydgoszcz, would gather pace. Among those who would fall victim to the executioners was Stefan Starzyński, Warsaw's redoubtable mayor, who was arrested by the Gestapo in following month and sent to the city's Pawiak prison. It is thought that the SS murdered him in or around Warsaw shortly before Christmas 1939. His body was never found.[55]

Following Starzyński's example, others refused to surrender. The day before the capitulation, Śmigły-Rydz's order for the creation of an underground resistance organization had been entrusted to Michał Karaszewicz-Tokarzewski, a forty-six year old general who had already worked out a plan of action. In devising it, he drew on Poland's long, painful experience of foreign occupation. Taking the pseudonym "Torwid," Karaszewicz-Tokarzewski gathered about him a group of some fifteen officers and charged them with setting up active resistance cells to secure and secrete weapons, funds, and ammunition; preparing methods of covert communication; and establishing facilities to forge essential documents. Recruitment was simple. As one colonel recalled, though the men were to wear civilian clothes, they would remain soldiers of the Polish Republic, ready to receive the orders of their superiors: "Have no doubts," the colonel said to his men in his valedictory address. "We shall meet again to fight shoulder to shoulder to victory. . . . I am not saying 'Adieu'—only 'Au revoir.'"[56] The plans certainly did not lack ambition. Under Torwid's leadership, the Służba Zwycięstwu Polski (SZP, In the

Service of Poland's Victory) aimed to encompass the whole country, despite the two occupation regimes, and extended beyond purely military resistance into the political sphere, with a Supreme Defense Council to direct its actions. As such, it would be the forerunner of the formidable Armia Krajowa (AK, Home Army), the largest and most effective underground resistance movement of the war.[57]

At that moment, of course, for many Varsovians, such ideas must have appeared as so much "pie in the sky." Many soldiers were inclined to believe German promises of good treatment and considered that the risks of continued resistance outweighed the benefits.[58] There were also more urgent priorities to be considered, such as clearing the dead and making the city's ruins habitable once again. It would be no easy task. When he dared to venture out of his shelter, Władysław Szpilman returned home in a depressed state. "The city no longer existed," he later recalled. "At every corner I had to make detours round barricades constructed from overturned trams and torn-up paving slabs. Decaying bodies were piled up in the streets. The people, starving from the siege, fell on the bodies of horses lying around. The ruins of many buildings were still smouldering."[59] Even the victors were dismayed. When SS-*Major* Walter Schellenberg arrived in Warsaw, the city made one of the most disturbing impressions of his entire wartime career: "I was shocked at what had become of the beautiful city I had known—ruined and burnt-out houses, starving and grieving people . . . everywhere the sweetish smell of burnt flesh. No running water anywhere." Warsaw, he remembered, was "a dead city."[60]

In such circumstances, many in the capital were justifiably more concerned with the everyday necessities of life and death, rather than politics and grand strategy. But for those able to raise their eyes to the horizon, critical questions remained, not least among them how the collaboration between Hitler's Germany and Stalin's Soviet Union would develop, now that their common foe had been destroyed, and where Warsaw would sit within that new constellation of power. They could not have known, but just as Varsovians were emerging from their cellars and shelters into a fragile, nervous peace, that very question was being decided in Moscow.

JOACHIM VON RIBBENTROP, HITLER'S VAIN, POMPOUS FOREIGN minister, arrived in the Soviet capital on September 27. Whereas his earlier visit had been one overwhelmingly characterized by nervous tension, his return had an air of celebration about it. The invasion and destruction of Poland—the "territorial and political reorganization" anticipated in the Secret Protocol to the Nazi–Soviet Pact—was almost complete, and the cooperation between German and Red Army forces, though minimal, had nonetheless proceeded without major incident. Barely a month after its establishment, the strategic relationship between Berlin and Moscow had borne significant fruit, overturning the old status quo in Europe and providing a territorial windfall to both parties. Little wonder, then, that Ribbentrop was treated to all the ceremonial pomp the Soviet state could muster, including a gala performance of *Swan Lake* and a twenty-four-course celebratory banquet.[61]

After the mutual congratulations, there was serious work to be done when the two sides convened in the Kremlin that night. The looming defeat of Poland meant that some of the provisions of the Secret Protocol were due for revision—loose ends had to be tied up. The mood was thoroughly congenial, however, even "friendly." Ribbentrop described being back in Moscow as like being in a "circle of old comrades," while Stalin was, if anything, even more effusive, promising that if Germany were to get into difficulties, Hitler could rest assured that "the Soviet people would come to Germany's aid."[62]

There were a number of items on the agenda, including the fate of the Baltic states—which were still independent, though under increasing pressure from Stalin—and the further shaping of the German–Soviet relationship. The "friendly collaboration" between Hitler and Stalin had achieved much already, Ribbentrop explained, but there was more to be done. Given that Germany and the Soviet Union shared a common enemy—Britain—the foreign minister went on, it would be desirable to issue a joint declaration to document the cooperation between the two states "before the whole world" and affirm their agreement on basic foreign policy matters. With a flourish, Ribbentrop then produced a draft for Stalin's consideration.

A central point for discussion was the issue of the final delineation of the German–Soviet frontier—what Ribbentrop called the "solution of the Polish question." On this topic, the German foreign minister had a particular request. While acknowledging that the line agreed in the Secret Protocol followed the rivers Pissa, Narew, Vistula, and San,* he asked that a revision might be considered. Given the relative sizes of Germany and the USSR, he continued, and the fact that Germany lacked forests and oil reserves, he asked if the line might be revised eastward to the river Bug, which would leave the forests around Białystok and the oilfields of Galicia in German hands. In addition, he suggested that the idea of leaving a rump Polish state—which had been left open by the Secret Protocol—should be formally abandoned. Any autonomous Polish territory would only be a source of constant disruption, he said: a "clear division" of Poland was more desirable.[63]

Meeting again the following day, Stalin showed himself very amenable to Ribbentrop's ideas. He had long advocated closer collaboration with Germany, he declared, and "one need only read the works of Lenin to recognize that England was always hated and cursed by the Bolsheviks." Regarding Poland, he agreed that any rump state would inevitably be a source of friction—it would do everything it could "to play Germany and the Soviet Union off against one another." He concurred, then, that Poland should—once again—disappear from the map. That led to the question of the German–Soviet frontier, which, like Ribbentrop, Stalin viewed as unsatisfactory, as it would divide Poland's ethnic core territory, and thereby provide yet another potential source of difficulties. It would be preferable, he suggested, to leave what he called "ethnic Polish territory" in German hands, and move the frontier to the river Bug. The Galician oilfields, however, would remain under Soviet control, though he promised to sell Germany half of the region's oil production, or exchange it for coal. Finally, he added that, by way of compensation for the lost territory, he would accept the transfer of Lithuania into the Soviet "sphere of influence."[64]

---

* Interestingly, had this original agreement been maintained, Warsaw itself would have straddled the German–Soviet frontier, as it is bisected by the river Vistula.

A Red Army guard on the German–Soviet frontier: the "boundary of peace."
Muzeum II Wojny Światowej, Gdańsk

With that, a large-scale map of the Polish Republic was produced from the German embassy and laid out across the conference table, and a black line was drawn to mark the new German–Soviet border. The line began at the East Prussian frontier, on the river Pissa, and ran southwest to Ostrołęka before turning southeast, to meet the river Bug near Ostrów Mazowiecka. It then followed the course of the Bug southeastward past Brest—where Wehrmacht and Red Army forces had paraded a week before—and proceeded on southward to Krystynopol (Chervonohrad), where it followed the river Sołokija westward before winding its way down, following the upper reaches of the river San, to the border with Hungary at the village of Sianki in the Beskid Mountains.

When they had finished, Poland had been neatly divided into two almost equal halves: Germany took 201,000 square kilometers (77,600 square miles) of territory, along with 20 million inhabitants; and the Soviet Union took 188,500 square kilometers (72,780 square miles) with a population of 12 million. Ribbentrop and Stalin then signed the map to signify the agreement. Ribbentrop added his signature in a flourish of red pencil, giving the date of "28 IX 39"; Stalin signed with a swirl of blue, adding an initial next to two adjustments. "Is my signature clear enough for you?" he asked his guest.[65]

That day, the text of the German–Soviet Boundary and Friendship Treaty was published. It stated that Germany and the USSR considered it "exclusively" their task to restore order in the region following "the collapse of the former Polish state." Between them, they would establish the frontier, and they alone would administer the territories on either side of that line; the map was appended to the treaty for the sake of clarity. Furthermore, in an addendum, they agreed not to tolerate "Polish agitation" in their respective areas and promised to collaborate in the suppression of such activity.[66] With that—consumed by its enemies and abolished with a scribble of colored pencil—Poland ceased to exist.

FOR ALL THE BRAVERY OF THE POLISH FORCES THAT CONTINUED to defy the invaders, what remained for the Wehrmacht and the Red Army was merely a process of mopping up. The fortress complex of Modlin was still obstinately holding out, despite dire shortages of munitions, food, and medical supplies, and after enduring days of concentrated aerial, artillery, and ground assault by an enemy vastly superior in numbers and equipment. For all the privation, however, morale was still good. "Until the last moments," one captain recalled, "the soldiers did not think of surrendering or throwing down their weapons. The only complaints one heard were due to the decreasing food rations and the shortage of cigarettes."[67] One senior officer noted that the shortage of bread was "the most terrifying thing."[68] Another, stationed at the western edge of the Modlin enclave, suggested that his men were buoyed by a sense of moral purpose, in contrast to their opponents:

> The Germans were heroes when they could freely drop bombs on defenseless villages and towns. They performed wonders of courage, flying over the heads of innocent civilians at the lowest altitude, sparing

no woman or child. But here, at modest Zakroczym, they cannot cross a distance of 300 meters (985 feet). They no longer advance in a triumphant march. . . . They cannot reach our trenches even by crawling on their bellies, for our positions are defended by men aware of the purpose of the fight, convinced that their role is not only to hold Zakroczym or Modlin but to preserve the entire nation.[69]

Though the moral case was undimmed, once Warsaw had capitulated the defense of Modlin lost whatever strategic rationale it still had. At dawn on September 28, a staff officer arrived from the capital, having been sent through the German lines, to bring word that Warsaw had surrendered under "honorable conditions." After brief consideration, the commander of Modlin, Brigadier-General Wiktor Thommée, decided it was time to end the fight. He gave the order to cease firing and sent an emissary to begin negotiations on a surrender.[70]

The capitulation did not go smoothly everywhere: lines of communication were frayed, and passions on both sides were running high. Many prisoners were routinely beaten. One recalled how Germans had surrounded his group of around twenty men and ordered them to keep their hands up. Those who dropped their arms from exhaustion were beaten and kicked. When an officer dared to remind their captors of their duty of care to the prisoners, he was hit with a rifle butt.[71]

It was the defenders of Zakroczym who paid most dearly for their defiance. That morning, Polish troops there were instructed to cease firing and raise white flags, much to their evident consternation.[72] What followed is disputed, but shortly thereafter, German troops of the Kempf Armored Division, including elements of the SS-Deutschland Regiment, stormed the Polish lines. As the Poles were rounded up, about sixty of their number were shot out of hand. A battalion commander in the 2nd Legions Infantry Regiment, Captain Tadeusz Dorant, was killed with a flamethrower.[73] German accounts suggest the attack was made in error; Polish sources are less charitable.[74]

It would not prove to be an isolated incident. Over the day, the killing spree continued. Prisoners were massacred in the Jewish cemetery and in Zakroczym itself, where dozens of civilians were also murdered in a rampage. As a military surgeon would later testify, the killing was seemingly indiscriminate: "Next to the Jewish cemetery, over a dozen soldiers were shot after they had surrendered. The same happened in Gałachy. Some soldiers were burned alive. When passing cellars where the elderly and children were hiding, the Germans threw in hand grenades."[75]

By the following morning, as the survivors were being marched through Zakroczym, the evidence of the slaughter was all around:

> Burnt-out ruins everywhere, smoke still rising from some of the houses. . . . Before us more ashes of farms and vegetable fields plowed in deep, jagged furrows: the work of bombs and artillery shells. To the right and left, the field is strewn with the bodies of our fallen brothers-in-arms. . . . Here and there, there are only shreds of human flesh blown apart by exploding bombs. A German NCO walking next to me beholds this harvest of death with horror. Shocked by the sight, he tells me that "history will write about your heroic resistance." I hold my tongue. I cannot tell him what I really think.[76]

It has been estimated that some 500 Polish soldiers were slaughtered at Zakroczym, along with 100 civilians.[77]

On the morning of September 29, Modlin itself formally capitulated. With terms agreed the previous day, Thommée traveled to the small town of Jabłonna, on the road to Warsaw, where, on a windswept country lane, he met his counterpart, General Adolf Strauss, commander of the German 2nd Army Corps. There, they agreed to the handover of the fortress complex. The terms offered were essentially the same as those agreed the previous day in Warsaw, except that special provision was requested for the 4,000 wounded inside the Citadel; in addition, given that Modlin's food supplies were exhausted, it was asked that the garrison be fed as a matter of urgency.[78] That afternoon, Thommée returned to the fortress under a clear blue sky, for once devoid of enemy aircraft. It was "as though the world had changed in those few hours," he mused. "A free man turns into a slave. I no longer have anything to do, the battle

Modlin surrenders: "A free man turns into a slave."
Ian Sayer Archive

is over. Nothing makes one happy, everything brings grief and shame. Wouldn't it have been better to have died in these walls?"[79] As he pondered these questions, the Modlin defensive area was being prepared for surrender: rifles were stacked, helmets discarded, documents burned, and ammunition hidden. Soon afterward, some 25,000 officers and men marched into German captivity.[80]

Far to the north, meanwhile, the complex of defenses at Hel was still holding out, though that action, too, was nearing its end. Over the previous weeks, the Germans had pummeled Hel's coastal artillery positions both from the air and from the battleships *Schlesien* and *Schleswig-Holstein*, which patrolled the Bay of Danzig. A few days earlier, the privations endured by the Hel garrison had led to a brief mutiny among the troops guarding the landward front, sparked—it was said—by German leaflets encouraging the defenders to surrender, with the promise that they would not be harmed and would be returned to their families. Despite the rebellion, morale remained robust: when the area commander, Rear-Admiral Józef Unrug, visited the main Laskowski battery on the tip of the peninsula on September 30, he was greeted with demands from the men that they should fight on. According to one eyewitness, Unrug's face filled with grief and he thanked the soldiers, adding that he wished that all his men were as courageous.[81] He then asked his gun commanders how much food and munitions they had left. The replies could not have pleased him. Food had been all but exhausted, and none of the batteries had enough ammunition for more than fifteen minutes of firing. The guns that had shot down an estimated fifty enemy aircraft, sunk a minesweeper, damaged both the battleships in the bay, and contributed to the most protracted defensive operation of the September campaign had finally exhausted their supplies.[82]

That afternoon, Unrug issued orders for all of Hel's batteries to hold their fire and prepare to surrender. Spurning the opportunity to escape to Britain, he vowed to remain with his men and go into captivity. After securing a ceasefire, he destroyed the garrison's sensitive documents, evacuated those unit commanders who wished to escape, and sent a delegation to the German headquarters in the Kasino Hotel in Zoppot, where a formal capitulation was signed on October 1. The Germans occupied Hel the following morning. Fritz-Otto Busch, a German naval correspondent who accompanied the forces that took control of the harbor, was shocked by the "picture of absolute destruction": the sleek upturned flank of the destroyer *Wicher*, lapped by the waves, and the shattered superstructure of the minelayer *Gryf*, poking up out of the oil-stained water.[83] Polish dead amounted to around 100, with as many wounded. That day, 3,600 seamen and soldiers were taken captive, along with Rear-Admiral Unrug, who—true to his oath—would insist on speaking to his German captors only through an interpreter.[84]

With the surrender of Hel, the last remaining pocket of Polish resistance was the motley collection of forces commanded by Brigadier-General Franciszek Kleeberg, which was slowly making its way westward toward the river Vistula. Now around 18,000 strong, with its crowds of refugees and camp followers, its horse-drawn wagons, horses and cattle in tow, and its multifarious troops, the Polesie Independent Operational Group could easily have turned into something of a rabble.

General Franciszek Kleeberg, who surrendered the last regular Polish forces at Kock in October 1939. *public domain*

But that was not the case. At its heart was strict military discipline: it was still first and foremost an army. As one of its officers, Colonel Adam Epler, put it, "Every unit was in a constant state of readiness for battle."[85] Little wonder, perhaps, that the Red Army tended to shadow Kleeberg's group rather than confront it, often withdrawing when the two came too close.

It was a lesson that Soviet forces would learn to their cost in a number of engagements west of Włodawa on September 29 and 30. After skirmishes at Jabłoń and Parczew, battle was joined around the village of Milanów, where the Polish 79th Regiment met a Red Army advance with heavy machine guns and artillery fire. As the Soviet attack crumbled, the Poles went onto the offensive, launching an infantry assault, which soon turned into a rout. By the time the battle was over, 100 Red Army dead littered the field and 60 prisoners had been taken. According to Epler, they would later beg not to be returned to Soviet lines and were willingly incorporated into Kleeberg's group, with which they fought "gallantly to the very end."[86]

Pushing ever westward, Kleeberg was by now aware of the fall of Warsaw, and he altered his plans accordingly. Avoiding the capital, he planned to head—via Dęblin on the Vistula, where he hoped to be able to secure supplies of ammunition—to the forests of the Świętokrzyskie (Holy Cross) Mountains, 150 kilometers (90 miles) to the southwest, to continue the fight. As he explained to his officers, "Warsaw has fallen, there is no point in going to aid the capital or carry out diversions. The only option we have left is small warfare: guerrilla operations that can be carried out in large forest areas. This war will prove that, in spite of everything, we continued to fight."[87] According to Epler, the news of Warsaw's fall had little impact on morale. On the contrary, his soldiers took heart from the reactions of civilians in the towns and villages they encountered. "They looked upon us as if we were spectres or ghosts from another world," he wrote. "The women blessed the marching columns and the men stood silently gazing long after the last soldier had passed their dwellings." Their role, he said, was simple: "to remain united, to end on a battlefield in one last struggle, so that nobody—comrade, superior or subordinate—would be able to say that we did not do our best."[88]

That last struggle was looming. On October 1, the day that Hel surrendered, Kleeberg's group arrived in the area of Kock, north of Lublin. There, German forces of the 13th Infantry Division anticipated a simple surrender, on the assumption that the Poles were outnumbered and morale was low. They were to be disappointed. Polish forces were still capable of springing a surprise, even to their own side. Zofia Chomętowska recalled seeing a detachment of cavalrymen form up that day: "There is commotion in the market square. The jingle of stirrups; the quartermasters of the 1st Lancers Regiment. They look magnificent, we haven't seen such an army in a long time."[89]

The following day, the Germans attempted to persuade the Poles to submit with an assault on the village of Serokomla, at the heart of the area under Kleeberg's control. For civilians caught up in the fighting, it was a terrifying experience. One recalled the shocking intensity of the attack: "Shells fall all around the village, but we cannot see the enemy. It is difficult to determine where they are firing from. They must be all

Hitler reviews his victorious 8th Army in Warsaw.
Narodowe Archiwum Cyfrowe

around us. . . . If we're not killed in this battle it will be a miracle."[90] Yet the Germans met with spirited resistance and were beaten back by units of Polish cavalry and infantry.

Over the next couple of days, the Poles were sufficiently emboldened to go over to the offensive; though pushed westward, they still sought to drive the Germans back from some of the villages, and they scored a few successes. Colonel Epler recalled the taking of Charlejów on October 4, sending German troops there into a headlong flight. "This was the last splendid testimony of our soldiers of 1939," he later wrote, "a final pursuit of fleeing Germans."[91]

Though the Poles were successful in isolated skirmishes, the wider picture was bleak. The Germans had brought up reinforcements, and Polish forces were now surrounded and facing insuperable odds. Leaflets were dropped on their positions, urging them to surrender. "We acknowledge your gallantry," the notes read, but added a harsh truth: "Stop fighting. You are alone."[92] As if to confirm that fact, Hitler visited

Warsaw on October 5, arriving as a conqueror. After being driven through the rubble-strewn streets, he arrived at a saluting base on the Aleja Ujazdowskie, one of the city's main boulevards. There, among the remains of once opulent villas and former embassies, a dais had been constructed. A huge German war flag had been hung behind it between yellowing trees. For two hours, Hitler took the salute of the victorious German 8th Army, which filed past in massed ranks of infantry, cavalry, and motorized artillery. Tellingly, the wider city was in lockdown, its prominent persons held hostage to ensure the good behavior of the others. Its inhabitants learned of Hitler's presence only through rumor and hearsay.[93]

That evening, Kleeberg called for a conference with his senior commanders to assess their prospects for continuing the fight. He told them that, after the three-day battle at Kock, they had exhausted their ammunition, and there was no possibility of replenishing their supplies. Their losses had been heavy, and morale was fading. The commanders then gave their assessments: they were still fighting, they said, but ammunition was low. Regretfully, they concurred that there was nothing to be gained by further resistance. Kleeberg concluded the meeting with the words, "We have nothing with which to reproach ourselves. We have done our duty to the last, and some time, when our country will ask us for an account, we shall be able to answer every question. Tell your soldiers that they knew how to fight for the honour of their Fatherland." Underlining the seriousness of his predicament, Kleeberg's closing words were accompanied by the cacophony of incoming artillery fire.[94]

With that, emissaries were sent to request a ceasefire and to agree to capitulation terms with the Germans. The following morning, October 6, at eleven o'clock, over 1,000 officers and 15,000 men of the Polesie Independent Operational Group would march, in perfect order, into German captivity. Poland's defensive war had come to an end. Many of them marched with the words of Kleeberg's emotional final address ringing in their ears:

Soldiers! I have gathered you under my command from faraway Polesie, from the banks of the Narew, from the units that resisted demoralization in Kowel, to fight until the end. . . . You showed courage at a time of doubt and you remained faithful to your country until the end. Today we are surrounded and running out of ammunition and food. Continued resistance offers no hope, but will only shed soldiers' blood, which could still be useful. It is a commander's privilege to take responsibility for his decisions. Today I take it at the hardest time, ordering you to stop further pointless bloodshed, so as not to waste soldiers' lives. I thank you for your courage and obedience, and I know that you will take up arms again when you are needed.

Appropriately, he ended with the opening line of the Polish national anthem: "Jeszcze Polska nie zginęła" (Poland is not yet lost).[95]

CONCLUSION

WITH THE SURRENDER OF GENERAL KLEEBERG AND HIS MEN at Kock, Poland's defensive war finally ended. It had been an unequal fight. Not only had Germany enjoyed a numerical advantage over the Poles, but the military hardware and doctrine of the two countries sometimes appeared to belong to two different ages of warfare. Though the Poles fought well, they were outgunned and outfought in every theater. By the time Stalin's Red Army—the largest military force in the world at that time—entered the fray, the Poles were already reeling. Faced with both German *and* Soviet forces, they had little chance.

Poland's losses consequently far outstripped those of its opponents. Though statistics are still confused and contested, Polish military deaths incurred in fighting the Germans are estimated at a little over 60,000—around four times those of Hitler's forces.[1] Polish military losses in fighting against the Soviets are extremely difficult to quantify but have been estimated at around 18,000.[2] Soviet military deaths, which were certainly massaged downward for propaganda purposes, were mendaciously claimed at the time to have totaled only 1,500, but must have been considerably greater.[3] Polish civilian deaths, meanwhile, are reckoned at around 100,000, with some 16,000 falling victim to extrajudicial killing by German military and security forces during the period of the military campaign.[4] The total death toll—civilian and military—from the five weeks of fighting in Poland may have reached as high as 200,000.

Poland's defensive war of 1939 was no side-show. But apart from the human cost, it was also significant for what it foreshadowed about the conflict to come. For one thing, the Polish campaign saw the widespread bombing of towns and cities, very often with no military component present on the ground, and no meaningful antiaircraft defense. Of course, aerial bombing was already an established tactic by 1939, having first been used by the Italians in Tripolitania in 1911, and the bombing of civilians had featured in every conflict since, most infamously at Guernica during the Spanish Civil War. However, the sheer scale of the targeting of civilian populations during the Polish campaign— witnessed at Wieluń, Warsaw, Frampol, Sulejów, and a thousand other locations—far outstripped anything that had been seen before. Arguably for the first time, the concept of a front line in warfare became completely redundant; as one Warsaw resident noted, "The front is actually above us—the war is being fought overhead."[5] Despite the countless protestations to the contrary, the deliberate bombing of civilians—by all sides—would become one of the salient features of the world war to follow. The road to Coventry and Dresden began at Wieluń.

The ferocity with which the Germans bombed Polish towns in 1939 hints at the second foreshadowing that the Polish campaign provided: that of the deliberate blurring of the distinction between combatants and noncombatants. This, again, was a phenomenon that had been witnessed before—indeed, it had been almost ever-present in warfare, from the Sack of Magdeburg to the Rape of Nanking—but the war against Poland took it to another level. Almost every town and village in Poland witnessed an atrocity in the autumn of 1939, whether against civilians or against prisoners of war—Poles and Jews alike. As might have been expected, Polish Jews found themselves victims of persecution, humiliation, and worse at German hands. With its large proportion of orthodox *Ostjuden*, Eastern Jews, Poland appeared to conform precisely to the Nazi nightmare vision, becoming an object lesson in the dangers of racial miscegenation. Yet German ire was not reserved exclusively for Poland's Jews in 1939; indeed, in that early phase it was targeted more toward ordinary Poles, who often found themselves on the receiving end of brutal and murderous reprisals. For the first time, the chaotic conditions of the war permitted the racist, exterminatory impulses of Nazism to be fully expressed: neither the Wehrmacht nor the SS hesitated to begin the process of "ethnic cleansing" in the territories under their control.

The numbers of noncombatants killed by the Germans during the September campaign are particularly shocking when compared to those who were murdered during the French campaign of May–June 1940. Whereas the German invasion of France and the Low Countries led to three notable massacres of POWs or civilians—at Vinkt, Wormhoudt, and Le Paradis—the German invasion of Poland produced, on average, more than fifteen such massacres for *every day* of the campaign—testament to the significance of the racial component in the barbarization of German conduct.[6]

In addition, of course, there are those Poles who were murdered by the Soviets during the Red Army's invasion after September 17. Though there are no coherent statistics for these, the total is likely many thousands. Both of the invading forces applied a brutal, binary, totalitarian logic: a racist binary in the German case, a class binary in the Soviet one. There were discomfiting parallels: while the Germans might decide a prisoner's fate by whether or not he was circumcised, the fate of the Soviets' prisoners might turn on the condition of their hands. Those with soft, uncallused palms were more likely to be singled out as potentially dangerous intellectuals. Wherever one was captured, the end result was often indistinguishable: the wanton killing of civilians and POWs.

It is worth remembering that, just as the Polish campaign foreshadowed the hideous barbarization of warfare that would be increasingly in evidence as the Second World War progressed, so it also prefaced more than five brutal years of occupation and oppression for Poland itself. Poland's tribulations did not end with Kleeberg's submission on

October 6—far from it. They persisted through twenty-one months of division and occupation by the Germans and Soviets, and thereafter right up to 1945, as Poland was transformed into a giant laboratory for the racial theories of Hitler's SS: a Nazi dystopia in which populations were expropriated, deported, or murdered on a whim; a world in which the horrors of the Holocaust were but a prelude to a grand racial and territorial reordering that would have seen cities such as Warsaw disappear from the map and entire races consigned to oblivion. It should come as no surprise, therefore, that the 200,000 Polish dead of the September campaign were but the first of the estimated 5.5 million Poles—fully one-fifth of the population—that would be killed in the Second World War.

The last foreshadowing from the Polish campaign is perhaps the most famous: the use of the Blitzkrieg. That German military doctrine, which foresaw the use of fast-moving armored spearheads to cut deep into the enemy's rear to prevent the creation of a coherent phased defense, came to be seen as the key to Germany's successes in the first half of the Second World War. Many popular history books still laud the Wehrmacht's campaign in Poland as the very apogee of Blitzkrieg, a view that—needless to say—was first floated by contemporary German propaganda. This is to flatter German forces, however. For all the undeniable magnitude of the German victory, it can only be attributed in part to this military idea, which was only imperfectly applied in 1939, and which some historians have disputed even existed at all.[7]

German forces were undoubtedly more mobile than their opponents' forces. They were also, on the whole, better equipped and better led. But to attribute their victory solely to the supposed employment of Blitzkrieg is a gross oversimplification that willfully ignores the other factors that contributed to Poland's defeat. The first of these is perhaps the most obvious: Poland was geographically doomed. It was flanked on three sides by Germany and its ally Slovakia, with the equally hostile Soviet Union to the east; it also consisted primarily of flat terrain largely lacking in natural obstacles—the great North European Plain—which is perfect for the effective use of tanks and motorized infantry. Even when the Poles were able to defend prepared positions, therefore—such as at

Mława or Węgierska Górka—they were forced to withdraw to counter the risk of being outflanked and surrounded. In addition, the weather played its capricious part. The summer of 1939 was one of the driest on record in Central Europe, and rainfall in Poland that August was barely two-thirds of what it had been in previous years. Consequently, the river systems that might feasibly have been exploited to form an additional line of defense—most notably the Narew in the north and the Warta in the west—lacked the volume of water to make that a viable proposition.

There were also failings of the Poles' own making. For one thing, the Polish High Command's obsession with military secrecy—itself a throwback to Piłsudski's time—meant that Polish units had no direct contact with troops on their flanks, were not permitted to know the grand strategic plan, and were unable to coordinate their movements effectively. While the Germans were moving faster and hitting harder, the Poles were effectively blind and deaf.

More seriously, Poland's comparative economic weakness in the interwar years meant that, for all its size, the Polish army was ill prepared to face the Germans in 1939. A rather telling statistic here is that the entire Polish defense budget for the five years to 1939 amounted to only 10 percent of the Luftwaffe's budget for 1939 alone.[8] Financially, at least, it was David against Goliath. The main problem resulting from this disparity was not the predominance of the cavalry in Polish forces—as we have seen, those troops fought as mobile infantry and could be surprisingly effective. Rather, it was the lack of armor. Poland in 1939 had only two armored brigades, yet in the Germans they faced an opponent with seven armored divisions and a numerical superiority in armored vehicles of more than 5:1.[9] A similar disparity pertained in the air, where Polish pilots—for all their undoubted valor—were outnumbered and outgunned by the Luftwaffe, their largely obsolete P.7 and P.11 fighters often struggling to even engage with the sleek Messerschmitts of their enemy.

Once battle had been joined, other shortcomings were swiftly made manifest. As has been shown, the decision to station Polish forces along the frontier, while politically understandable, was militarily catastrophic, raising the likelihood of a swift encirclement by a superior, more mobile enemy. The resulting inability to stem the German advance then forced other errors, most notably among them Śmigły-Rydz's decision to evacuate the High Command to Brest on September 7, and thereafter to Romania, all of which fatally impaired his dwindling ability to exert any meaningful influence on events.

The Soviet invasion on September 17 not only disrupted the organization of any coherent defense in Poland's east—were such a thing possible—but also dashed the High Command's last hope: the mass evacuation of men and materiel to the Romanian frontier, the so-called Romanian bridgehead. With that, Poland's fate was effectively sealed, and soon thereafter, only the besieged garrisons of Warsaw, Modlin, and Hel continued to resist, as well as those splintered and scattered forces still adrift between the German and Soviet lines.

Poland's defeat in 1939 was the child of many fathers, therefore, which makes it all the more peculiar that the simplistic mythology of an all-conquering Blitzkrieg has persisted for so long. Where the story of Poland's defensive war is known at all, beyond Poland, it is often this myth—of "cavalry against tanks," the desperate Polish lancers taking on the armored might of the Wehrmacht—that takes center stage. It was a story first publicized, unsurprisingly, by the organs of German propaganda, a way of ridiculing the enemy while producing a stereotype of Polish foolhardiness and German superiority. Ordinarily, perhaps, that story might—like other German propaganda myths—have quietly died off, enduring the death of a thousand corrections. But in Poland's case, it seemed that nobody after the war had a vested interest in correcting it: the Germans had many more egregious crimes to expiate, the Soviets were not minded to defend the prewar Polish regime, and the British and French were seemingly content to allow the narrative of Poland as an inept and incompetent ally to prevail. Only Poles in exile tried to speak the truth, but, seen all too often as the archetypal "Cold Warriors" and serial disturbers of the peace, they would make little headway against the combined forces of ignorance and inertia.

On the Soviet side, meanwhile, another myth took hold that was just as durable as the German one and just as insidious: the idea that the Red

Army did not invade Poland at all in 1939. Stalin went to great lengths to preserve the fiction of the Soviet Union's "neutrality" in that first year of the war, maintaining that his armies marched into Poland on the spurious premise of protecting that country's Byelorussian and Ukrainian populations from its supposed collapse, and that they had been ordered to keep their distance from the Germans. Hitler even lent a shoulder to the wheel, proclaiming in Danzig that the war had been won in three weeks, in an attempt to relieve the Red Army of the political burden of sharing the "glory of victory." In the postwar period, with Stalin anxious to obliterate all evidence of his collaboration with Hitler, the invasion was whitewashed again, portrayed as a simple police action and excised from the Soviet narrative of the war. The overriding mythology of a blameless Red Army, and of the "peace-loving" Soviet Union as the perennial victim, would brook no contradiction.

Yet, as this book has demonstrated, the Red Army's entry into Poland was no benign intervention to restore order or protect the rights of embattled minorities: it was a military invasion, a "lightning strike" to destroy the remaining Polish forces and capture the territory promised to Stalin under the Nazi–Soviet Pact. And though the fighting that followed in eastern Poland was of shorter duration than that against the Germans, and of a rather different character, it was no less bitter, unleashing a vicious class war against soldiers and civilians alike. In the postwar years, as Poland was resurrected under communist control, this subject, too, disappeared, consigned to the proscribed list, one of the forbidden "black spots" of Polish–Soviet history. Only after 1989 could it be told at all.

And what of the other outside actors in the Polish drama of 1939— the British and the French? Their role is perhaps the least immediately toxic, predicated as it was—unlike that of the Germans and the Soviets—on the desire to avoid war rather than foment it, but it was scarcely effective or considered. The root problem, aside from a certain imperial arrogance, was that Anglo-French policy was based on a misconception: the belief that if the Poles were sufficiently galvanized by their support, then the mere specter of war would be enough to bring Hitler to his senses and curb German aggression. But the Poles needed little goading. They were always going to fight for their independence: their proud military tradition, as well as their history of occupation and partition, surely dictated that. What they needed was the thing that would not be forthcoming: genuine material assistance—action, not words.

Moreover, the possibility that Hitler might not be brought to reason was not entertained in London and Paris. Meat was never put onto the bones of the resulting alliance with the Poles in that troubled summer of 1939 despite the airy promises of Gamelin and Ironside. The British and French declared war on Hitler on September 3—their sense of national honor would permit nothing less—but they did nothing in the short term to aid their ally. Theirs was still largely a rhetorical war—a Phoney War, a *Drôle de Guerre*—even though very real battles were being fought in Poland in the fervent expectation of Allied assistance. Those who portray Allied policy toward Poland in September 1939 as crudely Machiavellian are off the mark: it was more benign—and more naïve—than that. But in its end effect—in the popular hopes that it raised, in the strategies that it influenced, in the expectations that it aroused—it amounted nonetheless to the betrayal of an ally.

Like all history, Poland's defensive war of 1939 was a complex affair—in the fevered diplomacy that prefaced it, just as in the military campaigns that it, in turn, unleashed. With its armored trains and cavalrymen, it seems a throwback to the battlefields of the past, while at the same time its hideous novelties of aerial bombing and the targeting of civilians pointed to the horrors that were to follow. As the opening campaign of the Second World War—which cost some 200,000 lives and contained all the wicked hallmarks of the later conflict—it surely warrants our attention and understanding, rather than being passed over in a couple of paragraphs, or remaining still mired in the mythologies and propaganda battles of the vilest totalitarians of the twentieth century. Most of all, it is a story from which the voices of its primary victims—the Poles themselves—have been excluded for far too long. One hopes that this book might begin the process of restoring them to their own narrative.

APPENDIX 1

POLISH ARMY ORDER OF BATTLE
September 1, 1939

Pomeranian Army (commander: General Władysław Bortnowski)

9th Infantry Division, 15th Infantry Division, 27th Infantry Division, Pomeranian National Defense Brigade, Chełmno National Defense Brigade
Operational Group East
    4th Infantry Division, 16th Infantry Division
Czersk Operational Group
    Pomeranian Cavalry Brigade, Kościerzyna National Defense Brigade, Chojnice Detatchment

Modlin Army (commander: General Emil Krukowicz-Przedrzymirski)

8th Infantry Division, 20th Infantry Division, Nowogródek Cavalry Brigade, Mazowiecka Cavalry Brigade, Warsaw National Defense Brigade

Narew Independent Operational Group (commander: General
Czesław Młot-Fijałkowski)
18th Infantry Division, 33rd Infantry Division, Podlaska Cavlary
Brigade, Suwalska Cavalry Brigade

Poznań Army (commander: Major-General Tadeusz Kutrzeba)

14th Infantry Division, 17th Infantry Division, 25th Infantry Division, 26th Infantry Division, Wielkopolska Cavalry Brigade, Podolska
Cavalry Brigade

Łódź Army (commander: General Juliusz Rómmel)

2nd Legions Infantry Division, 10th Infantry Division, 28th Infantry
Division, Kresowa Cavalry Brigade, Sieradz National Defense Brigade
Piotrków Operational Group
    30th Infantry Division, Wołyńska Cavalry Brigade

Kraków Army (commander: General Antoni Szylling)

6th Infantry Division, 7th Infantry Division, 11th Infantry Division,
Kraków Cavalry Brigade, 10th Motorized Cavalry Brigade
Silesian Operational Group
    23rd Infantry Division, 55th Infantry Division
Bielsko Operational Group
    21st Mountain Infantry Division, 1st Mountain Brigade

Carpathian Army (commander: Major-General Kazimierz Fabrycy)

22nd Mountain Infantry Division, 2nd Mountain Brigade, 3rd Mountain Brigade, Carpathian National Defense Brigade
Carpathian Army Reserve
    24th Infantry Division, 38th Infantry Division

APPENDIX 2

GERMAN ARMY ORDER OF BATTLE
September 1, 1939[1]

Army Group North (commander: Colonel-General Fedor von Bock)
Army Group Reserve
10th Panzer Division, 73rd Infantry Division, 206th Infantry Division, 208th Infantry Division

Third Army (commander: General Georg von Küchler)
I Corps
  Panzer Division Kempf, 11th Infantry Division, 61st Infantry Division
XXI Corps
  21st Infantry Division, 228th Infantry Division
Brandt Corps
  Goldap Infantry Brigade, Lötzen Infantry Brigade
Wodrig Corps
  1st Infantry Division, 12th Infantry Division
Third Army Reserve
  217th Infantry Division, 1st Cavalry Brigade

Fourth Army (commander: General Günther von Kluge)

I Frontier Guard Corps
    207th Infantry Division
II Corps
    3rd Infantry Division, 32nd Infantry Division
III Corps
    Netze Infantry Brigade, 50th Infantry Division
XIX Motorized Corps
2nd Motorized Division, 3rd Panzer Division, 20th Motorized
Division, Panzer Lehr-Regiment
Fourth Army Reserve
    II Frontier Guard Corps
XII Frontier Guard Corps
    23rd Infantry Division, 218th Infantry Division

Army Group South (commander: Colonel-General Gerd von Rundstedt)

Army Group Reserve
VII Corps
    27th Infantry Division, 68th Infantry Division
    62nd Infantry Division, 213th Infantry Division, 221st Infantry
    Division, 239th Infantry Division

Eighth Army (commander: General Johannes von Blaskowitz)

X Corps
    24th Infantry Division, 30th Infantry Division
XIII Corps
    10th Infantry Division, 17th Infantry Division, SS Motorized
    Regiment "Leibstandarte Adolf Hitler"
XII Frontier Guards Corps
XIV Frontier Guards Corps

Tenth Army (commander: General Walther von Reichenau)

IV Corps
4th Infantry Division, 46th Infantry Division
XI Corps
18th Infantry Division, 19th Infantry Division
XIV Motorized Corps
13th Motorized Division, 29th Motorized Division
XV Motorized Corps
2nd Light Division, 3rd Light Division
XVI Panzer Corps
1st Panzer Division, 4th Panzer Division, 14th Infantry Division,
31st Infantry Division
Tenth Army Reserve
1st Light Division

Fourteenth Army (commander: General Wilhelm List)

VIII Corps
5th Panzer Division, 8th Infantry Division, 28th Infantry Division,
SS-Germania Motorized Infantry Regiment
XVII Corps
7th Infantry Division, 44th Infantry Division, 45th Infantry
Division
XVIII Corps
2nd Panzer Division, 3rd Mountain Division, 4th Light Division
XXII Corps
1st Mountain Division, 2nd Mountain Division
Slovak Army "Bernolak"
1st Infantry Division, 2nd Infantry Division, 20th Infantry
Division

APPENDIX 3

RED ARMY ORDER OF BATTLE
September 17, 1939[1]

BYELORUSSIAN FRONT
(COMMANDER: GENERAL MIKHAIL KOVALEV)

Third Army (commander: Komkor Vasily Kuznetsov)

4th Rifle Corps
    27th Rifle Division, 50th Rifle Division, 18th Tank Brigade
Lepelska Army Group
    5th Rifle Division, 24th Cavalry Division, 22nd Tank Brigade, 25th
    Tank Brigade

Fourth Army (commander: Komkor Vasily Chuikov)

8th Rifle Division, 29th Rifle Division, 32nd Tank Brigade
23rd Rifle Corps
    52nd Rifle Division, Dniepr Military Flotilla

Tenth Army (commander: Komkor Ivan Zakharkin)

11th Rifle Corps
6th Rifle Division, 33rd Rifle Division, 121st Rifle Division

Eleventh Army (commander: Komkor Nikolai Medvedev)

16th Rifle Corps
2nd Rifle Division, 100th Rifle Division
3rd Cavalry Corps
7th Cavalry Division, 36th Cavalry Division, 6th Tank Brigade

Dzerzhinsk Mechanized Cavalry Group
(commander: Komkor Ivan Boldin)

5th Rifle Corps
4th Rifle Division, 13th Rifle Division
6th Cavalry Corps
4th Cavalry Division, 6th Cavalry Division, 11th Cavalry Division
15th Tank Corps
2nd Tank Brigade, 27th Tank Brigade, 20th Motorized Brigade,
21st Tank Brigade

Ukrainian Front
(Commander: General Semyon Timoshenko)

Fifth Army (commander: Komdiv Ivan Sovetnikov)

8th Rifle Corps
44th Rifle Division, 81st Rifle Division, 36th Tank Brigade
15th Rifle Corps
45th Rifle Division, 60th Rifle Division, 87th Rifle Division

Sixth Army (commander: Komkor Filipp Golikov)

17th Rifle Corps
> 96th Rifle Division, 97th Rifle Division, 10th Tank Brigade, 38th Tank Brigade

2nd Cavalry Corps
> 3rd Cavalry Division, 5th Cavalry Division, 14th Cavalry Division, 24th Tank Brigade

Twelfth Army (commander: Komandarm Ivan Tyulenev)

13th Rifle Corps
> 72nd Rifle Division, 99th Rifle Division

4th Cavalry Corps
> 32nd Cavalry Division, 34th Cavalry Division, 26th Tank Brigade

5th Cavalry Corps
> 9th Cavalry Division, 16th Cavalry Division, 23rd Tank Brigade

25th Tank Corps
> 4th Tank Brigade, 5th Tank Brigade, 1st Motorized Brigade

SELECTED BIBLIOGRAPHY

ARCHIVES AND LIBRARIES

Archiwum Akt Nowych, Warsaw
Archiwum Muzeum Marynarki Wojennej, Gdynia
Archiwum Narodowe w Krakowie, Oddział w Tarnowie
Archiwum Wschodnie, Ośrodek Karta, Warsaw
Biblioteka Muzeum Wojska Polskiego, Warsaw
Biblioteka Narodowa, Warsaw
British Library, London
Bundesarchiv, Berlin
Bundesarchiv-Militärarchiv, Freiburg
Centralna Biblioteka Wojskowa, Dział Zbiorów Specjalnych, Warsaw
Centralna Biblioteka Wojskowa, Warsaw
German Historical Institute Library, London
Ian Sayer Archive, Spain
Imperial War Museum Archive, London
Institut für Zeitgeschichte, Munich
Library of the School of Slavonic and East European Studies, University
    of London
Mass Observation Archive, University of Sussex Library
Muzeum II Wojny Światowej, Gdańsk
Muzeum Poczty Polskiej, Gdańsk
Muzeum Ziemi Zawkrzeńskiej, Mława

Narodowe Archiwum Cyfrowe, Warsaw
The National Archives, London
National Archives and Records Administration, Washington, DC
Naval Historical Branch, Portsmouth
Polish Institute and Sikorski Museum Archive, London

Books

Aksamitowski, Andrzej, and Wojciech Zalewski. *Mława 1939.* Warsaw, 2008.

Anders, Władysław. *An Army in Exile: The Story of the Second Polish Corps.* London, 1949.

———. *Bez ostatniego rodziału.* Warsaw, 2008.

Banac, Ivo, ed. *The Diary of Georgi Dimitrov, 1933–1949.* New Haven, CT, 2003.

Bance, Alan, trans. *Blitzkrieg in Their Own Words: First-Hand Accounts from German Soldiers, 1939–1940.* St. Paul, MN, 2005.

Bębnik, Grzegorz. *Wrzesień 1939 r. w Katowicach.* Katowice, Poland, 2012.

Bekker, Cajus. *The Luftwaffe War Diaries.* New York, 1994.

von Below, Nicolaus. *At Hitler's Side: The Memoirs of Hitler's Luftwaffe Adjutant, 1937–1945.* London, 2004.

Bethel, Nicholas. *The War Hitler Won: September 1939.* London, 1972.

Böhler, Jochen. *Auftakt zum Vernichtungskrieg: Die Wehrmacht in Polen 1939.* Frankfurt am Main, 2006.

———. *Der Überfall: Deutschlands Krieg gegen Polen.* Frankfurt am Main, 2009.

———. *"Grösste Härte . . .": Verbrechen der Wehrmacht in Polen, September/Oktober 1939.* Osnabrück, Germany, 2005.

———. *Zbrodnie Wehrmachtu w Polsce: Wrzesień 1939—wojna totalna.* Kraków, 2009.

Borodziej, Włodzimierz, and Sławomir Dębski, eds. *Polish Documents on Foreign Policy, 24 October 1938–30 September 1939.* Warsaw, 2009.

Borowiak, Mariusz. *Admirał Unrug, 1884–1973.* Warsaw, 2009.

———. *Westerplatte: W obronie prawdy.* Gdańsk, Poland, 2001.

Bryan, Julien. *Warsaw.* New York, 1959.

Buchner, Alex. *Der Polenfeldzug 1939.* Leoni am Starnberger See, Germany, 1989.

Carruthers, Bob. *Poland 1939: The Blitzkrieg Unleashed.* Barnsley, England, 2011.

Carton de Wiart, Adrian. *Happy Odyssey.* London, 2007 [1950].

Chinciński, Tomasz. *Forpoczta Hitlera.* Gdańsk, Poland, 2010.

Chinciński, Tomasz, and Paweł Machcewicz, eds. *Bydgoszcz 3–4 września 1939.* Warsaw, 2008.

Chomętowska, Zofia. *Na wozie i pod wozem: Wspomnienia z lat 1939–1940.* Warsaw, 2008.

Churchill, Winston. *The Second World War.* Vol. 1, *The Gathering Storm.* London, 1948.

Colville, John. *The Fringes of Power: Downing Street Diaries, 1939–1955.* Vol. 1, *September 1939–September 1941.* London, 1985.

Cynk, Jerzy B. *The Polish Air Force at War: The Official History.* Vol. 1, *1939–1943.* Atglen, PA, 1998.

Czyżewski, Ludwik. *Wspomnienia dowódcy obrony Zakroczymia w 1939 r.* Warsaw, 1973.

Danchev, Alex, and Daniel Todman, eds. *Field Marshal Lord Alanbrooke: War Diaries, 1939—1945.* London, 2001.

Datner, Szymon. *55 dni Wehrmachtu w Polsce: Zbrodnie dokonane na polskiej ludności cywilnej w okresie l.ix 25.x. 1939 r.* Warsaw, 1967.

Davies, Norman. *God's Playground: A History of Poland.* Vol. 1, *The Origins to 1795.* Oxford, 1982.

———. *God's Playground: A History of Poland.* Vol. 2, *1795 to the Present.* Oxford, 1981.

Degras, Jane, ed. *Soviet Documents on Foreign Policy.* Vol. 3, *1933–1941.* Oxford, 1953.

Derdej, Piotr. *Westerplatte-Oksywie-Hel 1939.* Warsaw, 2014.

Dobroszycki, Lucjan, Marian Drozdowski, Marek Getter, and Adam Słomczyński, eds. *Cywilna obrona Warszawy we wrześniu 1939 r. Dokumenty, materiały prasowe, wspomnienia i relacje.* Warsaw, 1964.

Documents on German Foreign Policy, 1918–1945. Series D, vols. 5–7. London, 1954–1957.

Domarus, Max, ed. *Hitler: Reden und Proklamationen, 1932–1945*, vols. 2 and 3. Wiesbaden, Germany, 1973.

Drescher, Herbert. *Warschau und Modlin im Polenfeldzug 1939: Berichte und Dokumente.* Pforzheim, Germany, 1991.

Drozdowski, Marian Marek, ed. *Archiwum Prezydenta Warszawy Stefana Starzyńskiego.* Warsaw, 2004.

Drzycimski, Andrzej. *Westerplatte: Special Mission.* Gdańsk, Poland, 2015.

Eberle, Henrik, and Matthias Uhl, eds. *The Hitler Book: The Secret Dossier Prepared for Stalin.* London, 2005.

Elble, Rolf. *Die Schlacht an der Bzura im September 1939.* Freiburg, Germany, 1975.

Emmerling, Marius. *Luftwaffe nad Polską 1939.* Vol. 3, *Stukaflieger.* Gdynia, Poland, 2006.

Epler, Adam. *The Last Soldier of the Battle of Poland, September 1939*. Edinburgh, 1944.

Flisowski, Zbigniew, ed. *Westerplatte*. Warsaw, 1974.

Foreign Relations of the United States, 1939, General, Volume I. Part 1, Events Leading to the Outbreak of War in Europe, September 1, 1939. VIII. Final Efforts to Preserve Peace in Europe; Appeals by President Roosevelt to Germany and Italy, August 22–31, 1939, and Part 2, Beginning of European Phase of World War II. I. Invasion of Poland by Germany and Entry of the British and French into the War, September 1–16, 1939. Eds. Matilda F. Axton, Rogers P. Churchill, Francis C. Prescott, John G. Reid, N. O. Sappington, Louis E. Gates, and Shirley L. Phillips. Washington, DC: Government Printing Office, 1956.

French, David. *Raising Churchill's Army: The British Army and the War Against Germany, 1919–1945*. Oxford, 2000.

Gardiner, Juliet. *Wartime Britain, 1939–1945*. London, 2004.

Garliński, Józef. *Poland in the Second World War*. Basingstoke, 1985.

Gibson, Hugh, ed. *The Ciano Diaries, 1939–1943*. Garden City, NY, 1946.

Gluza, Zbigniew, ed. *Rok 1939: Rozbiór Polski*. Warsaw 2009.

Gorlitz, Walter, ed. *The Memoirs of Field Marshal Wilhelm Keitel*. New York, 2000 [1966].

Grabowska-Chałka, Janina. *Stutthof: Informator historyczny—przewodnik*. Gdańsk, Poland, 2011.

Groehler, Olaf. *Selbstmörderische Allianz: Deutsch-russische Militärbeziehungen, 1920–1941*. Berlin, 1992.

Gross, Jan. *Revolution from Abroad: The Soviet Conquest of Poland's Western Ukraine and Western Belorussia*. Princeton, NJ, 2002.

Grzelak, Czesław. *Sowiecki najazd 1939 r.: Sojusznik Hitlera napada polskie Kresy—relacje świadków i uczestników*. Warsaw, 2017.

———. *Szack–Wytyczno 1939*. Warsaw, 1993.

Guderian, Heinz. *Panzer Leader*. London, 1952.

Halifax, Earl of. *Fulness of Days*. London, 1957.

Hargreaves, Richard. *Blitzkrieg Unleashed: The German Invasion of Poland, 1939*. Barnsley, England, 2008.

Henderson, Nevile. *Failure of a Mission: Berlin, 1937–1939*. London, 1941.

Hoffmann, Heinrich. *Hitler Was My Friend*. Barnsley, England, 2011 [1955].

Hollingworth, Clare. *The Three Weeks' War in Poland*. London, 1940.

Jacobsen, Hans-Adolf, ed. *Generaloberst Halder Kriegstagebuch*. Vol. 1, *Vom Polenfeldzug bis zum Ende der Westoffensive* Stuttgart, 1962.

Jurga, Tadeusz, and Władysław Karbowski. *Armia "Modlin" 1939*. Warsaw, 1987.

Juszkiewicz, Ryszard. *Bitwa pod Mławą 1939*. Warsaw, 1979.

Karpov, Vladimir. *Marshal Zhukov: Ego soratniki i protivniki v dni voĭny i mira*. Moscow, 1992.

Karski, Jan. *Story of a Secret State: My Report to the World*. London, 2011 [1944].

von Kielmansegg, Johann Graf. *Panzer zwischen Warschau und Atlantik*. Berlin, 1941.

Klemperer, Victor. *I Shall Bear Witness: The Diaries of Victor Klemperer, 1933–1941*. London, 1998.

Klessmann, Christoph, ed. *September 1939: Krieg, Besatzung, Widerstand in Polen. Acht Beiträge*. Göttingen, Germany, 1989.

Kochanski, Halik. *The Eagle Unbowed: Poland and the Poles in the Second World War*. London, 2012.

Komorowski, Krzysztof, ed. *Boje Polskie 1939–1945: Przewodnik encyklopedyczny*. Warsaw, 2009.

Korwin-Rhodes, Marta. *The Mask of Warriors: The Siege of Warsaw, September 1939*. New York, 1964.

Kozłowski, Eugeniusz, ed. *Wojna obronna Polski 1939*. Warsaw, 1979.

Krausnick, Helmut. *Hitler's Einsatzgruppen: Die Truppen des Weltanschauungskrieges, 1938–1942*. Frankfurt am Main, 1998.

Kunert, Andrzej, and Zygmunt Walkowski. *Kronika kampanii wrześniowej 1939*. Warsaw, 2005.

Kutrzeba, Tadeusz. *Bitwa nad Bzurą (9–22 września 1939): Przyczynek do historii kampanii polsko-niemieckiej w obszarze: Poznań-Warszawa we wrześniu 1939*. Warsaw, 1957.

———. *Wojna bez walnej bitwy*. Warsaw, 1998.

Lehnstaedt, Stephan, and Jochen Böhler, eds. *Die Berichte der Einsatzgruppen aus Polen 1939*. Berlin, 2013.

Leixner, Leo. *From Lemberg to Bordeaux: A German War Correspondent's Account of Battle in Poland, the Low Countries and France, 1939–1940*. London, 2017.

Linge, Heinz. *With Hitler to the End: The Memoirs of Adolf Hitler's Valet*. London, 2009.

Lubs, Gerhard. *Infanterie-Regiment Nr. 5*. Bochum, Germany, 1965.

von Luck, Hans. *Panzer Commander*. London, 1989.

Macleod, Roderick, and Denis Kelly, eds. *The Ironside Diaries, 1937–1940*. London, 1962.

Maczek, Stanisław. *Od podwody do czołga: Wspomnienia wojenne, 1918–1945*. London, 1961.

Magnuski, Janusz, and Maksym Kolomijec. *Czerwony blitzkrieg, wrzesień 1939: Sowieckie wojska pancerne w Polsce*. Warsaw, 1994.

Markowska, Marta, ed. *The Ringelblum Archive: Annihilation—Day by Day.* Warsaw, 2008.

Matthäus, Jürgen, and Frank Bajohr, eds. *The Political Diary of Alfred Rosenberg and the Onset of the Holocaust.* Lanham, MD, 2015.

Mehner, Kurt, ed. *Die Geheimen Tagesberichte der Deutschen Wehrmachtführung im Zweiten Weltkrieg, 1939–1945.* Vol. 1, *1. September 1939–30. April 1940* Osnabrück, Germany, 1995.

Mel'tyukhov, Mikhail. *17 Sentyabr' 1939: Sovetsko-pol'skie konflikty, 1918–1939.* Moscow, 2009.

Mende, Erich. *Das verdammte Gewissen: Zeuge der Zeit, 1921–1945.* Munich, 1982.

Meyer, Georg, ed. *Generalfeldmarschall Wilhelm Ritter von Leeb: Tagebuchaufzeichnungen und Lagebeurteilungen aus zwei Weltkriegen.* Stuttgart, 1976.

Michaelis, Rolf. *SS-Heimwehr Danzig 1939.* Bradford, England, 1996.

Miniewicz, Janusz. *Ośrodek oporu Węgierska Górka 1939.* Poznań, Poland, 2000.

Mirowicz, Ryszard. *Edward Rydz-Śmigły: Działalność wojskowa i polityczna.* Warsaw, 1991.

Misch, Rochus. *Hitler's Last Witness: The Memoirs of Hitler's Bodyguard.* Barnsley, England, 2014.

Moorhouse, Roger. *Berlin at War: Life and Death in Hitler's Capital, 1939–45.* London, 2010.

———. *The Devils' Alliance: Hitler's Pact with Stalin, 1939–1941.* London, 2014.

Noakes, Jeremy, and Geoffrey Pridham, eds. *Nazism, 1919–1945.* Vol. 3, *Foreign Policy, War and Racial Extermination.* Exeter, England, 1988.

Ostrowski, Stanisław. *W obronie polskości Ziemi Lwowskiej: Dnie pohanbienia, 1939–1941. Wspomnienia.* Warsaw, 1986.

Overy, Richard. *1939: Countdown to War.* London, 2009.

Pertek, Jerzy. *Mała flota wielka duchem.* Poznań, Poland, 1989.

Phillips, Janine. *My Secret Diary.* London, 1982.

Piesakowski, Tomasz. *The Fate of Poles in the USSR, 1939–1989.* London, 1990.

Polish Historical Commission. *Polskie Siły Zbrojne w Drugiej Wojnie Światowej: Kampania Wrześniowa 1939. Przebieg działań od 1 do 8 września,* vol. 1, part 2. London, 1954.

Polish Ministry of Foreign Affairs. *The Polish White Book.* Vol. 1, *Official Documents Concerning Polish–German and Polish–Soviet Relations, 1933–1939.* London, 1941.

Polish Ministry of Information. *The German Fifth Column in Poland.* London, 1941.

Polonius, Alexander. *I Saw the Siege of Warsaw.* Glasgow, 1941.

Porwit, Marian. *Komentarze do historii polskich działań obronnych 1939 r.* Vols. 1–3. Warsaw, 1983.

———. *Obrona Warszawy, wrzesień 1939: Wspomnienia i fakty.* Warsaw, 1979.

Prażmowska, Anita. *Britain, Poland and the Eastern Front 1939.* Cambridge, 1987.

Prenatt, Jamie. *Polish Armour of the Blitzkrieg.* Oxford, 2015.

Prugar-Ketling, Bronisław. *Aby dochować wierności: Wspomnienia z działań 11. Karpackiej Dywizji Piechoty. Wrzesień 1939.* Warsaw, 1990.

Prüller, Wilhelm. *Diary of a German Soldier.* New York, 1963.

Przybylski, Jerzy, ed. *Kontradmirał Xawery Stanisław Czernicki.* Gdynia, Poland, 2002.

———, ed. *Ostatnia wachta: Mokrany, Katyń, Charków.* Gdynia, Poland, 2000.

Raack, Richard. *Stalin's Drive to the West, 1938–1945: The Origins of the Cold War.* Stanford, CA, 1995.

Raczyński, Edward. *In Allied London.* London, 1962.

Ruwski, Tadeusz. *Piechota w II wojnie światowej.* Warsaw, 1984.

Rees, Laurence. *World War Two Behind Closed Doors: Stalin, the Nazis and the West.* London, 2008.

Reibig, Willi. *Schwarze Husaren: Panzer in Polen.* Berlin, 1941.

Riefenstahl, Leni. *The Sieve of Time.* London, 1992.

Roberts, Andrew. *The Holy Fox: A Life of Lord Halifax.* London, 1991.

Rokicki, Paweł, Anna Piekarska, et al. *A więc wojna: Ludność cywilna we wrześniu 1939 r.* Warsaw, 2009.

Rómmel, Juliusz. *Za honor i ojczyznę: Wspomnienia dowódcy armii "Łódź" i "Warszawa."* Warsaw, 1958.

Rossino, Alexander. *Hitler Strikes Poland: Blitzkrieg, Ideology, and Atrocity.* Lawrence, KS, 2003.

Rotfeld, Adam, and Anatoly Torkunov, eds. *White Spots, Black Spots: Difficult Matters in Polish–Russian Relations, 1918–2008.* Pittsburgh, 2015.

Rowecki, Stefan "Grot." *Wspomnienia i notatki, czerwiec–wrzesień 1939.* Warsaw, 1957.

Rudnicki, Klemens. *Last of the Warhorses.* London, 1974.

Ryś, Kazimierz. *Obrona Lwowa w 1939 roku.* Palestine, 1943.

Schenk, Dieter. *Die Post von Danzig: Geschichte eines deutschen Justizmords.* Reinbek, Germany, 1995.

Schindler, Herbert. *Mosty und Dirschau 1939.* Freiburg, Germany, 1971.

Schmidt, Paul. *Hitler's Interpreter.* London, 1951.

Semiryaga, Mikhail. *Tainy Stalinskoi Diplomatii, 1939–1941.* Moscow, 1992.

Shepherd, Ben H. *Hitler's Soldiers: The German Army in the Third Reich.* London, 2016.

Sosabowski, Władysław. *Freely I Served: The Memoir of the Commander, 1st Polish Independent Parachute Brigade, 1941–1944.* Barnsley, England, 2013.

Sosnkowski, Kazimierz. *Cieniom września.* Warsaw, 1989.

Speer, Albert. *Inside the Third Reich.* London, 1970.

Spiess, Alfred, and Heiner Lichtenstein. *Das Unternehmen Tannenberg.* Wiesbaden, Germany, 1979.

Stachiewicz, Wacław. *Wierności dochować żołnierskiej: Przygotowania wojenne w Polsce 1935–1939 oraz kampania 1939 w relacjach i rozważaniach szefa Sztabu Głównego i szefa Sztabu Naczelnego Wodza.* Warsaw, 1998.

Stachura, Peter. *Poland Between the Wars, 1918–1939.* Basingstoke, 1998.

Stanicki, Zygmunt. *Obrona Warszawy w 1939 roku.* Warsaw, 1961.

Stawecki, Piotr. *Oficerowie dyplomowani wojska Drugiej Rzeczypospolitej.* Wrocław, Poland, 1997.

Strychalski, Jerzy. *Bitwa pod Kałuszynem.* Siedlce, Poland, 1985.

Sword, Edward Roland. *The Diary and Despatches of a Military Attaché in Warsaw, 1938–1939.* London, 2001.

Sword, Keith, ed. *The Soviet Takeover of the Polish Eastern Provinces, 1939–1941.* Basingstoke, 1991.

Szawłowski, Ryszard, ed. *Wojna polsko-sowiecka 1939.* Warsaw, 1997.

Szpilman, Władysław. *The Pianist: The Extraordinary Story of One Man's Survival in Warsaw, 1939–45.* London, 1999.

Szymański, Antoni. *Zły sąsiad: Niemcy 1932–1939 w oświetleniu polskiego attaché wojskowego w Berlinie.* London, 1959.

Trevor-Roper, Hugh, ed. *Hitler's War Directives, 1939–1945.* London, 1964.

Tym, Wacław, and Andrzej Rzepniewski, eds. *Kępa Oksywska 1939: Relacje uczestników walk lądowych.* Gdańsk, Poland, 1985.

von Vormann, Nikolaus. *Der Feldzug 1939 in Polen: Die Operationen des Heeres.* Weissenburg, Germany, 1958.

Wardzyńska, Maria. *Był Rok 1939: Operacja niemieckiej policji bezpieczeństwa w Polsce: "Intelligenzaktion."* Warsaw, 2009.

Warlimont, Walter. *Inside Hitler's Headquarters, 1939–1945.* London, 1964.

Watt, D. C. *How War Came: The Immediate Origins of the Second World War, 1938–1939.* London, 1989.

Wegner, Bernd, ed. *From Peace to War: Germany, Soviet Russia and the World, 1939–1941.* Oxford, 1997.

Weinstein, Frederick (Fryderyk Winnykamień), ed. *Auszeichnungen aus dem Versteck: Erlebnisse eines polnischen Juden 1939–1946.* Berlin, 2006.

Williamson, David G. *Poland Betrayed: The Nazi–Soviet Invasions of 1939.* Barnsley, England, 2009.

Włodarkiewicz, Wojciech. *Lwów 1939.* Warsaw, 2003.

Wojciechowski, Witold. *Pamiętnik z wojny na morzu, 1939–1943.* Gdańsk-Gdynia, Poland, 2014.

Wojewoda, Maciej, and Jakub Wojewoda. *Bitwa nad Bzurą: Pierwsza wśród wielkich bitew II Wojny Światowej.* Warsaw, 2016.

Woodward, E. L., and R. Butler, eds. *Documents on British Foreign Policy, 1919–1939.* Third Series, vol. 4. London, 1951.

Wordzyński, Artur. *W odwrocie i walce.* Gdańsk, Poland, 2013.

Wróbel, Janusz, ed. *Wieluń był pierwszy: Bombardowania lotnicze miast regionu Łódzkiego we wrześniu 1939 r.* Łódź, Poland, 2009.

Zaborowski, Leszek, ed. *Chronicles of Terror.* Vol. 1, *German Executions in Occupied Warsaw.* Warsaw, 2018.

Zaloga, Steven. *Poland 1939: The Birth of Blitzkrieg.* Oxford, 2002.

Zaloga, Steven, and Victor Madej. *The Polish Campaign 1939.* New York, 1985.

Zamoyski, Adam. *The Forgotten Few: The Polish Air Force in the Second World War.* London, 1995.

Zarzycki, Edmund. *Działalność hitlerowskiego Sądu Specjalnego w Bydgoszczy w latach 1939–1945.* Bydgoszcz, Poland, 2000.

Zwarra, Brunon. *Wspomnieniu Polaków-Gdańszczan.* Gdańsk, Poland, 2002.

NOTES

PROLOGUE

1. Alfred Spiess and Heiner Lichtenstein, *Das Unternehmen Tannenberg* (Wiesbaden, Germany, 1979), 79.

2. Ibid., 80.

3. Report of Staatsanwaltschaft Düsseldorf, December 1969, Bundesarchiv, B162/20571, 9.

4. Spiess and Lichtenstein, op. cit., 81.

5. William Shirer, *The Rise and Fall of the Third Reich: A History of Nazi Germany* (London, 1964), 629.

6. Jeremy Noakes and Geoffrey Pridham, eds., *Nazism, 1919–1945*, vol. 3, *Foreign Policy, War and Racial Extermination* (Exeter, England, 1988), 743.

7. Tomasz Chinciński, "Piąta kolumna," *Polityka*, November 4, 2009. See also Polish Ministry of Foreign Affairs, *The Polish White Book*, vol. 1, *Official Documents Concerning Polish–German and Polish–Soviet Relations, 1933–1939* (London, 1940), Doc. 116, 124–126.

8. List of victims from *Polska Zbrojna*, August 30, 1939.

9. Guzy interrogation, Archiwum Narodowe w Krakowie Oddział w Tarnowie, 33/226, sig. V141.

10. Jochen Böhler, *Der Überfall: Deutschlands Krieg gegen Polen* (Frankfurt am Main, 2009), 63.

11. "The Overture," Alfred Naujocks deposition, p. 9, Ian Sayer Archive.

12. Bundesarchiv, R9350/774.

13. "Polens Schande," *Völkischer Beobachter*, August 31, 1939, 1.

14. Spiess and Lichtenstein, op. cit., 156–176.

15. See the deposition of SS-*Unterscharführer* Josef Grzimek in Bundesarchiv, B162/20571.

16. Spiess and Lichtenstein, op. cit., 129.

17. Naujocks deposition, op. cit., 9b.

18. Quoted in Dennis Whitehead, "The Gleiwitz Incident," *After the Battle* 142 (2008): 13.

19. Naujocks deposition, op. cit., 15.

20. Jürgen Runzheimer, "Der Überfall auf den Sender Gleiwitz im Jahre 1939," *Vierteljahrshefte für Zeitgeschichte* 10 (1962): 415.

21. Polish text quoted in Roger Moorhouse, *Trzecia Rzesza w 100 Przedmiotach* (Kraków, 2018), 180.

22. Naujocks deposition, op. cit., 18.

23. Böhler, op. cit., 70.

24. See the deposition of *Kriminalsekretär* Karl Nowak in Bundesarchiv, B162/20571.

25. See the deposition of Alfred Naujocks in Bundesarchiv, B162/1490, 2–3.

26. See, for instance, "Polen-Überfall auf reichsdeutschen Sender Gleiwitz," *Völkischer Beobachter*, September 1, 1939, 1–2; "Ueberfall auf Gleiwitzer Sender," *Oberschlesischer Wanderer*, September 1, 1939, 1.

CHAPTER 1: "WESTERPLATTE FIGHTS ON"

1. Andrzej Drzycimski, *Westerplatte: Special Mission* (Gdańsk, Poland, 2015), 54.

2. Ibid., 46.

3. Deposition of Wiktor Białous-Bielas, Karta Archive, Warsaw, AW/I/0034.

4. "Kriegstagebuch des Linienschiffes *Schleswig-Holstein*," September 1, 1939, 4:48 a.m., Naval Historical Branch, Portsmouth, PG713.

5. Białous-Bielas deposition, op. cit.

6. Drzycimski, op. cit., 63.

7. Andrzej Drzycimski and Janusz Górski, *The Redoubt Westerplatte* (Gdańsk, Poland, 2015), 45.

8. Willi Aurich, quoted in Dieter Schenk, *Die Post von Danzig: Geschichte eines deutschen Justizmords* (Reinbek, Germany, 1995), 77.

9. "Kriegstagebuch," op. cit., August 27, 1939.

10. Ibid., August 31, 1939.

11. Richard Hargreaves, *Blitzkrieg Unleashed: The German Invasion of Poland, 1939* (Barnsley, England, 2008), 103.

12. "Kriegstagebuch," op. cit., Beilage, report by *Kapitänleutnant* Merten, September 1, 1939.

13. Białous-Bielas deposition, op. cit.

14. "Kriegstagebuch," op. cit., September 1, 1939.

15. Drzycimski, op. cit., 65.

16. "Kriegstagebuch," op. cit., September 1, 1939, 7:20 a.m.

17. Ibid., September 1, 1939, 8:55 a.m.

18. Pająk, quoted in Zbigniew Flisowski, ed., *Westerplatte* (Warsaw, 1974), 89.

19. Rolf Michaelis, *SS-Heimwehr Danzig 1939* (Bradford, England, 1996), 32.

20. "Kriegstagebuch," op. cit., September 1, 1939, 1:00 p.m.

21. Ibid., Beilage.

22. Hans-Adolf Jacobsen, ed., *Generaloberst Halder Kriegstagebuch*, vol. 1, *Vom Polenfeldzug bis zum Ende der Westoffensive* (Stuttgart, 1962), 55.

23. Sucharski, quoted in Flisowski, op. cit., 50.

24. Alfons Flisykowski interrogation record, courtesy of Muzeum Poczty Polskiej, Gdańsk, Poland, p. 5.

25. Schenk, op. cit., 61.

26. Bob Carruthers, *Poland 1939: The Blitzkrieg Unleashed* (Barnsley, England, 2011), 88.

27. Anton Winter, quoted in Michaelis, op. cit., 22.

28. Schenk, op. cit., 61.

29. Flisykowski, op. cit., 5.

30. Testimony of Franciszek Milewczyk, from Janina Skowrońska-Feldmanowa bequest, Jagiellonian University Archives, Kraków, DLXXXVI/13.

31. Schenk, op. cit., 67.

32. Ibid., 66.

33. Ibid., 67.

34. Max Domarus, ed., *Hitler: Reden und Proklamationen, 1932–1945*, vol. 3 (Wiesbaden, Germany, 1973), 1307.

35. Albert Speer, *Inside the Third Reich* (London, 1970), 236; Wahl, quoted in Wilhelm Deist, Manfred Messerschmidt, Hans-Erich Volkmann, and Wolfram Wette, *Ursachen und Voraussetzungen des Zweiten Weltkrieges* (Frankfurt am Main, 1989), 25.

36. Heinz Linge, *With Hitler to the End: The Memoirs of Adolf Hitler's Valet* (London, 2009), 116; Birger Dahlerus, *The Last Attempt* (London, 1948), 119.

37. Domarus, op. cit., 3:1313.

38. Ibid., 3:1314.

39. Halder, quoted in ibid., 1317.

40. *Documents on German Foreign Policy*, Series D, 1937–1945, vol. 7, *The Last Days of Peace, August 9–September 3, 1939* (London, 1956), Weizsäcker circular, September 1, 1939, Doc. 512, p. 491.

41. William Shirer, *The Rise and Fall of the Third Reich: A History of Nazi Germany* (London, 1964), 721.

42. Quoted in Miroslav Ferić, *Pamiętnik wojenny pilota 111 Eskadry Myśliwskiej im. Tadeusza Kościuszki*, vol. 1, p. 5, Central Military Library, Warsaw, Rps 126.

43. Diary of Alma Heczko, Karta Archive, Warsaw, AW/II/1297/2K; testimony of Konstanty Peszyński, Karta Archive, Warsaw, AW/II/3448.

44. Broadcast of Roman Umiastowski, cited in Hargreaves, op. cit., 121.

45. Władysław Szpilman, *The Pianist: The Extraordinary Story of One Man's Survival in Warsaw, 1939–45* (London, 1999), 24–25.

46. Quoted in *Express Poranny*, September 2, 1939, 1.

47. Quoted in Hargreaves, op. cit., 84.

48. Testimony of Wacław Sawicki, Karta Archive, Warsaw, AW/II/3185.

49. Józef Garliński, *Poland in the Second World War* (Basingstoke, 1985), 12–13; Steven Zaloga, *Poland 1939: The Birth of Blitzkrieg* (Oxford, 2002), 23.

50. Witold Wojciechowski, *Pamiętnik z wojny na morzu, 1939–1943* (Gdańsk-Gdynia, Poland, 2014), 30–34.

51. Steven Zaloga and Victor Madej, *The Polish Campaign 1939* (New York, 1985), 31.

52. Quoted in Cajus Bekker, *The Luftwaffe War Diaries* (New York, 1994), 37.

53. Szpilman, op. cit., 23; Alexander Polonius, *I Saw the Siege of Warsaw* (Glasgow, 1941), 24; Marta Korwin-Rhodes, *The Mask of Warriors: The Siege of Warsaw, September 1939* (New York, 1964), 8.

54. Janine Phillips, *My Secret Diary* (London, 1982), 47–48.

55. Herbert Schindler, *Mosty und Dirschau 1939* (Freiburg, Germany, 1971), 101.

56. Ibid., 127.

57. Hozzel, quoted in Peter C. Smith, *Ju 87 Stuka: Luftwaffe Ju 87 Dive Bomber Units 1939–1941* (London, 2006), 20.

58. The precise timing of the Wieluń raid is disputed. I have concurred with Jochen Böhler, Grzegorz Bębnik, and Sławomir Abramowich, who cite Luftwaffe records showing it to be 5:40 a.m., rather than 4:40 a.m.

59. Quoted in Bekker, op. cit., 32–33.

60. Sławomir Abramowich, "Tragedia Wielunia w świetle materiałów śledztwa Oddziałowej Komisji Ścigania Zbrodni Przeciwko Narodowi Polskiemu," in Janusz Wróbel, ed., *Wieluń był pierwszy: Bombardowania lotnicze miast regionu łódzkiego we wrześniu 1939 r.* (Łódź, 2009), 134.

61. Józef Musiał, quoted in Joachim Trenkner, "Ziel Vernichtet," *Die Zeit,* July 2003.

62. Quoted in ibid.

63. The crash, at Neuhammer (now Świętoszów), is discussed in John Ward, *Hitler's Stuka Squadrons: The JU 87 at War, 1936–1945* (Staplehurst, England, 2004), 57.

64. Grzegorz Bębnik, "Wieluń, 1 września 1939," in Wróbe, op. cit., 54.

65. Abramowich, op. cit., 112–115.

66. Palusinski, quoted in David G. Williamson, *Poland Betrayed: The Nazi–Soviet Invasions of 1939* (Barnsley, England, 2009), 71. Ellipses and other insertions in Williamson.

67. Jerzy B. Cynk, *The Polish Air Force at War: The Official History,* vol. 1, *1939–1943* (Atglen, PA, 1998), 74.

68. Gabszewicz's trophies are on display in the Polish National Army Museum in Warsaw.

69. Quoted in Ferić, op. cit., 11.

70. Cynk, op. cit., 73.

71. Polish Institute and Sikorski Museum Archive, London (hereafter "PISM"), General Staff report, September 1, 1939, AII 9/5.

72. Cynk, op. cit., 74; PISM, General Staff report on enemy aerial activity, September 1, 1939, AII 9/14.

73. PISM, Corps District Command V situation report, September 1, 1939, AII 9/14/8.

74. PISM, Ministry of Military Affairs situation report, September 3, 1939, AII 11/15/2.

75. Cynk, op. cit., 74.

76. Johann Graf von Kielmansegg, *Panzer zwischen Warschau und Atlantik* (Berlin, 1941), 14–15.

77. Wilhelm Prüller, *Diary of a German Soldier* (New York, 1963), 13.

78. Account courtesy of Mr. Robin Schäfer.

79. Leo Leixner, *From Lemberg to Bordeaux: A German War Correspondent's Account of Battle in Poland, the Low Countries and France, 1939–1940* (New York, 2017), 11.

80. Hans von Luck, *Panzer Commander* (London, 1989), 28.

81. Generalkommando VII AK, *Wir zogen gegen Polen: Kriegserinnerungswerk des VII Armeekorps* (Munich, 1940), 74.

82. Ibid., 75.

83. Leixner, op. cit., 30.

84. Janusz Miniewicz, *Ośrodek oporu Węgierska Górka 1939* (Poznań, Poland, 2000).

85. Krzysztof Komorowski, ed., *Boje polskie 1939–1945: Przewodnik encyklopedyczny* (Warsaw, 2009), 471.

86. Generalkommando VII AK, op. cit., 75.

87. Andrzej Aksamitowski and Wojciech Zalewski, *Mława 1939* (Warsaw, 2008), 19–22.

88. Eyewitness account of Staff Sergeant Mikołaj Bujan, Zawkrze Land Museum Archives, MZZ/fk/380. Translated by Anastazja Pindor.

89. Account quoted in Ryszard Juszkiewicz, *Bitwa pod Mławą 1939* (Warsaw, 1979), 93.

90. Aksamitowski and Zalewski, op. cit., 37.

91. Quoted in Hargreaves, op. cit., 118.

92. Heinz Guderian, *Panzer Leader* (London, 1952), 70.

93. Zaloga and Madej, op. cit., 110.

94. PISM, Bortnowski letter, April 10, 1947, PISM B.1.25a.

95. Bortnowski, May 17, 1962, quoted in PISM, B.1.25a/3.

96. Paul Malmassari, *Armoured Trains: An Illustrated Encyclopaedia, 1825–2016* (Barnsley, England, 2016), 201–202.

97. *Kriegstagebuch der Generalkommandos XIX AK* (hereafter "KTB XIX AK"), US National Archives, T314, roll 611, p. 17.

98. Polish Historical Commission, *Polskie Siły Zbrojne w Drugiej Wojnie Światowej: Kampania Wrześniowa 1939. Przebieg działań od 1 do 8 września*, vol. 1, part 2 (London, 1954), 70n.

99. Major Stanisław Malecki, "The 18th Pomeranian Lancers Regiment in the War of 1939," PISM, B.1.28g.

100. Komorowski, op. cit., 187.

101. Malecki, op. cit.

102. Guderian, op. cit., 71.

103. KTB XIX AK, 29.

104. Quoted in Hargreaves, op. cit., 15n.

105. Zbigniew Zieliński, "Bitwa pod Mokrą," *Niepodległość i Pamięć* 16/2, no. 30 (2009): 127.

106. Peter Chamberlain and Hilary Doyle, *Encyclopedia of German Tanks of World War Two* (London, 1999), 20–30.

107. Zieliński, op. cit., 129.

108. Jan Kamiński, *Od konia i armaty do spadochronu: Wspomnienia uczestnika II wojny światowej* (Warsaw, 1980), 17.

109. Willi Reibig, *Schwarze Husaren: Panzer in Polen* (Berlin, 1941), 14.

110. Włodzimierz Tabaka, quoted in Władysław Dziewicki, *Dzieje pułku ułanów podolskich, 1809–1947* (London, 1982), 167.

111. Mirosław Dziekoński, quoted in ibid., 170.

112. Reibig., op. cit., 16–17.

113. Dziewicki, op. cit., 162.

114. Zieliński, op. cit., 129.

115. Hargreaves, op. cit., 120.

116. Jochen Böhler, *Auftakt zum Vernichtungskrieg: Die Wehrmacht in Polen 1939* (Frankfurt am Main, 2006), 131.

117. Szymon Datner, *55 dni Wehrmachtu w Polsce: Zbrodnie dokonane na polskiej ludności cywilnej w okresie I.ix-25.x. 1939 r.* (Warsaw, 1967), 184, 187.

118. Ibid., 171, 183.

119. See Böhler, op. cit., 115–117; Datner, op. cit., 173.

120. Maria Wardzyńska, *Był rok 1939: Operacja niemieckiej policji bezpieczeństwa w Polsce "Intelligenzaktion"* (Warsaw, 2009), 98.

121. Rada Ochrony Pomników Walki i Męczeństwa, *Przewodnik po upamiętnionych miejscach walk i męczeństwa: Lata wojny, 1939–1945* (Warsaw, 1966), 104.

122. Erwin Kartzewski, "Verzeiht mich bitte, dass ich noch lebe," blog post, December 28, 2012, www.erwin-kartzewski.blogspot.de.

123. Datner, op. cit., 110.

124. Tomasz Ceran, "Anti-Polonism in the Ideology of National Socialism," *Totalitarianism and 20th Century Studies* 1 (2017): 218–239.

125. Adrian Carton de Wiart, *Happy Odyssey* (London, 2007 [1950]), 156.

126. *Die Wehrmachtberichte 1939–1945*, vol. 1, *1. September 1939 bis 31. Dezember 1941* (Munich, 1985), 1.

CHAPTER 2: THE TYRANNY OF GEOGRAPHY

1. Quoted in Norman Davies, *God's Playground: A History of Poland*, vol. 1, *The Origins to 1795* (Oxford, 1982), 521–522.

2. Ibid., 526.

3. Daniel Beer, *The House of the Dead: Siberian Exile Under the Tsars* (London, 2016), 137.

4. Norman Davies, *God's Playground: A History of Poland*, vol. 2, *1795 to the Present* (Oxford, 1981), 147–148.

5. Stefan Kieniewicz, Andrzej Zahorski, and Władysław Zajewski, *Trzy powstania narodowe: Kościuszkowskie, listopadowe, styczniowe* (Warsaw, 1992), 357–361.

6. Quoted in Norman Davies, *White Eagle, Red Star: The Polish–Soviet War 1919–1920 and the "Miracle on the Vistula"* (London, 2003), 21.

7. Ryszard Mirowicz, *Edward Rydz-Śmigły: Działalność wojskowa i polityczna* (Warsaw, 1991), 110.

8. Quoted in Davies, *God's Playground*, 2:396.

9. See Robert Service, *Stalin: A Biography* (London, 2004), 180–183.

10. Quoted in Davies, *God's Playground*, 2:393.

11. Seeckt, quoted in Halik Kochanski, *The Eagle Unbowed: Poland and the Poles in the Second World War* (London, 2012), 35.

12. Peter Stachura, "National Identity and the Ethnic Minorities in Early Inter-War Poland," in Peter Stachura, ed., *Poland Between the Wars, 1918–1939* (Basingstoke, 1998), 62.

13. Norman Davies, *Heart of Europe: The Past in Poland's Present* (Oxford, 2001), 107.

14. Paul N. Hehn, *A Low Dishonest Decade: The Great Powers, Eastern Europe, and the Economic Origins of World War II, 1930–1941* (New York, 2005), 72.

15. See Steven Zaloga and Victor Madej, *The Polish Campaign 1939* (New York, 1985), 11; Steven Zaloga, *The Polish Army, 1939–1945* (London, 1982), 4.

16. Józef Garliński, *Poland in the Second World War* (Basingstoke, 1985), 12.

17. Jamie Prenatt, *Polish Armor of the Blitzkrieg* (Oxford, 2015), 6.

18. David R. Higgins, *Panzer II vs 7TP: Poland 1939* (Oxford, 2015), 74.

19. Jerzy Cynk, *The Polish Air Force at War: The Official History*, vol. 1, *1939–1943* (Atglen, PA, 1998), 29.

20. John Ellis, *The World War II Databook* (London, 2003), 237, 240; Cynk, op. cit., 56.

21. Quoted in Andrzej Suchcitz, "Poland's Defence Preparations in 1939," in Stachura, op. cit., 117.

22. Zaloga and Madej, op. cit., 17–18.

23. Suchcitz, op. cit., 117–118.

24. Max Domarus, ed., *Hitler: Reden und Proklamationen, 1932–1945*, vol. 2 (Wiesbaden, Germany, 1973), 927.

25. E. L. Woodward and R. Butler, eds., *Documents on British Foreign Policy, 1919–1939*, Third Series, vol. 4 (London, 1951), 552.

26. Quoted in Frank McDonough, ed., *Neville Chamberlain, Appeasement and the British Road to War* (Manchester, 1998), 81.

27. Włodzimierz Borodziej and Sławomir Dębski, eds., *Polish Documents on Foreign Policy, 24 October 1938–30 September 1939* (Warsaw, 2009), 126.

28. Roderick Macleod and Denis Kelly, eds., *The Ironside Diaries, 1937–1940* (London, 1962), 80.

29. Józef Beck, *Final Report* (New York, 1957), 198–199; Kochanski, op. cit., 49–50.

30. Timothy Snyder, *Black Earth: The Holocaust as History and Warning* (London, 2015), 105.

31. Quoted in Hans-Bernd Gisevius, *To the Bitter End* (Boston, 1947), 363.

32. Jürgen Matthäus and Frank Bajohr, eds., *The Political Diary of Alfred Rosenberg and the Onset of the Holocaust* (Lanham, MD, 2015), 156.

33. Instructions quoted in A. J. P. Taylor, *English History, 1914–1945* (Oxford, 1965), 447.

34. Anthony P. Adamthwaite, *The Making of the Second World War* (London, 1977), 218–219.

35. Sir Stafford Cripps to the Foreign Office, July 16, 1940, The National Archives, London (hereafter "TNA"), FO 371/24846, f.10 N6526/30/38.

36. Quoted in Ivo Banac, ed., *The Diary of Georgi Dimitrov, 1933–1949* (New Haven, CT, 2003), 115.

37. Quoted in Richard Raack, *Stalin's Drive to the West, 1938–1945: The Origins of the Cold War* (Stanford, CA, 1995), 24.

38. *Documents on German Foreign Policy*, Series D, 1937–1945 (hereafter *DGFP*), vol. 7, *The Last Days of Peace, August 9–September 3, 1939* (London, 1956), No. 56, p. 64, Ribbentrop to Schulenburg, August 14, 1939.

39. Quoted in Mikhail Semiryaga, *Tainy stalinskoi diplomatii, 1939–1941* (Moscow, 1992), 57.

40. Peter Kleist, *Zwischen Hitler und Stalin, 1939–1945* (Bonn, 1950), 55.

41. Quoted in Laurence Rees, *World War Two Behind Closed Doors: Stalin, the Nazis and the West* (London, 2008), 10.

42. For the text of the nonaggression pact and the Secret Protocol, see Roger Moorhouse, *The Devils' Alliance: Hitler's Pact with Stalin, 1939–1941* (London, 2014), 305–306.

43. Vladimir Karpov, *Marshal Zhukov: Ego soratniki i protivniki v dni voiny i mira* (Moscow, 1992), 124.

44. Statistical breakdown from OSS report no. 2325 from August 22, 1944, quoted in *Litanus* 27, no. 3 (1981).

45. Quoted in Jane Degras, ed., *Soviet Documents on Foreign Policy*, vol. 3, *1933–1941* (Oxford, 1953), 367.

46. Andor Hencke, "Die deutsch-sowjetischen Beziehungen zwischen 1932 und 1941," unpublished protocol, Institut für Zeitgeschichte, Munich, MA 1300/2, p. 11.

47. Donald Cameron Watt, *How War Came: The Immediate Origins of the Second World War, 1938–1939* (London, 1989), 480.

48. TNA, FO 371/23686/N4146/243/38, August 26, 1939.

49. Henry "Chips" Channon, quoted in Irene Taylor and Alan Taylor, eds., *The Secret Annexe: The World's Greatest War Diarists* (London, 2004), 436.

50. "The Russo-German Deal," *The Times*, August 23, 1939, 13.

51. Alexander Polonius, *I Saw the Siege of Warsaw* (Glasgow, 1941), 14.

52. Adrian Carton de Wiart, *Happy Odyssey* (London, 2007 [1950]), 153–154.

53. Ibid., 154.

54. Borodziej and Dębski, op. cit., 360–361.

55. Max Domarus, ed., *Hitler: Reden und Proklamationen, 1932–1945*, vol. 3 (Wiesbaden, Germany, 1973), 1257.

56. Nevile Henderson, *Failure of a Mission: Berlin, 1937–1939* (London, 1941), 307–308.

57. Domarus, op. cit., 3:1257.

58. Watt, op. cit., 489.

59. Garliński, op. cit., 13–14.

60. Domarus, op. cit., 3:1258.

61. *DGFP*, vol. 7, Doc. 286, p. 296.

62. Borodziej and Dębski, op. cit., 180.

63. Edward Raczyński, *In Allied London* (London, 1962), 20.

64. *DGFP*, vol. 7, Doc. 271, Attolico note, August 25, 1939, pp. 285–286.

65. Walter Gorlitz, ed., *The Memoirs of Field-Marshal Wilhelm Keitel* (New York, 2000 [1966]), 89.

66. Kulik interrogation, Ian Sayer Archive.

67. Original document in the Ian Sayer Archive.

68. Herbert Schindler, *Mosty und Dirschau 1939* (Freiburg, Germany, 1971), 20.

69. Herzner debrief, Ian Sayer Archive.

70. Alfred Spiess and Heiner Lichtenstein, *Das Unternehmen Tannenberg* (Wiesbaden, Germany, 1979), 116.

71. Quoted in Schindler, op. cit., 48.

72. See Władysław Steblik, "Niemiecki napad na Przełęcz Jabłonkowską w nocy z 25 na 26 VIII 1939," *Wojskowy Przegląd Historyczny* 10, no. 4 (1965): 287–299.

73. Kulik interrogation, op. cit.

74. Herzner debrief, op. cit.

75. General Józef Kustroń, quoted in Schindler, op. cit., 98.

76. Domarus, op. cit., 3:1264.

77. Wacław Stachiewicz, *Wierności dochować żołnierskiej: Przygotowania wojenne w Polsce 1935–1939 oraz kampania 1939 w relacjach i rozważaniach szefa Sztabu Głównego i szefa Sztabu Naczelnego Wodza* (Warsaw, 1998), 448.

78. Jan Karski, *Story of a Secret State: My Report to the World* (London, 2011 [1944]), 9.

79. Henderson, op. cit., 308–311.

80. Quoted in Domarus, op. cit., 3:1266.

81. Walter Warlimont, *Inside Hitler's Headquarters, 1939–1945* (London, 1964), 27.

82. Stachiewicz, op. cit., 443.

83. See Gailiński, op. cit., 12; Rafał Białkowski, "Plan Operacyjny 'Zelint,'" *Biuletyn DWS* 7 (2010): 15.

84. Hugh Trevor-Roper, ed., *Hitler's War Directives, 1939–1945* (London, 1964), 38.

85. *DGFP*, vol. 6, *The Last Months of Peace, March–August 1939* (London, 1956), Doc. 754, Moltke to German Foreign Ministry, August 1, 1939, pp. 1035–1043.

CHAPTER 3: A FRIGHTFUL FUTILITY

1. The National Archives, London (hereafter "TNA"), PREM 1/331A, telegram to Prime Minister, September 1, 1939, quoted in Richard Overy, *1939: Countdown to War* (London, 2009), 73.

2. For audio of the BBC radio announcement, see "BBC News—Lionel Marson Reports on Invasion of Poland—September 1, 1939," YouTube, posted September 6, 2016, https://youtu.be/ktn_P5z5MK4.

3. Moyra Charlton, quoted in Terry Charman, ed., *Outbreak 1939: The World Goes to War* (London, 2009), 103.

4. Mass Observation extract, quoted ibid., 95.

5. TNA, CAB 23/100, Minutes of Cabinet Meeting, September 1, 1939, p. 443.

6. Quoted in Włodzimierz Borodziej and Sławomir Dębski, eds., *Polish Documents on Foreign Policy, 24 October 1938–30 September 1939* (Warsaw, 2009), 392.

7. TNA, CAB 23/100, Minutes of Cabinet Meeting, September 1, 1939, pp. 444–445.

8. Quoted in Charman, op. cit., 93.

9. TNA, CAB 23/100, Minutes of Cabinet Meeting, September 1, 1939, Annex, p. 458.

10. Hansard, HC Deb, September 1, 1939, vol. 351, cols. 126–132.

11. Charman, op. cit., 100.

12. Max Domarus, ed., *Hitler: Reden und Proklamationen, 1932–1945*, vol. 3 (Wiesbaden, Germany, 1973), 1326.

13. Nevile Henderson, *Failure of a Mission: Berlin, 1937–1939* (London, 1940), 272.

14. Paul Schmidt, *Hitler's Interpreter* (London, 1951), 155.

15. Quoted in Henrik Eberle and Matthias Uhl, eds., *The Hitler Book: The Secret Dossier Prepared for Stalin* (London, 2005), 47.

16. Henderson, op. cit., 279.

17. "For Freedom Against Brutal Oppression," *Daily Telegraph*, September 2, 1939, 1, 10.

18. "Communist Appeal to the British People," *Daily Worker*, September 2, 1939, 1.

19. Robert Rhodes James, ed., *Chips: The Diaries of Sir Henry Channon* (London, 1993), 211.

20. Respondents Christopher Tomlin and Pam Ashford, quoted in Simon Garfield, ed., *We Are at War: The Remarkable Diaries of Five Ordinary People in Extraordinary Times* (London, 2005), 20–21.

21. Respondent quoted in Charman, op. cit., 116; entries for September 2, 1939, from diarists 5456 and 5106, Mass Observation Archive, University of Sussex, Brighton.

22. His Majesty's Stationery Office, *The Navy List*, September 1939.

23. James Holland, *The War in the West: A New History*, vol. 1, *Germany Ascendant, 1939–1941* (London, 2015), 66.

24. David French, *Raising Churchill's Army: The British Army and the War Against Germany, 1919–1945* (Oxford, 2000), 63.

25. John Ellis, *The World War II Databook* (London, 2003), 231.

26. Alfred Price, *The Spitfire Story* (Leicester, England, 2002), 73.

27. Ellis, op. cit., 237.

28. Ibid., 245.

29. French cabinet minutes reproduced in Anthony P. Adamthwaite, *The Making of the Second World War* (London, 1977), 222.

30. Quoted in Benjamin F. Martin, *France in 1938* (Baton Rouge, LA, 2005), 78.

31. Overy, op. cit., 78.

32. Hugh Gibson, ed., *The Ciano Diaries, 1939–1943* (Garden City, NY, 1946), 136.

33. Winston Churchill, *The Second World War*, vol. 1, *The Gathering Storm* (London, 1948), 362.

34. TNA, CAB 23/100, Minutes of Cabinet Meeting, September 2, 1939, p. 470.

35. Borodziej and Dębski, op. cit., 394.

36. TNA, CAB 23/100, Minutes of Cabinet Meeting, September 2, 1939, pp. 465, 466, 472.

37. Hansard, HC Deb, September 2, 1939, vol. 351, cols. 280–286.

38. Edward Spears, quoted in Overy, op. cit., 85.

39. Hansard, HC Deb, September 2, 1939, vol. 351, cols. 282–283.

40. Sir John Simon, quoted in Donald Cameron Watt, *How War Came: The Immediate Origins of the Second World War, 1938–1939* (London, 1989), 582.

41. Daladier speech, September 2, 1939, quoted in Charman, op. cit., 112.

42. Watt, op. cit., 583.

43. Richard Overy and Andrew Wheatcroft, *The Road to War* (London, 1989), 140.

44. TNA, CAB 23/100, Minutes of Cabinet Meeting, September 2, 1939, pp. 474, 478, 484.

45. Sir Reginald Dorman-Smith, quoted in Watt, op. cit., 588.

46. Quoted ibid., 588.

47. Chamberlain, quoted in Overy, op. cit., 88.

48. Quoted in Watt, op. cit., 579.

49. Andrew Roberts, *The Holy Fox: A Biography of Lord Halifax* (London, 1991), 164–168.

50. Earl of Halifax, *Fulness of Days* (London, 1957), 208, 211.

51. Churchill, op. cit., 361.

52. "British Determination Never Doubted," *The Times*, September 4, 1939, 4.

53. Schmidt, op. cit., 157.

54. Ibid., 158.

55. Alvar Lidell, quoted in Charman, op. cit., 157.

56. Part of the broadcast on audio at BBC, "Neville Chamberlain: Declaration of War," https://www.bbc.com/news/av/science-environment-41505713/neville-chamberlain-declaration-of-war; full text at "Radio Address by Neville Chamberlain, Prime Minister, September 3, 1939," Yale Law School, Avalon Project, https://avalon.law.yale.edu/wwii/gb3.asp.

57. Quoted in Juliet Gardiner, *Wartime Britain, 1939–1945* (London, 2004), 5.

58. Tilly Rice, quoted in Garfield, op. cit., 24.

59. Churchill, op. cit., 363.

60. Peter Coats, quoted in Charman, op. cit., 167.

61. John Colville, *The Fringes of Power: Downing Street Diaries, 1939–1955*, vol. 1, *September 1939–September 1941* (London, 1985), 20.

62. Domarus, op. cit., 3:1336–1338.

63. Henderson, op. cit., 285.

64. Quoted in Roger Moorhouse, *Berlin at War: Life and Death in Hitler's Capital, 1939–45* (London, 2010), 19.

65. Else Danielowski, *Kindheit und Jugend im nationalsozialistichen Deutschland*, CD produced by the Zeitzeugenbörse, Berlin, 2006.

66. Quoted in Moorhouse, op. cit., 20.

67. Victor Klemperer, *I Shall Bear Witness: The Diaries of Victor Klemperer, 1933–1941* (London, 1998), 295–296.

68. Ruth Andreas-Friedrich, *Der Schattenmann: Tagebuchaufzeichnungen, 1938–1945* (Frankfurt am Main, 1984), 64–65.

69. Herbert Döhring, *Hitlers Hausverwalter* (Bochum, Germany, 2013), 80.

70. Moorhouse, op. cit., 185.

71. "Poles Cheer Declarations," *Daily Telegraph*, September 4, 1939, 1.

72. Diary of Barbara Różicka, quoted in Dermot Turing, *X, Y & Z: The Real Story of How Enigma Was Broken* (Stroud, England, 2018), 129.

73. Anonymous diarist, quoted in Marta Markowska, ed., *The Ringelblum Archive: Annihilation—Day by Day* (Warsaw, 2008), 8.

74. Marta Korwin-Rhodes, *The Mask of Warriors: The Siege of Warsaw, September 1939* (New York, 1964), 14.

75. Stanisław Dmuchowski, Karta Archive, Warsaw, AW/I/0126.

76. Maciej Nowak-Kreyer, "Zuchwały rajd," *Polska Zbrojna*, September 2018.

77. "Wyprawa bombardierska eskadry liniowej Nr. 24 w godzinach rannych Dn.3.IX.39r. na kolumnę pancerno-motorową nieprzyjaciela w rejonie Jabłonka," *Bellona* 7 (1941).

78. Alexander Polonius, *I Saw the Siege of Warsaw* (Glasgow, 1941), 32.

79. Władysław Szpilman, *The Pianist: The Extraordinary Story of One Man's Survival in Warsaw, 1939–45* (London, 1999), 28.

80. Diary of Maria Komornicka, September 3, 1939, Karta Archive, Warsaw, AW/II/3611.

81. "Poles Cheer Declarations," op. cit.; Edward Roland Sword, *The Diary and Despatches of a Military Attaché in Warsaw, 1938–1939* (London, 2001), 53; *Warszawski Dziennik Narodowy*, September 4, 1939, 3; Charman, op. cit., 186–187.

82. Anita Prażmowska, *Britain, Poland and the Eastern Front 1939* (Cambridge, 1987), 152, 171.

83. *Foreign Relations of the United States*, 1939, General, Volume I, Part 1, Events Leading to the Outbreak of War in Europe, September 1, 1939, VIII: Final Efforts to Preserve Peace in Europe; Appeals by President Roosevelt to Germany and Italy, August 22–31, 1939. Eds. Matilda F. Axton, Rogers P. Churchill, Francis C. Prescott, John G. Reid, N. O. Sappington, Louis E. Gates, and Shirley L. Phillips (Washington, DC, 1956), Doc. 350, Ambassador in the United Kingdom (Kennedy) to the Secretary of State, August 23, 1939, Telegram 760C.62/942.

84. Memorandum of Lieutenant-General Stanisław Burhardt-Bukacki, Polish Institute and Sikorski Museum Archive, London, B.I.119E/2.

85. Polonius, op. cit., 34.

86. Paweł Starzeński, quoted in Zbigniew Gluza, ed., *Rok 1939: Rozbiór polski* (Warsaw 2009), 99.

87. Janine Phillips, *My Secret Diary* (London, 1982), 49–50.

CHAPTER 4: THE TEMERITY TO RESIST

1. Quoted in Johann Graf von Kielmansegg, *Panzer zwischen Warschau und Atlantik* (Berlin, 1941), 19.

2. Władysław Anders, *An Army in Exile: The Story of the Second Polish Corps* (London, 1949), 3.

3. Alex Buchner, *Der Polenfeldzug 1939* (Leoni am Starnberger See, Germany, 1989), 48–49.

4. Piotr Matusak, "Ciechanów w czasie II wojny światowej (1939–1945): Zarys problematyki badawczej," *Niepodległość i Pamięć* 23/1, no. 53 (2016): 154.

5. Władysław Sosabowski, *Freely I Served: The Memoir of the Commander, 1st Polish Independent Parachute Brigade, 1941–1944* (Barnsley, England, 2013), 24–25.

6. Anders, op. cit., 3.

7. Testimony of Konstanty Peszyński, Karta Archive, Warsaw, AW/II/3448.

8. Ibid.

9. Ibid.

10. Erich Mende, *Das verdammte Gewissen: Zeuge der Zeit, 1921–1945* (Munich, 1982), 79.

11. Stanisław Maczek, *Od podwody do czołga: Wspomnienia wojenne, 1918–1945* (Edinburgh, 1961), 59.

12. Ibid., 63–64.

13. Krzysztof Komorowski, ed., *Boje polskie 1939–1945: Przewodnik encyklopedyczny* (Warsaw, 2009), 467.

14. Jan Karski, *Story of a Secret State: My Report to the World* (London, 2011 [1944]), 10–11.

15. Marian Porwit, *Komentarze do historii polskich działań obronnych 1939 r.*, vol. 1 (Warsaw, 1983), 207.

16. Quoted in Gerhard Lubs, *Infanterie-Regiment Nr. 5* (Bochum, Germany, 1965), 179.

17. Helmut Baier, quoted in Alan Bance, trans., *Blitzkrieg in Their Own Words: First-Hand Accounts from German Soldiers, 1939–1940* (St. Paul, MN, 2005), 32.

18. Richard von Weizsäcker, *Vier Zeiten: Erinnerungen* (Berlin, 1997), 78.

19. Heinz Guderian, *Panzer Leader* (London, 1952), 71.

20. Indro Montanelli, "Con le truppe del Reich sul fronte orientale," *Corriere della Sera*, September 6, 1939, 1.

21. Quoted in Lubs, op. cit., 182.

22. Testimony of Adam Zakrzewski, Paris, January 20, 1940, Polish Institute and Sikorski Museum Archive, London (hereafter "PISM"), B.I.28a, p. 42.

23. *Kriegstagebuch des Generalkommandos XIX AK* (hereafter "KTB XIX AK"), reports from the afternoon of September 2, 1939, US National Archives, T-314, roll 611, pp. 32–33.

24. Ibid., pp. 33, 42, 53.

25. Major Józef Wojtaszewski, quoted in Zbigniew Gluza, ed., *Rok 1939: Rozbiór polski* (Warsaw, 2009), 102.

26. Guderian, op. cit., 72.

27. Testimony of Czesław Cichoński, Paris, December 12, 1939, PISM, B.I.26f, p. 4.

28. Zakrzewski testimony, op. cit., 54; Porwit, op. cit., 217.

29. Zakrzewski testimony, op. cit., 48–49.

30. *Unteroffizier* Pries, quoted in Bance, op. cit., 26.

31. Wolfgang Reischock, quoted in Christoph Klessmann, ed., *September 1939: Krieg, Besatzung, Widerstand in Polen. Acht Beiträge* (Göttingen, Germany, 1989), 160.

32. KT XIX AK, 56.

33. Polish Historical Commission, *Polskie Siły Zbrojne w Drugiej Wojnie Światowej: Kampania Wrześniowa 1939. Przebieg działań od 1 do 8 września*, vol. 1, part 2 (London, 1954), 381.

34. Diary of General Kazimierz Ładoś, September 3, 1939, PISM, B.1.4e/1.

35. Nikolaus von Vormann, *Der Feldzug 1939 in Polen: Die Operationen des Heeres* (Weissenburg, Germany, 1958), 77.

36. Peter Hoffmann, *Hitler's Personal Security: Protecting the Führer, 1921–1945* (New York, 2000), 134.

37. Quoted in Richard Hargreaves, *Blitzkrieg Unleashed: The German Invasion of Poland, 1939* (Barnsley, England, 2008), 136.

38. Heinrich Hoffmann, *Hitler Was My Friend* (Barnsley, England, 2011 [1955]), 117.

39. Ibid., 117; Guderian, op. cit., 73.

40. Quoted in Bance, op. cit., 27.

41. Quoted in ibid., 27.

42. Karl Krause, Herbert Döhring, and Anna Plaim, *Living with Hitler* (Barnsley, England, 2018), 72.

43. Montanelli, op. cit.

44. See Markus Krzoska, "Der 'Bromberger Blutsonntag' 1939," *Vierteljahrshefte für Zeitgeschichte* 60 (2012): 241.

45. Polish Ministry of Information, *The German Fifth Column in Poland* (London, 1941), appendix 1, 149–152.

46. Peszyński testimony, op. cit.

47. Testimony of Czesław Cichoński, PISM, B.I.26f., p. 5.

48. Testimony of Maciej Nowacki, Karta Archive, Warsaw, AW/II/2263/P.

49. Deposition No. 30, cited in Polish Ministry of Information, op. cit., 66–67.

50. Tomasz Chinciński, "Zeznania świadków złożone przed: Okręgową Komisją Badania Zbrodni Niemieckich w Bydgoszczy w latach 1945–1948 oraz Okręgową Komisją Badania Zbrodni Hitlerowskich w Bydgoszczy w latach 1967–1973," in Tomasz Chinciński and Paweł Machcewicz, eds., *Bydgoszcz 3–4 września 1939* (Warsaw, 2008), 589.

51. Polish Ministry of Information, op. cit., 59, 66.

52. Paweł Kosiński, "Ofiary pierwszych dni września 1939 roku w Bydgoszczy," in Chinciński and Machcewicz, op. cit., 266–268; Krzoska, op. cit., 248.

53. Karski, op. cit., 10.

54. Jochen Böhler, *Der Überfall: Deutschlands Krieg gegen Polen* (Frankfurt am Main, 2009), 121–122.

55. Grzegorz Bębnik, *Wrzesień 1939 r. w Katowicach* (Katowice, Poland, 2012), 85.

56. Clare Hollingworth, *The Three Weeks' War in Poland* (London, 1940), 19–20.

57. Testimony of Rafał K., cited in Alexander Rossino, *Hitler Strikes Poland: Blitzkrieg, Ideology, and Atrocity* (Lawrence, KS, 2003), 78–79.

58. Böhler, op. cit., 123–128.

59. Testimony of Stanisław Szarski, Karta Archive, Warsaw, AW/II/2925.

60. Hollingworth, op. cit., 26–27.

61. Quoted in Bogusław Sonik, "Krakowski Starzyński," *Dziennik Polski,* August 30, 2006, www.dziennikpolski24.pl/ar/1664746.

62. Testimony of Wincenty Bogdanowski, deputy mayor of Kraków, Jagiellonian University Manuscript Collection, 6/68=111 9869.

63. Zofia Piotrowiczowa, quoted in Zbigniew Gluza, *September 1939: The Partition of Poland* (Warsaw, 2009), 15.

64. Quoted in Hargreaves, op. cit., 130.

65. Piotr Derdej, *Westerplatte-Oksywie-Hel 1939* (Warsaw, 2014), 93.

66. Mariusz Borowiak, *Westerplatte: W obronie prawdy* (Gdańsk, Poland, 2001), 92.

67. Andrzej Drzycimski, *Westerplatte: Special Mission* (Gdańsk, Poland, 2015), 72.

68. Ibid., 77.

69. Quoted in Hargreaves, op. cit., 142.

70. Drzycimski, op. cit., 79–87.

71. Ibid., 89.

72. Konstanty Ildefons Gałczyński, "Pieśń o żołnierzach z Westerplatte," translated for the author by Bartek Pietrzyk.

73. Drzycimski, op. cit., 93, 96.

74. Quoted in Nicolaus von Below, *At Hitler's Side: The Memoirs of Hitler's Luftwaffe Adjutant, 1937–1945* (London, 2004), 36.

75 Willi Reibig, *Schwarze Husaren: Panzer in Polen* (Berlin, 1941), 24.

76. Ibid., 24.

77. Guderian, quoted in Bance, op. cit., 30.

78. Ibid., 30–31.

79. Kielmansegg, op. cit., 23–24.

80. Hollingworth, op. cit., 60.

81. Porwit, op. cit., 279.

82. Ibid., 245–247.

83. Krappe's diary, p. 6, Ian Sayer Archive.

84. Adam Kurus, "Częstochowa 1939: Zapomniana bitwa," *Dobroni,* May 17, 2012, https://dobroni.pl/n/czestochowa-1939/10283.

85. Testimony of Maria Komornicka, Karta Archive, Warsaw, AW/II/3611.

86. Vormann, op. cit., 75.

87. Jan Pietrzykowski, *Cień swastyki nad Jasną Górą: Częstochowa w okresie hitlerowskiej okupacji 1939–1945* (Katowice, Poland, 1985), 18.

88. Jochen Böhler, *Zbrodnie Wehrmachtu w Polsce: Wrzesień 1939—wojna totalna* (Kraków, 2009), 106–116.

89. Jochen Böhler, *"Grösste Härte . . .": Verbrechen der Wehrmacht in Polen, September/Oktober 1939* (Osnabrück, Germany, 2005), 106.

90. Quoted in David G. Williamson, *Poland Betrayed: The Nazi–Soviet Invasions of 1939* (Barnsley, England, 2009), 93.

91. Kielmansegg, op. cit., 26.

92. Jerzy B. Cynk, *The Polish Air Force at War: The Official History*, vol. 1, *1939–1943* (Atglen, PA, 1998), 77.

93. Jackiewicz, quoted in Williamson, op. cit., 93.

94. Kielmannsegg, op. cit., 26–27.

95. David Higgins, *Panzer II vs. 7TP: Poland 1939* (Oxford, 2015), 16–17, 20–21.

96. Testimony of Philipp Mamat, at LeMo, part of the website of the German Historical Museum, www.dhm.de.

97. Kurt Mehner, ed., *Die Geheimen Tagesberichte der Deutschen Wehrmachtführung im Zweiten Weltkrieg, 1939–1945*, vol. 1, *1. September 1939–30. April 1940*, part 1 (Osnabrück, Germany, 1995), 14.

98. Quoted in Williamson, op. cit., 94.

99. Kielmansegg, op. cit., 33–34.

100. Steven Zaloga and Victor Madej, *The Polish Campaign 1939* (New York, 1985), 123, 125.

101. Extract from the diary of Kazimiera Musiałowicz, unpublished manuscript in the collection of Katarzyna Myszkowska, Sulejów.

102. Tadeusz Kutrzeba, *Bitwa nad Burzą (9–22 września 1939): Przyczynek do historii kampanii polsko-niemieckiej w obszarze Poznań–Warszawa we wrześniu 1939* (Warsaw, 1957), 32.

103. Wacław Stachiewicz, *Wierności dochować żołnierskiej: Przygotowania wojenne w Polsce 1935–1939 oraz kampania 1939 w relacjach i rozważaniach szefa Sztabu Głównego i szefa Sztabu Naczelnego Wodza* (Warsaw, 1998), 484.

104. Porwit, op. cit., 281.

105. August Schmidt, *Die Geschichte der 10. Infanterie-Division* (Eggolsheim, n.d.), 28.

106. Fela Wiernikówna, quoted in Gluza, *September 1939*, 15.

107. Account of Samuel Goldberg, Imperial War Museum Archive, London, 06/521, pp. 109–110.

108. Quoted in Piotr Stawecki, *Oficerowie dyplomowani wojska Drugiej Rzeczypospolitej* (Wrocław, Poland, 1997), 192.

109. Deposition of Lieutenant-General Stanisław Kopański to the Historical Commission, London, 1947, PISM, B.I.7a, p. 25.

110. Andrzej Suchcitz, "Poland's Defence Preparations in 1939," in Peter Stachura, ed., *Poland Between the Wars, 1918–1939* (Basingstoke, 1998), 117.

111. Frederick Weinstein (Fryderyk Winnykamień), ed., *Aufzeichnungen aus dem Versteck: Erlebnisse eines polnischen Juden 1939–1946* (Berlin, 2006), 54–55.

112. Kielmansegg, op. cit., 23.

113. Goldberg account, op. cit., 112.

114. Quoted in Böhler, *"Grösste Härte . . ."*, 131.

115. The "Munich Letter," quoted in Jochen Böhler, *Auftakt zum Vernichtungskrieg: Die Wehrmacht in Polen 1939* (Frankfurt am Main, 2006), 172.

116. Helmut Krausnick, *Hitlers Einsatzgruppen: Die Truppen des Weltanschauungskrieges, 1938–1942* (Frankfurt am Main, 1998), 40.

117. Böhler, *"Grösste Härte . . . ,"* 115.

118. Quoted in Hargreaves, op. cit., 229.

119. Quoted in Böhler, *Auftakt zum Vernichtungskrieg*, 113–114.

120. Maria Wardzyńska, *Był rok 1939: Operacja niemieckiej policji bezpieczeństwa w Polsce "Intelligenzaktion"* (Warsaw, 2009), 96.

121. Ben H. Shepherd, *Hitler's Soldiers: The German Army in the Third Reich* (London, 2016), 53. See also Polish command report of operations of the 10th Cavalry Brigade by Major Franciszek Skibiński, PISM, B.I.58a, p. 10.

122. Testimony of Helena Szpilman, quoted in Böhler, *"Grösste Härte . . . ,"* 109.

123. Wardzyńska, op. cit., 94–96.

124. Quoted in Andreas Ulrich, "Hitler's Drugged Soldiers," *Der Spiegel*, May 2005.

125. Norman Ohler, *Blitzed: Drugs in Nazi Germany* (London, 2016), 78.

126. Quoted in Shepherd, op. cit., 51–52.

127. Rossino, op. cit., 205.

128. Quoted in Böhler, *"Grösste Härte . . . ,"* 42.

129. Rossino, op. cit., 161.

130. Szymon Datner, *55 dni Wehrmachtu w Polsce: Zbrodnie dokonane na polskiej ludności cywilnej w okresie l.ix-25.x. 1939 r.* (Warsaw, 1967), 114–117, 241.

131. Quoted in Böhler, *Auftakt zum Vernichtungskrieg*, 138.

132. Nowacki testimony, op. cit.

133. Rossino, op. cit., 64.

134. Franciszek Derezinski, quoted ibid., 64–65.

135. Datner, op. cit., 233.

136. Polish Ministry of Information, op. cit., Deposition No. 512, p. 60.

137. *Völkischer Beobachter,* September 9, 1939, 2.

138. Andrzej Kunert and Zygmunt Walkowski, *Kronika kampanii wrześnio-wej 1939* (Warsaw, 2005), 35.

139. Quoted in Gluza, *September 1939,* 14.

140. Adrian Carton de Wiart, *Happy Odyssey* (London, 2007 [1950]), 157.

141. Alexander Polonius, *I Saw the Siege of Warsaw* (Glasgow, 1941), 54.

142. Zofia Chomętowska, *Na wozie i pod wozem: Wspomnienia z lat 1939–1940* (Warsaw, 2008), 34.

143. Account held at Imperial War Museum Archive, London, PP/MCR/378.

144. Quoted in Gluza, *Rok 1939,* 108.

145. Wiktor Thommée, "Ze wspomnień dowódcy obrony Modlina," *Wojskowy Przegląd Historyczny* 4, no. 3 (1959): 184.

146. Marian Porwit, *Obrona Warszawy, wrzesień 1939: Wspomnienia i fakty* (Warsaw, 1979), 61.

147. Julien Bryan, *Warsaw* (New York, 1959), 18.

148. Wacław Lipiński, quoted in Gluza, *September 1939,* 18.

149. Porwit, *Obrona Warszawy,* 59.

150.Marta Korwin-Rhodes, *The Mask of Warriors: The Siege of Warsaw, September 1939* (New York, 1964), 41.

151. Polonius, op. cit., 50.

152. Korwin-Rhodes, op. cit., 34, 37.

153. Ibid., 46.

154. Quoted in Herbert Drescher, *Warschau und Modlin im Polenfeldzug 1939: Berichte und Dokumente* (Pforzheim, Germany, 1991), 316.

155. Komornicka testimony, op. cit.

CHAPTER 5: "POLAND IS NOT YET LOST"

1. *Robotnik,* September 9, 1939.

2. Georg Meyer, ed., *Generalfeldmarschall Wilhelm Ritter von Leeb: Tagebuchaufzeichnungen und Lagebeurteilungen aus zwei Weltkriegen* (Stuttgart, 1976), 174.

3. Alistair Horne, *To Lose a Battle: France 1940* (London, 1969), 141.

4. See Kevin Austra, "Operation Saar: A Lost Opportunity," *World War II Magazine,* September 1999.

5. Meyer, op. cit., 173.

6. Quoted in Ronald Atkin, *Pillar of Fire: Dunkirk 1940* (London, 1990), 28.

7. Quoted in Horne, op. cit., 140.

8. Adrian Carton de Wiart, *Happy Odyssey* (London, 2007 [1950]), 160.

9. *The Times,* September 8, 1939, 8; *Daily Mail,* September 8, 1939, 3.

10. See *Chwila*, September 6, 1939; *Słowo*, September 6 and 7, 1939; *Robotnik*, September 9, 1939; *Słowo*, September 9, 1939.

11. Testimony of Mieczysław Ptaśnik, Karta Archive, Warsaw, AW/II/3192.

12. Testimony of Maria Komornicka, Karta Archive, Warsaw, AW/II/3611.

13. Colonel Wojciech Fyda to Chief of II Bureau, Polish General Staff, September 11, 1939, Polish Institute and Sikorski Museum Archive, London (hereafter "PISM"), AII 18/16/2.

14. Norwid-Neugebauer to General Staff Warsaw, PISM, AII 22/7/2.

15. Daniel Todman, *Britain's War: Into Battle, 1937–1941* (London, 2016), 218; Alex Danchev and Daniel Todman, eds., *Field Marshal Lord Alanbrooke: War Diaries, 1939–1945* (London, 2001), 20.

16. Roderick Macleod and Denis Kelly, eds., *The Ironside Diaries, 1937–1940* (London, 1962), 107.

17. *Głos Narodowy*, September 8, 1939.

18. September 1939 overview at "British Military Aviation in 1939," Royal Air Force Museum, https://www.rafmuseum.org.uk/research/history-of-aviation -timeline/interactive-aviation-timeline/british-military-aviation/1939.aspx.

19. *Foreign Relations of the United States*, 1939, General, Volume I, Part 2, Beginning of European Phase of World War II, I: Invasion of Poland by Germany and Entry of the British and French into the War, September 1–16, 1939. Eds. Matilda F. Axton, Rogers P. Churchill, Francis C. Prescott, John G. Reid, N. O. Sappington, Louis E. Gates, and Shirley L. Phillips (Washington, DC, 1956), Doc. 434, Ambassador in France (Bullitt) to the Secretary of State, September 13, 1939, Telegram 740.0011.

20. A. J. P. Taylor, *English History, 1914–1945* (Oxford, 1965), 459.

21. Norwid-Neugebauer to Edward Śmigły-Rydz, September 10, 1939, Archiwum Akt Nowych, Warsaw, 2/1318/0/1/195/1.

22. Macleod and Kelly, op. cit., 106.

23. H. Kennard, September 11, 1939, The National Archives, London (hereafter "TNA"), CAB 66/1/216.

24. Appendix II to War Cabinet Committee report dated September 12, 1939, TNA, CAB 66/1/200.

25. Quoted in Eleanor M. Gates, *End of the Affair: The Collapse of the Anglo-French Alliance 1939–40* (London, 1981), 19–20.

26. War cabinet minutes of the meeting of the Supreme War Council, September 20, 1939, TNA, CAB 66/1/318–322.

27. Anita Prazmowska, *Britain, Poland and the Eastern Front 1939* (Cambridge, 1987), 184.

28. TNA, CAB 66/1/322, Annex B.

29. "House of Commons," *The Times*, September 14, 1939, 4.

30. Włodzimierz Borodziej and Sławomir Dębski, eds., *Polish Documents on Foreign Policy, 24 October 1938–30 September 1939* (Warsaw, 2009), Doc. 217, 420–422.

31. General Stanisław Burhardt-Bukacki to General Staff, Warsaw, September 14, 1939, PISM, AII 22/7/3.

32. Norwid-Neugebauer to General Staff, Warsaw, September 14, 1939, PISM, AII 22/7/2.

33. Stephan Lehnstaedt and Jochen Böhler, eds., *Die Berichte der Einsatzgruppen aus Polen 1939* (Berlin, 2013), Doc. 11, 85.

34. Quoted in Alexander Rossino, *Hitler Strikes Poland: Blitzkrieg, Ideology, and Atrocity* (Lawrence, KS, 2003), 70.

35. Quoted in Lehnstaedt and Böhler, op. cit., 90.

36. Testimony of Benon Brzezicha at "Pamięć Bydgoszczan: Archiwum Historii Mówionej," Biblioteka Główna Uniwersytetu Kazimierza Wielkiego, http://pamiecbydgoszczan.ukw.edu.pl/relacje/wrzesien-1939-roku-na-szwederowie.

37. Figures from Rossino, op. cit., 71–72.

38. Dorothee Weitbrecht, *Der Exekutionsauftrag der Einsatzgruppen in Polen* (Filderstadt, Germany, 2001), 21.

39. Edmund Zarzycki, *Działalność hitlerowskiego Sądu Specjalnego w Bydgoszczy w latach 1939–1945* (Bydgoszcz, Poland, 2000), 23.

40. Kurt Mehner, ed., *Die geheimen Tagesberichte der Deutschen Wehrmachtführung im Zweiten Weltkrieg, 1939–1945*, vol. 1, *1. September 1939–30. April 1940*, part 1 (Osnabrück, Germany, 1995), 23.

41. Heinz Guderian, *Panzer Leader* (London, 1952), 75.

42. *Oberst* Hans-Karl Freiherr von Esebeck, quoted in Alan Bance, trans., *Blitzkrieg in Their Own Words: First-Hand Accounts from German Soldiers, 1939–1940* (St. Paul, MN, 2005), 39.

43. Guderian, op. cit., 76.

44. Testimony of Captain Wacław Schmidt, PISM, BI 16/3.

45. Quoted in Leszek Bartoszyński and Franciszek Burdzy, "Wizna," *Żołnierz Polski* 37 (1964).

46. Seweryn Biegański, quoted in Zbigniew Gluza, ed., *September 1939: The Partition of Poland* (Warsaw, 2009), 23.

47. Quoted in Ludwik Zalewski, ed., *Obiekty obronne Ziemi Łomżyńskiej* (Łomża, Poland, 2013), 33.

48. Testimony of Lieutenant Adam Łempicki, PISM, BI 14c/4.

49. The Polish text is "Przechodniu, powiedz Ojczyźnie, żeśmy walczyli do końca, spełniając swój obowiązek."

50. Testimony of Lieutenant-Colonel Tadeusz Tabaczyński, PISM, BI 16/1.

51. See, for instance, "75. Rocznica bohaterskiej obrony pod Wizną," *Polska Newsweek*, October 9, 2014, https://www.newsweek.pl/wiedza/historia/bitwa -pod-wizna-major-raginis-rocznica-wrzesien-1939-newsweekpl/6q73kjm.

52. *Kriegstagebuch Armeegruppe Nord*, entries for September 8 and 9, 1939, US National Archives, T311-200.

53. Testimony of Dr. Walerian Terajewicz, PISM, BI 14d/6.

54. Szymon Datner, *55 dni Wehrmachtu w Polsce: Zbrodnie dokonane na polskiej ludności cywilnej w okresie l.ix-25.x. 1939 r.* (Warsaw, 1967), 314–317.

55. Leni Riefenstahl, *The Sieve of Time* (London, 1992), 259.

56. Jochen Böhler, *Auftakt zum Vernichtungskrieg: Die Wehrmacht in Polen 1939* (Frankfurt am Main, 2006), 195–197.

57. Riefenstahl, op. cit., 259.

58. Diary of W.K., Imperial War Museum Archive, London, 94/26/1, p. 4.

59. Testimony of Philipp Mamat, at LeMo, part of the website of the German Historical Museum, www.dhm.de.

60. Willi Reibig, *Schwarze Husaren: Panzer in Polen* (Berlin, 1941), 26.

61. Quoted in Peter Hoffmann, *Stauffenberg: A Family History, 1905–1944* (Montreal, 2003), 115.

62. W.K. diary, op. cit., 11.

63. Datner, op. cit., 358–359, 117.

64. Quoted in Marcin Bielesz, "Gwizd, huk, błysk, dym! 74 lata temu Niemcy zmietli całe miasto z powierzchni ziemi," *Gazeta Wyborcza*, September 13, 2013.

65. See Norman Davies, *Europe at War 1939–1945: No Simple Victory* (London, 2006), 297.

66. Quoted in Richard Hargreaves, *Blitzkrieg Unleashed: The German Invasion of Poland, 1939* (Barnsley, England, 2008), 152.

67. Klemens Rudnicki, *The Last of the War Horses* (London, 1974), 23.

68. Quoted in Rolf Elble, *Die Schlacht an der Bzura im September 1939* (Freiburg, Germany, 1975), 100.

69. Colonel Marian Porwit, Foreword, in Tadeusz Kutrzeba, *Bitwa nad Bzurą (9–22 września 1939): Przyczynek do historii kampanii polsko-niemieckiej w obszarze Poznań–Warszawa we wrześniu 1939* (Warsaw, 1957).

70. Czesław Ławniczak, quoted in Maciej Wojewoda and Jakub Wojewoda, *Bitwa nad Bzurą: Pierwsza wśród wielkich bitew II Wojny Światowej* (Warsaw,

2016), 24; Roman Bąkowski, "Mój wrzesień: Wspomnienia z bitwy nad Bzurą," *Kutnowskie Zeszyty Regionalne* 4 (2000): 426.

71. Elble, op. cit., 119; Hans Breithaupt, *Die Geschichte der 30. Infanterie-Division 1939–1945* (Bad Nauheim, 1955), 24–25.

72. Bąkowski, op. cit., 426.

73. Christian Kinder, *Männer der Nordmark an der Bzura: Aus den Gefechtshandlungen einer Infanteriedivision in Polen* (Berlin, 1941), 27.

74. Franciszek Rackowiak, quoted in Wojewoda and Wojewoda, op. cit., 25.

75. Stanisław Stapf, quoted ibid., 30.

76. Quoted in Hargreaves, op. cit., 155.

77. Bąkowski, op. cit., 426.

78. Elble, op. cit., 148.

79. Nikolaus von Vormann, *Der Feldzug 1939 in Polen: Die Operationen des Heeres* (Weissenburg, Germany, 1958), 132.

80. Elble, op. cit., 141.

81. Quoted ibid., 132.

82. Hargreaves, op. cit., 158.

83. Walter Gorlitz, ed., *The Memoirs of Field-Marshal Wilhelm Keitel* (New York, 2000 [1966]), 95.

84. Johann Graf von Kielmansegg, *Panzer zwischen Warschau und Atlantik* (Berlin, 1941), 62.

85. Quoted in Wiktor Thommée, "Ze wspomnień dowódcy obrony Modlina," *Wojskowy Przegląd Historyczny* 4, no. 3 (1959): 194.

86. Sergeant Józef Skórka, quoted in Wojewoda and Wojewoda, op. cit., 41.

87. Kurt Meyer, *Grenadiers* (Mechanicsburg, PA, 2005), 6.

88. Quoted in Piotr Bauer, *17 Pułk Ułanów Wielkopolskich im. Króla Bolesława Chrobrego w obronie Ojczyzny 1939 r.* (Gostyń, 1978), 56.

89. Quoted in Edmund Makowski and Kazimierz Młynarz, eds., *Dni klęski, dni chwały: Wspomnienia Wielkopolan z wrzeénia 1939* (Poznań, Poland, 1970), 295.

90. Kutrzeba, quoted in Alex Buchner, *Der Polenfeldzug 1939* (Leoni am Starnberger See, Germany, 1989), 116.

91. Lieutenant-Colonel Jan Maliszewski, quoted in Wojewoda and Wojewoda, op. cit., 50.

92. Kielmansegg, op. cit., 68.

93. Bąkowski, op. cit., 430.

94. Quoted in Wojewoda and Wojewoda, op. cit., 41.

95. Indro Montanelli, "Cavalli contro autoblindo," *Corriere della Sera*, September 13, 1939. Translated by Dr. Alex Standen.

96. See William Shirer, *Berlin Diary, 1934–1941: The Rise of the Third Reich*, illus. ed. (London, 1997 [1941]), 106; William Shirer, *This Is Berlin: Reporting from Nazi Germany, 1938–40* (London, 1999), 88.

97. Günther Grass mentioned the scene in his 1959 novel *The Tin Drum*, and Andrzej Wajda gave an early cinematic representation of it in his film *Lotna* of the same year.

98. For Zgierz and Łowicz, see Rossino, op. cit., 169–170.

99. Datner, op. cit., 391, 416.

100. Wojewoda and Wojewoda, op. cit., 45.

101. Jochen Böhler, *"Grösste Härte . . .": Verbrechen der Wehrmacht in Polen, September/Oktober 1939* (Osnabrück, Germany, 2005), 80.

102. Böhler, *Auftakt zum Vernichtungskrieg*, 224.

103. Stanisław Klejnowski, quoted in Szymon Datner, *Zbrodnie Wehrmachtu na jeńcach wojennych armii regularnych w II wojnie światowej* (Warsaw, 1961), 54–55.

104. Kielmansegg, op. cit., 70.

105. Hargreaves, op. cit., 163.

106. Tomasz Owoc, *Prisoners of War in Occupied Kraków, 1939–1945* (Kraków, 2016), 42.

107. Bąkowski, op. cit., 432.

108. Ludwik Czyżewski, *Wspomnienia dowódcy obrony Zakroczymia w 1939 r.* (Warsaw, 1973), 16.

CHAPTER 6: OF "LIBERATORS" AND ABSENT FRIENDS

1. Bernardo Bellotto (1721–1780) was the nephew of the better-known "Canaletto," Antonio Canal, but also styled himself in the same way.

2. Władysław Sosabowski, *Freely I Served: The Memoir of the Commander, 1st Polish Independent Parachute Brigade, 1941–1944* (Barnsley, England, 2013), 30.

3. Testimony of Maria Komornicka, Karta Archive, Warsaw, AW/II/3611.

4. Colonel Hans-Karl Freiherr von Esebeck, quoted in Alan Bance, trans., *Blitzkrieg in Their Own Words: First-Hand Accounts from German Soldiers, 1939–1940* (St. Paul, MN, 2005), 40–42.

5. Testimony of Lieutenant Andrzej Żyliński, *Szarża kawalerii pod Kałuszynem 11–12 wrzesień 1939 r.*, reproduced at 1939: Kampania Wrześniowa, www.1939.pl/kampania-wrzesniowa/relacja-andrzej-zylinski/index.html.

6. Marek Sarjusz-Wolski, "Bitwa pod Kałuszynem 1939," in Kamil Janicki and Anna Winkler, eds., *Polskie triumfy: 50 chwalebnych bitew Polaków, o których każdy powinien pamiętać* (Kraków, 2018), 428.

7. Tadeusz Jurga and Władysław Karbowski, *Armia "Modlin" 1939* (Warsaw, 1987), 283.

8. Sarjusz-Wolski, op. cit., 434; Jerzy Strychalski, *Bitwa pod Kałuszynem* (Siedlce, Poland, 1985), 14.

9. Władysław Anders, *An Army in Exile: The Story of the Second Polish Corps* (London, 1949), 6.

10. Wiktor Thommée, "Ze wspomnień dowódcy obrony Modlina," *Wojskowy Przegląd Historyczny* 4, no. 3 (1959): 179.

11. General Tadeusz Kutrzeba, quoted in ibid., 190.

12. Alexander Polonius, *I Saw the Siege of Warsaw* (Glasgow, 1941), 123–124.

13. Lola Halama, *Moje nogi i ja* (Warsaw, 1984), 70.

14. Marta Korwin-Rhodes, *The Mask of Warriors: The Siege of Warsaw, September 1939* (New York, 1964), 100.

15. Władysław Szpilman, *The Pianist: The Extraordinary Story of One Man's Survival in Warsaw, 1939–45* (London, 1999), 34–35.

16. Stefan Starzyński, quoted in Zbigniew Gluza, ed., *Rok 1939: Rozbiór Polski* (Warsaw, 2009), 124.

17. Komornicka testimony, op. cit., September 10, 1939.

18. Szpilman, op. cit., 33.

19. Korwin-Rhodes, op. cit., 105.

20. Ibid., 114.

21. Szpilman, op. cit., 35–36.

22. Testimony of Stanisław Dmuchowski, Karta Archive, Warsaw, AW/I/0126.

23. Julien Bryan, *Warsaw* (New York, 1959), 18–19.

24. Ibid., 20–21.

25. Quoted in Gluza, op. cit., 108.

26. Szpilman, op. cit., 37.

27. Account of Mikołaj Bujan, entry for September 16, 1939, Zawkrze Land Museum Archive, Mława, MZZ/fk/380.

28. Sosabowski, op. cit., 37.

29. Ibid., 39.

30. Hans-Adolf Jacobsen, ed., *Generaloberst Halder Kriegstagebuch*, vol. 1, *Vom Polenfeldzug bis zum Ende der Westoffensive* (Stuttgart, 1962), 77.

31. See Sosabowski, op. cit., 37–38; Herbert Drescher, *Warschau und Modlin im Polenfeldzug 1939: Berichte und Dokumente* (Pforzheim, Germany, 1991), 420.

32. Cajus Bekker, *The Luftwaffe War Diaries* (New York, 1994), 57.

33. Komornicka testimony, op. cit.

34. Polonius, op. cit., 136.

35. Nigel Nicolson, ed., *Harold Nicolson: Diaries and Letters*, vol. 2, *1939–1945* (London, 1967), 30.

36. *Documents on German Foreign Policy*, Series D, 1937–1945 (hereafter *DGFP*), vol. 7, *The Last Days of Peace, August 9–September 3, 1939* (London, 1956), Doc. 567, Ribbentrop to Schulenburg, p. 541.

37. *DGFP*, vol. 8, *The War Years, September 4 1939–March 18 1940* (London, 1954), Doc. 5, Schulenburg to Ribbentrop, p. 4.

38. Mikhail Mel'tyukhov, *17 sentyabrya 1939: Sovetsko-pol'skie konflikty, 1918–1939* (Moscow, 2009), 339, 344.

39. John Erickson, "The Soviet March into Poland, September 1939," in Keith Sword, ed., *The Soviet Takeover of the Polish Eastern Provinces, 1939–1941* (Basingstoke, 1991), 10.

40. *DGFP*, vol. 8, p. 44.

41. Mel'tyukhov, op. cit., 355.

42. See Roger Moorhouse, *The Devils' Alliance: Hitler's Pact with Stalin, 1939–1941* (London, 2014), 127–131.

43. Quoted in Czesław Grzelak, *Sowiecki najazd 1939 r.: Sojusznik Hitlera napada polskie Kresy—relacje świadków i uczestników* (Warsaw, 2017), 42–43.

44. *DGFP*, vol. 8, pp. 60–61.

45. Ibid., 69, 76, 79.

46. Włodzimierz Borodziej and Sławomir Dębski, eds., *Polish Documents on Foreign Policy, 24 October 1938–30 September 1939* (Warsaw, 2009), Doc. 218, 423.

47. Text in Stefania Stanisławska, ed., *Sprawa polska w czasie drugiej wojny światowej na arenie międzynarodowej: Zbiór dokumentów* (Warsaw, 1965), 83–84.

48. Henryk Batowski, "17 September 1939: Before and After," *East European Quarterly* 27, no. 4 (1993): 528; Olaf Groehler, *Selbstmörderische Allianz: Deutsch-russische Militärbeziehungen, 1920–1941* (Berlin, 1992), 116; Natalia S. Lebedeva, "Poland Between the Soviet Union and Germany, 1939–1941: The Red Army Invasion and the Fourth Partition of Poland," in Adam Daniel Rotfeld and Anatoly V. Torkunov, eds., *White Spots, Black Spots: Difficult Matters in Polish–Russian Relations, 1918–2008* (Pittsburgh, 2015), 191.

49. Borodziej and Dębski, op. cit., 427.

50. Steven Zaloga, *Poland 1939: The Birth of Blitzkrieg* (Oxford, 2002), 80; Albin Głowacki, "Poland Between the Soviet Union and Germany, 1939–1941: The Red Army Invasion and the Fourth Partition of Poland," in Rotfeld and Torkunov, op. cit., 164.

51. Erickson, op. cit., 13.

52. Quoted in Alexander Hill, "Voroshilov's 'Lightning' War: The Soviet Invasion of Poland, September 1939," *Journal of Slavic Military Studies* 27, no. 3 (2014): 413.

53. Lebedeva, op. cit., 189–190.

54. Mel'tyukhov, op. cit., 331.

55. Hill, op. cit., 411.

56. See Moorhouse, op. cit., 9; testimony of Janina Król, Karta Archive, Warsaw, AW/I/0407.

57. Testimony of Captain Stefan Gołębiowski, Polish Institute and Sikorski Museum Archive, London (hereafter "PISM"), B I 70/H.

58. Stanisławski testimony, Karta Archive, Warsaw, AW/I/744.

59. Steven Zaloga and Leland S. Ness, *Companion to the Red Army, 1939–1945* (Stroud, England, 2009), 158.

60. Hill, op. cit., 415–416.

61. Testimony of Professor Kazimierz Antonowicz, Karta Archive, Warsaw, A/I/0009.

62. Hill, op. cit., 417.

63. Erickson, op. cit., 17; Głowacki, op. cit., 164.

64. Colonel Marceli Kotarba to II Bureau, General Staff, PISM, AII 25/12/4.

65. Order from Colonel Kaftański, September 17, 1939, PISM, AII 25/12/3.

66. Ryszard Szawłowski, "The Polish-Soviet War of 1939," in Sword, op. cit., 35, 39.

67. Documents on the defense of Sarny, PISM, B I 96/H.

68. Mel'tyukhov, op. cit., 386.

69. Szawłowski, op. cit., 37.

70. Testimony of Witold Żółkiewski, Karta Archive, Warsaw, AW/I/0677.

71. Quoted in Jan T. Gross, *Revolution from Abroad: The Soviet Conquest of Poland's Western Ukraine and Western Belorussia* (Princeton, NJ, 2002), 21–22.

72. Testimony of Stefan Kurylak, Imperial War Museum Archive, London, 78/52/1.

73. Ibid.

74. Testimony of Stanisława Kupczykowska, Karta Archive, Warsaw, AW/II/236A/Ł.

75. Author interview with Mieczysław Wartalski, London, September 2011.

76. Testimony of Władysław Olesiński, Karta Archive, Warsaw, AW/II/1388.

77. Mel'tyukhov, op. cit., 360.

78. Jan Karski, *Story of a Secret State: My Report to the World* (London, 2011 [1944]), 14.

79. Testimony of Kazimierz Odyniec, in Czesław Grzelak, *Szack—Wytyczno 1939* (Warsaw, 2001), 108.

80. Reproduced in Olesiński testimony, op. cit.

81. Gross, op. cit., 22–23.

82. Bujan account, op. cit., entry for September 17, 1939.

83. Testimony of Konstanty Peszyński, Karta Archive, Warsaw, AW/II/3448.

84. Testimony of Adolf Koc, Karta Archive, Warsaw, AW/I/0352.

85. Testimony of Henryk Kundzicz, Karta Archive, Warsaw, AW/I/0432.

86. Mel'tyukhov, op. cit., 372.

87. Peszyński testimony, op. cit.

88. Walery Choroszewski, quoted in David G. Williamson, *Poland Betrayed: The Nazi–Soviet Invasions of 1939* (Barnsley, England, 2009), 122.

89. Account of Bruno Hlebowicz, in Ryszard Szawłowski, ed., *Wojna polsko-sowiecka 1939*, vol. 2, *Dokumenty* (Warsaw, 1997), 57.

90. Account by Lieutenant Władysław Tomaszewski, PISM, B I 70/H.

91. Gołębiowski testimony, op. cit.

92. Account of Grażyna Lipińska, in Szawłowski, *Wojna polsko-sowiecka*, 2:70.

93. Testimony of Janusz Puchciński, Karta Archive, Warsaw, AW/I/0652.

94. Lipińska account, op. cit., 73–74. See also testimony of Władysław Wasilewski, PISM, B I 70/H.

95. Kundzicz testimony, op. cit.

96. Hill, op. cit., 409; Szawłowski, *Wojna polsko-sowiecka*, 2:36.

97. Mel'tyukhov, op. cit., 478–479.

98. Tomasz Piesakowski, *The Fate of Poles in the USSR 1939–1989* (London, 1990), 36.

99. Czesław Grzelak, ed., *Wrzesień 1939 na Kresach: W relacjach* (Warsaw, 1999), 384.

100. Testimony of Henryk Jaroszyński, Karta Archive, Warsaw, AW/I/0292.

101. Mel'tyukhov, op. cit., 482.

102. Gross, op. cit., 43.

103. Testimony of Father Józef Anczarski, Karta Archive, Warsaw, AW/II/1224/2K.

104. Testimony of Jerzy Piwoński, Karta Archive, Warsaw, AW/I/624.

105. Gross, op. cit., 44.

106. Testimony of Dariusz Dąbrowski, Imperial War Museum Sound Archive, London, 10450.

107. Testimony of Henryk Meszczyński, Karta Archive, Warsaw, AW/I/0508.

108. Testimony of Józef Bartoszewicz, Karta Archive, Warsaw, AW/I/0026.

109. Vladimir Abarinov, *The Murderers of Katyń* (New York, 1993), 101 et. seq.

110. Anczarski testimony, op. cit.

111. Account of Major-General Andrei Yeremenko, quoted in Grzelak, *Sowiecki najazd 1939 r.*, 50.

112. Anczarski testimony, op. cit.

113. Testimony of Kazimierz Rodziewicz, Karta Archive, Warsaw, AW/I/0672.

114. Zofia Chomętowska, *Na wozie i pod wozem: Wspomnienia z lat 1939–1940* (Warsaw, 2008), 94.

115. Olesiński testimony, op. cit.

116. Quoted in Gross, op. cit., 36.

117. Testimony of Andrzej Ramułt, Karta Archive, Warsaw, AW/I/0663.

118. Chomętowska, op. cit., 30n.

119. Quoted in Gross, op. cit., 37.

120. Kupczykowska testimony, op. cit.

121. Ibid., 34.

122. Testimony of Stanisław Ossowski, Karta Archive, Warsaw, AW/II/3301.

123. Karski, op. cit., 16–17.

124. Daniel Gerould, ed., *The Witkiewicz Reader* (Evanston, IL, 1992), 275.

125. Winston Churchill, *The Second World War*, vol. 1, *The Gathering Storm* (London, 1948), 400; John Colville, *The Fringes of Power: Downing Street Diaries, 1939–1955*, vol. 1, *September 1939–September 1941* (London, 1985), 24.

126. Nicolson, op. cit., 34.

127. Norman Mackenzie and Jeanne Mackenzie, eds., *The Diary of Beatrice Webb*, vol. 4, *The Wheel of Life* (London, 1985), 438–440.

128. Dorothy Sheridan, ed., *Among You Taking Notes . . . : The Wartime Diary of Naomi Mitchison, 1939–1945* (London, 1985), 40.

129. Harry Pollitt, *How to Win the War* (London, 1939), passim.

130. See Moorhouse, op. cit., 109–114.

131. "Stalin Shows His Hand," *The Times*, September 18, 1939.

132. Raczyński to Halifax, September 17, 1939, The National Archives, London (hereafter "TNA"), FO 371/23103 C14996.

133. Quoted in Keith Sword, "British Reactions to the Soviet Occupation of Eastern Poland in September 1939," *Slavonic and East European Review* 69 (1991): 89.

134. Broadcast message to Warsaw, reproduced in Polish Ministry of Foreign Affairs, *The Polish White Book*, vol. 1, *Official Documents Concerning Polish–German and Polish–Soviet Relations, 1933–1939* (London, 1941), Doc. 143, 140.

135. Churchill, op. cit., 403.

136. Sword, "British Reactions," 98.

137. David Dilks, ed., *The Diaries of Sir Alexander Cadogan, OM, 1938–1945* (London, 1971), 218.

138. Supreme War Council Minutes, September 25, 1939, TNA, CAB 66/1/399.

139. Dilks, op. cit., 219.

140. Supreme War Council Minutes, op. cit.

141. Polonius, op. cit., 164–165.

CHAPTER 7: "INTO THE ARMS OF DEATH"

1. Heinz Linge, *With Hitler to the End: The Memoirs of Adolf Hitler's Valet* (London, 2009), 122.

2. Max Domarus, ed., *Hitler: Speeches and Proclamations, 1932–1945. The Chronicle of a Dictatorship*, vol. 3: *1939 to 1940* (Würzburg, Germany, 1997), 1802–1804.

3. Ibid., 1807.

4. Ibid., 1808.

5. Linge, op. cit., 123.

6. Wacław Tym and Andrzej Rzepniewski, eds., *Kępa Oksywska 1939: Relacje uczestników walk lądowych* (Gdańsk, Poland, 1985), 257–258.

7. Ibid., 36.

8. An image of the grave can be seen on Dąbek's Wikipedia page at https://pl.wikipedia.org/wiki/Stanisław_Dąbek.

9. Charles W. Sydnor Jr., *Soldiers of Destruction: The SS Death's Head Division, 1933–1945* (Princeton, NJ, 1977), 41.

10. Tym and Rzepniewski, op. cit., 189.

11. Richard Hargreaves, *Blitzkrieg Unleashed: The German Invasion of Poland, 1939* (Barnsley, England, 2008), 175.

12. Quoted in Marius Emmerling, *Luftwaffe nad Polską 1939*, vol. 3, *Stuka-flieger* (Gdynia, Poland, 2006), 10.

13. Testimony of Eugeniusz Maciejewski, "Wspomnienia z obrony Helu w 1939," typescript (Gdynia, Poland, 1960), 18, Polish Navy Museum Archive, Gdynia.

14. Tym and Rzepniewski, op. cit., 371.

15. Krzysztof Komorowski, ed., *Boje Polskie 1939–1945: Przewodnik encyklopedyczny* (Warsaw, 2009), 114.

16. Tym and Rzepniewski, op. cit., 377.

17. Maciejewski testimony, op. cit., 20.

18. Max Domarus, ed., *Hitler: Reden und Proklamationen, 1932–1945*, vol. 3 (Wiesbaden, Germany, 1973), 1316.

19. Linge, op. cit., 123.

20. Walter Warlimont, *Inside Hitler's Headquarters, 1939–1945* (London, 1964), 38.

21. Roman Bąkowski and Waldemar Nadolny, *Baterie Artylerii Przeciwlotniczej* (Hel, Poland, 2005), 8–12.

22. Mariusz Borowiak, *Admiral Unrug, 1884–1973* (Warsaw, 2009), 253.

23. Paul Schmidt, *Hitler's Interpreter* (London, 1951), 163.

24. Maciejewski testimony, op. cit., 20–21.

25. Ibid., 23.

26. Wiesław Arlet, quoted in Janina Grabowska-Chałka, *Stutthof: Informator historyczny—przewodnik* (Gdańsk, Poland, 2011), 18–19.

27. *Danziger Vorposten*, September 13, 1939, 10.

28. Quoted in Hermann Kuhn, ed., *Stutthof: Ein Konzentrationslager vor dem Toren Danzigs* (Bremen, 2016), 99.

29. Ibid., 97.

30. Quoted in ibid., 39.

31. Wanda Ruczkal, quoted in Grabowska-Chałka, op. cit., 52.

32. Testimony of Wacław Lewandowski, displayed at Muzeum Stutthof w Sztutowie, Poland. Also in Archiwum Muzeum Stutthof, *Relacje i wspomnienia, relacja Wacława Lewandowskiego*, 208.

33. Mieczysław Filipowicz, quoted in *Westerplatte w 7 odsłonach* (Gdańsk, Poland, 2017), 97.

34. Bolesław Kowalczyk, quoted in Grabowska-Chałka, op. cit., 50.

35. Kuhn, op. cit., 96.

36. Quoted in ibid., 96.

37. Lewandowski testimony, op. cit.

38. Paul Malmassari, *Armoured Trains: An Illustrated Encyclopaedia, 1825–2016* (Barnsley, England, 2016), 360.

39. Hans Baur, *I Was Hitler's Pilot* (Barnsley, England, 2013 [1958]), 102.

40. Nikolaus von Vormann, *Der Feldzug 1939 in Polen: Die Operationen des Heeres* (Weissenburg, Germany, 1958), 176.

41. Wiktor Thommée, "Ze wspomnień dowódcy obrony Modlina," *Wojskowy Przegląd Historyczny* 4, no. 3 (1959): 179n.

42. Tadeusz Krawczak and Janusz Odziemkowski, *Polskie pociągi pancerne w wojnie 1939 r.* (Warsaw, 1987), 102.

43. Erhard Jähnert, *Mal oben—mal unten: Einer, der immer dabei war* (Bad Kissingen, Germany, 1992), 32–33.

44. Thommée, op. cit., 191.

45. Ludwik Czyżewski, *Wspomnienia dowódcy obrony Zakroczymia w 1939 r.* (Warsaw, 1973), 26.

46. Ibid., 56.

47. Rochus Misch, *Hitler's Last Witness: The Memoirs of Hitler's Bodyguard* (Barnsley, England, 2014), 30–31.

48. Czyżewski, op. cit., 38.

49. Klemens Rudnicki, *The Last of the War Horses* (London, 1974), 41.

50. Mario Appelius, *Una guerra di 30 giorni: La tragedia della Polonia* (Milan, 1940), 185.

51. Rudnicki, op. cit., 42.

52. Quoted in Herbert Drescher, *Warschau und Modlin im Polenfeldzug 1939: Berichte und Dokumente* (Pforzheim, Germany, 1991), 530–531.

53. Johann Adolf Graf von Kielmansegg, *Panzer zwischen Warschau und Atlantik* (Berlin, 1941), 73.

54. Quoted in Drescher, op. cit., 548.

55. Ibid., 550.

56. Testimony of Fritsch's adjutant, Lieutenant Rosenhagen, *Der Spiegel* 34 (1948): 18.

57. Baur, op. cit., 102.

58. See, for instance, Johnny von Herwarth, *Against Two Evils* (London, 1981), 171.

59. Victor Klemperer, *I Shall Bear Witness: The Diaries of Victor Klemperer, 1933–1941* (London, 1998), 300–301.

60. Julien Bryan, *Warsaw* (New York, 1959), 36.

61. John Ker Davis, "Farewell to a Beleaguered City," *Foreign Service Journal*, July 1966, 47.

62. Bryan, op. cit., 37, 39.

63. Quoted in Lucjan Dobroszycki, Marian Drozdowski, Marek Getter, and Adam Słomczyński, eds., *Cywilna obrona Warszawy we wrześniu 1939 r. Dokumenty, materiały prasowe, wspomnienia i relacje* (Warsaw, 1964), 143.

64. Michalina Mazińska, quoted in Leszek Zaborowski, ed., *Chronicles of Terror*, vol. 1, *German Executions in Occupied Warsaw* (Warsaw, 2018), 36.

65. Marta Korwin-Rhodes, *The Mask of Warriors: The Siege of Warsaw, September 1939* (New York, 1964), 132.

66. Alexander Polonius, *I Saw the Siege of Warsaw* (Glasgow, 1941), 137.

67. Quoted in Emmerling, op. cit., 202.

68. Bryan, op. cit., 34.

69. Władysław Szpilman, *The Pianist: The Extraordinary Story of One Man's Survival in Warsaw, 1939–45* (London, 1999), 39.

70. Testimony of Maria Komornicka, Karta Archive, Warsaw, AW/II/3611.

71. Anonymous diarist, quoted in Marta Markowska, ed., *The Ringelblum Archive: Annihilation—Day by Day* (Warsaw, 2008), 18.

72. Polonius, op. cit., 154.

73. Testimony of Stanisław Dmuchowski, Karta Archive, Warsaw, AW/I/0126.

74. Jadwiga Zdanowa, quoted in Zbigniew Gluza, ed., *Rok 1939: Rozbiór polski* (Warsaw, 2009), 159.

75. Paweł Rokicki, Anna Piekarska, et al., *"A więc wojna": Ludność cywilna we wrześniu 1939 r.* (Warsaw, 2009), 189, 191.

76. Polonius, op. cit., 151–152.

77. Korwin-Rhodes, op. cit., 128.

78. Stanisław Lorentz, quoted in Rokicki et. al., op. cit., 195.

79. Korwin-Rhodes, op. cit., 137; Polonius, op. cit., 162.

80. Marian Marek Drozdowski, ed., *Archiwum Prezydenta Warszawy Stefana Starzyńskiego* (Warsaw, 2004), 292.

81. Korwin-Rhodes, op. cit., 146.

82. Polonius, op. cit., 163.

83. Quoted in Marian Marek Drozdowski, *Starzyński: Legionista, polityk gospodarczy, prezydent Warszawy* (Warsaw, 2006), 397.

84. Szpilman, op. cit., 39.

CHAPTER 8: IMPENITENT THIEVES

1. On Lauterpacht and Lemkin, see Philippe Sands, *East–West Street: On the Origins of Genocide and Crimes Against Humanity* (London, 2016).

2. Stanisław Maczek, *Od podwody do czołga: Wspomnienia wojenne, 1918–1945* (Edinburgh, 1961), 84–85.

3. Diary of General Władysław Langner, commander of Lwów garrison, Polish Institute and Sikorski Museum Archive, London (hereafter "PISM"), KOL 166, p. 14.

4. Report by Colonel Stanisław Maczek, PISM, B I/58A, p. 21.

5. Max Domarus, ed., *Hitler: Reden und Proklamationen, 1932–1945*, vol. 3 (Wiesbaden, Germany, 1973), 1350.

6. See Ronald Smelser and Enrico Syring, eds., *Die Militärelite des Dritten Reiches* (Frankfurt am Main, 1995), 502.

7. Quoted in Richard Hargreaves, *Blitzkrieg Unleashed: The German Invasion of Poland, 1939* (Barnsley, England, 2008), 191.

8. Ibid., 191.

9. Wojciech Włodarkiewicz, *Lwów 1939* (Warsaw, 2003), 80.

10. Ibid., 91.

11. Langner diary, op. cit., 19.

12. Bruno Shatyn, *A Private War: Surviving in Poland on False Papers, 1941–1945* (Detroit, 1985), 122.

13. Jochen Böhler, *Auftakt zum Vernichtungskrieg: Die Wehrmacht in Polen 1939* (Frankfurt am Main, 2006), 213.

14. Shatyn, op. cit., 122.

15. Langner diary, op. cit., 20.

16. Langner to Commander-in-Chief, September 14, 1939, PISM, AII 24/17/1.

17. Hermann Frank Meyer, *Blutiges Edelweiß: Die 1. Gebirgs-Division im Zweiten Weltkrieg* (Berlin, 2008), 29.

18. Tadeusz Rawski, *Piechota w II wojnie światowej* (Warsaw, 1984), 45.

19. Rosamund Rolle, *Kazimierz Sosnkowski: Servant of the White Eagle* (London, 1944), 29.

20. *Der Polenfeldzug im Tagebuch eines Gebirgsartilleristen* (Innsbruck, 1940), quoted in Hargreaves, op. cit., 195.

21. Bronisław Prugar-Ketling, *Aby dochować wierności: Wspomnienia z działań 11. Karpackiej Dywizji Piechoty. Wrzesień 1939* (Warsaw, 1990), 77.

22. Hargreaves, op. cit., 197.

23. Prugar-Ketling, op. cit., 71.

24. Ibid., 71.

25. Kazimierz Sosnkowski, *Cieniom września* (Warsaw, 1989), 135.

26. Prugar-Ketling, op. cit., 79.

27. Ibid., 90.

28. Generalkommando VII AK, *Wir zogen gegen Polen: Kriegserinnerungswerk des VII Armeekorps* (Munich, 1940), 90–91.

29. Sosnkowski, op. cit., 178.

30. Langner diary, op. cit., 26.

31. Sosnkowski, op. cit., 171–172.

32. Włodarkiewicz, op. cit., 175.

33. Copy of a Soviet leaflet, "Do wojsk Polskich!," in the possession of the author.

34. Copy of a leaflet in the possession of the author.

35. Langner diary, op. cit., 27.

36. Maczek report, op. cit., 33.

37. Langner diary, op. cit., 29.

38. Testimony of Michał Gawroński, Karta Archive, Warsaw, AW/I /0183.

39. Diary of Alma Heczko, Karta Archive, Warsaw, AW/II/1297/2K.

40. Władysław Langner, "Ostatnie dni obrony Lwowa 1939," *Niepodległość* 11 (1978).

41. Testimony of Janina Król, Karta Archive, Warsaw, AW/I/0407.

42. Langner diary, op. cit., 34.

43. Account of Lieutenant-Colonel Kazimierz Ryziński, in Kazimierz Ryś, *Obrona Lwowa w 1939 roku* (Palestine, 1943), 171–172.

44. Włodarkiewicz, op. cit., 176.

45. Heczko diary, op. cit.

46. Stanisław Ostrowski, *W obronie polskości Ziemi Lwowskiej: Dnie pohanbienia, 1939–1941. Wspomnienia* (Warsaw, 1986), 44.

47. Langner, "Ostatnie dni obrony Lwowa 1939."

48. Langner diary, op. cit., 37.

49. Ostrowski, op. cit., 45.

50. Antoni Szymański, *Zły sąsiad: Niemcy 1932–1939 w oświetleniu polskiego attaché wojskowego w Berlinie* (London, 1959), 188.

51. Langner diary, op. cit., 39.

52. Ibid., 40.

53. Ibid., 41.

54. Ibid., 48.

55. Langner, "Ostatnie dni obrony Lwowa 1939."

56. Langner diary, op. cit., 52.

57. Stanisław Czuruk, quoted in Paweł Rokicki, Anna Piekarska, et al., *"A więc wojna": ludność cywilna we wrześniu 1939 r.* (Warsaw, 2009), 129.

58. Account of Adam Huk, in Ryś, op. cit., 177.

59. Testimony of Janina Przyszlak, Karta Archive, Warsaw, AW/I/0649.

60. Adam Epler, *The Last Soldier of the Battle of Poland, September 1939* (Edinburgh, 1944), 39, 52.

61. Jan T. Gross, "Sovietisation of Poland's Eastern Territories," in Bernd Wegner, ed., *From Peace to War: Germany, Soviet Russia and the World, 1939–1941* (Oxford, 1997), 63.

62. Roger Moorhouse, *The Devils' Alliance: Hitler's Pact with Stalin, 1939–1941* (London, 2014), 49.

63. Protocol, signed in Mińsk-Mazowiecki, on German–Soviet cooperation, PISM, AII 27/57.

64. Natalia Lebedeva, "The Red Army Invasion and the Fourth Partition of Poland," in Adam Daniel Rotfeld and Anatoly V. Torkunov, eds., *White Spots, Black Spots: Difficult Matters in Polish–Russian Relations, 1918–2008* (Pittsburgh, 2015), 194–195.

65. Nikita Khrushchev, *Khrushchev Remembers* (London, 1971), 112.

66. Major-General Andrei Yeremenko, quoted in Czesław Grzelak, *Sowiecki najazd 1939 r.: Sojusznik Hitlera napada polskie Kresy—relacje świadków i uczestników* (Warsaw, 2017), 48.

67. Testimony of Nela Boratyn, Karta Archive, Warsaw, AW/I/0063.

68. *Kriegstagebuch des Generalkommandos XIX AK* (hereafter "KTB XIX AK"), reports from September 14, US National Archives T-314, roll 611, pp. 124–125; Heinz Guderian, *Panzer Leader* (London, 1952), 81.

69. KTB XIX AK, 130; Dr. Frahm, quoted in Alan Bance, trans., *Blitzkrieg in Their Own Words: First-Hand Accounts from German Soldiers, 1939–1940* (St. Paul, MN, 2005), 51.

70. KTB XIX AK, 153.

71. Vasily Laskovich, quoted in Yury Rubashevsky, "Radost' byla vseobshchaya i triumfal'naya," *Vechernii Brest*, September 16, 2011, www.vb.by/article .php?topic=36&article=14200.

72. KTB XIX AK, 173.

73. Ibid., 164, 168.

74. Guderian, op. cit., 82–83.

75. KTB XIX AK, 179.

76. Guderian, op. cit., 82.

77. Janusz Magnuski and Maksym Kołomijec, *Czerwony blitzkrieg, wrzesień 1939: Sowieckie wojska pancerne w Polsce* (Warsaw, 1994), 72.

78. Raisa Shirnyuk, quoted in Vasily Sarychev, "V poiskach utrachennogo vremeni," *Vechernii Brest*, archived at www.vb.by/sarychev/content/75/main .php.

79. German eyewitness account from a 1939 postcard, reproduced at "Parade," Río Wang, http://riowang.blogspot.com/2009/09/brest-nazi-soviet -military-parade-23_25.html.

80. Shirnyuk, quoted in Sarychev, op. cit.

81. Ibid.

82. Stanislav Miretski, quoted in ibid.

83. Boris Akimov, quoted in ibid.

84. Semyon Krivoshein, *Mezhdubur'ye: Vospominaniya* (Voronezh, 1964), 261.

85. Testimony of Marian Paszkiewicz, New Records Archive, Warsaw, 2/2113/0/1.8/77.

86. Testimony of Mieczysław Wiąckiewicz, Karta Archive, Warsaw, AW/I/861.

87. Testimony of Barbara Soós, Karta Archive, Warsaw, AW/II/3460.

88. Zofia Chomętowska, *No wozie i pod wozem: Wspomnienia z lat 1939–1940* (Warsaw, 2008), 48.

89. Ibid., 42, 57, 60, 70.

90. Quoted in Stanley S. Seidner, "Reflections from Rumania and Beyond: Marshal Śmigły-Rydz in Exile," *Polish Review* 22, no. 2 (1977): 45.

91. Wojciech Rojek, "Wojenne losy polskiego złota," *Bankoteka*, Special Issue 3 (2014): 6.

92. Agnieszka Michalak, "Mission Impossible," *Kaleidoscope* (Warsaw), January 2017, 71.

93. Diary of Henryk Zygalski, courtesy of Anna Zygalska-Cannon.

94. See Dermot Turing, *X, Y & Z: The Real Story of How Enigma Was Broken* (Stroud, England, 2018).

95. Jerzy Przybylski, ed., *Kontradmiral Xawery Stanisław Czernicki* (Gdynia, Poland, 2002), 16–18.

96. Marcin Graczyk, *Admiral Świrski* (Gdańsk, Poland, 2007), 192–193.

97. Testimony of Franciszek Kornicki, Imperial War Museum Archive, London, 01/1/1.

98. Adam Zamoyski, *The Forgotten Few: The Polish Air Force in the Second World War* (London, 1995).

99. Quoted in Miroslav Ferić, *Pamiętnik wojenny pilota 111 Eskadry Myśliwskiej im. Tadeusza Kościuszki*, vol. 1, p. 94, Central Military Library, Warsaw, Rps 126.

100. Biography of Oswald Krydner, unpublished manuscript, 11.

101. Zamoyski, op. cit., 33.

102. Wojciech Dziedzic, "Armia 'Kraków' i Armia 'Lublin' w pierwszej bitwie tomaszowskiej: Kalendarium oraz wybrane aspekty działań i próba oceny," in Tadeusz Guz, Wojciech Lis, and Ryszard Sobczuk, eds., *Bitwy pod Tomaszowem Lubelskim w 1939 roku* (Lublin, 2010).

103. Stefan "Grot" Rowecki, *Wspomnienia i notatki, czerwiec–wrzesień 1939* (Warsaw, 1957), 112.

104. Ibid., 113.

105. Ibid.

106. Alex Buchner, *Der Polenfeldzug 1939* (Leoni am Starnberger See, Germany, 1989), 153.

107. Testimony of Captain Zenon Starkiewicz, PISM, B I 85/D.

108. VII Army Corps chronicle, quoted in Hargreaves, op. cit., 186.

109. Testimony of Captain Marian Kowalczyk, PISM, B I 85/D, p. 50.

110. General Józef Giza, quoted in Rowecki, op. cit., 23.

111. Józef Szyrmer, quoted ibid., 125–126.

112. Władysław Anders, *An Army in Exile: The Story of the Second Polish Corps* (London, 1949), 9.

113. The first was at Piotrków on September 5. See Marian Porwit, *Komentarze do historii polskich działań obronnych 1939 r.*, vol. 2, (Warsaw, 1983), 331–332.

114. Anders, op. cit., 10.

115. Ibid., 11.

116. Ryszard Szawłowski, *Wojna polsko-sowiecka 1939*, vol. 1, *Monografia* (Warsaw, 1997), 224–225.

117. Corporal Włodzimierz Rzerzycki, quoted in Ryszard Szawłowski, *Wojna polsko-sowiecka 1939*, vol. 2, *Dokumenty* (Warsaw, 1997), 162.

118. Tadeusz Skoczek, ed., *Dziedzictwo i pamięć września 1939 na Mazowszu* (Warsaw, 2013), 72.

119. Quoted in Szawłowski, op. cit., 1:228.

120. Ibid., 1:377.

CHAPTER 9: "TO END ON A BATTLEFIELD"

1. Marta Korwin-Rhodes, *The Mask of Warriors: The Siege of Warsaw, September 1939* (New York, 1964), 155.

2. Alexander Polonius, *I Saw the Siege of Warsaw* (Glasgow, 1941), 174–175.

3. Korwin-Rhodes, op. cit., 147.

4. Testimony of Maria Komornicka, Karta Archive, Warsaw, AW/II/3611.

5. Korwin-Rhodes, op. cit., 159.

6. Polonius, op. cit., 177.

7. Ibid., 175.

8. Ibid., 175–176.

9. Ibid., 176.

10. Jochen Böhler, *Der Überfall: Deutschlands Krieg gegen Polen* (Frankfurt am Main, 2009), 171.

11. Antony Beevor, *Arnhem: The Battle for the Bridges 1944* (London, 2017), 63; Frederick Taylor, *Coventry: Thursday 14 November 1940* (London, 2015), 282. One should add that the Coventry raid was primarily composed of incendiaries, but the comparison still stands.

12. Colonel Tomaszewski, quoted in Herbert Drescher, *Warschau und Modlin im Polenfeldzug 1939: Berichte und Dokumente* (Pforzheim, Germany, 1991), 730.

13. Testimony of Mikołaj Buja, Zawkrze Land Museum Archive, MZZ/ fk/380.

14. Quoted in Nicholas Bethell, *The War Hitler Won: September 1939* (London, 1972), 139.

15. Korwin-Rhodes, op. cit., 159; Lucjan Dobroszycki, Marian Drozdowski, Marek Getter, and Adam Słomczyński, eds., *Cywilna obrona Warszawy we wrześniu 1939 r. Dokumenty, materiały prasowe, wspomnienia i relacje* (Warsaw, 1964), 144.

16. Ludwik Hirszfeld, *Historia jednego życia* (Warsaw, 1977).

17. Polonius, op. cit., 181.

18. Zygmunt Stanicki, *Obrona Warszawy w 1939 roku* (Warsaw, 1961), 33.

19. Tomaszewski, quoted in Drescher, op. cit., 731–732.

20. Sliwiński, quoted in ibid., 734.

21. Lipiński, quoted in Zbigniew Gluza, ed., *Rok 1939: Rozbiór Polski* (Warsaw, 2009), 162.

22. Ibid., 162.

23. Polonius, op. cit., 189.

24. Xaver Kotheder, quoted in Richard Hargreaves, *Blitzkrieg Unleashed: The German Invasion of Poland, 1939* (Barnsley, England, 2008), 249.

25. Testimony of Jan Grzybowski, in Paweł Rokicki, Anna Piekarska, et al., *"A więc wojna": Ludność cywilna we wrześniu 1939 r.* (Warsaw, 2009), 198.

26. Władysław Szpilman, *The Pianist: The Extraordinary Story of One Man's Survival in Warsaw, 1939–45* (London, 1999), 40.

27. Quoted in Drescher, op. cit., 737.

28. Quoted in ibid., 739.

29. Mieczysław Niedziałkowski, quoted in ibid., 739.

30. Ivánka, quoted in Gluza, op. cit., 165.

31. Text given in ibid., 164.

32. Juliusz Rómmel, *Za honor i ojczyznę: Wspomnienia dowódcy armii "Łódź" i "Warszawa"* (Warsaw, 1958), 338–339.

33. Report by Stanisław Riess, Polish Institute and Sikorski Museum Archive, London (hereafter "PISM"), LOT A I 3/1e.

34. Rómmel, op. cit., 339.

35. Ibid., 358–359.

36. Michael Peszke, *Battle for Warsaw, 1939–1944* (Boulder, 1995), 29.

37. Zofia Chomętowska, *Na wozie i pod wozem: Wspomnienia z lat 1939–1940* (Warsaw, 2008), 70, 88.

38. Seaman Stanisław Bartkiewicz, quoted in Zbigniew Wojciechowski, "Zbrodnia w Mokranach," in Jerzy Przybylski, ed., *Ostatnia wachta: Mokrany, Katyń, Charków* (Gdynia, Poland, 2000), 38.

39. Mikhail Mel'tyukhov, *17 sentyabrya 1939: Sovetsko-pol'skie konflikty, 1918–1939* (Moscow, 2009), 426.

40. Adam Epler, *The Last Soldier of the Battle of Poland, September 1939* (Edinburgh, 1944), 40.

41. See Czesław Grzelak, *Szack—Wytyczno 1939* (Warsaw, 1993), 166.

42. Ibid., 178.

43. Korwin-Rhodes, op. cit., 169.

44. Komornicka testimony, op. cit.

45. Tadeusz Kutrzeba, *Wojna bez walnej bitwy* (Warsaw, 1998), 368.

46. Kutrzeba, quoted in Drescher, op. cit., 773.

47. Stanisław Sosabowski, *Freely I Served: The Memoir of the Commander, 1st Polish Independent Parachute Brigade, 1941–1944* (Barnsley, England, 2013), 42.

48. Ibid., 43.

49. Quoted in Alex Buchner, *Der Polenfeldzug 1939* (Leoni am Starnberger See, Germany, 1989), 176; Hargreaves, op. cit., 255.

50. Rómmel, op. cit., 365.

51. Sosabowski, op. cit., 42.

52. Korwin-Rhodes, op. cit., 174.

53. See Roger Moorhouse, *Berlin at War: Life and Death in Hitler's Capital, 1939–1945* (London, 2010), chap. 6.

54. Alexander Rossino, *Hitler Strikes Poland: Blitzkrieg, Ideology, and Atrocity* (Lawrence, KS, 2003), 15.

55. IPN report, Warsaw, 2014, on the probable fate of Stefan Starzyński, at "Zacończenie śledztwa w sprawie zabójstwa Prezydenta m. st. Warszawy Stefana Starzyńskiego," Instytut Pamięci Narodowej, https://ipn.gov.pl/pl/dla-mediow/komunikaty/11943,Zakonczenie-sledztwa-w-sprawie-zabojstwa-Prezydenta-m-st-Warszawy-Stefana-Starzy.html.

56. Sosabowski, op. cit., 45.

57. Józef Garliński, *Poland in the Second World War* (Basingstoke, 1985), 40–41.

58. Testimony of Stanisław Dmuchowski, Karta Archive, Warsaw, AW/I/0126.

59. Szpilman, op. cit., 40–41.

60. Walter Schellenberg, *Schellenberg* (London, 1965), 27–28.

61. See Roger Moorhouse, *The Devils' Alliance: Hitler's Pact with Stalin, 1939–1941* (London, 2014), 74.

62. Quoted in Robert Conquest, *Stalin: Breaker of Nations* (London, 1991), 224; reminiscences of Gustav Hilger, quoted in Ingeborg Fleischhauer, "Der

deutsch-sowjetische Grenz- und Freundschaftsvertrag vom 28. September 1939," *Vierteljahrshefte für Zeitgeschichte* 39, no. 3 (1991): 458.

63. Fleischhauer, op. cit., 455–456.

64. Ibid., 457–460.

65. Moorhouse, *Devils' Alliance*, 51.

66. The text of the German–Soviet Boundary and Friendship Treaty is available at Yale Law School, Avalon Project, http://avalon.law.yale.edu/20th _century/gsbound.asp.

67. Testimony of Captain Stanisław Skierski, quartermaster, 8th Infantry Division, PISM, B I/20A/1.

68. Wiktor Thommée, "Ze wspomnień dowódcy obrony Modlina," *Wojskowy Przegląd Historyczny* 4, no. 3 (1959): 201.

69. Ludwik Czyżewski, *Wspomnienia dowódcy obrony Zakroczymia w 1939 r.* (Warsaw, 1973), 82.

70. Thommée, op. cit., 201.

71. Account of Edward Lisowski, in Kazimierz Szczerbatko, *Zakroczym* (Zakroczym, 1999), 26.

72. Czyżewski., op. cit., 84.

73. Szymon Datner, *Zbrodnie Wehrmachtu na jeńcach wojennych armii regularnych w II wojnie światowej* (Warsaw, 1961), 60–61; Czyżewski, op. cit., 91.

74. See, for instance, Drescher, op. cit., 867; Czyżewski, op. cit., 89.

75. Sylwester Fabiszewski, quoted in Szczerbatko, op. cit., 29.

76. Czyżewski, op. cit., 96.

77. Datner, op. cit., 61.

78. Drescher, op. cit., 868.

79. Thommée, op. cit., 203.

80. Buchner, op. cit., 180.

81. Testimony of Stefan Zwolenkiewicz, sound recording, Polish Navy Museum Archive, Gdynia, Poland, (hereafter "PNMA"), 171R.

82. Testimony of Eugeniusz Maciejewski, "Wspomnienia z obrony Helu w 1939" (Gdynia, Poland, 1960), typescript, p. 26, PNMA.

83. Busch, quoted in Hargreaves, op. cit., 262.

84. Mariusz Borowiak, *Admiral Unrug, 1884–1973* (Warsaw, 2009), 253.

85. Epler, op. cit., 44.

86. Ibid., 48–51.

87. Quoted in Eugeniusz Kozłowski, ed., *Wojna obronna Polski 1939* (Warsaw, 1979), 702–703.

88. Epler, op. cit., 53.

89. Chomętowska, op. cit., 113.

90. Ibid., 118.
91. Epler, op. cit., 67.
92. Ibid., 67.
93. Komornicka testimony, op. cit.
94. Epler, op. cit., 69–70.
95. Kozłowski, op. cit., Doc. 557, p. 1005.

CONCLUSION

1. Eugeniusz Kozłowski, *Wojna obronna Polski 1939* (Warsaw, 1971), 851.

2. Tadeusz Panecki, "Militarny udział Polski II wojnie światowej," in Tadeusz Panecki, ed., *Polski wysiłek zbrojny w II wojnie światowej: Bilans, wnioski i doświadczenia* (Warsaw, 1999), 31.

3. G. F. Krivosheev, ed., *Soviet Casualties and Combat Losses in the Twentieth Century* (Barnsley, England, 1997), 57–59.

4. Paweł Kosiński and Piotr Łysakowski, "Z największą brutalnością: Zbrodnie Wehrmachtu w Polsce w 1939 r.," *Biuletyn IPN* 8–9 (2004): 128–130.

5. Quoted in Marta Markowska, ed., *The Ringelblum Archive: Annihilation— Day by Day* (Warsaw, 2008), 8.

6. According to Szymon Datner, there were over 600 massacres carried out by German forces over the thirty-six days of the conflict. See Szymon Datner, *55 dni Wehrmachtu w Polsce: Zbrodnie dokonane na polskiej ludności cywilnej w okresie l.ix-25.x. 1939 r.* (Warsaw, 1967), 358–359.

7. On this, see Karl-Heinz Frieser, *The Blitzkrieg Legend: The 1940 Campaign in the West* (Annapolis, MD, 2005).

8. Steven Zaloga and Victor Madej, *The Polish Campaign 1939* (New York, 1985), 11.

9. Ibid., 107.

APPENDIX 2: GERMAN ARMY ORDER OF BATTLE

1. From Nikolaus von Vormann, *Der Feldzug 1939 in Polen* (Weissenburg, 1958), 202–209, and Steven Zaloga and Victor Madej, *The Polish Campaign 1939* (New York, 1985), 188–190.

APPENDIX 3: RED ARMY ORDER OF BATTLE

1. From Mikhail Mel'tyukhov, *Sovetsko-pol'skie voiny, 1918–1939* (Moscow, 2001).

INDEX

ROGER MOORHOUSE studied history at the University of London and is a visiting professor at the College of Europe in Warsaw. He is the author of several books on World War II history, including *Berlin at War* (shortlisted for the Hessell-Tiltman Prize) and *The Devils' Alliance*. He lives in the United Kingdom.